MARK GERTLER

MARK GERTLER

Biography of a painter, 1891-1939

John Woodeson

UNIVERSITY OF TORONTO PRESS

First published in 1973 in Canada and the United States of America
by University of Toronto Press
Toronto and Buffalo

ISBN 0-8020-2060-7

Originally published in Great Britain in 1973
by Sidgwick and Jackson Limited

Printed in Great Britain

For Merry

Author's Note

For biographical information I am indebted to many of Mark Gertler's relatives, and in particular to the following: his son Luke (who also provided most valuable help with the catalogue), his widow Marjorie Kostenz, sister-in-law Mrs D. Blundell, niece Mrs Renée Diamond and niece Mrs M. Jacques and her husband. Other relatives and friends who were helpful include Miss Sally Charton, Mrs Irving Joseph, Mr Albert Morris and his son Leslie.

I would like to express my gratitude for the help and information provided by the following people and organizations:
Mrs Clare Armstrong; the Hon. Dorothy Brett; Professor Quentin Bell; Lord Bernstein; Mrs Lilian Bomberg; The British Museum (Readers Room and Department of Manuscripts); Mr David S. Burleigh; Mr Noel Carrington; Mr David Carrington; Mrs M. Clifton; Mr Michael Chase; Mr Andrew Causey; Miss Maria Donska; Mrs Barbara Duce; Mr Raymond Drey; Mr Anthony d'Offay; Mrs Olga Edwards; Mr Maurice Farquharson; the Fine Art Society; Dr A. S. Fulton; Mr Frederick Gore; the late Mrs Spencer Gore; the late Miss Sylvia Gosse; Mr Alan Gwynne-Jones; Mrs Angelica Garnett; Miss Julia Gowing; the Greater London Council Photographs and Map Library; Lady Juliette Huxley; Mrs Mary Hutchinson; Mrs Hellerman; Mrs Jean Hogh; Mr Darsie Japp; *Jewish Chronicle*; Mr John Lumley; the Leicester Galleries; Mr Joseph Leftwich; Lady Pansy Lamb; Mr Paul Levy; Mrs Nora Meninsky; Mr Henry Moore; Mrs Dorothy Morland; Mrs Elizabeth Manson; Mrs Mary Mitchell; Mr Richard Morphet; Mr John Nash; Mrs Kathleen Nevinson; the New York Public Library; Mr J. B. Priestley; Mrs Frances Partridge; the Piccadilly Gallery; the Regent Street Polytechnic; Mr Cyril J. Ross; Mr David F. Rutherston; Roland Browse & Delbanco; Miss Lydia Sherwood; Mr Gilbert Spencer; Mrs Silver;

Mrs R. D. Schweder; Mrs Alix Strachey; the Slade School; the University of Texas; The Tower Hamlets Local History Library; Mrs Julian Vinogradoff; Mr Mark Wayner; the Witt Library (and in particular Mr Sunderland and Mr Hodge); Mr & Mrs Ethelbert White; Mr Hubert and Mr Robert Wellington; Mrs Sarah Whitfield.

I am especially grateful for their help and advice to the staff of the Courtauld Institute of Art (in particular to Mr Alan Bowness, Dr John Golding and Mr Christopher Green), to the staff of the publishers Sidgwick and Jackson (in particular to Mr William Armstrong and Mr Fraser Harrison), and to the following:

Mr Julian Agnew; Mrs Barbara Bagenal; Mr Robert Bevan and Mrs Natalie Bevan; Mr Richard Carline; the Contemporary Arts Society; Mrs Pamela Diamand; Mr Duncan Grant; Mr David Garnett; Mr Michael Holroyd; Mrs Betty Powell; Sir John Rothenstein.

Acknowledgements and appreciation are offered to the owners of the pictures reproduced and to the copyright holders of the following material from which I have quoted:

Adrian Allinson's unpublished Memoirs; copyright holder Miss M. Mitchell-Smith

Clive Bell, *Pot Boilers*, 1918

Quentin Bell, Introduction to *Mark Gertler – Selected Letters*

Clive Bell, *New Statesman*, 24 May 1941

Jacques Emile Blanche, *Portraits of a Lifetime*, (J. M. Dent & Sons, London, 1937)

Charles Booth, *Life and Labour of the People of London* (Macmillan, London, 1896 etc.)

Gilbert Cannan, *Mendel* (T. Fisher Unwin, London, 1916)

D. Carrington, unpublished letters; copyright holder Mrs Frances Partridge

George Charlton, 'The Slade', *Studio*, October 1946

Valentine Dobrée, *Listener*, 15 May 1941

Roger Fry, *New Statesman*, 12 February 1921

David Garnett, *Carrington, Letters and Extracts from Her Diaries* with biographical note by Noel Carrington (Jonathan Cape, London, 1971)

David Garnett, *The Flowers of the Forest* (Chatto & Windus, London, 1955)

Lloyd P. Gartner, *The Jewish Immigrant in England 1870-1914* (George Allen and Unwin, London, 1960)

Beatrice, Lady Glenavy (Beatrice Campbell), *Today We Will only Gossip* (Constable, London, 1964)

Mark Gertler, *Selected Letters*, edited by Noel Carrington; Introduction by Quentin Bell (Rupert Hart-Davis, London, 1965)

Mark Gertler, unpublished letters; copyright holder Mrs M. Kostenz

Christopher Hassall, *Edward Marsh*, (Longmans, London, 1959)

Michael Holroyd, *Lytton Strachey*, Heinemann 1968, Penguin Books, 1971

Augustus John, Foreword to C. Gray, *Peter Warlock*

D. H. Lawrence, Letters, ed. H. T. Moore (Viking Press, New York, 1962)

A. B. Levy, *East End Story* (Constellation Books, London, 1951)

Sylvia Lynd, *Mark Gertler*, Leicester Galleries catalogue 1941

Ottoline: The Early Memoirs of Lady Ottoline Morrell, edited by Robert Gaythorne-Hardy (Faber and Faber, London, 1963)

John Middleton Murry, *Between Two Worlds* (Jonathan Cape, London, 1935)

Paul Nash, *Outline* (Faber and Faber, London, 1949)

C. R. W. Nevinson, *Paint and Prejudice* (Methuen, London, 1937)

Sir John Rothenstein, *Summer's Lease* (Hamish Hamilton, London, 1965), *Modern English Painters* (Eyre & Spottiswoode, London, 1956)

Sir William Rothenstein, *Men and Memories*, vol. 2 (Faber and Faber, London, 1932) and unpublished letters

Bertrand Russell, *Autobiography*, Allen and Unwin

C. Russell and H. S. Lewis, *The Jew in London* (T. Fisher Unwin, London, 1900)

Michael Sadler, *M. E. Sadler* (Constable, London, 1949)

Randolph Schwabe, 'Three Teachers', *Burlington Magazine*, June 1943

George R. Sims, *Living London* (Cassell, London, 1902)

Osbert Sitwell, *Laughter in the Next Room* (Macmillan and Reprint Society, London, 1949)

Gilbert Spencer, *Stanley Spencer* (Victor Gollancz, London, 1961)

Frank R. Swinnerton, *The Georgian Literary Scene* (J. M. Dent, London, 1938)

Leonard Woolf, 'S. S. Koteliansky', *New Statesman*, 5 February 1955

Lastly, for the help which they gave in various ways, I thank my own relatives: Mrs Agnes Kerr, Mrs Owo Bilbo, my brother Martin and his wife Ann, and my sister Margaret.

Above all I thank my wife, Merry, for all her help both in research and in writing. Without the never-ending generosity with which she gave her time and effort this book could not have been written.

Contents

Illustrations

All paintings and drawings illustrated are by Mark Gertler. Exact titles, owners and full details are listed in the Catalogue on pp. 357 to 391.

PART ONE

'Come, we shall meet in England!'

'I was at the end of the row on the floor, next to my mother.' – MARK GERTLER

CHAPTER I

'Golda, take warning'

The picture of Golda Gertler in the Tate Gallery, London[169] was painted in 1911 when she was forty-seven, but the lines of her face, and the quiet watchful tension of the eyes, make her look much older.

When she took her children to the station at Przemysl, Galicia, in 1896 she was thirty-two, and it was her second attempt to emigrate. Half a dozen years earlier the family had left Przemysl and managed to reach London. But with the failure of Golda's husband Louis to make any sort of living there, poverty had forced them to return to Przemysl after a few months. The London Jewish Board of Guardians, who were trying to discourage the immigration of destitute aliens, paid their fares back.[1] During their brief stay in London another child, Max, or, as he later became known, Mark, had been born in the slum lodging house where they lived.

A small cathedral city of 50,000 people, Przemysl lay in the border country between Russia, Austria and Poland, on a tributary of the Vistula, about sixty miles west of Lvov. It had become important in the tenth century as a fortress on the old route leading south through the Carpathian passes, and the neighbouring countries had squabbled over it ever since.

Here Mark grew up, gradually becoming aware of the poverty and violence that surrounded him. In an account written many years later, in which he combined his own recollections with those of his family, he described their life after the return to Przemysl: 'Louis and Golda were not received exactly with enthusiasm by their relatives, who realized that something would have to be done. and who had by this time decided that my father was a good-for-nothing, especially those on my mother's side, who had often warned her, she used to relate so frequently, not to marry him, "for if you do, Golda, take warning you will never have enough to eat."[2] However they all clubbed together and managed to put up enough money to buy Louis a small inn on the outskirts of the town. It was doomed from the start, being most unfortunately situated between two other more important inns. "The only customers we got", Mark wrote, "always arrived already drunk, with all their money spent, from one or other pub, and refused to pay for what they drank at our place – which resulted nearly every night in murderous fights between my father and his customers, who were mainly soldiers.'

Louis had courage – in order to get out of the army to marry Golda sixteen years earlier he had resorted to the device of self-inflicted wounds – and he was very strong. In the brawls at the inn he usually fought, not with his fists, but using the sides of both hands in chopping movements. And on one occasion he knocked a soldier unconscious with a heavy glass.

'A story I want to relate', Mark wrote, 'is to show the sort of thing that used to happen on really bad nights. Once, my brother tells me, we were warned that a whole troop of drunken soldiers were making towards us in a very menacing mood. My father ordered the doors to be locked and barred and as many heavy objects as could be moved to be shoved up against them. Sure enough a few minutes later there were noises, bangings and shoutings, and even swords thrust in between the crevices of the doors. This went on for so long and my mother and sisters became so terrified, that my father decided at last to scramble out unseen from a back window and get help from some neighbouring people and officers, who between them managed somehow to restore order and disperse the soldiers.'

Mark was an attractive child, with large, dark eyes in a pale, thin face and one of the more harmless diversions of the soldiers was to play with him: 'Often, those very rough young men would agree to pay for their drinks only on condition that I was produced, when they would proceed to play and joke with me. As this meant dragging me out of my cradle my mother often cursed them in her heart – but produced me all the same, for sometimes, she said, she would hardly dare to think of what ructions they would kick up if she had failed to do so. Finally they somehow arranged to have a complete officer's uniform made for me and the correct number of stars fixed to the collar – and amused themselves by very seriously saluting me and awaiting my return salute. This apparently was a great game . . .

'How the inn came to an end, and what happened later, my mother used to tell in a derisive manner in order to "show up" what a simpleton my father was; for she always used to blame him for our failures and tell us how much better things would have turned out, had he waited and taken her advice. Her Yiddish was extremely expressive and in translating it I shall try and keep to her kind of expression and phrasing: "Oh, what an inn that was – what a hell – and how does your *tuttalla* (derisive way of referring to my father) wind up with that inn? Perhaps, sell it? No fear! Not he! One day, in he comes, with that smile of his – of course I know already what that smile means – and says to me, 'Golda don't worry any more, no more inn, we've got something better than that inn now.' 'Oh, tell me,' I says, 'What have we got better, tell me, be quick!' And what do you think he tells to my unhappy self? – 'BOOTS!' 'Oh! God help me,' I says, 'Boots? What do you mean boots?' 'BOOTS,' he says. Well I go and look and what do I see. Oh woe for my troubles, not even a single pair of boots!!! All odd, all odd, as I live today. God help me, all Odd! 'Why did you not wait for my advice,' I says. But not he, he even gets angry, if you please, and runs out. A few days later, as sure as I live, he returns with the same smile and says, 'Golda you didn't like the boots, eh?' 'No I did *not* like the Boots,' I says. 'All right,' he says, 'Come and look here.' And what does he show me this time – perhaps something valuable, you may think? No, even worse, BUTTONS! A sack full of buttons, and *such* buttons. Where could he have got such buttons from, that's all I wondered. I have never seen such buttons, not even on Christians' garments, let alone Jewish ones. Well, what more can I tell you; you know your *tuttalla*. Soon there was nothing in the house to eat."

'Her story is hardly an exaggeration of what actually happened,' Mark wrote. 'As for the buttons, the story my brothers tell of that used to fill me with pity for my father. Apparently he actually went out into the market place with both my brothers – he, a very, very proud man, and in that market place, where he was so well known, managed to articulate in a sort of shy undertone, "Buttons, Buttons." My brothers tell me that during the many hours they stood there, only one customer approached and even that one was unable to find the kind of buttons she wanted.

'After the buttons failure he could stand it no longer. One day he said, "Let me have a clean shirt, Golda, for this evening I go to America," and my mother was left without means and five children.'

Such an occurrence had always been common among Jewish families, for though ties were extremely strong, and infidelity rare, it was quite normal for a husband to emigrate on his own to try and establish a new home for his family. The wife was left to fend for herself until the husband, perhaps as much as ten years later, sent word.

Left in Przemysl with her five children, Deborah, Harry, Jack, Sophie, and Mark (the youngest by seven years) Golda's situation in Przemysl became desperate. The comfortable home, which she had left at the age of sixteen to marry Louis, was already far behind her; she was unable to look to her father for help since he had married again and her step-mother had no interest in her plight. Her life had become one long period of struggle against increasing hardship.

Poverty was widespread in Przemysl, with its population swollen by Jewish refugees from Russia, and infant mortality up to the age of five years was over fifty per cent.

'Fortunately,' Mark wrote, 'my eldest brother was just old enough to start work and I suppose contributed a little to the upkeep of the household. My mother did what she could to support us; at one time, she slaved away in a Jewish restaurant, her only wages being food left over from the day. This she carried home to us, tired and worn out after her long day's work. At times we were reduced to extremes; one day, for instance, when my eldest brother was seen to be approaching the house, the few crusts that we had were quickly hidden away, in case he took more than his share. This story my mother used to repeat with tears in her eyes.'

Once Mark was supposed to be asleep, when he heard his mother say to his eldest brother Harry, 'Harrish, it is cold and Maxalla will suffer. Could you not bring home with you from the factory a warm little coat?' Harry replied, 'All right, all right, I'll try perhaps, mother.' 'If you succeed we'll say father sent you a present for Maxalla from America.' The next evening at the same time Harry arrived. Mark was impatient: it was hard for him to keep up the pretence of sleep. 'I kept cocking one eye open every second,' he recalled, 'and sure enough, my brother extricates from inside his trousers a coat! A coat I was to wear a long time and get to love very much, though I knew it was not my father who sent it.'

All the children would take part in the struggle for survival by stealing vegetables from market wagons with the aid of spiked sticks; or, when at play, in the country between the mountains and the river, by watching for a chance to raid unguarded potato fields.

The poor in Przemysl, whether Jew or Christian, were always liable to ill-treatment: Mark's elder brother Jack came home one day with a cut across his face from a whip. He had splashed mud over the boots of an army officer.

Jews in the area were not persecuted systematically, though prejudice was strong and the people willing to believe grotesque stories of Jewish outrages against Christian children. But accounts of persecution were brought in continually by the Jews who poured in from outside, swelling the number of refugees in Galicia to nearly a million, all of them strongly aware of events in the past two decades across the border. In the early 1880s the hostility of the Russian Government to its five million Jews, already mostly confined to a 'Pale of Settlement' in Russia and Poland, had erupted in the widespread slaughter of the Pogroms, and in 1884 Bismarck's edict drove the Poles from Prussia as well.

After almost five years of struggle and hardship in Przemysl. Golda at last received a letter from Louis in America which raised her hopes and cheered her heart. 'I have prospects,' it said. 'Come, we shall meet in England! I know what to do there and if what I do there is not good, we shall go on to America where I know still better what to do.' Although Golda usually distrusted Louis' optimistic moods and felt that nothing good would come of it, she was at this time ready for any change as she felt that their condition could hardly be worse – and at least the family would be united again.

So for the second time Golda set out from Przemysl. The trail of the tens of thousands of Jewish emigrants from Eastern Europe to the West which she was following was a hazardous one. A contemporary observer, describing the arrival of a Jewish immigrant boat in England, wrote, 'Many of them . . . have already been despoiled of the little money they had. At the frontier they are sometimes detained for two or even three days in order that they may be robbed by harpies in collusion with certain subordinate officials. In some cases a man when he asks for a ticket at the frontier railway station is refused by the booking clerk. He is told that tickets can only be issued to emigrants through an agent. The agent then introduces himself, and on one plea or another succeeds in involving the immigrant in expenses which leave him with scarcely anything in his pocket at the journey's end.'[3]

Mark remembered little of the voyage. 'From what I used to hear of it from my brothers and sisters it was, for the most part, like a nightmare,' he wrote. 'We travelled in some sort of cattle boat herded very close together, the journey lasting for weeks, and most of the time in rough seas, when they were all sick and in a dreadful plight . . . it is quite at the end of the journey, our landing, in fact, when my memory comes to life . . . I am standing on a wooden floor; there is land, England; England is moving towards me – not I to it. It is sort of *gyrating* towards me. I am standing by my family all ready with heavy packages straining from their necks – pressing their backs – all available limbs are grasping rebellious packages. My mother strains her eyes and says, "Oh, woe is me, but I cannot see your father! He is not there, he is not there, what shall I do?" Everybody is pushing and shoving. It doesn't feel friendly. All is chaos, selfish and straining. I am being pushed and hustled. Some women are screaming and men shouting roughly.'

The scenes that took place when these Jewish immigrant boats arrived were commented upon by a number of contemporary witnesses. The *Jewish Chronicle* said, 'The process of robbery and chicanery . . . is quite as active in London as it is on the Russian frontier,' and an accurate observer gave this account: 'There are a few relations and friends awaiting the arrival of the small boats filled with immigrants: but the crowd gathered in and about the gin-shop overlooking the narrow entrance of the landing-stage are dock loungers of the lowest type and professional "runners". These latter individuals, usually of the Hebrew race, are among the most repulsive of East London parasites; boat after boat touches the landing-stage, they push forward, seize hold of bundles or baskets of the new-comers, offer bogus tickets to those who wish to travel forward to America, promise guidance and free loading to those who hold in their hands addresses of acquaintances in Whitechapel, or who are absolutely friendless. A little man with an official badge (Hebrew Ladies' Protective Society) fights valiantly in their midst for the conduct of unprotected females, and shouts or whispers to the others to go to the Poor Jews' Temporary Shelter in Leman Street. For a few moments it is a scene of indescribable confusion; cries and counter-cries; the hoarse laughter of the dock loungers at the strange garb and broken accent of the poverty-stricken foreigners; the rough swearing of the boatmen at passengers unable to pay the fee for landing. In another ten minutes eighty of the hundred new-comers are dispersed in the back slums of Whitechapel; in another few days, the majority of these, robbed of the little money they possess, are turned out of the "free lodgings" destitute and friendless.'[4]

Out of the chaos surrounding the Gertlers on their arrival appeared a familiar face, a friend of Louis's from Przemysl. 'Golda! Golda! Here I am – Louis Weinig – don't you know me? Louis will be later – at Liverpool Street station – later. Come, where are you all – Tema – Sosha – Harrish – Jankel – Max – come, Golda!'

Later they stood forlornly outside Liverpool Street station, looking rather like gypsies. Some passers-by threw coins, and Mark, dressed in his Hungarian coat of deep orange-coloured leather, decorated with gold-and-scarlet braid, vermilion tam-o'-shanter and top boots up to the knees, started a song and a sort of Russian dance, and still more money was thrown.

Louis was late. 'While we waited,' Mark recalled, 'on my eldest brother's neck I saw a vein sticking out – the enormous bundle hanging from his shoulder was straining it. As long as I live I shall continue to see that swollen vein. The bundle contained most of our bedding – feather beds. My father arrives at last – there is a sort of wave of emotions which entangles us, but I am not very moved by this – only the vein on my brother's neck is telling on me. But later

I see a bright-coloured shop – Gardiners of Whitechapel. "Mother, does the King live here?" "No my son, in London nearly everybody has such large and brightly lit houses – this is *London*, my son." Yes, this was London! Yes, although I was born in it, I saw London, experienced London for the first time then . . . and my only language was Yiddish. . . .'

Louis Weinig's family lived in two rooms in a tenement in Shoreditch, and it was in one of these two rooms that the seven members of the Gertler family were housed for the night. Louis Weinig and his family slept in the other. 'How exactly we were accommodated I don't know,' Mark wrote, 'but this is how it appeared to me when I awoke in the middle of the night. I was at the end of the row on the floor – next to my mother, then the others all on the floor, covered in sacks. The vision of them somehow filled my heart with overwhelming sadness – I cried, but quietly, not to awaken my mother. And that is the first real fit of depression I remember experiencing. It is curious that I should have felt it like that – for it was not as if I were accustomed to more luxurious circumstances. Yet as I sat there in the quiet of the night I was filled with a sort of pathos and a feeling of gloom which remains as vivid today as it was then; and I have always remembered it besides, as being the first fit of depression that I consciously suffered.'

CHAPTER 2

Chaida and sweatshops

The Weinigs alone were pleased that the family had come to England. As far as everyone else was concerned immigration was getting out of hand. People watched the arriving boat loads with depression and irritation and the wary tolerance of the authorities was becoming strained. England had never seen anything quite like Whitechapel at the turn of the century.

Lying to the east of the old City walls, it had always been more or less a transit camp for immigrants. This was as far as they got, coming into London from the Continent, before the City politely declined to allow them in. The same rather stony welcome was offered to successive groups of people running from persecution or poverty. They were barred from citizenship, but there would be no repression. If they cared to live outside the boundaries of the original City of London, they would be left alone to get on with it.

In the seventeenth century the Huguenots had arrived, forced out of France by Catholic persecution, and built up a district called Spitalfields, in the north of Whitechapel. Protected from French competition by customs duties, their silk-weaving industry prospered. Then the duty was lifted and trade declined. Later the invention of powered machinery drove them out of business altogether, and they dispersed, or relapsed into poverty.

The Sephardic Jews from Spain and Portugal, who came later, were richer and luckier. England absorbed them, and by the late nineteenth century they were an integral part of English commercial life. There was little trace of them left in Whitechapel, save for the magnificent synagogue, Bevis Marks. Immigrants in the nineteenth century consisted largely of poorer people from Germany and the east – the Ashkenazi Jews. At first they trickled in, but after the Russian Pogroms of the 1880s the movement across Europe became a flood. 'The turn of the century brought a decade of turmoil. In almost consecutive order, East European Jewry underwent the Rumanian "Exodus" of 1900, the Kishinev outrage of 1903, the outbreak of the Russo-Japanese War in 1904, the Revolution of 1905, and its trail of Pogroms lasting into 1906 . . . Waves of Rumanian wanderers, fleeing conscripts, Pogrom victims and, above all, Jews who simply despaired of improvement in Russia, streamed into the British Isles in proportions which bewildered those who tried to organize the flow.'[5]

The newcomers were pushing their way into an area which consisted of some of the worst slums in England. But several factors gave the Gertlers and their fellow Jews a chance:

Clothes, furs, umbrellas, boots and shoes – cheap goods that could be made in small workshops – would find a ready market in England. Secondly the better-off Jews there had become one of the world's most successful, accepted and well-organised Jewish communities, which helped the immigrants by means of various agencies. Also the immigrants, poor as they were, helped each other. Although the aim of each was to start a sweatshop and employ a few hands – people even more poverty-stricken than himself – and eventually to rent a house, then sublet it at rents even higher than his own, few were willing to see fellow Jews actually starve to death, and to prevent this various relief organizations were set up.

The Gertlers were joining a community of people who were on the way up. Their new environment was quite different from the stagnant misery they had left behind.

During the eighties and nineties the refugees, their drive for self-preservation sharpened by memories of the terror behind them, and now motivated by a new hope for the future, continued to take over Whitechapel. Faced with their tenacity, which showed itself in their willingness to club together to pay higher rents, living several families in a room if necessary, and their ability to survive on 'a red herring and a cup of coffee a day', the Christians fell back. They were pushed north along Commercial Street beyond the Great Eastern Railway line. To the east the farthest limit of the Jewish advance along Whitechapel Road and Commercial Road was marked by the Stepney Green area. To the south, down Leman Street, the advance was halted by the unyielding wall of the Irish community near the docks.

Within their enclave the Jews fought for food and gasped for air, as the overcrowding reached appalling proportions. Every day brought new arrivals, many of them destitute: at one point the Poor Jews Temporary Shelter in Leman Street was receiving five hundred a day.*

England reacted in various ways to this extraordinary situation. The middle classes were largely indifferent: no one wanted to live in Whitechapel anyway. Among the working classes in the East End hostility steadily increased: 'The aliens will not conform to our ideas,' said one report, 'and above all, they have no sort of neighbourly feeling . . . A foreign Jew will take a house, and he moves in on a Sunday morning, which rather, of course, upsets all the British people there. Then his habits are different. You will see the house with sand put down in the passages instead of oilcloth or carpet. These are little things, but they all serve to make a difference . . . He will use his yard for something. He will store rags there, perhaps, mountains of smelling rags, until the neighbours all round get into a most terrible state over it; or perhaps he will start a little factory in the yard, and carry on a hammering noise all night; and then he will throw a lot of waste stuff, offal, or anything like that – it is all pitched out; and in the evening the women and girls sit out on the pavement and make a joyful noise . . . on Sunday the place is very different to what the English are accustomed to.'[6]

The trade unions protected their members by keeping unskilled aliens out of the craft trades, and their presence in the big industrial centres of the provinces was not encouraged.

Philanthropic Christians were anxious about the misery in East London but didn't quite know what to do about the Jews. The extension of the underground to Aldgate had made it easier, however, to reach Whitechapel. Groups of various kinds had started settlements and were doing what they could, for Jews as well as Christians.

---

* Reliable counts of the Whitechapel population could never be made. Official figures, which were based on census forms and other papers depending on public co-operation, show the population of Stepney reaching a peak of just under 300,000 in 1901, the majority being Jewish. It had been claimed (N. E. Boulton, *Fortnightly Review*, February 1888) that thirteen years before, the density in the Jewish quarter had already risen to 600 an acre. After 1910 it steadily declined.

Of rather less use were the Christian Conversionist Societies, which sent missionaries to Whitechapel as an alternative to tours of duty in Africa. One, the London Society for Promoting Christianity among the Jews, had an income of £35,000 a year. But in spite of tempting bribes – 'Board and lodging at a specially provided house during the enquiry stage, constant charitable assistance after conversion, and the free education and free maintenance of Jewish children brought up in the Christian faith' – out of forty thousand Jews who were estimated to be in want, only twelve were baptized in a typical year, and even with these, the results were not entirely satisfactory: 'The Society has, however, one complaint against its converts. Inspired by the Jewish spirit of competing with former masters, and anxious to turn to some account their newly-acquired "talent" of Christianity, the youthful proselytes set up in business on their own account, collecting and spending the subscriptions of zealous Christians, with no respect to the monetary claims or superior authority of the mother society.'[7]

The Jewish authorities watched Whitechapel with sympathy, but irritation and apprehension grew as the immigrant rabble invaded an already teeming slum. They gave limited help and wished that the newcomers would go elsewhere. Referring to the march of Rumanian Jews across Europe to England in 1899–1900 the Jewish Board of Guardians commented, 'It is an outrage against the dictates of common sense and humanity, that such a senseless and hopeless movement should ever have been directed at these shores.'

For some weeks Louis and Golda with their five children shared the Weinig family's two rooms. Then Louis succeeded in getting a job smoothing walking-sticks with sandpaper at 12s. 6d. a week. 'A poor wage,' Mark wrote, 'yet we were all very cheerful, and very soon we were to have a home of our own. I can't imagine how it was managed on 12s. 6d. a week, but sure enough we got our home.' It consisted of one room in Zion Square. There they settled down, and Louis struggled to do his best for his family.

After about a year it was time for Mark to be sent to school, or *chaida*. This had to be paid for, but to forego it was unthinkable. He had to begin his education, which consisted in a study of the Law which had held the Jewish race together, so that he would become a good Jew, and instruction in the Hebrew Bible and prayers, so that he could begin to follow the synagogue service. These little *chaidarim* were run as private ventures by teachers of various types, ranging from rabbis to newly arrived immigrants supplementing a precarious living.[8]

Mark did not have far to go, as a *chaida* operated in the same square, only a few yards from his home. The teacher was a rabbi of about seventy 'with a long white beard which ended in two points', and the school consisted of one room with a long narrow table. At the head of this the old rabbi sat, with the children around the rest of it. He read the Old Testament to them in Hebrew, translating each sentence or sometimes each word into Yiddish, in a rapid, hardly intelligible monotone. 'We had to drone on after him, repeating the bits we could catch, and filling up the rest with noises that meant nothing whatsoever,' Mark admitted. 'Only occasionally, when he felt like it, would he pull us up, and choosing a boy quite indiscriminately, thump him. I must have been one of his favourites, for not only did I hardly ever get thumped, but he would even select me quite frequently from among the class, and let me sit on his lap, while the lesson proceeded. This, for me, was a very doubtful pleasure, for as he gabbled out the Hebrew and Yiddish his beard would travel up and down my cheek tickling intolerably – making me long even more than usual for the end of the lesson.

'The experience that stands out most clearly of my *chaida* days is not the Hebrew lessons or any stories of the Old Testament (we hardly understood a word he was reading anyway,) but ... *fried fish*! There was always a smell of fried fish in *chaida*, and occasionally the Old Testament would be abruptly closed and put aside as the old rabbitzin would enter from the kitchen with a piece of fried fish and some brown bread (the sort that contains caraway seeds) for the rabbi to eat. Now I was always a small eater, but watching the rabbi eating his fish I became fascinated, and I have never ceased to like fried fish. I mean of course fried fish done in the *Jewish* way – an entirely different affair from the fried fish you get ordinarily in restaurants.'

Zion Square lay just to the south of Whitechapel High Street, less than a hundred yards away, but cut off by a large block of buildings so that the square could only be approached from one direction. The district was described at the time as: 'Occupied chiefly in tailoring and cigar making. There are also many artisans, workers in furs and skins, bootmakers, hawkers, and labourers mostly of the casual order; a great number of Jews here, some comfortable, but many abjectly poor.'[9]

The dozen or so three-storey houses in a terrace round the sides of the square had been built in the eighteenth century. Front doors opened directly on to the unpaved ground and each house had a tiny yard at the back. 'They were small, slummy and had some-thing cottage about them – almost countrified,' Mark wrote. Most of the occupants made a living as tailors, and the rattle of their sewing-machines was the dominant sound. This and the noise of the children filled the square, which was only forty yards wide. The Gertlers' landlord, Mr Levy, was a bootmaker, and other occupants included a chandler at No. 8, a diamond-mounter at No. 4 and a silversmith. One non-Jew remained – a weaver, the last survivor of the previous inhabitants of the square.

'Our home', Mark wrote, 'consisted of a room with some kind of detached corner where my mother cooked and managed to produce enough food to keep us all alive.' Here Louis and Golda, Deborah, Harry, Jack, Sophie and Mark lived, crowded together, for the next three years. 'Our landlord and his wife were kind, decent people,' Mark wrote, 'and their leniency with regard to our rent was of course a great help, for the 12s. 6d. did not always work out, and often the weekly rent had to be delayed. Their youngest son Moisha, who was about my own age, soon became my "best pal", and I always remember him as my *first* best pal; for I have always had a "best pal" and I could name them all in succession.' Other friends of Mark's included a young Christian. But this friendship was frowned upon by Louis and Golda because of the difference in religion, and the boys had to meet in secret.

Mark always felt that the austerity forced on the family by poverty was transformed into a fine simplicity by the pious, intensely serious nature of Louis and Golda; they shared a character-istic common to most of the immigrant Jews – their religion was the religion of the ghetto. A writer at the time commented: 'It has been at once intensified and narrowed by ages of persecution, and consists largely in a devotion to the letter of the Law, which is by no means shared by those who have grown accustomed to a freer atmosphere and a wider range of thought...Judaism owes its strength and persistence, as well as its narrowness and impenetrability, to the stress of persecution ... It is generally recognized in Jewish circles that the stronghold of orthodoxy is in the East End where the foreign Jews congregate.'[10]

Outside his home and the *chaida*, the most familiar sight to Mark was the small synagogue to which he would be taken so often. 'It is a curious and touching sight to enter one of the poorer and more wretched of these places on a Sabbath morning,' wrote a contemporary. 'Probably the one you choose will be situated in a small alley or narrow court, or it may be built out in a back-yard. To reach the entrance you stumble over broken pavement and household debris; possibly you pick your way over the rickety bridge connecting it with the cottage property fronting the street. From the outside it appears as a long wooden building surmounted by a skylight, very similar in construction to the ordinary sweater's workshop. You enter... Add to the rhythmical cadence of numerous voices, the swaying to and fro of the bodies of the worshippers, expressive words of personal adoration – "All my bones exclaim, Oh! Lord, who is like unto Thee!" – and you may imagine yourself in a far-off Eastern land ... You step out, stifled by the heat and dazed by the strange contrast of the old-world memories of a majestic religion and the squalid vulgarity of an East End slum.'[11]

Fixed to the right-hand doorpost of the Gertlers' one-room home, and the homes of all the other Jews, was a *mezuzah*. This was an ornamented cage about three inches long, of metal, wood or glass, inside which, on a scroll of parchment, was the daily prayer beginning: 'Hear O Israel, the Lord our God, the Lord is one.' Visitors would make a gesture and the most devout would kiss it.

On Friday evenings the Sabbath candles were lighted, the cup of wine was drunk and Louis pronounced a blessing upon his children.

Excursions to outside entertainments were limited by lack of money and friendly callers provided most diversions. Louis

Weinig, in particular, would always be welcome. 'He was my father's life long friend and pal,' Mark wrote. 'He came from Przemysl also and was therefore our "lansman". He was a wit and famous for his comic stories.

'False modesty or any sort of modesty was not his, nor was it much indulged in by anybody in his world. When he told one of his stories he was quite frankly the hero, and mostly a very glowing hero. Nobody was critical, because modesty was not the fashion, and most people used conversation chiefly to boost themselves. The difference between him and the others was that he *was* funny. I remember looking forward to his visits. His *style* was the important element, not the matter, so one could hear him often without getting bored. His wife was a very frail woman always dying of consumption. There were several children and the poverty so great that the poor little woman was compelled to crawl about and do the housework, bring up the children and even help others who were as poor as herself, when she was obviously feverish and hardly able to stand. In our presence she would often be seized with a fit of coughing which generally ended in hemorage, yet she was always cheerful and sweet tempered.'

Louis, now forty, was still finding it a struggle to make a living. Nearly three years after settling in Zion Square he described himself officially as a 'traveller' when Mark's eldest sister Deborah got married. She was a fine-looking girl of twenty, and her husband had been chosen from among the many suitors brought by the matchmakers. Hopes raised by the marriage – to an apparently prosperous Russian-Jewish cabinet-maker – were dashed only a few months later, when he went bankrupt.

There seemed to be no point in searching in England outside Whitechapel for a living. Anywhere else Louis would run into language difficulties, and he had in any case to stay close to his fellow Jews where there would be *chaidarim* for his children, synagogues, and kosher shops selling food prepared according to the Law of the Jews. And only a hundred yards or so from Zion Square was the all important *Beth Din*, or Court of Judgement. For Jew to fight Jew in a Gentile court of law was considered a scandal; a contemporary writer noted, 'Family quarrels, trade and labour disputes, matrimonial differences, wife desertions, even reckless engagements, and breach of promise cases – in short all the thousand and one disputes, entanglements, defaults and mistakes of every-day life are brought before the Beth Din to be settled or unravelled by the mingled lights of the Pentateuch, the Talmud, and the native shrewdness of the Hebrew Judge'.[12] In Whitechapel Louis was among a self-contained Jewish community, with its own shops, ritual baths, a hospital in Stepney Green, and two burial grounds nearby, one for Sephardic Jews, the other for the Ashkenazi. In all these the custodians spoke Yiddish. Shop signs were in Yiddish and there were local Yiddish papers. Even the agencies of the Christian world spoke it: Stepney was looking for a Yiddish-speaking librarian in 1907 and the policemen were learning Yiddish.

There was no need to go outside Whitechapel, and Golda, for one, wouldn't even have thought of it. As a community, it was organized for survival. Though the Gertlers had no relatives or friends at first, other than the Weinigs, insecurity was tempered by the thought of the various charities and institutions they could turn to in case of desperation: the Jewish Board of Guardians, the Sabbath Meals Society, the soup kitchen for the Jewish poor, the Jewish Lodging house in Gun Street, and the Friendly societies. There was also the English poor law, though this was hardly ever resorted to by the Jewish immigrants.

It would not have occurred to Louis, even had it been easy, to get a permanent and reasonably paid job working for someone else. His object was to start a small workshop and be his own master. His children would work for him, the family would be kept together, and problems of working on the Sabbath would be avoided. He had learnt something about the fur trade in America and there were only two hurdles to be overcome. It was necessary to persuade a manufacturer to give him 'out-work', or to get credit for skins with which he could work. Then he had to get the necessary machines. There were some thirty agents of the Singer Sewing Machine company looking for business and it was often possible to get a starting loan from the Board of Guardians.

Their landlord's workshop was a small room holding four or five people. 'Moisha and I used to spend most of our time there,' Mark

Early pictures painted in Mark's house at 14 Spital Square, Whitechapel. *Above left* May Berlinsky, she lived nearby **(1)**; *above right* self-portrait **(2)**; *below* 'A Family Scene' —his mother Golda, sister Sophie and brothers Jack and Harry. **(3)**

Now in the Tate Gallery, this picture of Golda Gertler was exhibited publicly in London while the artist was only nineteen and still a student. (4)

Golda and Louis painted as 'The Apple Woman and her Husband' (5). *Below* Golda in her kitchen. (6)

Right 'Dora Carrington'; Mark was her first lover. **(7)**

In 1912 Mark broke away from the naturalistic style which he had been taught, and at which he had already become so proficient.

Below 'The Violinist' 1912. **(9)**

Above 'Family Group' 1913; 'the bareness, eloquent and intimate, speaks of poverty and stresses the human aspect of the little family' (Mary Sorrell). **(8)**

Above 'Mrs T. E. Harvey', 1912, wife of the warden of Toynbee Hall, one of Mark's early supporters. (**10**)

Right 'Vanity' 1912.
(**11**)

Right 'The Rabbi and his Grandchild' (May 1913). Mark painted a number of pictures of the old Jews in Whitechapel, many of them refugees from persecution in Russia. (**12**)

With this portrait of Golda Mark Gertler succeeded in creating a new kind of picture while still retaining the realism of his earlier work. His aim was to suggest 'suffering and a life that has known hardship. It is barbaric and symbolic'. **(13)**

'Jewish Family'; another attempt to show the character of the people among whom he lived. **(14)**

'Rabbi and Rabbitzin', 1914; 'a hint of what the century was to experience in the way of ruthless metallic form and fierce sculptural statement' (Quentin Bell). **(15)**

recollected, 'playing in and around the machines, over which the "hands" used to sit bent and huddled, treadling, treadling away hour after hour. These "hands", mere boys and girls, who appeared to me then as very adult people indeed, worked an incredible number of hours at a stretch, couped up in that dirty, airless little room. I remember one youth, called Marx, vividly, because he worked more persistently than the others at what was called "overtime". Probably more ambitious than the rest to make a little extra money in order to save up for marriage and a "home", he worked from early morning until late at night and sometimes past – not even leaving the workshop for meals; every now and then a chunk of bread and butter, overlaid with a thin spread of pinky, watery jam and a cup of tea was brought up to him, which he would swallow rapidly, so that he could go on treadling out more and more of that stuff he was paid to produce. He was tall, very thin, and very white, and he came to a tragic end. All that toil and labour was utterly wasted, for one day he was discovered pacing the square, when he ought to have been working at his machine, spinning a few gold sovereigns in the air and murmuring as each piece clinked to the ground, "What is money, what is money." That unfortunate youth was discovered asking himself the meaning of money – the striving for which had so enfeebled his brain, and ultimately landed him in an asylum.'

The Levy's workshop was by no means unusual. A published description of a tailor's sweatshop said: 'In Hanbury Street we found eighteen workers crowded in a small room measuring eight yards by four yards and a half, and not quite eight feet high. The first two floors of this house were let out to lodgers who were also Jews. Their rooms were clean but damp as water was coming through the rotting wall . . . The sink was not trapped, the kitchen range was falling to pieces, while the closet was a permanent source of trouble. A flushing apparatus had been provided, but this discharged the water *outside* the pan; the water consequently came out under the seat and flowed across the yard to the wall opposite, which was eaten away at its base . . . The top room . . . had at times to hold eighteen persons, working in the heat of the gas and stove, warming the pressing irons, surrounded by mounds of dust and chips from the cut cloth, breathing an atmosphere full of woollen

3—MG * *

particles containing more or less injurious dyes it is not surprising
that so large a proportion of working tailors break down from
diseases of the respiratory organs.'[13] However, other writers commented: 'The poor Jew is not easily demoralized and can spend his
life without respect of circumstances in the unflagging pursuit of an
end . . . It might be much better for his health to work steadily for
ten hours a day in a factory, but under the present system, he finds
life fuller and richer in interest.' . . .[14] 'Whatever the evils of
sweating, master-workmen relations inside the workroom were at a
free and easy level. A highly informal atmosphere reigned inside the
shop. The worker often began his day in the master's workshop-
dwelling before the crack of dawn, and took breakfast coffee from
the kitchen.'[15] The Trades Union Congress, reporting on sweating in
1894, criticized the Jews' individualism: 'these people are incorrig-
ible; they were either sweaters or sweated.'

CHAPTER 3

'What's his Christian name?'

'It was of course understood that I must be sent to *chaida* and learn
how to become a good Jew,' Mark later recalled, 'but about the
ordinary schools, or board schools, as they were then called, my
parents lived in blissful ignorance. They had no idea that a child
was, or could be, forced by law to attend them. So one day, there
came a great knocking at the street door, the kind of rat-tat-tat that
forebodes trouble; and when my mother arrived, breathless and
fearful, and opened the door, she was confronted by a very angry
man, who was quite unable to make her understand what he was
angry about, for my mother's English, never very good, was at that
time very embryonic indeed. After a good deal of shouting on both
sides, Mrs Levy was sufficiently aroused from her cooking to come
to my mother's aid. It was then discovered that the angry man was
an inspector of board schools, and was demanding my presence at

the school *immediately*; and he told them I should have been sent to school long ago.'

Golda explained, with the help of Mrs Levy's English, that she hadn't the least idea that it was necessary to send children to school at a certain age, but that now she *did* know she would take Mark to school whenever he suggested. As all this had happened towards the end of the week, it was agreed that Mark should be taken to school the following Monday morning.

'On the morning of that important day', Mark recorded, 'both my mother and me awoke much too early – nervous and flustered – to prepare for this fearful event. My mother washed my face, neck, and hands, combed my hair through with the fine combs she used when looking for things, then again with the ordinary combs and brush and at last, after a period that seemed an age, I was all ready – dressed in my sailor suit to set out for school. When we arrived, we were told to join a queue of people who were waiting there for the same purpose as ourselves. It was a hot day, and as soon as we joined the queue, my mother for some reason lifted me into her arms and held me there in a manner she used when I was younger. I felt uncomfortable but did not protest, and soon I began to notice beads of sweat gather like pearls on her forehead and temples, then join and trickle down her cheeks in thin glistening streams. Then I heard a woman saying, "Why do you carry such a big boy in your arms Mrs, ain't he old enough to stand?" I felt ashamed and tried to wriggle down, but my mother gathered her arms around me tighter and held me there, not deigning even to answer the woman.

'At last our turn came to approach the desk, at which a man was sitting, very stern and angry – making us feel from the start that we were somehow in the wrong, and that he jolly well meant to "let us have it". "Put that boy down at *once*. He's not a babe! Name of Gertler, I see. What's his *Christian* name?" Of course my mother could make nothing of it at all, until a woman at the back came to the rescue. "Mux," she said. "Mux!" said the man. "Never heard such a name; no such name in *this* country. We'll call him *Mark Gertler*." And nodding to a woman nearby and pointing his pen at me he said "next!"

'The woman separated me from my mother and, taking me by
the hand, she led me away.'

The regular school hours caused Mark much strain. His brothers
and sisters were fairly close to each other in years, and there was
between them and him a considerable gap. 'I was always referred to
as the "babe",' Mark confessed, 'and was perhaps for this reason my
mother's darling. She did all she could for us, within her means, and
was completely self-sacrificing. But unfortunately, like most of the
people in the world she lived, some of the most important things in
connection with the upbringing of a child were quite unknown to
her. I consider the most disastrous of these was the fact that we were
allowed to go to bed at any old hour; the result was that I never got
enough rest. I was a very nervous, highly strung and emotional
child, somewhat undersized, thin and pale, yet I would hardly ever
be put to bed before the rest of the family, which meant midnight,
and on weekends, when there were gatherings, long past that hour.
It was when I first started going to school that I began feeling the
strain of it. I shall always remember the awful mixture of exhaustion and despair I felt every morning when I had to make myself
get up in time for school; for I was very conscientious, and terrified
of losing a mark, and every morning the strain made me weep and
cry as I dressed – "It is late already, I shall be late." '

Settles Street, a big board school of some fifteen hundred children, was less than two hundred yards from Zion Square. Mark had
only to go round two corners and cross two streets, and since they
were quiet back streets he could make the journey alone. But he
discovered there were other hazards than getting knocked down by
the horse traffic.

Soon after he started at the school, Louis arranged as a special
treat to give him pocket money – a farthing a day. 'When at last I
was dressed and got through my cup of tea and bread and butter, I
began to feel consoled and happy at the prospect of the farthing,'
affirmed Mark. 'I used to carry it clasped tightly in my fist, happily
contemplating which of the various sweets I should buy that day, at
a special little shop that I used to pass on my way to school. Now
for a while all went well; I would, after much deliberation, at last
decide upon a jar of sweets, and pointing at it with one hand and

producing the hot farthing from the other, receive in return the little bag of sweets. But one day as I emerged from the shop with my bag, a girl, perhaps a little older than myself, but who looked formidably larger to me, approached, and quietly but very definitely robbed me of my sweets. When I recovered from my astonishment I cried.

'But alas, my troubles had only begun. The next morning as I was hopping and skipping along with my farthing, having by that time completely forgotten about the big girl, I was brought up sharp only a yard or so from the shop by the sight of my enemy! Yes, there she was, large and formidable, standing there waiting. I stopped. She approached, and without even allowing me to enter the shop she opened my fist, withdrew the farthing and, as if to add insult to injury, she smacked my face and walked off! This time I was just stunned, I did not even want to cry; but the injury, the pain, was profound. For the first time in my life I realized the existence of *injustice*. It seemed that I was being hurt, and was apparently going to be so hurt every day, though I had done nothing wrong to deserve it! And there was nothing, nothing I could do. I walked on to school brooding. It still did not occur to me to resist, and the situation itself became too important – too painful even – to be divulged or complained of. And so the thing grew into a dreadful secret inside me, and daily I suffered the same injury, the same indignity.

'This unfortunate episode came to an end somewhat abruptly. Although each day when I reached home I made no complaint, my family must have noticed at last that something was very wrong, and began cross-questioning me. At first I just refused to give up my painful secret; they then tried to guess – "Is it this, Is it that" – no, no, I kept shaking my head. At last I broke down under their sympathetic enquiries, and told them the whole story. It was arranged then that my sister Sophie should accompany me to school next morning, and catch the girl and give her "what's what". But next morning, as we approached the little shop, my tyrant soon realized the situation, turned tail and fled as hard as she could, and never again waylaid me.'

In the summer of 1899 Louis moved his family out of Zion

Square to No. 8 Bacon Street, about half a mile to the north. Mark left Settles Street School in July and started the following March at another board school in Deal Street. He was now able to speak and read English, though still unable to write in the language.[16]

As in Settles Street, nearly all the twelve hundred children in Deal Street were Jews, and about half had been born overseas; Yiddish was the language of the yard.*

The school was big, bare and ugly; however it was clean and quite new, put up only four years previously as one of the new generation of purpose-built board Schools. Deal Street, lying just to the north of Whitechapel High Street, had the common trouble of the district – noise. The din of wheels and horses, and above all human voices, was such that special sound-proofing techniques had been tried in the construction of the school.[17]

Following the usual pattern the building consisted of a triple sandwich: infants on the ground, then the boys, with girls on the second floor. On every floor was a hall and seven classrooms, where, in each, sixty Jewish boys would sit in short trousers, single-breasted jackets buttoned almost up to the neck, wearing caps, while the master, in a hat, would attempt to make them speak English.

The influence of these schools was surprisingly strong. As a contemporary put it, 'The newly arrived Russo-Jewish immigrant is, in all essentials, a mediaeval product, and his children grow up into something like the type of modern Englishmen. The evolution which the older Anglo-Jewish families have accomplished by the growth and effort of hundreds of years is in Whitechapel being compressed into a single generation.[18]

Mark was quiet, conscientious and well liked at the school: a

* In the records Mark's name got no further in its progress to Anglicization, being still recorded as 'Marks'. Accuracy about his birth-date was fair: the year was right, the month wrong. At least, it was a month earlier than that given on his birth certificate.

Though Louis and Golda were willing to obey the laws of England, to send Mark to board school and fill up any forms required of them, they showed no great zeal for accuracy. No one ever remembered what Mark's real birth-date was. He himself followed this tradition of vagueness by giving it later as 1892. Mark's birth certificate, which listed his mother's name as Kate instead of Golda, was the first of a long trail of inaccurate documents scattered by the family in England.

book presented to him as a prize on one occasion bore the inscription, 'For the most popular boy in the form.' Later he was to look back on the school with mild approval: 'It did me very well', he said once.

The teaching included rudimentary drawing lessons, but Mark's interest in drawing was aroused more by the outside world. Excited by a poster advertising a beef extract and some pictures by a pavement artist, he began drawing on the stones of his back yard. His family bought him some simple materials. Mark himself recalled: 'As a boy I was utterly ignorant of everything connected with art, but I longed to draw and paint, right from the very beginning. The shops, full of the brilliant colours of meat and fish, vegetables and fruit, were a continual joy, and my mother would sometimes get things for me, which I would paint. Until I left school, at the then statutory age of fourteen, I had no contact with the artistic world except the pavement artists. Such institutions as the public art galleries were not even names to me.'[19]

At home Golda encouraged him and delighted in his pictures. But the obsessive side of his character began to show and the family worried when he ignored meals and went on drawing for hour after hour, oblivious to the world about him. There were occasional scenes when they took away his colours and forced him to have a meal or go out to get some fresh air. 'After all, they didn't know he was talented,' a relative said later, 'they wanted him to eat.'

On the Sabbath nearest to his thirteenth birthday in 1904, Mark had his *Barmitzvah* ceremony. From eight in the morning, in a praying shawl and skull cap, he sat through the morning service in the synagogue waiting to read, in the customary sing-song chant, the part of the Law which he had studied at night during the previous months.

At the little party later he made the customary speech thanking his parents for all they had done. His speech pleased everyone and its unusual eloquence made a deep impression on his brothers and sisters. Afterwards they trooped off to Oscar Baumgart's photographic studio in Commercial Road, where Mark's skull cap was changed for a mortar board, and he was posed in jacket and knee breeches. The photograph showed a pale, rather undersized, round-headed, small-featured boy, with clear observant eyes set wide apart. In front of him he gripped the Bible rigidly in his small hands. According to Jewish custom, he was now of age, a man. It was time to make decisions. But round the mouth and behind the eyes hung a nervous, frightened air.

No. 8 Bacon Street, the property of a Mr Skurnick, was not a pleasant place to live. It was one of a terraced row of cheaply built dwellings, mostly of four storeys, with crabbed arched doorways opening on to the street. Above the sullen, badly proportioned windows, projecting courses of brick formed a meaningless decoration. From a narrow frontage the house rambled interminably back for eighty feet – a long thin strip of gloomy rooms – almost entirely surrounded at the sides and back by other houses built directly on to it. The one at the rear was a sawmill, and its noise mingled with that from the twenty-three-track railway only 160 feet away.

This was the reality of the overcrowding described in a survey of parts of East London at the time: 'Nearly all available space is used for building, and almost every house is filled up with families ... Houses of three rooms, houses of two rooms, houses of one room – houses set back against a wall or back to back, fronting it may be on to a narrow footway, with posts at each end and a gutter down the middle ... Another sort of filling up which is very common now is the building of workshops, and access to them is had through the houses. One I know of is arranged floor by floor, communicating with the respective floors of the house in front by a system of bridges. These workshops obstruct the light, and shut out the air ... Worse again is the solid backward extension, whether for business premises or as tenements, or as common lodging houses, of the buildings which front the street; and this finally culminates in quarters where house reaches back to house, and means of communication are opened through and through, for the convenience and safeguard of the inhabitants in case of pursuit by the police.'[20]

To add to other difficulties the water supply was erratic. It had hardly improved in the twelve years since an investigation of Whitechapel by the Jewish Board of Guardians had reported; 'The water supply was amazingly bad. The inspector visited altogether

1,747 Jewish houses, and counted 1,621 without flushing water in their indoor or outdoor water closets.'[21]

The people of Bacon Street were put in the category 'very poor, chronic want' by a contemporary survey.[22] This applied more to the north side; on the other, where the Gertlers lived, there was in fact a certain rough variety. It was occupied mainly by cabinet-makers, but a fried-fish shop at No. 20, and a rag-and-bone yard at 30, added their smells to the sharp reek of timber. Between them and No. 8 was the inevitable pub (there were very few blocks in the district without at least one, open twenty hours a day and much frequented). Next door on the other side, at Nos 4 and 6, a tin-plate worker plied his noisy trade, and next to him on the corner was a workers' coffee room.

The street itself lay just to the north of the Great Eastern Railway, which marked the limits of the area occupied by the Jewish community, so that English was heard as well as Yiddish; people with names such as Evans, Meadows, Houghton and Webb lived alongside the Shifferblatts, Lebofskys and Moses.

Mark had much farther to walk to school than from Zion Square. It took about fifteen minutes to get home at nights, and there was little temptation to linger. In winter the only light came from the dim gas jets of the occasional street lamps, and the windows of the back street shops. These were open until late, but their feeble lights shone no more than a few yards.

Many of the narrow streets and courts were dim even on a bright summer's day. The sun might gild the upper stories of the buildings and flood down between the high walls, but it could never reach the bottoms of the courts.

Certain streets were best avoided. About four hundred yards to the west of the school was Dorset Street, which, with its fourteen registered common lodging houses, had never been reputable even before the 'Jack-the-Ripper' murders there a few years earlier. A contemporary of Mark's said, 'There is nothing that can describe how very bad Dorset Street was, the way the people lived; it was most horrible. And people were immoral, openly immoral; and for those days this was dreadful. The children were so badly clad, without shoes, often naked. The parents just lazed around with

beer. It was *dreadful* – always fights in and outside the tenements.'[23]

To the south of the school was Wentworth Street, known locally
as 'the Ripper Street', scene of another of the series of murders. To
the north, between the school and Mark's home, some of the streets
were occupied by non-Jewish poor, and the tensions which were
shortly to result in the anti-Jewish Aliens Act of 1907 (which
limited immigration) were becoming evident now in these
Christian streets.*

What racial animosity there was showed mainly in the street
fights between children, and it was necessary to watch out for the
gangs waiting with sticks and stones to intercept boys from the
predominantly Jewish schools. A school friend of Mark's said, 'The
school was in a very poor slum area. The reason for the absence of
non-Jews was the racial fighting, and the schools tended to
segregate. The area was very dark and frightening, with frequent
screams and drunken fights, and homeless people asleep in corners
or on steps.'[24]

A year or so after his *Barmitzvah*, when he left school in January
1906, Mark made a decision: he was going to be a painter. The
family were baffled; they had never heard of such a thing as a
professional artist. The supreme aim of this poverty-stricken community was to earn a living. 'Louis didn't understand what an artist
was,' one member of the family wrote. 'To him a Jew could not be
an artist; he thought everyone should learn a trade.' But in a
second-hand bookshop Mark had come across a life of the Victorian
painter W. P. Frith, which showed that a poor man with talent
could become immensely rich and end by painting the Royal
Family. And a hopeful sign was that Mark's drawings had been
called brilliant by Henrietta Adler, the daughter of the Chief Rabbi.
She had come across him when doing social work in the schools.

Mark was determined to find a way of living which was less
materialistic than that of the people around him, and his skill in

---

* 'Broken windows and other forcible arguments have not infrequently been
used to convince the unlucky Jew, who has had the temerity to take up his abode
in these streets, that for him, at least, they are not desirable homes.' (C. Russell &
H. S. Lewis, *The Jew in London*, T. Fisher Unwin, London, 1900, p. XXXIX).

drawing offered a chance of this. For the first time his family became aware of how stubborn he could be.

'Paint I must and would,' he wrote later. 'Take the clerkship in the timber trade which my father had found for me I would not.'[25]

Fortunately, Louis had at last managed to set up a little fur-sewing business, and the family had moved in January 1905 to No. 56 Leman Street. Louis, helped by the elder sons, had raised the family above the level of bare subsistence, and it was agreed to give Mark a chance. 'But', Mark recalled, 'how to set about it was the problem, and we were in despair.'

Their visitors, to whom Golda always showed Mark's drawings, included no one with any influence or knowledge of the world of art. 'Finally,' Mark wrote, 'a family friend, a Scottish fur traveller, promised to take my rather vague aspirations in hand. He discovered the Regent Street Polytechnic, and led me along to a Mr Gaskell, who was kindness itself, but very damping as to the monetary feasibility of an artist's career. However, a sudden inspired gesture of faith in my abilities, delivered by our friend, carried the day.'[26]

Mark started at the polytechnic with high hopes. His childhood was over. Its miseries and discomforts had left him with an unusually strong will to survive, to work and to succeed. The East End had given him a knowledge of life and an intensity of vision which would help him to produce fine pictures. Unfortunately it had also left him with a tendency to fits of violent depression, and health which was at best uncertain.

For those who saw them, the reports of the Medical Officers of Health for the area usually made depressing reading. In 1900 the Whitechapel M.O.H. had confessed, 'I know of nothing which has caused me more trouble ... than the one burning question of "overcrowding" ... Just those diseases which are caused or aggravated by the necessity for living in crowds, and by exposure in all kinds of weather, such as "constitutional" diseases, and diseases of the respiratory system, claim more victims from our own people ... than for the rest of London.' Another survey reported: 'Stoop and pallor marked the physique and countenance of immigrant workers, and one characteristic immigrant disease, tuberculosis, ended the lives of many ... Nine per cent (of the known

Jewish cases in London) died in one year. The victims were largely tailors, boot and shoe makers, furriers, and cap makers, and cigarette makers.'[27]

Twenty per cent of the deaths of inmates of Whitechapel lodging houses in 1900 were caused by tuberculosis. In 1910, the Medical Officer of Health disclosed that it accounted for over twelve per cent of the deaths in the district from all causes. In some streets, of which Bacon Street was one, there were as many as four deaths from it in this year.

PART TWO

'My nice friends amongst the upper class'

'What more does one want but a room, materials and the National Gallery?' – MARK GERTLER

CHAPTER 4

Self-help and cherubim

Once at the Polytechnic, Mark worked with an application as single-minded as any immigrant in Whitechapel and, in the next two years, he laid the foundations for one of the fastest rises to fame that Britain had seen in a young artist.

A variety of choices presented themselves for his first journeys out of the East End. He could take a steam train on the underground Circle Line and walk down to the Polytechnic from Portland Road station; or he could walk down Whitechapel to the City and take the new electric tube direct to Oxford Circus. If he had time to spare there was the horse-drawn tram, which took a roundabout route to Bloomsbury; from there he could walk. The most interesting, though least comfortable way, was by bus. As the vehicle bumped and rattled along behind its two horses, it offered the enjoyment of unfamiliar sights in the West End: the ostentatious luxury of the private carriages, occasional motor cars, smart restaurants, hotels and shops with illuminated electric signs.

From Oxford Circus, Mark walked along Upper Regent Street, which was dignified and quiet. Among the staid, rather tired Classical stucco England's biggest educational institute was a cheerful sight. The upper part, save for a statue of Minerva, was similar to its neighbours – its windows flanked by columns on which was mounted the full quota of entablatures and pediments. Below, every window was plastered with posters, advertising evening classes in cabinet-making, plumbing, bricklaying, engineering, cookery, elocution, sign-writing, painting, tailoring and carriage-building, courses in mathematics, science and art, a day school for young boys and girls, university degree courses, cheap tours and the Biograph programmes. They almost surrounded the enormous white lettering on the windows at either side of the entrance: 'Polytechnic, Young Men's Christian Institute.'

Inside, the large hall was paved with mosaic, its ceiling supported by columns. Allegorical frescoes on the walls illustrated the aims and work of the institution. Behind rose a bewildering maze of dark staircases, passages and rooms of various sizes, all packed with students.

This was the original of the several London polytechnics. 'They accommodate over thirty thousand boys and stand like forts in the sea of London temptations to youthful dissipation, ignorance and idleness', was a contemporary appraisal.[28]

An article in *The Times* had described a visit to the Regent Street Polytechnic. 'The visitor . . . will find every room occupied by numbers of lads and young men from seventeen years old upwards, either harmlessly amusing themselves or studying in class . . . In the larger hall the gymnastic instructor is taking his numerous energetic class through their exercises. From fifty to one hundred lads are there, most of them in flannels, and forgetting the workshop and the counter in the physical delight of exercise . . . It is no exaggeration to say that nothing that the University gymnasiums can show can at all compete with or approach the skill of these young men, these auctioneers' clerks, tailors, and carpenters of London. It adds a new dignity to the draper's counter to reflect that the young man who stands behind it and measures you a yard of ribbon, may, when he is stripped among his fellows in the evening, show a figure almost as fine as Captain Webb's, and go through a performance not unworthy of a Leotard'.[29]

Mark's fellow students in the art department were a very mixed bunch. Some were training to be teachers, but most had jobs already. They were practical designers, lithographers, book illustrators, draughtsmen for stained glass, fashion artists, modellers, decorators and cabinet-makers. Most used the school as a place in which to improve their skill in order to earn more money at their trade, and various classes had been designed to meet their needs. The emphasis was on practical, or applied art. Very few besides Mark had the idea of concentrating only on painting or 'fine art', and, of these, most aimed simply at being accepted by the Royal

Academy so that they could set up successfully as professional portrait painters. 'The polytechnic authorities have neither time nor inclination to give a smattering to amateurs; they aim to make the actual craftsmen masters of their trades', an observer commented. 'The classics and purely literary studies receive comparatively little attention.'[30] In one way this suited Mark: his own attitude was nothing if not professional. Only later did a fundamental difference between himself and most of the other students become evident.

The common background of working-class struggle helped to smooth over another important difference. For the first time Mark's days were to be spent surrounded by Gentiles, and at first he felt very isolated.

'The polytechnic differs from most of its English imitaters in being distinctively a religious institution,' a writer observed, 'and Christianity is the pivot of the whole'.[31] Bible-study classes and Christian endeavour meetings were always being held somewhere in the building, and many clubs for leisure activities tried to foster friendships. But the fur traveller's choice was a lucky one. The polytechnic was one of the few Christian-inspired institutions that were willing to offer good fellowship without forcing religion upon the recipients. Yet no record shows that Mark took notice of the elaborate organization of good will, or indeed of any of the various clubs, and his name was not found later in any list of old boys' activities. He was there simply to learn to paint.

For his first year Mark enrolled in the elementary classes for drawing in light and shade and drawing wooden models. He also went in for design and still-life painting – an ambitious programme – and settled into a routine of hard work.

The head of the art department, G. Percival Gaskell, became interested in Mark and took him to the National Gallery— his first sight of a big national collection. Gaskell was a well-qualified man, a practical painter with a good knowledge of art history.[32]

As well as teaching his art classes, Gaskell was usually giving a course of art history lectures at the polytechnic or elsewhere in London. In the autumn of 1906 he was doing a special series of twenty on Dutch and Flemish painters, and during a visit with

Mark to the National Gallery he talked further on seventeenth-century Dutch still-life painters and later painters, such as Chardin, with a similar approach. Mark was deeply impressed by a small Chardin still life, and listened to Gaskell emphasizing that the important thing in painting was not to go for bright colours – which hardly existed in nature anyway – but to get subtleties of tones right, and to convey the existence of atmosphere between the observer and the objects. This kind of painting struck an immediate response in Mark: 'I at once went ahead', he wrote, 'working along the lines of strictest academic realism, of the old Dutch still life schools.'[33]

At the end of his first year, in the summer of 1907, he sat with the others for the Board of Education examinations. When the results were announced he had failed in one subject, design, and been awarded second-class certificates in the other three, including still-life painting in oils. He was doing very well, but not exactly brilliantly, and Louis was finding it a strain to keep him at the school. 'My family were very poor, and the fees were insuperable, small though they were,' Mark recalled.

He decided to try the Jewish Board of Guardians for help. They referred him to Isidore Spielmann and the Educational Aid Society. But everyone was away for the summer: 'It will be necessary for us to take a further opinion before we can come to a definite decision,' they wrote vaguely on 2 August 1907.

In the new term Mark put in again for oil painting of still life. He decided to try another of the more advanced classes – figure drawing, starting with drawing casts and hoping to progress to the life classes. He gave up design.

Mark's painting was now coming along rapidly. A series of little still lifes showed that he had already learnt the practical trade of reproducing the forms, colours and tones of simple groups of subjects in oils.[34]

But the money crisis could no longer be avoided; the few ideas he had for getting financial help had failed and he would have to take a job.

Next door to the polytechnic were Clayton and Bell, 'Gold

Medallists, Paris 1889 and Glass painters to H.M. the King'. Three
steps led up to their discreet front door and the two wide windows
behind railings looked extremely sober compared with the brash
advertisements of the 'poly'.

In answer to his application Mark received an ornate little letter;
'Messrs. Clayton & Bell present their compliments to Master Mark
Gertler and beg to inform him that they will be very pleased to
give him a six months' trial in their studio at the rate of 5s. per
week . . . and if matters progress satisfactorily during such period
they would increase his salary to 7s. 6d. per week. Messrs Clayton
and Bell offer these terms for Master Gertler's consideration as an
alternative to an Apprenticeship, as they understand that a premium
might prove an obstacle. Master Gertler could commence operations on Monday 30 December 1907 – if the terms were agreeable.'

With his days taken up by his job, Mark became a night-school
boy, one of the nine thousand earnest, white-faced, perpetually
tired youths who hurried into the polytechnic after a ten-hour day
to yawn through another two and a half hours from seven o'clock
onwards.

He began to discover more of London's institutions, a world of
order, space, regularity, serious purpose, self-help, stone floors,
carbolic and ugliness.

At weekends he could study in the reference rooms of the
Whitechapel Public Library – open and crowded until ten o'clock
every night weekdays and Sundays. A contemporary wrote that this
place recalled 'memories of eager plodding young men and women
ambitious for success and often attaining it . . . including a poet and
a painter of genius who both died too young, Isaac Rosenberg and
Mark Gertler.'[35]

He found his way to another institution open to poor boys. Like
the polytechnic, the Toynbee Hall Settlement was Christian but
willing to give help without strings. It had been founded in the
1880s with the idea that Oxford students should actually live in the
East End to understand and help with the problems of its people.
Whitechapel gaped at the consequent island of middle-class civilization which grew up. 'Come down and see,' a writer urged. 'You
think of Whitechapel as the prowling ground of Jack the Ripper, as
a labyrinth of reeking slums, or a Ghetto crowded with foreign

Jews chaffering in Yiddish over piles of old clothes. Yet when you have passed through the arched entry of Toynbee Hall you might imagine your self in the "quad" of some old college at Oxford or Cambridge. There is a feeling of refinement and distinction in the very air.'*

Mark looked rather frail, undersized and dependent. But his unshakable determination to succeed was to arouse the sympathy and catch the imagination of many.

The warden of Toynbee was Thomas Harvey, in his early thirties, a Quaker, and originally from Leeds. Behind him lay Christchurch College, Oxford, the universities of Berlin and Paris, and work in the British Museum. He had been a resident at Toynbee since 1900, becoming warden in 1906. Mark found it hard

---

* G. Sims, *Living London*, (Cassell, 1902) Vol. 1. The account continues, 'In front an ivy-clad porch; on one hand a turreted library rising from its cloistered foundations; on the other, a dovecote and a clock tower. The illusion is deepened when you enter the spacious dining hall and hear the unmistakable 'Varsity accent of the diners.' This was a fair description of the atmosphere of the low brick buildings, with their pointed roofs and latticed windows, which rambled round the cosy 'quad', but the residents, as they were called, got through a lot of useful work. 'When the company have separated', Sims continued, 'you learn that three or four have gone off to manage clubs for working-men or for the "old boys" of some neighbouring Board school: one is going round arranging for parental payments to the Children's Country Holiday Fund, and another is presiding over a conference on old age pensions, or the water supply; this one is to give a "University Extension" lecture, and that one is taking a class of pupil teachers in his own room; while a couple of others have volunteered to patrol the streets – narrow and gloomy like mountain gorges, bounded on either hand by the forbidding fronts of common lodging houses – to investigate a complaint that the street lighting is not equal to the needs of such a doubtful locality. Festoons of fairy lamps begin to twinkle and glow among the creepers that beautify the "quad" and presently the people of the neighbourhood will flock in to enjoy an open-air concert... In the Tenant's Defence Association we halt at a door placarded with an inscription in Hebrew and English. Behind a table at the far end of the room sits a sharp yet benevolent-looking attorney, with a venerable Hebrew interpreter sitting on the edge of a desk close by. An old lady stands in front of the table pouring forth, with tearful voice and gestures of despair, a Yiddish tale of woe. "What's that – what's that?" asks the presiding genius. "She says," replied the old interpreter, "that her landlord has taken all the doors off their hinges because she wouldn't get out when he wanted her to; and it's terribly draughty." '

not to feel impatient at first with Harvey's Quaker liberalism, his rather unworldly humanity and tolerance. Yet he was a man who naturally commanded respect and his talk opened up new vistas of culture. The acquaintance became a friendship; Mark had a sympathizer who was to come to the rescue at a crucial moment in later life.

At home Mark spent every spare minute working at his drawing. After the family had moved to Leman Street, while he was still at school, he had got into the habit of working in Golda's kitchen. Most days he would be accompanied home after school by a friend (Cyril Ross) who said later, 'There was no proper art master at Deal Street School and the drawing lessons weren't much use. Neither of us was interested in games. I liked going home with Mark to practise drawing simple objects: vegetables, pots and pans. His drawing always seemed extraordinary to me, so accurate, clean and perfect; it was correct from the very start. We would spend hours working on the floor in the dim gaslight, while his mother washed clothes in the cement copper in the corner. Sometimes the steam would get so thick we had to stop and wait for it to clear.'

The house was a great improvement on their previous domiciles. Built less than a hundred years earlier as one of a short terrace, its four storeys and basement of red brick looked solid and quite spacious, with three windows on each floor. Golda had her own kitchen and Louis had taken more rooms in the house for his furrier's workshop. The yard at the back was large by East End standards, being twenty feet square. The front door, at the top of a few steps, was protected from the street by iron railings.

True, the overall appearance was ugly: bricks projected in patterns over the windows and in horizontal courses every few feet, in a style similar to the public lavatories in the district. Yet the street itself was interesting. Instead of living in back streets, the Gertlers now had a home in one of the district's main roads. It led down from Whitechapel (from the corner occupied by Gardiners, the shop which had made such an impression on the infant Mark) towards the docks. Electric street lamps had been installed, and in addition to the inevitable pubs (three within sixty yards of the Gertlers) and a lodging house at No. 66 ('working man's home – good beds' proclaimed the sign outside), there were a number of more impressive buildings to look at: opposite was the Jewish working-girls' club, the East End mission to the Jews and the enormous Co-operative Wholesale Society; on the Gertlers' side were wool warehouses, a police station, and the Poor Jews' Temporary Shelter. All these were interspersed with coffee rooms, shops, the premises of dealers – cork merchants, flour factors, clock makers – and those of one or two solicitors and doctors.

Every day Mark made the journey to the little glass-painting firm, where his task consisted in the production of charcoal cherubim. 'I longed to be free of its restrictions, and to get forward with my own real work,' he recalled. 'There are, however, redeeming memories. Stock cartoons were prepared in advance, and the call from the shop of " 'Ere Bill! Bring down Our Lord number two, will you?" retains a gentle humour still.'

At the polytechnic evening classes, the quality of Mark's work was beginning to stand out among that of the four hundred-odd students. Yet only fifteen were as young as he; three-quarters were adult men and women, and many were already established. In 1908 several of them managed to get pictures accepted by the Royal Academy exhibition.[36] Three landscapes by Gaskell himself and paintings by two of his assistants were also on show. However, though Mark did not know it, the teaching methods promoted by the Board of Education and used at the polytechnic were already being condemned in more advanced circles. This was especially true in the subjects of design, in which he had failed, and in drawing from plaster casts, at which he was now toiling. In spite of all his efforts, when the examinations came round again in the summer of 1908 he failed in this subject.

What saved him was his natural flair for and love of oil painting, the medium to which he would always remain faithful. His beautiful little still lifes were already starting to reflect his strong feelings for the quality and texture of his subjects. Although in the examination in oil painting of still life he was awarded only a second-class pass, he had better luck when in company with some of the other advanced students he entered for the National Art Competition, and his work went in alongside that of fifteen thousand other hopefuls across the country. For his entry Mark painted an arrangement of a pot and a melon in front of a willow-pattern tray,[170] and when the results were announced he had been awarded a Bronze Medal.[37]

Things now began to happen quickly. Clayton and Bell had, rather reluctantly, renewed his job after the first six months, writing to his father: 'We did not intend our letter to convey to you any evidence of dissatisfaction on our part, as your son's conduct and efforts in respect of his work have been all that we could wish. We were unable to satisfy ourselves, upon the evidence of his first six months' work, that he would do justice to himself by following our branch of Art work; but we are glad to have your permission for him to work on for a further probationary period of six months, by the end of which time we expect he will be working with greater freedom.'

But with a positive sign of his success Mark renewed his application to the Jewish Educational Aid Society. Their first referee, S. J. Solomon,* was doubtful, but the second was to take a different view: 'I have been told that you wish to show your work to a practising painter, and I shall be very glad to look at any you will send . . . or bring to me,' wrote the well-known Jewish painter William Rothenstein on 3 October 1908.† And so, accompanied by his elder brother Jack, who helped to carry his paintings, Mark journeyed to Rothenstein's home in Hampstead. He rang the bell of the imposing house while Jack slipped away.

The door was opened by Rothenstein's son John, who remembered Mark as 'a being very much alive, a shortish, handsome boy with apricot-coloured skin and a dense mop of dark brown hair so stiff that it stood on end. He looked nervous, sullen and somehow hectic. I took him for a barrow boy but he told me he had been sent to see my father!'[38] Rothenstein, always very helpful to the young,[39] looked closely at Mark's work and sent him away feeling much encouraged.

---

* Solomon J. Solomon, R.A., 1860–1927, portrait and subject painter.

† William Rothenstein, 1872–1945, the son of a German Jewish wool merchant living in Bradford, had trained at the Slade School and in Paris. He was already widely known for his portraits and other pictures in art and literary circles in England, France and Germany. Later he became Principal of the Royal College of Art and was knighted in 1931.

Next day a letter arrived from him for Louis. 'Your son, as you will know, came here yesterday and brought me a number of his paintings. It is never easy to prophesy regarding the future of an artist but I do sincerely believe that your son has gifts of a high order, and that if he will cultivate them with love and care, that you will one day have reason to be proud of him. I believe that a good artist is a very noble man, and it is worth while giving up many things which men consider very important, for others which we think still more so. From the little I could see of the character of your son, I have faith in him and I hope and believe he will make the best possible use of the opportunities I gather you are going to be generous enough to give him.'

Golda carefully framed this letter and hung it on the wall of her kitchen.

Rothenstein was friendly with the authorities at the Slade School of Art, and he persuaded the Educational Aid Society to pay for Mark to go there. The Society's secretary wrote, 'You are to become a student at the Slade School of Art, and Mr Rothenstein has very kindly agreed to personally look after your studies. This will include the valuable privilege of occasionally working at his studio. So I think you ought to consider yourself very lucky and determine to make the most of the opportunity now offered you – as I am sure you will.'

The Slade agreed that Mark could start at once, and, on 13 October, within a few days of his visit to Rothenstein, he found himself enrolling at one of the country's most famous art schools. Even Clayton and Bell, though ruffled, had helped: 'The suddenness of the removal of your son from our Studio is quite unusual with us, a full week's notice being the rule; but we have no desire to place any obstacles in the boy's way and will consequently release him. He will also take with him our heartiest good wishes for a successful career.'

CHAPTER 5

The surgical eye

Several hurdles awaited Mark when he started at the Slade School, which was part of University College in Gower Street, Bloomsbury: the first being an interview with the Professor, Brown. This did not go too badly, though for some it could be an unnerving experience: 'Waiting outside Brown's room could easily revive unhappy memories for those who had had their share of waiting to see their headmasters at other schools. And entering his room could deepen the feeling of utter gloom: the room sadly needed redecorating, the walls were bare, and there was nothing anywhere to suggest the glory of the place. Brown sat at the table, leaning back in his chair. Behind him stood Tonks and Steer, each with one arm on the mantelpiece. It all seemed so still and silent that they might have passed for a tableau at Madame Tussauds. Brown would be wearing an ageing black frock coat with here and there some smudges of paint on it. Being interviewed by him was not encouraging; one almost felt that he hated the sight of students. His face seemed flushed with anger, and it was only years later that I realized that he suffered from a distressing shyness.'[40]

Many students found Brown, with his grey hair, moustache and chin-tuft, protruding jaw and grave eyes behind spectacles, a rather grim figure. 'He was a somewhat gruff, hard bitten man, of great feeling, with something of the Victorian military man about him, such as the Colonel who had spent his life on the North West frontier, surrounded by savages.'[41]

The Antique Room, on the first floor, was where Mark first saw his new fellow students at work. Casts of Classical and Renaissance sculpture were scattered everywhere, around the walls, on plinths, on trestle-tables, or simply lying on the floor: heads, busts, torsos, complete figures, here and there an odd foot. Among these and various overhanging plants the students worked, most of them seated astride wooden donkeys: each had written his name on the sheet of Michelet paper pinned to a board in front of him and was copying a cast with pencil or charcoal, using bread as an eraser.

It was evident that the students here were quite different from those at the polytechnic, the most obvious distinction being that of social class. Some of the students were rich and titled. Others thought of their families as very hard up, but there were always one or two servants. England belonged to the middle class, and they were the middle class – even if in some cases they questioned its values. One student described the Slade as, 'like a typical public school seen in a nightmare . . . Certainly, in atmosphere, it differed very little from St Paul's at its chilliest . . . It required all my so-called public-school training to take my place at the Slade.'[42]

Compared with the others, Mark's clothes, speech and personal habits were all wrong, and his background not only lower class but positively amazing. A fellow student wrote, 'Mark was sensitive about his origin and background . . . Lacking the education which the rest of us had received, his ignorance was expressed with a naivety and solemnity that sent us into fits of laughter.'[43]

Though there was little anti-semitism as such at the Slade, some students were wary: 'I was silly enough to feel some antipathy to Gertler because he was a Jew,' one student later confessed.[44]

Another shock was that the drawing teacher, Tonks, condemned his methods of work. This was all the more serious because succeeding as an artist had already become for Mark the basis of his plan of living; his ability was to be his passport, and on it everything depended.

But his road to success now lay only through the Slade, since this was the choice of his sponsors. Rothenstein himself had been at the school and had sent his younger brother Albert* there; it had established a reputation as the most dynamic school in Britain. Its revolutionary approach had produced artists such as Augustus John and William Orpen, whose unconventional painting was talked about in a way previously reserved for young poets and playwrights. Its teachers – Professor Brown with his two assistants,

* Albert changed his surname to Rutherston.

Henry Tonks and Wilson Steer – were practising painters.* They
were the dominant members of an exhibiting group, the New
English Art Club, which had built itself a circle of buyers and
gained platforms for its views in the press.† The group was
attacking, with some success, the uninspired attitudes of the Royal
Academy. Even the venerable dealers Agnews, in Bond Street, had
admitted the importance of the Slade-trained artists by including
them in an exhibition of modern painting in 1906.

It was in drawing, above all, that the school excelled, and Tonks
was by far the strongest personality on the staff; only by gaining his
approval could a pupil hope to get on. Paul Nash, who arrived two
years after Mark, described his first encounter: 'Tonks was the Slade
and the Slade was Tonks. As a new student I sought an interview
and confidently displayed my drawings . . . His surgical eye raked
my immature designs. With hooded stare and sardonic mouth, he
hung in the air above me, like a tall question mark, backwards and
bent over from the neck, a question mark, moreover, of a derisive
rather than an inquisitive order. In cold discouraging tones he
welcomed me to the Slade. It was evident he considered that neither
the Slade, nor I, was likely to derive much benefit.'[45]

'He was very tall and grim with a distinct resemblance to the
"Iron Duke",' recalled a later colleague. 'His criticisms must be
some of the most scathing in history. A typical beginning, in a slow,
horrified voice, would be like this: "What is it? . . . *what* is it? . . .
Horrible . . . *Horrible*! . . . is it an insect?" '[46] William Rothenstein
described how: 'Young ladies of the best families were known to
weep at Tonks's acid comments on their work; yet young ladies of

---

* Frederick Brown, 1851–1941, Wilson Steer, 1860–1942, and Henry Tonks,
1862–1937, were friends and painted together. Wilson Steer was one of the best
painters of the time in England, concentrating mainly on landscapes. Tonks had
trained in medicine, becoming a Fellow of the Royal College of Surgeons. He
began to attend evening art classes under Brown, who was then at the Westminster Technical Institute, in 1888. When Brown was appointed Slade Professor in
1893 he offered Tonks a job as his assistant and Tonks gave up medicine. Tonks
became interested in painting groups of figures in interiors and the play of light
on them, and he is remembered for these, and for his caricatures and gifts as a
draughtsman.

† Critics such as D. S. MacColl, Roger Fry, Frank Rutter and C. J. Holmes
were all supporters.

the best families flocked to the Slade to throw themselves before Tonks's Jaganath progress through the life rooms. There was a time when poor Tonks had to walk the streets not daring to go home, lest ladies be found at his door awaiting his arrival with drawings in their hands, whose easels had been passed by, and in whose hearts was despair.'[47]

Yet in spite of his daunting manner, Tonks had a sense of humour, and he respected courage. Occasionally, very occasionally, a student could hold his own. Once a new student, a very tall, heavy man, in private life an amateur pugilist, was sitting on a low donkey. 'Tonks, from his great height, bent over him and said cuttingly, "I suppose you think you can draw." The student collected himself, rose slowly to an even greater height than Tonks and, looking down, replied with suppressed fury, 'If I thought I could draw, I shouldn't come here, should I?" '[48]

Tonks was in fact a kindly, shy man. The caricatures which he drew from time to time as a change from painting were brilliant and savage, but not primarily designed to wound. He wrote once, 'I have always felt my particular caricatures are too homely for publication. I have no skill and they are therefore for the amusement (I hope they are amused) of my friends.'[49]

Here was the man whose approval Mark had to win, a task made slightly easier by some qualities that the two had in common, the sixteen-year-old slum boy, and this ex-surgeon of forty-six. Tonks had got his chance to give up medical work and follow his real interest, drawing, very late in life. This late start and a feeling of time lost lay behind, and partly accounted for, his complete dedication to art. 'He talked of dedication, the privilege of being an artist; that to do a bad drawing was like living with a lie, and he proceeded to implant these ideals into his students by a ruthless and withering criticism. His features gave the impression of severity and sadness . . . (the students) used to chant, "I am the Lord thy God, thou shalt have no other Tonks but me".'[50]

This was Mark's first contact with a community and a personality to whom pictures were not only of infinitely greater importance than fabric designs, tiles or furniture, but more important than anything else in life, and all-important as an end in themselves.

Tonks was a dedicated and obsessive fanatic, and Mark was made of the same material. Tonks's enthusiasm reinforced his own, and Tonks, as a living demonstration of dedication to art, fired Mark for ever with the same qualities, so that for the rest of his life he was to give the impression to everyone who met him that, in art, nothing short of the best would do, and everything must be sacrificed to achieve it.

Mark settled down to struggle with the new methods of drawing. At least now he had inspiring company and favourable conditions. Life was opening out. The new spaciousness of University College made the polytechnic seem cramped and ramshackle. Every day, as he came to the college gates, his eye could take in the side sweep of lawns between the U-shaped range of buildings. The wing on the left housed the Slade School and in the centre was the attractive ivy-covered doorway, set in a semi-circular projection of the wall. Directly facing the gates and about two hundred yards away, rose the magnificent columned portico of the main college, behind which entrance halls stretched away in both directions, flooded with light from a long row of tall windows. The ceilings were so high that the halls could have comfortably contained a whole street of little East End houses.

And now, even in the East End, Mark had a little more space, for a few months earlier Louis had managed to rent the whole of a sizeable house, No. 14 Spital Square. With a basement and four floors, there was adequate room for the family and the workshop, while the Square was quiet and traffic-free – dingy and run down, perhaps, but still a cut above the rest of the area.

Lying east of Liverpool Street station, behind Bishopsgate, it had been built by Huguenots nearly two hundred years before, and for over a hundred years until the industry decayed, the wealthier master-weavers had lived in the solid, beautifully proportioned houses.

The Slade method of teaching was in the French tradition, and laid great emphasis on working from the live model. After only a short preliminary training with casts in the Antique Room, the students were allowed for the last hour of each day into the Life

Rooms, and then, after only a few terms, spent all their time there. The mens' Life Room was thus the very heart of the school.* This vast basement room, 'a gloomy vault of a place that seemed to smell like a chapel', extended upwards through two stories. Over the students' heads a balcony in the wall at ground-floor level connected with the professor's room, and they sometimes became aware of Tonks or Brown brooding over them. Here they worked, in a thick atmosphere of tobacco smoke, warmed by a coke stove on the model's throne and hot water pipes on the North wall.

When they first entered, students were duly deferential. Adrian Allinson, a fellow student of Mark's, described his own first day: 'Timidly and apprehensively I shuffled to the rear of the serried rows of silent workers. The unexpected heat and tobacco fug and the sudden sight of a naked woman enthroned before forty men increased my discomfiture. With shaking fingers I arranged the paper on my drawing board and began sharpening the all too fragile sticks of vine charcoal, when a chorus of voices sang out, "Change". Whereupon, to my surprise, the model took up an entirely new pose before I had got a single line on to the paper. This was "life drawing" with a vengeance. I had been unaware that the last hour of the day was devoted to short poses, the drawings of which should train the eye to quick reactions. Realizing that it was senseless for me yet to attempt drawing at high speed, I decided to make a dispassionate examination of the model, the first adult female I had ever seen stripped. Museums and the Antique Room had already made me familiar with the sculptor's versions of woman in stone and bronze; but these were "Art" – static and remote as the days in which they had been created. Nymphs and Goddesses, they belonged to the realm of imagination, and the thought that some Greek or Roman girl had actually posed for those statues never entered my head. The figure before me with its pink and soft flesh, breathing and ever so slightly swaying, though like, was yet utterly unlike the sculptured replicas. Moreover, though the body and limbs were relatively immobile, the lady's eye roved and her glance as it rested on one or other of the men seemed to share dark and unholy secrets with them. In all probability the

* The female students had a separate Life Room, much smaller, on the first floor.

poor girl, bored and tired out by the day's work, was merely thinking of her cup of tea and a quick release from the stuffy enclosure.'[51]

The Slade advocated a return to concentrated study of the Old Masters, especially those of the Renaissance. The methods which the Board of Education and the Royal Academy Schools set out for art teaching were rejected on almost every point. The Board thought a student should spend months at a time producing an elaborately finished, highly detailed drawing. The Slade encouraged the student to work fast – the casts in the Antique Room were moved frequently, and the model poses in the Life Room were changed after a week or two, so that the student could not spend too long on one work. Thus his eyes were trained to search quickly for the vital lines of his subject.

In the second place the board emphasized the use of stump and charcoal, chalk and india-rubber to stimulate, by shading and stippling, the subtle variations in surface texture and the play of light on a static subject. Thus at the polytechnic Mark had been taught the importance of correctly observing these variations in tone. Now at the Slade, he found that Tonks showed little interest in tone in drawing – it was too often used as a cover for bad draughtsmanship. Instead Mark was urged to draw with the point, to place each line as a courageous statement which could be judged right or wrong.

There was a third important difference. Students were directed by the Board to make a drawing by first fixing the outline with the aid of actual measurements and a plumb line. The outline was then filled in. Again this method was rejected by Tonks, who wanted the drawing kept open and warned pupils against committing themselves too early to a contour.

The Slade was above all a school of drawing. Painting was under the direction of Wilson Steer and instruction, though sensitive, was erratic: nervous students who waited a long time for his comments on their work after he had sat down behind them, had been known to turn round and find him asleep. 'Painting and colour developed at the Slade by trial and error ... There was some doubt about teaching colour and life painting was not compulsory. It was in the ratio of about two weeks life painting to three months for life drawing.'[52]

But Steer was a fine painter and helped by his example to emphasize the importance of 'pure' painting, devoid of the trivial subject matter associated with the Royal Academy. To despise this august institution was *de rigueur* among staff and students at the Slade. It had reduced painting to a formula and art to a social event, the Academy Exhibition taking its place among the Epsom Spring Meeting, Ascot, Goodwood and the Richmond Horse Show.

It represented the commercial success which an artist could obtain by painting anecdotal subjects: 'Darbies & Joans, deeds of derring-do or sacrifice, young girls praying while dogs looked on with human eyes expressing reverence mixed with envy; true-blue religion, sudden death and beef-on-the-hoof or hunting; sex, provided it showed coy and pretty maidens fleeing from wicked conquerors; loot and rape...if and when they were daintily wrapped up in the theme that men would be men in the Good Old Days!'[53]

Mark had a lot to learn very quickly about matters other than art, though his nervousness in these first years was well hidden. 'He seemed extremely sure of himself in a quite sensible way; though tolerated and respected he was not much liked,' one student affirmed. 'He was smallish, delicately made, pretty in an almost girlish fashion. His complexion was noticeably transparent and his appearance generally marred by the film of yellow ear wax which I remember as one of his most noticeable features. It seemed to me characteristic.'[54]

Contact with the girl students was ruled out by Mark's diffidence towards them, and in any case only the older and more confident boys braved Tonks's disapproval of chatting in the corridors. 'This isn't a matrimonial agency,' he once observed to a boy and girl talking in the hall.

To talk to the models was even more of a risk. It was only thirty years since the use of naked models was so controversial that the professor could not be in the women's Life Room when both students and model were there: first the girls had to file out, then the teacher would go in and mark the drawings.

At the beginning of Mark's second term a new student, C. R. W. Nevinson, joined. He was two years older, much more experienced and confident, and quickly established himself as one of the leaders. Having taken a liking to Mark, he adopted him, and brought him into closer contact with the other students.*

The end of the year brought triumphant success. John Fothergill, a senior student, thought Mark's work was so good that he should try straight away to get it shown publicly. In May Mark wrote, not without trepidation, to Rothenstein: 'I have a question to ask you which has been worrying me the last few weeks. Fothergill – I will say it right away – wants me to send my "Onions", to the New English and on that account made the frame for it. The idea has always seemed so absurd to me that I was ashamed to ask you when I saw you, but what will he say if I don't send it? What shall I do?' Rothenstein encouraged him, 'You are doing quite rightly in submitting your still life to the jury of the New English. You must not worry too much as to your progress, about which I have no kind of doubt ... Get away into the fields whenever you get a chance, and spend as much of your time as you can in the open air. Come up to Hampstead some day soon, and we will go for another walk on the Heath. Please remember me kindly to your people.' (12 May 1909).

The New English jury was not sufficiently impressed to accept the picture, but Lesser, secretary of the Jewish Educational Aid Society, stepped in and bought it for a pound.

The great event came in May: Mark had succeeded in mastering the new methods to such an extent that he not only achieved his certificate in painting but won one of the two Slade scholarships, and with it the prestige of the 'Scholar', who was supposed to help keep order and assist the younger students. Worth £35 a year for two years, it paid the fees (£21 a year) and left enough for materials, lunches and fares. It made further help from the Jewish Society unnecessary, relieved the strain on his family, and was

---

* C. R. W. Nevinson, 1889–1946, was the son of the author, war correspondent and philanthropist H. W. Nevinson, 1856–1941, and he had studied painting at St John's Wood before going to the Slade in 1908. In 1914 he became closely associated with the Italian Futurist movement, and in 1914–17 painted the war pictures for which he is best known.

evidence to them that from now on Mark could stand on his own feet and might be destined for great things. 'How proud and happy you will be feeling at your son's success,' Rothenstein wrote to Golda on 22 May 1909. 'You may be quite sure he has deserved it, and that his beginning is an indication of the path which he is to follow. Everyone who meets him feels that he is one day going to express the beauty he feels so deeply . . . He has already won for himself many friends, and the honourable place he has now won in the Slade School will be an immense stimulus to him.' But Rothenstein was concerned about overwork: 'Please see that he gets out as much as possible; we shall always be glad to see him here.'

It was Golda's hour of triumph too. Unable to reply to Rothenstein in English herself, she asked Mark to do it for her: 'On behalf of my mother,' he wrote, 'I desire to express to you her most heartfelt thanks for your kind letter, which completed the over-whelming happiness my success brought her. When she reflects on all that you have done for me she does not quite know how to express her gratitude. As for myself, I cannot sufficiently express my own gratitude for the kindness you have shown me.'

CHAPTER 6

Upon the crest of the wave

Many doors were opened to Mark by his friendship with Nevinson.

This first companion in the world outside the East End cut a very dashing figure, usually wearing, 'a large bow tie, bewaisted coat, socks and handkerchiefs of a delicate peacock blue, and a slight growth of whiskers à la Rapin about the ears.'[55] His background was exciting and impressive (a famous father, and travels on the Continent) and he could drop a surprising number of interesting names or tell stories about the artistic life of Paris. 'Because of his bulbous forehead, high cheekbones, flat nose and crinkly hair, Nevinson received the nickname of "Bucknigger" . . . He had a

5—MG * *

temperament that gravitated between easy bursts of laughter
(usually at his own witticisms) and deep depression.'[56]

Among his other traits, many appealed to Mark: sensitive and far
from complacent, with wide-ranging sympathies, Nevinson was
something of a rebel, and had a strong dislike for the public-school
milieu in which he had been temporarily immersed. To most of the
students Whitechapel was *terra incognita* and journeys there were
quite an adventure; as one wrote, 'The jostling crowds of Russian,
Polish and Central European Jews has so transformed this corner of
London that I felt I was going abroad but minus the expense and
discomfort entailed.'[57] But Nevinson's view of it, because his
parents had been associated with Toynbee Hall, was much deeper.
'Whitechapel had no terrors for me,' he wrote, 'and being what
Augustus John called a man cursed with an educational tendency, I
was delighted to be able to help Gertler, I hope without patronage,
to the wider culture that had been possible for me through my birth
and environment. At any rate, I loved it, and his sense of humour
prevented me from becoming a prig. Often, indeed, the pupil was
able to teach the master a great deal, and it is impossible to convey
the pleasures and enthusiasms we shared in the print room of the
British Museum, in South Kensington, and in the National Gallery.
We also shared the joys of eating, and I am proud and glad to say
that both my parents were extremely fond of him.'[58]

For his part, being so conscious of the barrier of class between
himself and the other students, Mark was overjoyed to win a friend
from among them: 'Just one other thing that makes me so happy,
that is my nice friends amongst the upper class,' he confided to
Rothenstein. 'They are so much nicer than the rough "East Ends" I
am used to. My chief friend and pal is young Nevinson, a very,
very nice chap. I am awfully fond of him. I am so happy when I am
out with him. He invites me down to dinners and then we
go on Hampstead Heath talking of the future. Oh! so enthusiastically!'

The Nevinsons, like Rothenstein, lived in Hampstead, so that
Mark was finding help and support for the second time in this
district. The trees and hills and wide spaces of the Heath enchanted
him. There was nothing like this in Whitechapel where, apart from
one or two tiny pockets of green such as Finsbury Square and

Christchurch Yard, the rows of low houses and narrow streets stretched on for mile after mile.

Nevinson's parents were a striking couple. His father was a liberal, a free thinker, and a famous writer; his mother spent her time on good causes. Being sympathetic to Mark's problems and aware of the odds against him, they set out to help by introducing him to important potential patrons such as Professor Sadler, of Leeds University. Even more important was the chance they gave him – his first – of becoming familiar, not only with the workings and comfortable way of life of a middle-class household, but with a family in which ideas were common currency, and concern about matters outside their own problems a normal thing. If there was talk of the problems of making more money and improving one's social position it was much more likely to refer to people in the East End or Central Africa than to the Nevinsons themselves. Unlike Mark's family, they did not live perpetually on top of each other. There was a spaciousness and freedom about their lives: each had his own interests, yet could be tolerant of the other's enthusiasms.

Mark and Nevinson became very friendly with three other students – Adrian Allinson, Edward Wadsworth and David Sassoon – and Mark found that they also were not, as they had at first appeared, merely rich, conventional, public-school men.

Allinson's background, like Nevinson's, was liberal, unorthodox and humanitarian. He too had found English public schools not wholly congenial: he had been expelled for trying to persuade his school friends that there was no God. But as with all the others except Mark, there was enough money in the family to give him a good start. 'Had I been born of poor parents the chances of my being given a course of training at the Slade would have been infinitely remote,' he observed.

Edward Wadsworth had begun as an engineering student. He had travelled to Munich, and while there had slipped into an art school in his leisure time and become converted. David Sassoon was a relation of the famous Anglo-Indian banking family, shy and generous: 'He has done me many little kindnesses,' noted Mark. 'He is a chap that does you a kindness *without fuss* from his heart.'

Allinson saw their roles in musical terms: 'We formed a quintet that became inseparable in work and play. Nevinson and

Wadsworth, as first and second violins, led, Gertler and I followed
as viola and 'cello with Sassoon occasionally audible in the background in the part of double bass.'⁵⁹

Although his new friends made Mark's evenings a little more
varied, the days saw no slackening in the pace of work, even during
holidays. 'The following is how I spend each day,' he wrote to
Rothenstein from Andover, where a visit to a farm had been
arranged for him. 'Paint from 10 a.m. to 1 p.m. Draw from 2 to 4
p.m. Paint from 5 to 8.30 p.m. Work altogether from 10 a.m. until
8.30 p.m.'

At the Slade Tonks was completely won over: 'I am in
Paradise. Everything is going excellently, and could not be
better,' Mark told Rothenstein. 'Tonks has been encouraging me
greatly; besides praising some paintings I have done in holidays, he
told me that I have made good progress in school and that I can tell
my people so. Imagine my joy. I shall come and see you next
Tuesday and bring some drawings *only*, although I should like you
to see paintings too, but for them I am going to be impertinent
enough to ask you down to *my* place for tea, where we will make
you taste some "Passover" food, which I am sure you will like.
Will you come?'

With good friends, no money worries and nothing to distract
him from concentrating his energy in work, he was happier than he
had thought possible. 'I must indeed thank you for your most kind
and encouraging letter,' he wrote to Rothenstein. 'It made me feel
much happier and braced me up like the sea an invalid. Reading it,
I felt encouragement dancing in the very atmosphere about me and
the earnest interest you take for my benefit are there convincingly
displayed. My world is a World of Beauty and joy . . . all is bliss
and I am in ecstasies of joy. So I must thank you once more and
only hope that *you* may always have cause for happiness as I have
today. Lastly I must thank "Providence" one hundred times for
being able to put my heart and soul to such an *Art*.' The basis of
his exaltation was his work, and only doubts about this could shake
him. His happiness 'could be marred only by one thing "progress",
and if at any time I am encouraged on that point my world
becomes perfect.'

In the summer of 1910 he collected more prizes, winning a £3 first for head painting and a £2 second for painting from the cast. His friend Allinson won one of the year's scholarships and Stanley Spencer won the other. 'The Slade at that date . . . was in one of its periodical triumphal flows, when from the unknown deeps arise a few gifted ones,' Paul Nash remembered later. 'And now, upon the crest of the wave, were riding nearly half a dozen – Stanley Spencer, Mark Gertler, William Roberts, Edward Wadsworth, Charles Nevinson.*

In his way, Spencer was as much of an outsider as Mark, though far less vulnerable. Each day he caught the 8.50 a.m. train from his village, Cookham, and 5.08 p.m. saw him safely on the train back home, where tea with his secure, comfortable family could not be missed.

Darsie Japp, another student, recalled: 'In his (always dirty) Eton collar he looked very much the schoolboy. He and I used to eat our lunch alone in the empty life room. He *always* had hard-boiled egg sandwiches.'[44]

Allinson also wrote a description of Spencer: 'With his hydro-cephalic forehead crowned by a cockatoo-like crest of hair, and a receding chin sparsely dotted with unshaven hairs, Spencer was a sheer delight for my caricaturist's pencil, and his apparent lack of humour tempted me to excesses of exaggeration.'

A Sketch Club competition was held every month, the winner receiving a prize of three guineas. Allinson recorded: 'A perverse kink in Spencer's make-up prevented his working to the set subject, so that though month after month his designs earned the highest praise, on account of their failure to illustrate the theme he never received the award. It was high time to rectify this lamentable situation, particularly as I knew that a little cash would be very welcome to him. So for the ensuing competition I executed not only my own design but also an imitation Spencer, that besides exhibiting all his mannerisms conformed, as regards the subject, to the rules of the competition. When seen on the wall amongst the rest of the drawings, students and professors alike took it to be authentic. The latter in particular were happy in the thought that

* Paul Nash, *Outline*, p. 90. Spencer had joined the Slade in October 1908. Paul Nash and William Roberts began in October 1910.

dear Stanley was coming into his own at last. I had, of course, to take him into my confidence so that my practical joke should achieve its aim. Alas, our genius, without a glimmer of a smile, said to me, "Oi think this will affect moy career Oi do, Oi'm going to tell the Pro.," and he promptly ran off to Tonks and blew the gaff. Shortly afterwards I was invited into the latter's private sanctum, his baleful lack-lustre eye fixed mine, and his words, "Allinson, you have a very dangerous talent here; beware how you use it," choked the bubble of laughter in my throat. As he was a gifted satirist when he felt so inclined, I had expected that he would enjoy the jest himself. He added that he had intended at the criticism to say he did not consider the work quite up to Mr Spencer's usual standard, which I hardly thought a sporting way out of the predicament.'[59]

Mark was now quite a figure among the students. His short haircut and shabby neat clothes were left behind. To Nevinson he looked 'with his curly hair, like a Jewish Botticelli . . . the genius of the place and besides that the most serious, single-minded artist I have ever come across. His combination of high spirits, shrewd Jewish sense and brilliant conversation are unmatched anywhere.'[60] The pupil had become the master, Nevinson confessed. 'Had Gertler, for instance, told me seriously that I was wasting my time, I should have been heart broken.' He now worked 'under the influence of Gertler.' Paul Nash was struck by Mark's 'Swinburn locks and blue shirt'. He impressed another by 'a certain force of personality and his quick intelligence . . . he seemed so sure of himself – he had very great talent.'[61]

One of the key qualities of Mark's personality began to show at this time – an ability to turn even the dullest events of daily life into a continuous, hilariously funny comedy. 'He was the "charmer" of our little circle,' said Allinson. 'Younger than the rest of us, he possessed good looks of an order that are usually described as "sweetly pretty"; but though his features were feminine in their delicacy of chiselling, he was not in the least effeminate. A devotee of the music hall, particularly of low comedy, and possessing exceptional powers of mimicry and burlesque, he would enchant us with his rendering of turns seen at the Bedford or the Middlesex. His humour was a continual delight.'

Paul Nash recalled Mark's 'imitation Oxford accent, one of the best of his clever repertoire'; other subjects for humour were not wanting. 'At this time the Slade was full with a crowd of men such as I have never seen before or since,' Nevinson wrote. 'There were two outsize Germans who were dwarfed by a giant of a Pole with scowling brows, tight check trousers and whiskers eight inches long. Mr Fothergill was an exquisite in dark blue velvet suiting, pale-yellow silk shirt and stock, with a silver pin as large as an egg, and patent court shoes with silver buckles.'[62] One student had previously worked on the Hampstead and Golders Green tube as an engineer. Naturally enough he was dubbed 'Tube Manager'. Paul Nash wrote: 'A very nice man arrived every morning in a taxi, wearing dancing pumps. He was called The Duke . . . The butt of the school, however, was a delightful person called "Have-a-Smoke", from his ingratiating habit of offering everyone a cigarette on every occasion. He was impervious to ridicule and seemed to live in a world of his own. "Have-a-Smoke" once commissioned Gertler to paint his wife, watching him the while. At every successful touch of the brush, "Have-a-Smoke" called out, "Good stroke, Gertler, oh, good stroke!" Gertler told us he felt as if he were playing cricket . . .'[63]

Among the older students who were taking notice of Mark were Robert Ihlee and Maxwell Lightfoot, who was five years Mark's senior. They lived together in a first-floor flat on the Hampstead Road.

The son of a commercial traveller in Liverpool, Lightfoot had come to the Slade from Chester School of Art and become one of its most brilliant students.[64] 'He was the best draughtsman of the 1909–10 year,' Darsie Japp maintained. 'He and Ihlee gave the tone to the life room . . . Ihlee, a Jew, was given to theorizing. Lightfoot was full of precepts, first principles of drawing, like, "You shouldn't paint the lips but the way the face juts out round them . . ." '

Lightfoot was friendly with the circle of lively young painters, including Harold Gilman and Spencer Gore, who had gathered round Sickert, in Fitzroy Street, and he discussed their ideas – many of which went beyond current Slade thinking – with Mark. The two became firm friends and when Lightfoot went away for the summer their discussions and exchanges of tips continued by letter:

'What are you going to do for the summer?' Lightfoot wrote to Mark from Wales. 'Where are you going? Wherever you go, and whatever you do, for God's sake go to nature for your *theme*. Even though your composition may suffer, your knowledge will benefit by it. If you can manage I would if I were you try and get with somebody that would be able to help you as you proceed. I know what an advantage it was for me to have Gore's criticism last year.'[65]

On 21 July 1910 a letter arrived congratulating Mark on his prizes and encouraging his idea of doing a big figure composition of Jews. 'I was very pleased to hear from Ihlee that you had been successful in winning some money at the Slade. I congratulate you, and hope that it will help you to put forth a great effort in the summer composition ... I remember you were going to do a Jewish picture for the competition. This I think is an excellent idea for you, who understand the people. If you can banish the idea of a set subject from your mind altogether, and let yourself have free scope, I have not the slightest doubt you will do a better picture, than if you tie yourself down to the subject as I did last year. I frankly admit mine was done for money – I needed it. Now I am using it to advantage, at least I hope so. All the same I think if I had not tied myself down so tightly I may have done a better picture.'

But this friendship was to come to an untimely end.

The students rarely looked outside the world of artists and artists' models for their companions. Although it was hard to make contact with the girls at the Slade, by the autumn of 1910, a few of the older students had begun to break down the barriers that separated them. Ways of making contact were provided by the annual winter balls and the summer picnics, both being great occasions. For the balls Tonks would lend the great silk skirted dresses he kept for his models. On the picnics, which Mark particularly enjoyed, the transport was by horse and wagon; these, packed with students, food and beer, would usually make their slow way to Epping Forest. One year they went to Burnham Beeches and the Spencer family walked from Cookham to watch the cricket; Professor Brown was batting and Mark was in the team. Other friendships were made during breakfast parties on Regents Park Lake and occasional visits to each others' studios.

Among the more or less light-hearted encounters, some alliances gave rise to deeper emotions. Allinson later recorded: 'Having fallen under the spell of a well-known artists' model Lightfoot engaged to marry her . . . It seemed incredible that his love should have blinded him to an aspect of his fiancée that was common knowledge to us all.' Lightfoot's family 'considered the girl an inferior' wrote Japp. But he went ahead and the wedding date was fixed.

Through Nevinson, Mark got an introduction to a little exhibiting group – the Friday Club – and in February 1911 the two friends, with Ihlee, Lightfoot and others, had the pride of seeing their pictures on show in the West End for the first time. The group borrowed the Alpine Club Gallery in Mill Street, and instead of the usual mountaineering exhibits visitors were able to see an exhibition 'from which can be gauged', as the *Morning Post* put it, 'the tendencies of the time even more easily than at the New English.'

Most of the artists were little known, being 'for the most part ladies who put forward their imitations of John,' as the *Globe* commented. But among the exhibitors were Roger Fry and two of his friends, Vanessa Bell and Duncan Grant, and it was probably their presence which induced the papers to take an interest in the show.★

Mark's name appeared in print in the majestic columns of the *Morning Post* in a list of 'admirable young artists' trained by Tonks. The greatest pleasure was a whole column in the *Sunday Times* devoted to the exhibition, under the heading, 'The Rising Generation'. Here Mark could see his work actually discussed: ' "Jews Arguing" of Mr Mark Gertler is more remarkable, for its vigorous and incisive rendering of form than for its colour, though this is brave and strong, and if, as I hear, Mr Gertler is only eighteen years of age, he has plenty of time in which to acquire distinction in colour and quality in pigment, and he shows a capacity, which, sooner or later, will force him to choose between being either a

★ The Friday Club had become much more prominent after Vanessa Bell had taken over as secretary a year or two previously. She made it lively and progressive, with meetings in the members' studios. The *Telegraph*, *Athenaeum*, and *The Times* reviewed the 1911 show and the latter referred to Lightfoot's drawings as 'full both of character and romance'. Lightfoot was doing very well. The previous autumn the New English had accepted his work and the newly formed Contemporary Art Society was interested in him.

popular Academy exhibitor or a superior person in the New English Art Club.' This was high praise for a student and Mark could feel well satisfied with his first exhibition.

His work caught the attention of one perceptive and very influential person: Vanessa Bell wrote to her husband Clive, 'One young man I have marked down as promising. His name is Mark Gertler and he has two other remarkable paintings; remarkable really only considering his age. But I think he may be going to be good!'

Appalling news came later in the year. On 27 September Lightfoot killed himself. The circumstances were slightly mysterious. Darsie Japp said later, 'When his family refused to become reconciled to the idea of his marrying the girl he cut his throat the day before what was to have been his wedding day.' Allinson's view was, 'Not until almost the eve of his marriage did he learn that he had set his heart upon a woman notoriously promiscuous and the discovery drove him to the extreme of suicide. We were all deeply shocked by the loss both to ourselves and to art.'

'Blasé as I was,' noted Nevinson, 'I felt bewildered when I witnessed the natural pride of the woman because a man had died for her.'[66]

Lightfoot was the first of Mark's friends to come to a violent end.

CHAPTER 7

Like one huge Rembrandt brought to life

It was as 'a newly risen star of realism', that Mark appeared to his contemporaries. He never forgot his origins, nor was he ashamed of them. His observations were reported with breathtaking candour and while he kept his family amused with stories of the students, to these he brought alive the East End furrier's family. 'I listened with interest and admiration to his remarks about his brothers,' wrote Darsie Japp. 'The admiration was for Gertler's unprejudiced description, not for the brothers.'

When Mark put still-life painting aside and used his new powers of technique to paint the people among whom he had grown up, it became evident that he had indeed watched the family relentlessly and missed nothing. It also became clear that his upbringing, whatever had been its effects on his mind and health, had provided one curious advantage – after all, none of his rivals at the Slade had lived in the same room as five of their subjects. For year after year Mark had watched them eating, arguing, undressing, sleeping and waking, a few feet away. Then he had watched their gradual trans-formation from poverty-stricken immigrants to a settled family who at least had enough to eat.

In 1909, he began work on a series of portraits of them, painting in the evenings, weekends and vacations; and after October 1910 he devoted even more time to these pictures, working at home and going into the Slade only three days a week.

Upstairs on the third floor at Spital Square the machines chat-tered away. Harry and Jack worked there and for the time being the family was self-sufficient.

Louis was never going to be a brilliant success at business and the others would still smile when he attempted a little trading, pleased one week at buying an article and even more pleased a few weeks later to get rid of it at a loss, lighting a cigar to celebrate the deal.

This unworldliness was allied to his extreme piety and he was intensely concerned that his children should live decently and avoid wrongdoing. This they respected. He was an established figure, too, among the people in the square, a certificate holder at the German Synagogue a few doors away, while at home no prayers or observances were omitted. Trivial amusements were frowned upon, and Mark's sister Sophie had to keep her dancing dress at a friend's in secret.

Louis's rule was quiet, and in Mark's paintings he was shown as a gentle, rather withdrawn figure with long moustaches and a neat, pointed beard. No trace remained of the violent streak which Mark had seen in the past, as when Louis attacked a hansom-cab driver for trying to overcharge, and once knocked down a teacher who had beaten Mark.

Nor was there any sure indication of the strength which had once been so formidable. Already, although only fifty-three, he seemed to be shrinking; his face was pale and rather unhealthy, the eyes dim behind the spectacles. His small success had come too late. One of Mark's most moving paintings was a little head and shoulders of Louis and Golda, their heads close together, looking out of the picture; Golda's arm encircled Louis's shoulder with a protective air.

Louis's strength, and perhaps his violence, had been passed on to Jack, who never had any trouble holding his own in the life of the streets. He belonged to an amateur boxing club and trained hard, with the aim of becoming a professional. A set of photographs showed him in different fighting postures, muscles bulging convincingly. But in his portrait it was Jack's gentleness that Mark chose to emphasize. A friend later called him, 'a softie, the type who gives away his last shilling'. None of the three brothers ever wavered in their affection for each other, but Jack and Mark had perhaps the closest relationship. It was usually Jack, for instance, who would carry Mark's paintings to prospective buyers. Throughout his life Mark was never without the very comforting knowledge that in an emergency Jack would come at once. And there were to be a number of such occasions. Mark's paintings of him depicted a sharp face with clear-cut features and indicated a quick intelligence and rather reckless gaiety. In 1910 they posed for a joint photograph in suits and boaters, looking bright, ambitious and very alike. By contrast, however, to the tension in Mark, Jack seemed more relaxed, smarter and perhaps even better looking. Jack learned how to make the most of what pleasures Whitechapel offered, becoming a well-known figure at the music halls and the Yiddish Theatre, and a skilful, prize-winning dancer. It was he who introduced Mark to these pastimes.

A problem for Harry and Jack was that the family wanderings and early struggles had left them with one serious disadvantage: their education was almost non-existent, so that neither could read either Yiddish or English. Nor, as would become apparent, did they have much talent for business. They did possess intelligence, courage and determination – but these qualities were relatively plentiful in Whitechapel.

The fur trade was notoriously hazardous and failures were frequent. For the present, however, things were not going badly, and by 1911 they even had a telephone installed.

Harry's skill and industry were to save Mark's career from coming to an abrupt halt half a dozen years later and many times thereafter. He married in 1910 and worked harder than ever at the business, taking more of the responsibility from Louis. Harry was quiet and steady. In Mark's portraits he looked neat and rather dapper in a stiff turnover collar, hair parted dead centre, carefully waved at the side.

Mark painted Golda more than anyone else, trying, in picture after picture, to produce a convincing image of his mother. For most of them he did not bother with a background or setting, and painted her so close up that in some pictures her face seemed only inches away from the onlooker. He drew her in sanguine and in pencil; with her head in a scarf; in a floral dress and in furs. And in one picture she was seated at her kitchen table preparing a meal.[171]

In the spring of 1911 he started on a portrait which he intended to try and have shown in the New English Art Club.[169]

It was never difficult to get Golda to sit; theatres, museums, pubs, restaurants and London West of the Bank were outside her knowledge or interest, and she was apprehensive of the Gentile world. Apart from shopping, visits to the synagogue and very occasional calls on friends in the district, she stayed at home. Her favourite pastime was to sit outside the front door watching the life of the square, or in her kitchen, hands folded over her ample stomach. She liked nothing better than for Mark to set up his easel to do yet another painting of her. He was her favourite son and his talent and success was bringing her great happiness. While she dreamed and Mark painted, hour after hour passed in silence.

Mark was very conscious of all he owed her: to his closest friends he never tired of repeating how marvellous she was – how she had held the family together and kept them alive in the years in Austria; for they would certainly have died without her.

In this picture he tried to show her shrewdness, and the observant eyes which had spotted one of the workers who was stealing furs by winding them round his body under his shirt. Golda had noticed that 'he comes in thin and goes out fat'. It was not a sentimental painting: Golda ruled her children. She could be demanding and selfish, binding them to her with stories of the misfortunes she had endured to bring them up, the hardness of her life and the inadequacy of Louis. The portrait was accepted and hung in the November 1911 New English show, as 'Portrait of an elderly woman'. Over the next sixty years it was to become one of the best known and most admired of Mark's pictures.*[169]

Painting in Golda's kitchen had its disadvantages. Accidents happened, especially in the dark evenings, as for example when one of the brothers, home late, groping round for the gas jet, walked into a wet canvas and spoiled it. It was decided that Mark should have a room in which to work and soon he was able to write to

* 'It shows a power of evoking an entirely convincing presence . . . remarkable also for a sheer capacity to paint . . . masterly.' (Sir John Rothenstein); 'The kind of thing that her son's teachers were trying to paint, but rarely with such a fine mixture of brilliance and sincerity.' (Professor Quentin Bell); 'Extraordinary power of drawing . . . grandeur of conception and psychological insight.' (Allan Gwynne-Jones: *Portrait Painters*, Phoenix House, 1950).

Rothenstein: 'I am now the proud possessor of a beautiful studio. It is situated in Commercial Street round the corner of where I live. Although it is on the top floor of a house in the middle of a noisy market place it is very comfortable. I am very happy and proud of it indeed. I am so independent: I sit at one end of the room and look across to the other and say, Look! This is all my own. I can do what I please: Sing, run, place my feet on the table, anything, and there is no one to stop me. I of course don't do those things, but sit and gloat over the quiet solitude of it. It is exactly what I used to look forward to, for what more does one want but a room, materials, and the National Gallery?'

Two houses away from the Gertlers, at No. 12 Spital Square, lived Solomon Jacob Berlinski with his sizeable family. His parents, Russian Jews, had arrived in the square over twenty-five years ago, after building up a business near Leman Street in Government surplus goods, and Solomon Jacob had carried on trading in military stores so that the family was now quite prosperous. Of the eight children, the two youngest, David and May, became close friends of Mark.

'Round about 1908 my hobby was photography,' David said later, 'and when Mark did a painting I used to photograph it . . . He loved to dress up himself or whoever he was painting. One picture was a self portrait in a fishing cap.'

To take the photographs the two boys would climb through a back window with the paintings on to a flat roof. One print from the big glass negatives shows Mark's head and shoulders, silhouetted among the chimneys, emerging over a very large composition on 'The return of Jephtha'.

Much of their leisure time was spent together. On Saturdays, forbidden to ride on the Sabbath, they went for long walks: to the Whitechapel Art Gallery, to Tower Bridge, where they would watch the ships go through, and to the Regents Canal to watch the barges.

As his friendship with May developed into a love affair Mark made a number of beautiful drawings and paintings of her. They showed a very young girl (she was sixteen in 1911) with a sturdy figure and a round face framed in long dark hair. In one painting,[67] looking pensive and serious, she sits at a table leaning on her elbows, one hand at her throat. Mark later described her as very like the girl in Rembrandt's picture at Dulwich College in London, and in fact he chose for her a very similar pose. It is inscribed 'To my young friend May Berlinski 1910'.

In another portrait she has acquired a touch of sophistication – an awareness of her attractiveness, and the vivid contrasts between her skin and dark eyes and hair are emphasized. A half-smile is on the full sensuous lips, the expression is gay and a little provocative.

On 10 May 1910, Mark wrote to Rothenstein, 'Although my praise, I know, has not much worth, I feel that as a "brother brush" (if you will give me leave to call myself that) I must congratulate you for the two very fine pictures you have at the Whitechapel Art Gallery. It is really impudent of me to write you this, but believe me it is from the bottom of my heart that I do so, for of all the fine things of that *very* fine show I like your pictures best. Of the two I like the "Jew" picture best, I spend all my time nearly looking at it. It is one of the finest things I know of *all* pictures and very proud I am to be able to say that the man who did it is my *kindest* friend.'

Rothenstein's interest in the Jews of Whitechapel as subjects for pictures had been stirred by a visit some years earlier to the Machzika Hadass Synagogue. Greatly impressed by what he saw, he rented a room nearby and visited Whitechapel many times to paint. Over a period of two years he had produced an immensely fine series of pictures of old men, one of which had found its way to the Tate Gallery. Others were on view at a one-man show in June 1910 at a dealers, for which he sent tickets to Mark.

The synagogue, situated as it was on the corner of Brick Lane and Fournier Street about two hundred yards from the Gertlers, was well known to Mark. Once, in the eighteenth century, a Huguenot church, it was later metamorphosed into a Wesleyan Methodist chapel then a Missionary Society establishment, before becoming the principal synagogue in the East End with a capacity of two thousand.[68]

Almost continuous prayers and services were held from 7 a.m. each day. For these it was the custom to make up the required quorum of ten people by employing some of the *minyan* (or quorum) men who waited about. They might be hard-up locals or, often, Rumanian or Austrian immigrant Jews straight from the ship, who would make their way there in search of shelter and in an attempt to earn a few shillings to get started.

It was these old men, their faces often showing the suffering and sadness of refugees from persecution, who inspired Mark, and he decided to make a series of pictures of them. Describing the synagogue he wrote, 'The whole scene inside, at any time of day, did certainly convey a scene "picturesque" to the extreme; like one huge Rembrandt brought to life. Scattered here and there, sometimes in groups, sometimes singly, were these magnificent old men with their long silver beards and curly hair, looking like princes in their rugs and praying shawls – swaying, bending, moaning at their prayers, passionate, ecstatic, yet casual and mechanical.' Some would shut out the world by facing the wall, or by drawing their shawls right over their heads, while others sat in an inner room poring over enormous books.

No drawing was allowed in the synagogue, but Mark persuaded them to come and sit for him. He was particularly interested in the old men just arrived from Poland and Russia, with their big felt hats and gabardine coats down to the ankles. They never shaved, and the long hair with ring curls reaching down to their sides were signs of their piety. Between 1909 and 1912 Mark drew and painted them often, head and shoulders and full length, singly and in groups.[69]

At the autumn exhibition of the New English in 1911 the portrait of Golda hung among the work of some of the most famous artists of the time, such as Sargent, Sickert, Mark's teachers Tonks, Brown and Steer, and Augustus John, the latter occupying three out of the four wall centres in the large gallery. Mark's picture was promptly bought by Professor Sadler, a very discerning collector, and later offered on loan to the Tate Gallery.

'I can hardly tell you how much pleasure your letter gave me,' Mark wrote to him on 30 November. 'That you like it, and have bought it, is to me a tremendous compliment. Last week I was awarded a British Institute scholarship, value £100, and believe me I do not value it as highly.

6—MG * *

'What also pleases me is that it will actually "rub shoulders" with those wonderful pictures I saw at your house. It is so nice to be encouraged. One works in such better spirits. In the ordinary way, you see, my profession is so depressing, and the terrible moments of hopelessness one gets are simply awful. For, oh! what a gulf there seems between the good work that has been done, and one's own.'

There were no irksome conditions on the scholarship: Mark could work where he liked and use the money to support himself. With this and the money from Golda's portrait he was about two years ahead. The winning painting was one of May Berlinski.

PART THREE

The Challenge

'As a boy in Whitechapel he had been attracted by the superabundant vitality of the Jewish girls, he told me, the girls of his own nationality; but it was an encounter with an English girl who happened to quote a phrase of great literature to him which gave him, in a single moment, a passion both for her and for a wholly different kind of life.' – SYLVIA LYND

'I went to the Indian Museum by myself. How I enjoyed it! I have discovered a lot of new things there which are simply magical! I wanted you so much to be with me. Tears came into my eyes as I looked at them all alone, in that deserted gallery. Oh! how genuine is the art of these ancients!' – MARK GERTLER TO CARRINGTON

CHAPTER 8

'Think of Christ, Michael Angelo'

Mark's pictures of his family did not please everybody. A painting 'A Playful Scene'[172], showing Golda asleep, with Sophie, egged on by Harry and Jack, tickling her ear with a straw was, both in theme and style, the kind of picture that Tonks and Steer were doing, but Mark was unable, or refused, to achieve their atmosphere of elegance and gentility. One student described it as, 'the interior of Gertler's comfortable bourgeois kitchen with his family cook[!] sitting dozing by the table on which was a glass of diluted tea meant to represent wine, and . . . Gertler's brothers mocking at her intemperance, each in a very artificial attitude. It was very well painted but somehow vulgar in spirit.'[70] A later critic, Clive Bell, commented on its 'ridiculous yet telling row of vulgarly expressive figures'. Yet interest in Mark and his pictures of the Jewish world was growing, and at the February 1912 Friday Club show the *Standard* declared that they were among the best things in the exhibition, and the *Westminster Gazette* referred to the 'character evinced by "Jew Praying".'[71] At the Slade, Mark's growing reputation stirred as much excitement as had that of William Orpen and Augustus John.

In the East End his family were in raptures when the *Jewish Chronicle* interviewed Mark and devoted a whole page to a description of his work.[72]

For a young student, still at art school, to get his pictures hung in the West End and favourably discussed by the critics, was then almost unknown, though later in the century this was to become not unusual. The older painters in the Slade–New English circle had reservations about this novelty, but for the moment Mark was their prodigy, exemplifying in his work the ideals which they taught.

Though until June he was technically still doing his fourth year, Mark now left classes and instruction and painted full time.

For the summer exhibition of the New English he painted Louis and Golda as 'The Apple Woman and her husband'[173]. The picture was accepted. By now the critics were watching the new-comer and praise rippled through the London Press – The *Sunday Times*, *Observer*, *Star*, *Westminster Gazette*, *Morning Post*, *Queen*, *Truth* – and out into the provinces in the *Manchester Guardian* and *Glasgow Herald*. Instead of merely passing mentions, Mark was now able to read long and detailed discussions of his work.[73]

Professor Brown wrote a congratulatory letter inviting Mark to put his name forward for election as a member of the New English; the new Society of Portrait Painters followed suit, and elected him. 'They are giving me a dinner . . .' wrote Mark. 'It will be rather fun having dinner with a lot of so-called artists. I shall probably be the youngest; they don't know my age; they will be surprised when I enter. Behold! I am here!'

Collectors were watching his progress. Professor Sadler instructed his son to report on Mark's latest work.[74] The indefatigable Rothenstein continued to arrange introductions to useful people: Mark met the Samuels family, John Sargent and the Wertheimers and the brother of a friend of Rothenstein, Sir George Howard Darwin, who become interested. 'I meant to catch you again at the Slade today to tell you how very much I liked your work,' he wrote to Mark. 'I was very much interested in your portraits, and the one of your brother remains in my memory as the best of all.'

A commission for a portrait[174] followed and for this Mark made trips to Cambridge, where dinner with the dons presented more problems of learning how the middle class lived. Mark learned – and laughed. 'I shall never forget his description of his visit to the Darwins at Cambridge,' said Nevinson. 'At dinner he was offered asparagus for the first time. Being accustomed to spring onions, he started at the white end first, and the beautifully mannered don followed suit in order not to embarrass him.'[75]

A visit to Sargent gave Mark the opportunity to see how fabulously rich a successful society portrait painter could become. Sargent's friend, Jacques-Emile Blanche, describes him at this time:

'The Van Dyck of Tite Street...had to make appointments six months or a year ahead with Royal Highnesses just as occupied as he. During the season, at the Grill room of the Hyde Park Hotel, he devoured his meals and gulped down his wine, his watch on the table in front of him. The cheese and dishes were all put on the table simultaneously, together with the newspapers: there was just half an hour for recharging the motor, for filling it with life-giving spirit, between the morning sitting and another, sometimes even two, in the afternoon. Stuffed with food, smoking Havana cigars as large as logs, with bloodshot eyes, puffing, he glanced through *The Times.*'[76] Sargent's friends, the Wertheimers, offered help: 'Mark Gertler was to be sent to Italy to study art, and great things were to be done for him. There was tremendous excitement among his people when Wertheimer's Rolls Royce arrived with a chauffeur and footman to take him and his paintings to be inspected. As he was putting his canvases in the back of the car the footman leaned forward and said, 'Be careful of the paint.' Gertler replied gaily, 'It's all right, they are quite dry.' The footman said, 'The paint on the car.'[77]

For their evening outings Mark and Nevinson found their way to the Café Royal in Regent Street. London's liveliest meeting place, it was very close in spirit to a French café; you could call for coffee, drinks or writing paper, sit all day talking, reading papers or playing games. It inspired several pictures. Charles Ginner, Harold Gilman, William Orpen and Adrian Allinson all painted the rococo interior crowded with mirrors, red plush benches, marble-topped tables, waiters with cloths round their waists, and a very assorted clientele. Dress was full of variety. Very popular with the more Bohemian was the newly fashioned Austrian velours hat – distorted into various fanciful shapes – with a corduroy coat and waving bow tie.

Writers' descriptions include Osbert Sitwell's 'smoky acres of painted goddesses and cupids and tarnished gilding . . . golden caryatids and . . . filtered, submarine illumination.' Augustus John summed up the various groups in the fly-blown rococo of the famous saloon: 'In one section under the bar, whose façade glittered with the almost Byzantine splendour of a steam roundabout, were the sporting fraternity, loud raucous-voiced men . . . [There was a] French colony playing dominoes . . . A gathering of unusually bulky and grave persons, collected from the vicinity of the British Museum, conversed in voices pitched like the squeaking of bats, so high as to be inaudible except to the trained ear (if I am not mistaken the females of this group alone *portaient barbe*) . . . A well-dressed gang of blackmailers, pimps, con men . . . secure in the well tried loyalty of the staff, laid their plans for the next operation . . . [There was a] body of exquisite Old Boys of the nineties, recognizable by their bright chestnut wigs and raddled faces . . . [and] within easy reach of the exit a mixed company of poets, prostitutes and portrait painters.'[78]

John himself, 'a tall, bearded figure, with an enormous black Paris hat, large gold ear-rings decorating his ears, with a carriage of the utmost arrogance,' was one of the Café's most striking personalities, dominating it with his presence as effortlessly as his pictures dominated the young artists. When he entered a respectful hush fell on the tables occupied by the art students.

Mark had seen this often enough and it made his pride all the greater when John now treated him as an equal. One day in the summer of 1912, when he went to the Café, 'Behold, *John* was there,' wrote Mark. 'He immediately came up to me and we talked and talked. I never knew what a beautifully simple man he was. He took me to see his work – asked me what I thought. But I was so excited and nervous that I didn't know what to say. Then we had lunch together and got so confidential that we told each other all about our lives. He told me that he loved his wife and, with *tears* actually in his eyes, he told me how he had just lost a charming little boy of his. He then proceeded to give me some very useful "tips" on tempera . . . We parted great friends and he told me he likes me very much. Isn't it splendid!'

Like the other young artists, Mark sometimes found it difficult not to be overcome by the influence of John in his work. Occasionally, as in a portrait of his sister Sophie, painted in February 1912, this influence almost swamped his own personality.[175]

Mark was discovering more about the world outside London. 'Our little Slade gang had "done" Paris during a hectic week of sight-seeing,' Allinson recorded. 'Galleries, museums and boîtes de nuit had all received their meed of attention. We had also dropped in at Julien's and there learnt that our own Slade was considered quite as good a training ground as this famous Parisian art school. Our visit was made at Easter and, the weather being bitterly cold, we had fortified ourselves with countless "babas au rhum".'[79]

Another trip was made, this time in May, and the city was 'all smiles and warmth'. Nevinson described it: 'We had all previously visited Paris, but the gang now went in force, with David Sassoon in addition. It was a ghastly trip, as we travelled steerage via Dieppe, and poor Gertler nearly died from sea-sickness, being revived only by French sailors hosing him in the early dawn. However, the Primitive Room at the Louvre compensated us for much and our enthusiasm was terrific. But how we despised Rubens!'[80]

As far as physical comforts went, Mark's life had become, if anything, even more austere. In April 1912 Harry and his wife Ann took a house in Elder Street, a road of terraced Georgian houses only a few yards from Spital Square, though much more dilapidated. Although the fronts had been well designed, with some handsome door-cases, the interiors were cramped and shoddy, the rooms being separated from the halls only by wooden partitions. Here, it was arranged, Mark would occupy the top floor.

The door of No. 32, two steps up from the pavement, had once been almost smart – arch-headed with moulded stucco pilasters on either side – but inside, above the basement, narrow dirty stairs wound up to the second floor.

There Mark had a landing, a small back room for sleeping and a room to work in at the front. It was low ceilinged, but adequate – about five yards square – with three narrow, slightly arched front windows facing east and tiny window seats. Looking out Mark could see the houses opposite (one floor higher than those on his side) looming above him and stretching away on either side, an interminable wall of plum-coloured brick. Mark and Harry found a bed, a chest, and a desk and a couple of chairs for the back room; with a chair for models in the studio, some coal for the fire and candles for light, the stage for Mark's daily struggle over the next few years was set.

The mood of exaltation which had carried him through several years of highly concentrated effort enabled him to accept the grubby discomfort and even to see a beauty in its harshness, simplicity and solitude.

'I hope you will find my picture worth seeing,' he wrote to a friend (6 May 1912) 'I have worked very earnestly at it, and put in a lot of love and care, but it still falls far short of the beautiful things I want to do.

'I have just come home from Cambridge and I have never before enjoyed a train ride so much; I enjoyed mostly when we passed the slums of Hackney and Bethnal Green. It reminded me so much of my early life and all its simplicity. The poverty, although striking, had a beautiful simplicity, which was to be envied. In one back yard there was a little girl minding a child: in another there was nothing but a dear little bird, who, with much curiosity, was inspecting a chimney-pot. It must have taken it for some huge and ruined Tower. One yard interested me very much. There was a Jewish boy, taking his Hebrew lesson from an aged rabbi. As usual, the rabbi was doing both the teaching and the learning, whilst the boy was vacantly thinking of his "pals" outside. How like my youth!! Only instead of "pals" I thought of art. Oh! . . . How curious life is!'

'That life is hard, is true,' he acknowledged a few weeks later. 'But isn't there something grand about it being hard? Isn't there something grand to try and bear up and give to the world all we can? Think of the good company we are in. Think of Christ, Michael Angelo. Angelo's life was very sad. How grand it is to think that a man that gave such marvellous things to the world got nothing in return but sadness and ill treatment from it! When a great friend of Michael Angelo's died, Michael said, "Now that he is gone and left me alone in this *deceitful* world I shall end my last few years in abject misery." Think of that! When he said that he had already given us that marvellous creation the "Entombment" in the National Gallery! So you see we have to try and see something beautiful in this hardness of life!'

This reverence for the finest art of the past kept Mark in a constant fever. In the street he would sometimes be overcome by gusts of emotion, and emerge from visions of great pictures to find himself clinging, dizzy and trembling, to railings or lamp-posts. At home one night he wrote, 'I write on my little desk by the light of a candle . . . Oh! I feel so inspired here – now – in my little room. It is midnight, all is quiet – quiet. My candle throws huge and awe inspiring shadows over the walls. The sky outside is Serenely Blue. I have no trees against it, but a chimney pot – and how majestic it looks! As I think, I think of the National Gallery with all its joys: Michael Angelo!!! Botticelli!!! Francesca!!!' (16 July 1912) . . . 'I have on my desk, as I write, some reproductions of Fra Angelico! – That beautiful monk knew how to paint! Dear, dear man – How I love you and your work. The dear man gave up his whole life to *Religion* and *Art* and did pictures on the walls of each fellow monk's cell.' (12 September 1912)

In July Epstein took him to the British Museum, 'and there revealed to me such wonders in works of art that my inspiration knew no bounds, and I came to the conclusion that Egyptian art is *by far, by far,* the greatest of *all* art. Oh! . . . it is, it is. We moderns are but ants in comparison. But ants! As I think of this great art my ambition doubles and redoubles! Oh! . . . if I am given many years in this world. I think, I think, I shall do great things! Things so great that they will surprise all men!'

But he had no illusion about the effort that would be needed. 'Of course you mustn't expect good pictures from me yet. It will yet take many years.' (16 July 1912)

CHAPTER NINE

'Dear Miss Carrington'

Mark had been seeing rather less of Nevinson, who had withdrawn himself slightly from the group of Slade friends to spend time with two of the girls at the school. Dora Carrington and the Honourable Dorothy Brett, daughter of Lord Esher, had been at the Slade since the autumn of 1910, and with Ruth Humphries, who had begun a year later, they formed a trio, 'governed in a vague gentle way by Brett'. Carrington however was the dominant personality.

Following the custom of the Slade, they were called, even among close friends, by their surnames.

Carrington already possessed the attraction that was to be felt by so many. 'She was both clever and good looking to an unusual degree . . . an amusing person with such very blue eyes, and such incredibly thick pig-tails of red gold hair,' wrote Paul Nash. 'I got an introduction to her and eventually won her regard by lending her my braces for a fancy dress dance. We were riding on the top of a bus and she wanted them then and there.'[81]

One day, when Nevinson and Carrington were on a walk of exploration down the river, they found themselves not far from Whitechapel. Nevinson talked of Mark and had the idea of taking Carrington to meet him.

The result was overwhelming.

Mark had noticed her when she first came to the Slade, without being particularly impressed. 'The first time I saw you', he wrote later, 'you only just looked attractive enough for me to look back. I looked back, saw a long plait and *turned in* toes; no good, I thought, and forgot all about it! Wonderful, how things happen.'

But now Carrington had changed and he was intrigued. 'Dear Miss Carrington,' he wrote after their meeting, 'I wonder if you could come and have tea with me on Thursday at five o'clock. I may want to draw you if you will be good enough to sit. Please try and come.'

In a matter of weeks Mark was under the spell that was to hold him for many years. He fell in love, helplessly and irretrievably, and asked her to marry him.

Carrington was very young, full of the sense of freedom that came with her first time away from home; she was much sought after and not even remotely ready to consider choosing a life partner. The proposal was much too sudden. She was working hard at her painting, determined to be taken seriously as an artist. In spite of its one or two brilliant female students, the Slade, until recently, had been very much a male preserve. At the end of the term in July, she won a Slade scholarship, the Melville Nettleship Prize for figure composition, and was awarded a second for figure painting.

Mark's attempt to take her by storm as a masterful lover was repelled without effort, and served only to make it clear that in this affair his love made him the more vulnerable and weaker of the two.

But his vitality and physical beauty were disturbing, and Carrington was attracted by his strangeness and intensity, and the glimpses he afforded both into the barbaric world of Whitechapel, refreshingly far removed from her own stuffy middle-class background,* and into his own life – one completely devoid of materialism, dedicated to art.

'There has seldom been a more exciting person than Gertler was when young,' said a friend. 'A Jew from the East End, with amazing gifts of draughtsmanship, amazing vitality, and a sense of humour and mimicry unique to himself – a shock of hair, the vivid eyes of genius, and the most beautiful hands'.[82]

Carrington loved him, she declared. If he would be patient and agree to be no more than friends for the time being, they could try this; but otherwise they must part.

One of the first casualties of the affair was the friendship between Nevinson and Mark. 'Our friendship must end from now,' Mark wrote, 'my sole reason being that I am in love with Carrington and I have reason to believe that you are so too. Therefore, much as I

---

* Carrington's mother, an ex-governess, and her father, a retired Indian Railways engineer, lived a very dull life in Bedford.

have tried to overlook it, I have come to the conclusion that rivals, and rivals in love, cannot be friends.

'You must know that ever since you brought Carrington to my studio my love for her has been steadily increasing. You might also remember that many times, when you asked me down to dinner, I refused to come. *Jealousy* was the cause of it. Whenever you told me that you had been kissing her, you could have knocked me down with a feather, so faint was I. Whenever you saw me depressed of late, when we were all out together, it wasn't boredom as I pretended but *love* . . . You are now evidently saying how silly Gertler has become! I know it and I cannot help it. If we meet in company we need make no fuss and just pretend that we are the same.' (July 1912)

Nevinson was ironical, writing to Carrington, 'I am distinctly amused at you two.' But underneath he was upset. 'All this worry has again succeeded in enlarging my liver, as unfortunately I have felt this loss of Gertler more intensely that I thought possible,' he went on. 'I suppose that I am cursed with an abnormally affection-ate temperament; after my first and only experiment of letting it loose on a girl five years ago, I have naturally ever since realized the hopeless misunderstanding and eventual quarrel that is bound to happen with a girl immensely liked . . . That my nature slowly and silently and almost unknown to myself has been letting itself loose on Gertler is my folly, never dreaming that sex would as usual come and ruin all, as it is bound to between men and women.'

Carrington tried to mend matters, but the friendship between the two young men was marred. 'As regards Nevinson, I am afraid I cannot go back to being his Friend. It is not jealousy at all,' wrote Mark unconvincingly. 'You see, I have lost interest in him – for no definite reason – so why should I be with a person for whose company I do not care? . . . Besides Nevinson will soon forget me. I shall soon pass out of his life as he has passed out of mine. When you come back [from holidays] he will be able to have you as a friend alright and I don't see why I should deputize until then.'

Fortunately Nevinson tried again and was able to avoid a com-plete break. 'Nevinson also wrote me, in return to my letter to him, how miserable my letter has made him', Mark said to Carrington. 'His letter has made me wretchedly miserable. I shall have to do my best to be friends with him too.' A little later he told Carrington, 'You will be interested to hear that since I wrote my letter Nevinson has come to see me and asked me to dinner to his place. And I have accepted . . . But I still feel the same about him.'

Mark needed someone to paint for. 'I find it almost impossible to paint without having some person at the back of my mind,' he declared to Carrington. 'I mean that ever since I got to know you I thought of you in every stroke I did. Now I find that I want you badly to see all that I paint and I keep wondering what you will think of my work. I can't bear the idea of developing without you and I am developing so quickly.'

He began a painting of Carrington. After the early days at the Slade she had cut her hair short. 'When she cut her thick gold hair into a heavy golden bell,' recalled Paul Nash, 'this, her fine blue eyes, her stutter, her turned-in toes, and other quaint but attractive attributes combined to make her a conspicuous and popular figure.' To Mark, her face was 'like a beautiful flower encased in a form of gold.'

The hair-cut had been a gesture of independence against Edwardian frills and fussiness, and the up-to-date idiom of Mark's picture of 1912 – clear hard outlines, large masses of almost flat col-our – was well suited for an image of the 'new woman'[176]. He aimed at simplicity: the simplest of poses in the simplest of garments. In a picture completely without clutter, he brought out the unity of the forms of her face and hair.

Mark saw her as an innocent child, and, although eighteen, she was still in many ways a child, with an enchanting, vivid imagin-ation and breathless, shy enthusiasms. She had her own way of doing everything. 'You have so often an air, as if you are in the thick of a great mystery,' he said to her once. A later friend of hers recalled, 'When she talked to me she seemed to be confiding a secret, and I was flattered. She made me feel like a child and she was a child herself.'[83] And to another she was 'a wild moorland pony'.

There was a sympathy and understanding between Mark and Carrington which never really failed even in the later torments of their long relationship. As companions they explored London together, and Mark was happy. 'I feel you are now my most intimate friend,' he wrote. 'I feel so happy now because I know the nicest person in the whole world. I believe it is a reward for having worked hard all my life.'

They walked on Hampstead Heath, enjoyed quiet suppers or held parties, spent evenings at the theatres and the bioscopes. Carrington always paid her way and free tickets were shared. He wrote recommending her to read John Masefield's 'The Widow in the Bye Street', and Keats ('interesting me enormously just now'); he urged her to see music-hall shows, ('If you possibly can, go to the Victoria Palace this week. There is the finest set of Rag Time niggers I ever saw. Wonderful!'); and described concerts ('I have not long come from a Wagner Concert, What a wonderful man is Wagner!! What a wonderful art is music!! – Oh! it was beautiful and inspiring! And how expressive! Love, Sorrow, Despair, Hope, Joy, all were expressed – Oh! – Wonderfully.').

She sent him flowers and books, including one on the painter Millet and a copy of *Les Miserables*, and tried to make him drink less, receiving in return weak explanations and exaggerated promises: 'That I was "rolling down" Shaftesbury Avenue is quite false! I wasn't at all *drunk*. I was *walking* down Shaftesbury Avenue with Nevinson and Odell because I met them at the Club. I had to have a *few* whiskies to keep Odell company who loves drink – but I didn't "roll" all the same.' Later he promised; 'I shall never drink again in your company.'

When they were apart they exchanged photographs as well as letters. One of Carrington on the beach at Seaford brought the comment, 'You are certainly a beautiful little person. I don't know anybody to equal you.'

Carrington and Mark had a common aim which drew them together. It was very much a comradeship between two young painters, in spite of Carrington's relatively junior status; they studied together in the National Gallery, Tate Gallery, British Museum and the South Kensington Museum. Reproductions, books, addresses of models and ideas for subject matter were exchanged. 'I have come across an interesting girl – a Jewess – with a Good head, not the ordinary Jewess', wrote Mark.

Advice was asked for and given: 'I shouldn't, if I were you, be too ready to change your scheme for your "Joy" picture, just because Allinson's is the same. *He* won't do much good at it,' said Mark.

Brett often accompanied them. Her family had a house in Mayfair, a box at the opera, and she had adopted Mark almost as a young brother (she was seven years older). From the start expeditions with her had involved struggling with some of the trappings of high life. 'I shall come in REAL *Evening dress*!!! No you must promise not to *laugh*,' he wrote to Carrington. (13 May 1912) 'You see, evening dress does not come natural to me. And the one I've got was given to me by Sassoon (But this is a Secret). I personally think the only fault is that the trousers are a little short. But with *your* experience of Braces you will know that with a little manipulation that fault can easily be mended – No one need know. The upper part of me will be perfect! I shall be able to look Aristocracy straight in the face.'

In spite of a mutual liking between Carrington and Golda, who called her 'herla', the hairless one, Mark was very conscious of the difference in class and could not always laugh at it. 'I am a poor workman's son, perhaps too rough for a lady like yourself,' he apologized once. 'Carrington I mean it. I am too rough for you.' And the subject was liable to come up in rows: 'You are the lady and I am the East End boy,' Mark threw at her on one occasion. 'Alas! or had I even been to a Public School like the gentleman of Hampstead [Nevinson].'

Carrington was a worrier. Sometimes she felt she was being a bore, or that she was interrupting his work. 'You mistake to think that anything you tell me about yourself bores me,' Mark reassured her. 'Few things interest me more ... Your friendship INSPIRES MY WORK, *not* as you say, spoils my life and work. You are *wrong*, *wrong*. Dear Carrington, Don't be unhappy as life is very inspiring and beautiful ... you are a source of inspiration to me.'

There were gaps in their time together when Carrington went home to her parents in the long Slade holidays, and even in term time meetings averaged only about four a month, but every few days they would write to each other.

To Mark she became an ideal of beauty and a symbol of purity, mixed up in his mind with his adoration of beauty in art. Her freshness and innocence, contrasted with the worldly materialism of his East End acquaintances, touched his heart. 'If only I could explain to you how *purely* I love you,' he wrote. 'I think you are the purest and *holiest* girl I have *ever* met and as long as you are with me you will remain so. I am going to devote my whole life to try and make you happy.'

In many ways this attitude suited Carrington, who did not want to have to cope with sex for some years yet, but she indicated a little disbelief which brought an agitated reply: 'Why should you suppose that I *only* like you for your sex? Do you know that if it was only sex I was after I could produce 1/2 dz. girls at any moment, who could serve me that way? From an East End Jewess, to an actress at the Savoy. So would I go with you – from whom I get *no* sex?'

Though this was an exaggeration, it was true that Mark was, as Nevinson put it, 'popular with the girls and adored by them'. His introduction to sex had been almost disastrous. Some years earlier Harry and Jack had taken it upon themselves to arrange an initiation – with a local prostitute. The experience had been repellent. Since then his relationship with May had helped him to get over his shyness, and there had been others, such as a girl from a seaside boarding house where some of the Gertler family had stayed. She had turned up in London where she and Mark became lovers, entering into an easy uncomplicated relationship. She asked him to help her find work as a model and he introduced her to the Café Royal circle.

His relationship with Carrington was fundamentally different. Carrington, besides having a fine vigorous body, so desirable that the sight of her often made him start trembling, had a personality and ideals which satisfied his romantic longings for a girl he could look up to; she was eminently worth waiting for, and he struggled to control his desire until she should be more mature. 'Ever since I've met you,' he told her, 'I am absolutely good and pure. You have that influence on me. You are to me the *one* thing outside painting worth living for . . . I love you so much that I could easily worship you . . . Whether I kiss you or do anything else to you it is with the purity of an angel, because I love your *Soul*.'

But how long could this state of affairs continue?

CHAPTER 10

Strange hats and strong opinions

Mark was having problems with his work. His attitude recently had been confident, even cocksure, and had irritated many. Now this changed. 'I am finding art absolutely beyond me,' he wrote to Brett late in the summer of 1912. 'The difficulty overwhelms me. It is immense! No one knows. I am at this moment disgusted with all that I have done so far. But still I am only twenty and I shall devote the whole of my life to it, and perhaps before I die I may do one thing that people will see is an addition to what has been done. At this moment I am very doubtful.'

In September he was still in difficulty: 'My work is progressing but slowly. I give up idea after idea.' To Carrington he explained: 'My work has been from a *Quantity* point of view – going so slowly, that I shall have *terribly little* to show you. But I am not sorry as I have been thinking and learning a great deal and I should *loathe* to turn out picture after picture (like a machine) of no value. It's not Quantity we want at all.

'Each day, I am struck with the enormity, the difficulty and the greatness of *Our Art*. My own incapacity appals me. Yet, each day, I learn so much, that I wonder at the little I knew yesterday. I abandon most of my ideas, so critical I am just now. Everything I have done so far is *nothing – nothing*. Unless I do something far far Greater soon I shall be very miserable and unhappy. The more I go on, the more difficult does my Art become to me. I have had such miserable nights lately – you don't know – some nights I couldn't sleep at all – so hopeless did my work and the future seem. Yet some youths would be happy in my position – Everybody seems to praise my work, and yet and yet – !'

He was, as it later became clear, beginning the critical struggle of his life, a struggle which was to end only with his death, and which perhaps caused his death: the fight to survive as an artist against the influence of what has been called the Parisian colossus – the great movements of Post-Impressionism, Fauvism, Cubism and their successors which, in the opinion of one critic, 'emasculated almost an entire generation of British artists'.

The more revolutionary of these developments had taken place in Paris in an astonishingly short space of time. In the first few years of the century a series of big retrospective exhibitions of the painters of the eighties and nineties who were to become known as Post Impressionists – Gauguin, Cézanne, Van Gogh and others – had been held. Their work had not been really familiar to the younger painters in Paris and these exhibitions triggered off a new wave of developments including Fauvism from 1905 (led by Matisse), and Cubism, from about 1907 (led by Picasso and Braque). These in turn stimulated others, and by 1910 the first purely abstract paintings had been produced by Kandinsky, and the tradition of naturalistic representational painting, which had lasted for several hundred years, was broken.

Because of its insularity the British art world knew little of events in Paris since the Impressionists of the seventies. Thus when Roger Fry organized a big show of modern work in London in 1910 the shock was great. Rapid though the pace had been in Paris, people had at least been able to see the work in the sequence in which it developed. The far less sophisticated Londoner had to cope with all the stages from Gauguin to abstraction at once. Other exhibitions had followed, books about the new art were published and excited discussion raged in the London art world.

To the Royal Academy it was simply unmentionable. The New English circle, as a progressive body, felt it should examine the new ideas, but its leading members were rather old to cope with a complete rethinking of all their aims and methods.

Tonks, for example, was not averse to new pictorial ideas as such, but the new doctrine had a number of unacceptable features. It was no longer concerned with representing the outer world directly: the emphasis lay in what went on in the artist's mind. 'I paint what I think, not what I see,' said Picasso. It finally demolished the idea that art and beauty were somehow necessarily connected. The human figure, so idealized in Renaissance art, might now be shown hideously distorted, or perhaps completely fragmented and indicated merely by a few signs.

Even more serious was the idea that a long training in drawing was unnecessary, and that a picture made up from old bus tickets might be an important visual experience.

Tonks, worried that the students might slacken their efforts to learn the skills he was trying to teach them, without gaining anything in return, advised them not to study the new art. Other established artists to whom Mark and his friends looked for a lead failed to provide it. The attitude of Sickert, who had known the French Post-Impressionist artists personally, was that they had some interesting ideas but were not crucially important.

Yet Mark was upset by the French pictures. He sensed the truth: he had spent years mastering techniques and a style which suddenly looked out of date. He could produce fine examples of a kind of picture which had little relevance to the new civilization which was ahead – heralded by the new ideas being put into circulation by people such as Bergson and Freud who were already shattering man's ideas about his identity, and Rutherford and Einstein, who were throwing new light on the reality of the external world. Young musicians and poets were exploring new ideas, and it was obvious that if the painters were not to take a back seat they had to do the same.

Years later, Mark said, 'The entry of Cézanne, Gauguin, Matisse, etc., upon my horizon was equivalent to the impact of the scientists of this age upon a simple student of Sir Isaac Newton.'[84]

If it was necessary to begin again, so be it. In a mood of humility and despair he toiled on. Sending a photograph of a painting to Carrington, he wrote of 'a beginner like myself', saying 'excuse please, my own *foolish* attempts that I send you'.

Sometimes he was almost tempted to give up. His work was much too important to him to allow any side-stepping of issues or aiming at anything less than the best: in the hard-working atmosphere of Whitechapel the idea of being a second-rate artist was ludicrous and offensive.

'I am *so* dissatisfied about my work,' he admitted to Carrington, 'so troubled am I lately and so useless do I feel as an artist, that, although it may seem funny I seriously thought of taking up some simple trade and so justifying my existence and being useful. What's the good of living if you are of no use? And Mediocre Art is not only useless but CRIMINAL. For we are merely imposing! I thought of being a *baker*. Three days a week, Bread is a *necessity* and I am at present more useless than the simplest baker! Please God! Give me some more talents so that I may be of some use . . . But I suppose I am young and there is yet time.

'Fancy, in the midst of all these thoughts, a poor woman and her son, a boy of fourteen, came to ask me advice; she thinks the boy has talents – ought he to be an artist? Oh! what could I say? The mother looked at me and envied me! They both thought what a happy man this must be. They were both nervous and "Sir'd" me. Did they know that though for so many years I had been studying, studying, working, working, pouring my very brains out into my art yet there I stood feeling, Oh! more ignorant than when I first started . . .

'*It's a hard life, it's a hard life*, was all I managed to mutter to the envious mother. They went away more bewildered than when they came. I dropped exhausted into an armchair, thinking of all my past life! How strange it all seemed! I remembered my childhood in Austria and the great *poverty*. No bread and my poor striving mother. Then I remembered my school days in London with my little urchin friends. They now sell newspapers at the Mansion House. Then came my Polytechnic days. Then I worked in a designing Firm for *a year*! which nearly broke my heart. Then the *Slade* . . . and here I am now an artist – supposed to be. Yes, I thought to myself, be a tailor, anything my dear boy, but not an artist. By this time the room was in gloom and my pictures all looked like mocking spectres, that were there to laugh at me. I could stand it no longer. So I went out and saw more unfortunate artists. I looked at them talking art – ancient art, modern art, Impressionism, Post-Impressionism, Neo-Impressionism, Cubists, Spottists, Futurists, Cave Dwellers, Wyndham Lewis, Duncan Grant, Etchells, Roger Fry! I looked on and laughed into myself, saying, give me the *Baker*, the *Baker*! And I walked home disgusted with them *all* and was glad to find my dear simple mother waiting for me with a nice roll, that she knows I like, and a cup of

Hot Coffee. Dear mother, the same mother of all my life, *twenty years*. You, dear mother, I thought, are the only *modern artist*. When you come back I will tell you a lot about my Mother.' (24 September 1912)

It was not a real dilemma. Dilemmas include alternatives. For Mark there was no way back to being a baker – or a furrier. 'If only, like my brothers, I was an ordinary workman, as I should have been,' he asserted to Carrington. 'But no! I must desire, desire. How I pay for those desires! By my ambition I am cut off from my own family and class and by them I have been raised to be equal to a class I hate! They do not understand me nor I them. So I am an outcast. As I look at my desk I laugh, for there are dozens of notices of me in the daily papers, a lot of them praising my talents. Oh! yes I am quite well known, and yet *alone*.' (December 1912)

Nothing outside his art, no beliefs or friendships, had yet proved enough to provide a strong reason for living; if his talent was failing, it would be impossible to continue. 'The more I go on the more I seem to realize that outside my *art* there is nothing to hope for – nothing!' he acknowledged. 'What sometimes fills me with dread is that more and more do I seem to get severed from my fellow creatures; sometimes it seems that I have nothing in common with *anybody* on earth. My real friends seem to be, rather, the sun, the moon, the trees, the sky and other things of natural beauty.'

In his worst moments, headaches and depression almost overwhelmed him, and his thoughts turned to suicide. 'So near death I feel now – at this moment in my little room, all alone,' he wrote once. The knowledge of Golda's love – and her need for him – then made all the difference. 'Yes it's very tempting – But I have a mother who *loves* and *lives* for me. So I mustn't. Yes! She is a great comfort to me and I mustn't be ungrateful.' (12 September 1912)

His basic aims were unchanged. 'How I should love to be able to express myself simply and beautifully in paint. I have no ambitions in life but that. I once told you how simple my desires are,' he wrote to Carrington. 'I shall keep doing little pictures for a long time – simple things – so that I can put my whole soul into trying to express my own feelings as forcibly and beautifully as I can. But oh! it makes me so sad and unhappy – I mean my incapacity . . . In life I have only one ambition, to justify my existence by paintings of great Beauty. BY MY DEAR, DEAR ART. I am sorry I said dear, dear art – it is not dear, because it gives me so much pain, but then all things we love give us pain.'

It was lucky for Mark that these months saw the development of an intimate friendship with another man – the closest and most inspiring working alliance he was ever to form with another young painter. John Currie had arrived in London from Bristol a few years earlier and had come into contact with the Slade painters when he spent half a term there in 1910. He had been a fellow exhibitor of Mark's at the February 1912 Friday Club,[85] and in the summer scored a great success at the New English, with his picture 'Some later Primitives and Madame Tisceron', which showed Currie, Mark, Nevinson, John and the proprietress of the Petit Savoyard café in Soho.

The *Standard, Morning Post, Star, Observer, Pall Mall Gazette, Truth, Queen* and others commented at length on the picture and Currie seemed all set for a brilliant future.

Mark and Currie were natural allies, both forthright, dedicated and burning with passion for art. Mark felt an ease with Currie which had never been possible with Nevinson. He could take time off from studying behaviour and manners and relax. It didn't matter that his clothes were wrong and his parents poor: Currie's birth certificate listed no father at all, and Currie knew what it was like to struggle out of a poor environment. He had been born in Ardwick, Lancaster, his mother being an Irish Catholic who had settled there and worked as a mantle maker. His father was said to be also of Irish origin, a builder and contractor for the North Staffordshire railway.

Their mutual friend Allinson found the intimacy between Mark and Currie natural. 'Both of them were ambitious and struggling to escape from their early environment,' he noted.

Professor Sadler, who became interested in Currie's work, said that he had 'the passion and instinctive piety of the Irish Catholic peasant', and Sadler's son Michael recorded: 'Currie had burning eyes, rather uncouth speech, and was a little rough in manner. Very humble-minded yet very confident of himself; he was simple and absorbed in his work – conscious of genius without being conceited, full of himself but not egoistic . . . He was a remarkable and attractive creature – square, dark-haired, handsome in a southern way.'[86]

Currie was possessive, and his attitude had stiffened Mark's annoyance with Nevinson over Carrington in the summer. 'You see I have a way of changing my friends,' Mark had written to Carrington (2 July 1912). 'Nevinson was once my friend, but now my *greatest* friend is Currie and Currie would consider it rather funny if I said tomorrow night I shall go out with Nevinson. It wouldn't be fair to Currie.'

Late in July 1912 Currie, his girl-friend Dolly Henry, and Mark had gone off together for a week's holiday in Ostend, and Mark had written to Carrington describing their time together: 'I am enjoying my stay here extremely. Our plan is to have a complete rest from work. This place is like one huge Soho! *Beautiful* children. It is very healthy. We bathe each morning in the sea. I have bought myself a very beautiful shirt . . . I have just come from a French café, where the music played so beautifully . . .'

But holidays were never very successful for Mark; he could not rest for long. 'I, of course, find it extremely difficult to go without work,' he added. 'Some moments hang heavily and wearily upon me, and my hand itches for the brush.'

Mark now had a close companion for discussion of the new ideas: Currie, a revolutionary by nature, was greatly stirred by them. Seven years older than Mark, he took the lead in putting them into practice.[87]

The all-important problem of finding a dealer who would adopt them became pressing for Mark and Currie. Only by this means could they hope to put on a really good exhibition of their pictures.

It was always difficult to find places to show work. They could not hope to get more than one or two pictures a year shown at the New English, and the only other established group professedly interested in advanced work was the International Society. This had started with high hopes under Whistler but by 1912 had congealed into middle age and was uninterested in innovations.

They could, of course, have sent pictures in to the Royal Academy, whose enormous annual shows attracted thousands of wealthy buyers and dominated the Press. Even critics such as Frank Rutter, one of the spokesmen for the progressive young, who spent the rest of the year attacking the Academy, would, when the show came round, devote to it whole pages of the *Sunday Times*. Both Mark and Currie had more than enough skill to paint the kind of pictures which would have been accepted. But the idea could not be seriously entertained for a moment.

One other possibility existed. In 1908 Frank Rutter, helped by Sickert, had started an English version of the Paris 'Independants' – an exhibiting society in which anyone who paid his subscription was entitled to show his works. Unlike the New English it was open to all comers and pictures did not have to get passed by a jury. The result of this Allied Artists Association was a series of annual exhibitions in the Albert Hall, so vast (several thousand works were on show) that Rutter supervised the hanging on a bicycle.

Almost every serious young artist took part. Yet Mark held aloof. From his point of view the two disadvantages were that the best work tended to be swamped by the thousands of inferior pictures and that prices were low. This followed the Sickertian principle of selling at any price to get the pictures in circulation. Sickert was a prolific genius;* but the idea was less attractive to Mark, who was a slow producer, conceiving and fashioning each work with the patience of a fifteenth-century artist making an altar-piece. Even when he got into his stride he rarely produced more than half a dozen important pictures a year.

The London dealers, for the most part, considered the work of young artists unprofitable and beneath their notice, though there were one or two exceptions.[88] The Chenil Gallery in Chelsea was the one to which Mark's contacts led: both William Rothenstein and Augustus John were associated with it. The proprietor, John Knewstub, was a good salesman and had successfully promoted the gallery as a place where interesting work could be found.[89] As the

---

* Walter Richard Sickert, 1860–1942, was one of the most hard-working painters of his time, besides being one of the most important. His work always sold, but he spent money at a great rate. Sometimes he would allow a dealer to carry off a dozen or more paintings for the sake of a relatively tiny sum in cash.

Daily Chronicle had put it, 'The little public that visits the Chenil
Gallery by the Town Hall in Chelsea, is not the general public of
Bond-street, or Trafalgar and Manchester Squares: it is a public of
artists, youthful and eager, who have strange hats and strong
opinions, and of connoisseurs who do their own buying, and who
are ill-content unless they possess a John, an Orpen, a Nicholson, an
Innes, or a Rousseau etching in a Rousseau frame.[90]

John had had two successful shows there, in 1910 and 1911, and
Knewstub agreed that to coincide with the next John exhibition
Mark and Currie could put on a joint display in another
room.

The show opened in December 1912 and Mark found himself,
according to the *Daily Chronicle*, 'one of the young bloods of the
Slade School showing us the newest new movement in art'. The
Observer thought that 'the group of artists who have gathered round
Mr John are considered to represent all that is most modern and
advanced in present day British Art'. The *Star*, urging its readers to
go to the Chenil 'to see what the younger men – the men of the
future – are doing', considered that 'the two most prominent
exhibitors here are Mr Currie and Mr Gertler'.

The galleries were very different in appearance from the big
West End showrooms, situated as they were in a house in the Kings
Road between the Town Hall and the Six Bells pub. Narrow and
unpretentious, it stood three storeys high with two rooms on each
floor, over a basement which was used for storage. Steps led from
the street up to the front door and the ground floor was run by
Knewstub as an artists' materials shop. Mark and Currie shared the
first-floor rooms, of which the front one looked out on to the street
over small iron balconies.

Some of Mark's pictures were in tempera, in which he had
become interested, getting help and advice from John and Currie.
When he had finished one he rejoiced, 'Just think, I have actually
done a painting in that wonderful medium tempera, the medium of
our old Great friends! . . . I love tempera.' (September 1912)

The portrait of Carrington was a success: 'I can praise without
qualification the precision of modelling and the bright, fresh colours
are admirable,' said the *Star*, adding that 'if Mr Gertler's future

work fulfils the promise of these paintings and drawings he will go far.'

The *Observer* praised the 'daring colour' of Mark's 'rather flatly painted heads, which have but the slightest suggestion of modelling. His work holds the fairest promise of future achievement.'

The two friends could congratulate themselves on the show, for their reputation had increased since the *Star* had coupled their names when reviewing the summer's New English Exhibition: 'Two new men have come forward with pictures that prove that the new movement is full of hope for the future.'

Knewstub was sufficiently impressed with the reaction to Currie's work to offer him a special show six months later, in July 1913, a chance of which Currie intended to make the most. Like Mark, he was a hard worker, and during the spring they spurred each other on to fresh efforts.

Currie's ardent, even violent feeling for Dolly Henry was fully returned. They had met three years previously, when she had been working as a dress model at Jay's in Regent Street.* He had asked her to sit for him and they soon became lovers. When his wife had discovered the affair, in August 1911, he had refused to give up Dolly, and had left his wife. Dolly was willing to throw in her lot completely with Currie, and in the autumn of 1912 they moved in together openly, ignoring the resulting gossip.

They took a flat at No. 1 St George's Square: a high, decaying Victorian terrace by Primrose Hill, and here Mark became a frequent visitor. 'Currie is a great joy to me and really my truest friend,' he noted.

The older man seemed to Mark to embody the ideal of an artist's life. His energy, 'like that of a steam engine', dominated the flat and made its poverty and untidiness of no account. Equally inspiring to Mark were both the passionate warmth of the couple's love for each other – after the cold innocence of Carrington – and the fury of enthusiasm with which Currie worked for his show. Other visitors shared Mark's admiration. The sculptor Gaudier-Brzeska – not an

* Her full name was Dorothy Henry. She came from Colchester, where her father was a commercial traveller, and had left in 1910, at the age of sixteen, to work in London.

easy man to impress – found Currie 'a great painter and a magnificent fellow'.

Dolly was a beautiful girl. One of Currie's paintings was a life-size nude of her in tempera which he showed in the January 1913 Friday Club under the title 'Reminiscence of Venus'. She was tall and heavy-limbed, her skin was soft, and though her movements were slow and sensual, her face was animated and gay under a thick mass of red-blond hair – the eyes curiously slanting, the chin tilting provocatively, the mouth wide. Another acquaintance found her 'an enchanting girl, a singularly kind and beautiful girl of a warm and affectionate temperament'.[91]

If she was willing to put up with the difficulties caused by her position, Dolly did not enjoy them, and Currie determined to get his freedom and marry her. They went to Colchester together to see Dolly's parents, and her mother later recalled, 'he wrote and asked my husband if he could become engaged to Dorothy and we consented; he told me he was getting a divorce from his wife'. His wife agreed and the future seemed bright.

Currie was a natural leader, and Mark and Dolly were often content to follow his initiative. The power of his presence was almost equal to that of Augustus John and, as with John, his exploits assumed a legendary character. 'He recited Yeats and Synge, and drank raw Irish whisky,' said Allinson. Nevinson considered that 'he had a Napoleonic complex and was non-moral because of an over-reading of Nietzsche'. Another wrote: 'He had great belief in himself and indeed showed great promise . . . Currie had a theory of life similar to that which induced Raskolnikoff in *Crime and Punishment* to kill an old woman for the sake of three thousand roubles. If he considered the possession of an article helpful to him, or desirable, he would take it without scruple as to its rightful ownership. Books which he coveted to assist him in the study of art, or even silver spoons from the tables of his hospitable friends, were thus converted to his use'.[92]

Having given his devotion, Mark was quite willing to be taken charge of in their outings together, though he limited his own participation in larceny to joint expeditions to steal paint and materials, and even these scared him. In Whitechapel crime was not a game but an unpleasant reality, and Golda's reaction if he were arrested did not bear thinking about.

In the evenings they sometimes gave parties or invited people to dinner. Sidney Schiff, the rich connoisseur and patron of artists, began to take an interest in them. 'On Saturday night Currie, Henry and myself went up to Schiff's for dinner,' Mark reported to Carrington in March 1913. 'There were a lot of people there, also a very graceful girl, who made me dance a ballet with her. I took the part of Nijinsky; I had on a jersey and a belt. Then we did a music-hall sketch.'

Sometimes the evenings would be spent just talking or reading. 'Currie is ill with rheumatism', Mark wrote in April, 'so most of my evenings are spent with him in his rooms. Henry makes supper. I enjoy these quiet and peaceful evenings very much.'

But it was a period, above all, of work for both Mark and Currie, and throughout the winter, and the spring of 1913, there were periods when Mark would remain in Whitechapel for weeks at a time. In September 1912 he had written, 'I am so interested in my work that I see *nobody* – not even Currie – I live in a sort of beautiful, half melancholy loneliness.' And towards the end of the spring, on 15 April 1913, he told Carrington, 'I have been working abnormally hard, so expect only to see my ghost. I haven't seen anybody for a week – not even Currie. In the evenings I just read. I went for a walk on the Embankment. Just the same as when I was a little boy. The picture I'm doing is very much like what I did as a little boy too.'

PART FOUR

'Chaotic and rawly alive'

'How adroitly he could have played their game had he chosen to stay with it.' – QUENTIN BELL

'I've made great friends with Gertler and Currie – especially Gertler, who I see a great deal of and think the greatest genius of the age.'

EDWARD MARSH TO RUPERT BROOKE

CHAPTER 11

'Lavishing money on these bloody artists'

Through his visits to the homes of Nevinson and Brett, Mark was beginning to have some idea of how the middle class lived, but his contacts with the famous had so far been negligible. In the summer of 1913 he found himself, quite suddenly, an object of interest to a man who moved at ease in the dazzling world of the Edwardian aristocracy.

It was Currie who introduced Mark to Edward Marsh.

The encounter took place at the Albert Hall, where Mark had gone with Currie and Gaudier-Brzeska to the Allied Artists exhibition; Marsh was inspecting the vast show of modern art and trying to make sense out of it all.* He was intrigued by the young artist; an invitation arrived soon after and was quickly accepted. 'Dear Mr Marsh, Thanks very much for inviting me. I shall be very pleased to come. Of course I remember you at the Albert Hall show. I shall be interested to see your pictures.'

Raymond Buildings, where Marsh lived, was a solid, rectangular block of grey brick towering like a cliff over the lawns of Gray's Inn. Going through the gate from Theobalds Road, Mark walked along the private road, past the entrances to flats, until he arrived at No. 5. The four in this section were mainly occupied by solicitors

---

* Edward Marsh, 1872–1953, son of a Master of Downing College, was at Cambridge with Bertrand Russell, Maurice Baring and Robert Trevelyan. He became Assistant Private Secretary to Mr Chamberlain and later Secretary to Winston Churchill. Interested in poetry as well as pictures (which he began to collect at the turn of the century), he was the propagandist, friend and biographer of Rupert Brooke, and the editor of the anthology *Georgian Poetry*; later knighted, he was a central figure in the cultural, social and political scene in London for several decades.

and accountants, but on the third floor, at the top of fifty-eight stone steps, was Marsh's flat. Pictures there certainly were: frame to frame they covered every inch of wall space in the flat. They stretched from floor to ceiling in the rooms, along the passages and over the bathroom door. They were almost exclusively English eighteenth- and nineteenth-century work, and there were no modern pictures, with the exception of a solitary Duncan Grant, 'Parrot Tulips'. Marsh had bought it at the previous December exhibition of the Camden Town Group.

Marsh himself, a young-looking forty, was impeccably dressed, courteous and sprightly, with 'a certain way of rearing his handsome head up, and across to one side. He had very fine eyes crowned by remarkable branching eyebrows, one of which curled round a bright monocle.'[93] He loved showing his collection. At these times his elegant urbanity would be overcome by his romantic and extravagant enthusiasms: all artists were wonderful and his own favourites were the greatest.

A friendship blossomed. Yet Mark was puzzled. Whatever Marsh wanted from him it did not seem to be his work. Marsh's interest in contemporary art was only just beginning to stir. 'I have made a very interesting friend lately; he knows your father,' Mark wrote to Brett in June, describing Marsh. 'I do not share his taste in art. He buys everybody's work except my own . . . He is a very nice man, but I am afraid he likes me, more than my work.' However it was all very flattering.

Marsh sent a letter to his close friend Rupert Brooke (who had given up his key of the flat a few months before to go on a long trip to America), describing Mark as 'a beautiful little Jew like a Lippo Lippi cherub' . . . 'Gertler is by birth an absolute little East End Jew . . . I am going to see him in Bishopsgate and be initiated into the ghetto. He is rather beautiful, and has a funny little shiny black fringe; his mind is deep and simple, and I think he's got the *feu sacré*.' (26 August 1913)

Being 'taken-up' had its difficult aspects. To Brett, Mark confessed, 'Mr Marsh took me to a first night of a play. Evening dress!!! I felt so awkward! Everybody in the theatre looked at me. I felt ashamed. I feel so uncomfortable in evening dress. I feel that there is always something wrong about my evening clothes especially as my friend

8—MG * *

wore a monical!!!' And other problems arose. 'My face looks so
dirty in comparison with those well washed gentry. I must use that
hard sponge again, that I bought.' Mark had never been able so far
to see much point in all this washing. 'I must tell you,' he wrote a
little later to Brett, 'that I do not wash much; I think it is a waste of
Labour. I only wash when I look dirty. I am sorry because I know
you would like me to do otherwise, but I cannot alter my habits.'
(September 1913)

When Marsh took him to friends for a weekend Golda had to
rush out and buy a pair of pyjamas. They were Mark's first: until
now he had always slept in his vest and underpants.

Yet Mark was never easy to overawe, and his belief that an artist
was classless, 'equal to the highest or the lowest', and should be
accepted everywhere, gave him courage. He resolutely did his best
to bridge the gap between them and treat Marsh as an equal,
taking him to the Café Royal music halls, East End theatres and
Yiddish plays, and inviting him to tea at Elder Street.

Marsh had been to Whitechapel before. As secretary to Winston
Churchill, who was Home Secretary, he had been present at the
astonishing siege of Sidney Street on 3 January 1911 when a
detachment of Guards with artillery fought a day-long battle with
two immigrant anarchists. Afterwards he had seen himself, an aloof
and immaculate spectator, on a newsreel of the event. The incident
had started a fresh wave of anti-immigrant feeling. 'Great Britain
cannot afford to maintain any longer her old attitude of tolerance
and indifference towards the aliens who come to her shores,'
declared the *Morning Post*. Some papers were more blunt: 'Many
of the immigrants ... are not fleeing from persecution but
prosecution, [they are] vultures and garbage mongers, the scum of
continental slums,' said the *Dublin Evening Mail*.

Elder Street was just over three-quarters of a mile from Sidney
Street. This time Marsh was going as the advance guard, as it were,
of a surprising number of distinguished people who were to make
their way to Whitechapel to see Mark. He stepped up the smelly
stairs of bare wood to Mark's rooms, like his own on the second
floor, looked at the pictures, sipped tea. The visit was a success. He
liked one picture, 'A Jewish Family',[177] which Mark was just finishing
so much that he bought it on the spot. Overjoyed, Mark wrote

to Brett and told her. 'Unfortunately I was so overwhelmed when he asked me the price that I only asked £35.' (September 1913) Currie was pleased. 'I knew you would like his work,' he said to Marsh.

Marsh's character and his way of life was a revelation to Mark. As the friendship developed it became evident that he was a remarkable man, one who had the entrée to all kinds of worlds.

In England people either were, or were not, 'in society'; Marsh was definitely in. On one hand he revolved gravely through the balls and circulated politely and wittily in the great country houses of the rich and titled, where one glittering weekend party followed another. Through his work, he had an equal acquaintance with the practical realities of Government, power and privilege, carrying out his duties with a light touch and apparent ease. A fellow civil servant, Harold Nicolson, later said of him, 'we thought it fitting that, suitably arrayed, he should spend his days in heavily carpeted rooms, locking and unlocking cabinet boxes with one of the four keys that dangled from a slim silver chain.'

But Marsh could not be despised as merely a social butterfly, or distrusted as a worldly politician. Aristocrats and politicians were not the only visitors to Raymond Buildings. Poets and writers flowed in and out by the dozen. The son of a former master of Downing College, Cambridge, and himself a product of the Cambridge of the nineties, where he was a fellow member of the Apostles Society with G. E. Moore and Bertrand Russell, Marsh was a fine scholar, at ease in Latin and Greek, and seemed to Mark to have read every book that ever existed. Eagerly Mark gobbled up recommendations of writers and poets, listened to readings of the newly published *Golden Journey* by Flecker, appreciated the perfect taste of his surroundings and enjoyed the excellent food of the housekeeper. Marsh had made his flat a little world of comfort as well as beauty.

The day at Raymond Buildings might begin with Marsh reciting poetry in his bath at the top of his voice. Breakfast was often a party. Marsh had brought out the anthology *Georgian Poetry* the previous December, and was involved with a wide circle of young writers which included Rupert Brooke, Gilbert Cannan, D. H. Lawrence, Katherine Mansfield, John Middleton Murry, and many others.* Any of these, when in London, might come to breakfast; they would exchange ideas, gossip and look out at the stately plane trees and lawns of the Inn. The day often ended with Marsh coming home in a hansom cab, after his round of work and dinner parties, and sitting down before his library table to read and edit more poetry until well into the night.

It was not long before Mark and Currie succeeded in convincing Marsh of the merits of modern painting in general, and their own work in particular. On 26 August 1913 he wrote to Brooke: 'Currie came yesterday. I have conceived a passion for both him and Gertler; they are decidedly two of the most interesting of *les jeunes*, and I can hardly wait till you come back to make their acquaintance... Gertler is only twenty-two – Currie I think, a little older, and his pictures proportionately better; he can do what he wants, which Gertler can't quite yet I think – but he will.' Before the end of the year he was saying, 'I've made great friends with Gertler and Currie – especially Gertler who I see a great deal of and think the greatest genius of the age.'

Under Mark's influence he began to take a greater interest in the French Post-Impressionist painters, as well as Mark's favourites among the Old Masters. 'Blake and Giotto are about the only people he will let me admire, so I am naturally rather narrow about the new International show,' Marsh joked. 'Of course I'm allowed Gauguin, Cézanne, etc.'

Marsh was comfortably off but not wealthy, and the money which he used to buy pictures had a curious origin: in 1812 the Prime Minister, Spencer Perceval, was shot and killed by an intruder in the House of Commons. Ever since, his descendants, of whom Marsh was one, had received regular payment from a Government grant. In August 1913 this 'murder money', as Marsh

---

* The group included W. H. Davies, John Drinkwater, T. E. Hulme, Ralph Hodgson, James Stephens and Siegfried Sassoon. Not far away in Devonshire Street was Harold Munro's Poetry Bookshop, which had published *Georgian Poetry*, and another group of friends were linked through Katherine Mansfield and John Middleton Murry with their magazine the *Blue Review*, previously *Rhythm*, which Marsh kept alive. It also published the works of Cannan and some of the others.

called it, was supplemented by a legacy from an aunt. Marsh decided to have his rooms done up and 'go a bust in Gertler, Currie and Cookham'. Brooke was not too happy about this: 'I hate you lavishing all your mad aunt's money on these bloody artists,' he wrote in September. But Marsh went ahead. His purchases over the next year were to make a big difference to Mark's life.

Mark was willing to share his good fortune and put his Slade friends in touch with this new source of money. David Bomberg, who had been a fellow student, was in difficulties, and Mark persuaded Marsh to buy a drawing.[94] Another Slade friend was Isaac Rosenberg, who had started in Mark's last year. 'He was a funny little man,' Mark recalled later, describing how Rosenberg, while they were drawing side by side, would pass him a piece of paper with a poem written on it. One day in November 1913 Mark took him along to the Café Royal to meet Marsh, and Rosenberg accompanied them on other outings. Marsh was interested and he helped. Other artists recommended by Mark included Paul Nash, who later recorded that when Marsh bought his work, it was 'at the instigation of Mark Gertler, whose advice Eddie was inclined to seek on matters of contemporary art.'[95]

Marsh began to share Mark's admiration for Stanley Spencer, or 'Cookham' as they called him after his home village. But a squabble between the two young artists prevented a meeting, and on 26 August 1913 Marsh was writing sadly, 'Gertler and Currie both admire "Cookham" more than anyone else. Gertler was to have taken me to see him (at Cookham) tomorrow, but it's had to be put off.' Mark had said, 'Dear Eddie, Kookham was so insultingly critical about my own work that I've done with him and could not think of going down to see him. You can go by yourself if you like.'

The importance of the paintings Spencer had begun to produce in mid 1912 had surprised everyone. It was obvious that he had become a powerful artistic personality with very decided ideas of his own. On this occasion he had written that Mark's work showed him to be 'quite incapable of understanding Cézanne', an insult indeed to Mark, who felt that he understood Cézanne a lot better than Spencer did. Spencer was as blunt as Mark himself, and inclined to be ham-fisted. A tactless letter of apology made Mark even more prickly; Mark explained to Marsh, 'His second letter says that it was not meant insultingly. That makes it worse. For then what he wrote were not insults, but truths . . . He seems to have already adopted the "Great Man" attitude, which I loathe like poison – I hate it!!! He has had much praise lately and he is spoilt. I will have nothing more to do with him.' (October 1913) Currie supported Mark. He thought Spencer's remark was unprovoked and 'the more acrimonious of the two', he told Marsh: 'the memory of such a blow would remain.*

The row blew over in a few months, but Marsh in the meantime had to make his own arrangements with Spencer. By the end of 1913 Spencer's big painting 'Apple Gatherers' was installed in Marsh's flat. The pictures by Duncan Grant, Gertler and Spencer looked rather strange among the quiet eighteenth-century works. Paul Nash, after visiting Marsh the following year, and staying in the spare room, commented, 'Apparently there had been a recent phase among the English progressives, which might have been called the apotheosis of the dwarf. Groups of dwarfs by Gertler and Spencer seemed to menace me from every wall.'[96]

CHAPTER 12

'They talk well, argue masterly'

To Mark, the standards generally observed in the society he had entered 'seemed to him as irrelevant to the actual circumstances of life as the rules of heraldry',[97] and he found it difficult not to be critical of many aspects of Marsh's way of life. He had earlier taken issue with Brett over the easy life of some cousins of hers: 'You must try and avoid the society of such people. They lead such soft and uselessly happy lives that they know nothing about life. Their life is too easy. They have had no hardships. God! They don't

* But Currie was troubled by a quarrel 'between the only two whose work I really care about'.

know what some experience here on Earth – the same Earth. "One touch of Nature makes the whole world kin," but some touches put miles of space between us.' (July 1913)

Sometimes an incident would bring him up short. An argument at the Café Royal developed into a brawl and several students were hauled off to the police station.[98] While the others were sent on their way with a good-humoured caution, Mark was charged and locked up until bail was found. The reason, he felt, was his East End address, compared to the St John's Wood and Chelsea abodes of the others.

Mark's reaction, when it came, was violent. After an outing with Marsh in December 1913 to see the latest Bernard Shaw play, *The Doctor's Dilemma*, he wrote to Carrington from Elder Street: 'I have just had a depressing night with Marsh at the theatre. To begin with I was in Evening dress and the play, Doctor's Dilemma, disgusted me. I cannot tell you how I hated Shaw last night for writing that play and for allowing such an insipid youth as Dennis Neilson-Terry and such a terrible woman as Lillah McCarthy to act in it! It was the artist part of the play that horrified me – the doctors were very good. I couldn't stand that terrible middle-class audience laughing in an enlightened way, when that insipid young artist was standing with painted lips and "charming" – justifying his artistic immorality in Shawese witticisms! How terrible! I wanted to scream, but I only got a terrible headache instead. How I should have loved to throw a rotten tomato at that weak and painted face of Terry! All this time Lillah McCarthy was standing on another part of the stage, wriggling into so-called beautiful and classic attitudes.

'It is said of Shaw that he has broken down the conventions of the upper middle classes, but I say that he has taken them out of the frying pan only to drop them into the fire!!! I could write you volumes on this subject, but I won't, chiefly because it makes me ill to think of it at all . . . Last night I couldn't sleep and I wanted to weep so, it upset me! I feel that I should like to excite all the working class to, one night, break into these theatres and destroy all those rich pleasure seekers! It was a relief to come home into my mother's kitchen. I looked at my father's thin bony suffering face and his working hands, all rough and hard, and I loved him. I thanked God that this *man* was my father. My father has never heard that name Bernard Shaw! – lucky man!'

He was more resolved than ever to keep his art anchored in the life he knew. 'As for realism,' he continued in his letter to Carrington, 'my work is real and I wanted it to be real. The more I see of life, the more I get to think that realism is necessary. There was not much reality going on in that theatre!' His basic aim was still, as he had once described it to Brett, 'to paint a picture in which I hope to express all the sorrow of Life.' When he painted his mother he wanted, he said, to 'try and get all that I feel about my mother.'

People who wanted merely pretty pictures were only to be despised. 'I am painting a portrait of my mother,' he had told Brett in July 1913[178]. 'She sits bent on a chair, deep in thought. Her large hands are lying heavily and wearily on her lap. The whole suggests suffering and a life that has known hardship. It is barbaric and symbolic. Ah! where is the prettiness! Where! Where!' The beauty that Mark sought was, as he put it, 'the beauty that trembles on the edge of ugliness.'

Later in the autumn he recorded, 'I have just started a picture of a mother feeding her baby. I am full of it. I am going to try and paint not the beauty of maternity, but the hardness of existence. I shall try to express all the poverty, strife and horror of life in the mother's face, whilst the child will be brutally and unconsciously sucking the very blood of the mother. Yet there will be a resignation about it all, a resignation that all we poor humans have to adopt, to make life tolerable. I shall not paint hurriedly but meditatively and shall take my time. If I get what I want it will be a fine picture.' His art could only have meaning, he felt, if he 'kept an eye on nature the whole time.'

While Mark struggled to sort out the confusion of emotions about class, society and morality into which his excursions to the upper class world had plunged him, a simultaneous battle of ideas about the new movement in art raged in his mind. His aim of realism raised a very serious question. Did he have a place in the new movement? Did it really have any relevance to what he wanted to express about life?

An art which had no obvious subject matter at all, such as the new abstract works of Kandinsky, was clearly not for him. And the cubists and many of the young British artists, such as Wyndham Lewis, Wadsworth and Bomberg, also seemed to be heading either for complete abstraction, or for an art which was concerned almost solely with pictorial problems. Hardly anyone else besides Mark among the talented young burned to express their feelings about the harshness of life.

Mark was worried; 'I don't want to be abstract and cater for a few hyper-intellectual maniacs. An over-intellectual man is as dangerous as an over-sexed man,' he wrote in December 1913. 'Besides I was born from a working man. I haven't had a grand education and I don't understand all this abstract intellectual nonsense! I am rather in search of reality, even at the cost of 'pretty decorativeness'. I love natural objects and I love painting them as they are – I use them to help me to express an idea . . .'

But it was more than just a matter of class. He reacted not only against the pleasure-seeking side of Marsh's life, but also against the Cambridge intelligentsia from which Marsh had sprung. They were interested enough in serious problems, but was their approach too intellectual, too thin-blooded?

In November 1913, Marsh took him for a weekend to Cambridge. They stayed with James Strachey Barnes, a cousin of the Strachey family. 'I enjoyed this weekend very much and am thankful to Barnes,' Mark wrote dutifully to Marsh. 'But it's always the same . . . They seem to be clever – very clever. They talk well, argue masterly, and yet, and yet there is something – something – that makes me dislike them. Some moments I hate them! . . . But if God will help me to put into my work that passion, that inspiration, that profundity of soul that I *know* I possess, I will triumph over those learned Cambridge youths. One of them argued *down* at me about painting!'

Marsh was upset, and Mark tried to soften his own bluntness. 'I do not for one moment include Jim [Barnes], I more than like him. I only meant the others; even those, I do not dislike. Only there does seem a bridge of tremendous lengths between such people and myself. I don't know what it is.' Wearily he went on, 'Perhaps it's merely difference of class. Anyhow, I have now definitely come to the conclusion that I am far happier alone. There is Grandier and dignity in Solitude. When I am amongst people of so called intellect, my soul gets torn to bits, my inspiration leaves me, and I get depressed. So it's my firm intention to see people as little as possible . . . if you write to Jim, do give him my love and tell him how much I like him . . .' At the bottom of the letter he scrawled a sad postscript: 'It is very good of you to be interested in me and to like me so much, thanks very much.'

'I value your friendship,' he said in another letter, 'Don't be offended with me – never be offended with me – for with my friends I must be frank. Frankness walks arm-in-arm with rudeness, and if ever I am rudely frank, don't think that I am insincere. Insincerity makes me so miserable that it pays to be sincere. Those are my feelings. Now we are friends, aren't we?'

Was it also possible that the new art was not only too cerebral but without a future? It was really very difficult for a young painter to assess its ultimate importance. The new movement was interesting and exciting, and there was no doubt that the artists were serious and highly talented. But could it be a diversion from the main road? A side-turning, perhaps leading to a dead end?

Certainly some thought so. Since Roger Fry's first exhibition of Post-Impressionist art there had been a number of others, and there had been ample opportunity to study the new ideas.[99] The opposition of many fairly enlightened critics had only hardened. Sickert, a fine painter whose subject matter had something in common with Mark's, was irritated at what he considered the over-praising of the French painters. He thought Futurism was 'a cul-de-sac', considered that the boom in Cézanne's pictures was 'owing to skilful operations by the international holders of picture stock', and considered there would be a time, 'when Cézanne is only remembered as a curious and pathetic by-product of the Impressionist group, and when Cubism has gone as lightly as it has come.'

Augustus John's attitude was important. He had spent much time in Paris and knew all about the new movement: he had even been to Picasso's studio and admired the strange 'Easter Island figures' he saw there. But he showed no signs of seriously adopting the new ideas from France, and had refused an invitation to take part in the

Second Post-Impressionist exhibition. Yet his reputation was still rising, and as far as many of the progressive critics were concerned he was the Leader of modern art in England and 'the head apostle of the new way of seeing and painting.'[100]

1912 had ended with Fry's second exhibition of Post-Impressionists and also the showing of John's picture 'Mumpers' at the New English. It was the latter event which, in the view of many critics, represented a turning-point in painting. Almost every paper printed a long discussion of it. The *Observer* hailed John as 'the leader of English Post Impressionism', and the *Illustrated London News* said: 'After a rocky impasse the roughest road is easy. After Picasso Mr John!'

The difficulty with this line of thinking was that the new art in Paris was not just an isolated French aberration: Picasso and Gris were Spanish, Kandinsky and Chagall, Russian, and Mondrian Dutch. Though they had all come to Paris, which was therefore the principal scene of action, the movement was clearly spread across Europe.

It was all very confusing. Sometimes Mark felt like rejecting all theories of art. 'The artists of today have thought so much about newness and revolution that they have forgotten art', he complained.

After finishing a painting of a woman, he wrote: 'My picture is now finished. I finished it yesterday. I worked very hard at it indeed and I think that I've succeeded to get something good into it. Anyway I've got the character of the woman and that's a great deal. I know it is not new, and our revolutionists would say of it that it was academic. I don't care. Newness doesn't concern me. I just want to express myself and be personal. When a bird is inspired it sings, it sings: it does *not* wonder if its manner of singing is different to a bird that sang a thousand years ago – it just sings!' (December 1913)

In his reaction against the soft life on the one hand, and his wariness of too intellectual an approach to life and art on the other, Mark found a supporter among Marsh's writer friends.

Gilbert Cannan had contacts in Whitechapel, loved the Yiddish theatre, and approved of many aspects of life in the East End.

Fascinated by Mark's exotic background, he conceived the idea of using his life as the basis of a novel, and Mark agreed to this. From then on, in between their meetings, at which he encouraged Mark to describe everything that happened to him and everything he thought, Cannan worked on the book. It was to be published in 1916 under the title of 'Mendel' – a Yiddish name which Mark's family had often used for him. Mendel was Mark, 'a being chaotic and rawly alive'. Many of the events were fictitious, and Cannan made a practice of mixing up some of the characters – the physique of one might be given the personality of another – but here and there, as Mark revealed in later years, his words were used almost verbatim.

In his description, for instance, of Mendel's confusion after an exhibition of modern French art, Cannan wrote, 'True, he had seen the same things in Paris and had not thought much of them, but so much had happened since then... For three weeks he lived between his studio and the Gallery, experimenting with their manners. Picasso baffled him altogether. These queer violent angular patterns actually hurt him; he was repelled by their intellectual intensity. Gauguin he found too easy, Van Gogh too incoherent. It was when he came to Cézanne that he was bowled out and reduced to impotence. He abandoned his experiments and made no attempt to work at all, but bought a reproduction of Cézanne's portrait of his wife and spent many days poring over it.'[101]

One of the dangers of the new art was that it was easy to adopt the superficial aspects of styles without really understanding them. Mark's wariness of this grew stronger as time went by. In January 1915 he was to write, 'An artist who has come back from Paris with all the "Latest Fashions", is to my mind the most dreadful of all living creatures. Oh! How they upset me. How I hate them!'

In guarding against the danger of simply imitating foreign fashions, Mark and Currie tried to paint pictures which would be firmly rooted in contemporary London life. Even some of the most conservative critics realized that the new art in Paris represented a valid response to the world, and a serious attempt to come to terms with it, but they reacted by saying that they did not have to approve of the twentieth century. This attitude could hardly be shared by vigorous young painters. Mark disliked many aspects of modern London life, but he was impressed by it.

Currie had quickly come to share Mark's desire for realism. Mark, as Cannan wrote in *Mendel*, 'had the further attraction for him that he was pure London, of the shifting motley London that Currie,* as a provincial adored. Currie's visit to Mendel in the East End had been one of the great events of his life . . . Together they would smash the English habit of following French art a generation late, and they would lay the foundation of a genuine English art, an art that grew naturally out of the life of the central city of the world.'[102]

If instead of merely following the new French ideas they could adapt them to a strong purpose of their own the possibilities became very exciting; even if it meant wasting hard-won skill in traditional oil-painting techniques, 'It was absurd to sit cramping over rules and difficult technicalities when the starting point of art lay so far beyond them.' 'I don't think skill, that is superficial skill, has much to do with the greatness of a picture,' Mark suggested to Brett. 'It has, in fact, been the cause of so many centuries of bad art. Thank God we "moderns" are finding out and soon, I think, we shall have art as great as it has ever been before, and *in our own way*. We have much to thank Cézanne for. He was a great, great man.' (September 1913)

* Cannan used fictitious names, but Gertler later identified the characters.

CHAPTER 13

'My types, they say, are ugly'

Golda knew nothing of these preoccupations, and would have been utterly baffled by them. But she had complete faith in Mark's talents. After his successes of a year or so before, the family had breathed sighs of relief and happiness. In their view he had justified all their sacrifices. He had gained an entry to the world of fashionable portraiture, and could look forward to being rich as well as famous. They would never understand why he was throwing his opportunities away.

Mark's problem was that, as Cannan put it in *Mendel*: 'It was impossible to explain to them about art, for they had neither words nor mental conceptions. Art was to them only a wonderful way of making money. A kind of magic that went on in the West End . . . It brought success and fame and money, and beautiful ladies in furs and diamonds and carriages and motor cars and fine clothes and rings on everybody's fingers.'[103] But now events were uncovering the real issues.

His family began to realize that something was going wrong. During 1913 his money was dwindling fast, and by July he was telling Brett, who had bought one of his drawings, 'I am getting very poor now. I cannot even afford models or outings in the evenings, and there is no hope of selling anything more, as my work is getting more and more personal, and therefore less and less understood. You see the curse is that even the most cultured buyer almost unconsciously looks for a little prettiness. Oh, he must have a little bit of it, else how can he hang it on his dainty wall! How could his white and scented wife look at it! How could one possibly go on eating asparagus in the same room! My types, they say, are *ugly*. But withal I am not a bit unhappy. I am working desperately hard and learning, learning daily.'

In *Mendel*, Cannan wrote, 'There came a terrible day when he had to tell them that he had not a penny in the world and that he was a failure. It would have gone hardly with him but for Jack, who espoused his cause, saying dramatically that he believed in his young brother as he believed in God, and that Mark should not be stopped for want of money.'[104] He scraped together a few pounds, and Harry and Louis then followed suit. This kind of thing obviously couldn't go on. 'The thing I hate looking forward to is living on my people', Mark confessed to Brett. 'They are so poor! If only I had a little income!' (July 1913)

In September Knewstub came to Elder Street and bought some work. Together with Marsh's purchase this relieved the situation. But it was clear that if Mark *did* throw in his lot completely with the new movement there was no chance of success in the worldly sense. He would be barred not only from the market of the Royal Academy and conventional collectors (a situation which he had already accepted), but from many of the circle of buyers round the New English group. His pictures would be hard to sell and there would be few commissions for portraits. And without these it was almost impossible for an artist to live in Britain.

He had no illusions about the situation. 'I think poverty is a terrible tragedy. A modern artist must have an income,' he declared to Marsh. (September 1913)

Having won his independence, could he risk alienating all his useful contacts and hence perhaps be forced to give up painting altogether and take a job? He had already passed up some opportunities. When Sargent had offered to help him to go to Italy to study, Mark had refused. The idea of blue skies was attractive, but he had felt that he would work better in his own home environment than following traditional lines in Italy; whereas the young people in London were excited by new ideas, there was little interest in modern art in Rome, and Mark believed that 'One must always live in cities that have a future, not merely a past – one mustn't be out of things.'

The question that really mattered was; Could he use his experience of life in the East End to make a new kind of picture?

The material in Whitechapel offered plenty of variety, in its unbearable way. He would wake in his dingy little room on the top floor in Elder Street to the noise of Harry and his family moving about below. Washing was difficult even if he felt like it: there were no baths or wash basins, only one sink on the ground floor, so normally he simply dressed and went straight over the road to Golda's kitchen for breakfast. This would be followed by his usual walk through Whitechapel before starting work.

The biggest problem during the day was noise. Ann had started to produce babies at the rate of one a year and the sound insulation of the house was poor. 'I can't write any more,' said Mark plaintively to Marsh on one occasion, 'as a baby is howling for all it's worth. Why so many babies? . . . How abominable it is to cram so many people into one small house.' Outside, the street was full of children screaming as they played, and the Yiddish language echoed along between the buildings. At one end the new electric trams screeched and clanged their way along Commercial Street and at the other heavy drays from the market came rumbling along the cobbles.

Spitalfields market was a rich source of smells. It was large, with 118 stall-holders, and East London's main distribution point for fruit and vegetables. Refuse collection in the district was never very efficient, and the stench of rotting fruit rose from the pavement outside Mark's window, mingling with the smells of dirt, people, and Kosher meat. The various small workshops around added their contribution from leather, rags and tobacco. Strongest of all was the smell of the trade by which the family lived. Once a furrier's workshop was started in a house the smell of the pelts became all-pervasive and could never be eliminated. There were four other furrier's workshops besides the Gertlers' in Spital Square, and more in the houses on both sides of Mark in Elder Street.

Concentration on work was difficult, though even so Mark often managed to lose himself in it. 'Today my father gave me a big row and almost wanted to hit me, because, whilst painting my mother, I forgot the dinner hour and went on painting till 2.30!' he wrote once. 'Oh! he was wild, he was so hungry. He dines at one o'clock! The meat and potatoes got burned! Everybody was annoyed with me. They said I love my art more than them!'

When he was prevented from working, depression closed in. Some days when the weather was bad, too dark to work and too wretched to go out, he sat for hours on end in his mother's kitchen by the fire, waiting until he could get on with his painting again.

There seemed no doubt that his work was suffering severely because of the discomfort of his surroundings. He had never known what it was like to be comfortable – except for moments in other people's houses – in his life. 'I am continually struggling against being overcome by the sordidness of my surroundings and family and by poverty,' he told Carrington. 'How I loathe poverty! However, I shan't grumble, for although there are so many people who have every comfort, there are also thousands of poor devils far more wretched than I.'

Mark's love for his family was as strong as ever, but gradually he came to think that 'it is hopeless to expect any spiritual understanding between our parents and ourselves.' In the evenings he might sit with them in Golda's kitchen. There, among 'its odd decorations from Tottenham Court Road, its dresser crammed with gilded china and fringed with cut green paper, its collection of his early pictures, almost all hanging crooked', time passed slowly. If trade was slack, Louis and Harry would play cards. Jack might join in, or sit toying with the front door key. This was so large – the lock was an enormous mortice type – that by common consent only Jack carried one; the house was never empty in any case and only Jack was ever out late. Golda might look through a Yiddish paper. Harry and Jack could not read it but were learning to pick out the headlines and main points in English papers. There were no books about.

The talk was mostly family gossip – endless recounting of their experiences in Austria and Whitechapel or discussions of the business. There was no formality or style. Only on Friday, before the Sabbath, would the family regularly sit down to a meal together. On other days food would be waiting all the time on the stove, as they came and went from the workshop.

There, Jack did the odd jobs, such as machining and nailing. Harry had become a skilful cutter. He was the craftsman upon whom the whole enterprise depended. The business consisted in making collars for women's coats and costumes. The workshop equipment was simple: sewing-machines, two or three long boards laid out on trestles, and piles of fur pelts. First the skins had to be matched up, then, after moistening, they were stretched out to

9—MG * *

cover a roughly chalked shape on a board, and nailed. When they
were dry Harry would take the board to his bench, lay his paper
pattern over the furs and cut round to the correct shape with his
furrier's knife. Then the boards would be stood up against the wall
to await the machinist.

Demand was highly seasonal: from about midsummer they
worked until eleven at night as trade built up, until the Lord
Mayor's show in November. This was popularly called the 'furriers'
funeral' because it marked the end of the 'season' and for the rest of
the year there was little to do. Harry and Jack might have done
better trying to find other jobs, but Louis maintained his 'absolute
refusal to receive his daily bread from any other hands than his
own, and his almost crazy refusal to let Harry and Jack go out and
work for other masters. They could work for their father because
he had authority over them.'[105]

It was a stifling, inbred kind of existence which oppressed Mark.
He was the only one with a definite purpose apart from making
money, and his activities provided one of the principal diversions.
'It's like having a play going on in the family,' they said. To Mark,
reflecting that they were still within a few hundred yards of
Liverpool Street station, their point of arrival in London, it
sometimes seemed that they were 'as much a part of the street as the
doors and windows of the houses'.

Jack had already tried to break away. Finding the restrictions
irksome he had asked Louis' consent to go to America. Louis had
refused. Then trouble with a girl had brought matters to a head.
Unable to discuss this kind of problem with his parents, Jack had
left for Paris. There he had stayed in the Jewish quarter working as
a machinist and playing the piano at dances in the evenings. After a
few months he had got bored and come back to London.

If Mark did leave Whitechapel, would his art suffer? Was his
life there one of its essential sources? After all he had never even
remotely *liked* the district. For a long time now he had been
sickened by his surroundings, living only for his art. 'I know what
art is,' Cannan described him as saying: 'it touches life at one point
and one point only, and there it gives a great light. If life is too
mean and beastly to reach that point, so much the worse for life. It

does not affect art, which is another world, where everything is beautiful and true – I know it; I have always known it. I have lived in that world. I live in it and I detest everything that drags me away from it, and makes me live in the world of filth and thieves and scoundrels.'[106]

To Carrington he explained, 'I thank God for at least having endowed me with the true spirit of an artist. By means of this true spirit I am raised for the most part of the time, far, far, above all these sordid and material cares and worries into a wonderful and higher world. A world of imagination and infinite beauty! It is in that world that I really live! It is only that part of my existence that makes life worth living for me. However, against my will though it be, I have to descend from my higher world into this – the material and the sordid. Yet in spite of much discouragement my life's plan is very simple. I just want to devote my whole life to working at what I feel and experience during my momentary stays in that higher world, by means of art.'

Whitechapel was squalid, but it was overwhelmingly alive. When he came back there from the West End, to Brick Lane for instance, as he recalled later, 'there was definitely "something different" – a greater vitality, perhaps: the rich dark-complexioned boys and girls seemed to move and talk with unusual intensity – as if life was fearfully important – momentous. The whole long narrow street itself seemed to vibrate with a quickened pulse, and a life of its own.' His companion on this occasion was excited with the dresses and hats in the shop windows. 'They were all in the very latest fashion, with just a touch of something else, just a touch of that charming vulgarity which made them so fetching – so different.'

Usually Mark could share in this vitality. 'I am still young and full of energy, and I know that tomorrow morning I shall get up with renewed vigour and go for it like a warrior! How wonderful that renewal of vigour is!! Just when one thinks that all is over and that there is nothing but death, suddenly, suddenly, it comes, it comes, like dawn it breaks! The heavy cloak of depression that so weighed and oppressed one's limbs drops, and eagerly with raised arm we embrace the New Hope! – that renewal of energy! How wonderful that it should happen so often! Ah! That's the beauty of youth!' (May 1913)

The East End offered any amount of unexploited subjects for painting. And the physical conditions were improving; the electric street lighting, underground railways and motor buses had brought an amazing transformation since he was a boy; and there seemed to be less poverty and less violence in the streets.

When Mark went out without his Slade friends and stayed in the East End, either alone or with Currie or Jack, he had a wide choice: he could pay a visit to Shevzik's Russian Steam Baths in Brick Lane, go to a music hall or cinema, or look for possible models, perhaps among the queues waiting with jugs for milk at one of the thirty-odd cowyards in the district. He could look at the soaring bulk of Hawksmoor's Christ Church, which was empty and disused, towering absurdly over the little streets, and stroll in its churchyard – locally known as Itchy Park because of the condition of its frequenters. If he wanted quiet in the evening, he might walk down to Tower Bridge to look at the still water and the ships at anchor, Once after such a stroll, he wrote, 'There was a beautiful half moon out. I was rather surprised to hear a tiny little child, sitting on a bench next to me, shouting to its mother "Oh! Muvver, ain't that nice?" and it was pointing to the moon!' When he wanted company there was Whitechapel High Street with its noisy, colourful crowds surging past the neat shop-keepers in suits and skull-caps; he could look at the fancy shows and shooting saloons, or the barrows with their flaring paraffin lights. He could pick up a girl, though there would be trouble from the respectable Harry and Ann if she wasn't out of Elder Street before night.

At home he would often sit up after midnight writing letters to Currie, Brett or Carrington.

Having painted the people around him in the East End in the style and manner which he had learnt at the Slade, Mark now set out to paint them again, this time developing a kind of picture which rejected most of the principles so dear to his teachers; and in the pictures which he created in the year or so following the autumn of 1912, Mark emerged as one of the leaders of the modern movement in London. In setting out to develop a kind of painting which was a complete break with the past, and yet be capable of conveying a high pitch of emotion about his subject matter, Mark had few serious rivals. The nearest were the younger painters of the Camden Town School, who were trying to develop what Harold Gilman and Charles Ginner called 'neo-realism', but it is arguable that in 1913 Mark was taking the lead in simplification and formalization,[107] in such pictures as 'Rabbi and his grandchild,'[179] 'A Family Group',[180] 'A Jewish Family',[177] 'The Artist's Mother',[178] and the slightly later 'Rabbi and Rabbitzin'.[180]

Besides painting his mother and family Mark was constantly on the lookout for interesting faces or other subjects.[108] As always he was fascinated by the old Jews of the district, and persuaded as many as possible to sit for him. One problem was that they could not believe he wanted them as they were: it was difficult to stop them cutting their beards and tidying themselves up for the sittings.

Sittings for paintings did not always go so smoothly. 'One of the things I have at present on hand is a picture which I call "Christ and the Elders",' Mark said to Brett in June 1913. 'Don't be surprised! It's merely a study of a lot of old Jews' heads round a young one – my brother. It's really a technical study of heads and hands, although I am interested in the subject, more than you would think. I have hopes for this picture.' But they were to be dashed. Writing to Rupert Brooke, Marsh gave news of the disaster: 'Gertler has had a temporary setback in a picture he is painting. He takes tremendous interest in Christ and wanted to paint him disputing with the doctors. It is apparently unheard of for a Jew to paint Christ, so to get his models (his brother and some Bishopsgate Rabbis) he made them think it was only going to be just any young Jew with any old Jews – he writes today that they have found out, and won't sit any more! Isn't it curious?' (26 August 1913)

The series of paintings in 1913 was made possible only by a strenuous and sustained effort, but throughout this period Mark's moods veered between elation and despair. In May he wrote to Carrington, 'Today my work went very badly and I was disgusted with my horrible incompetence. Sometimes it is really difficult to go on living. God knows when I shall do something that will please me! There are times when everything I do seems loathsome to me.'

'Good painting is so rare and beautiful an art, that it needs *tremendous* work and self-sacrifice to paint well,' he reported to Brett. 'I am working very, very hard and yet, would you believe it – if you were to come back this moment – I would have *nothing* to show you! No sooner do I finish a picture, than I paint it out. As I go on I get more and more critical about my own work. Nothing satisfies me, my people look upon me as a complete lunatic!!' (June 1913) In July, when he had nearly finished 'A Family Group', he wrote exhaustedly to Brett: 'Simplification is *terribly* difficult in art.'

By January 1914 he began to feel better: 'I am doing work now which is real work. Far better than anything I've done before.'

Most of the critics, not knowing what to make of Mark's new pictures, simply ignored them.*

The trouble was that the Tonks, Brown and Steer circle could now see clearly that he was rejecting the ideals of the New English group. They felt this the more keenly because he had been one of their star pupils. 'How adroitly he could have played their game had he chosen to stay with it,' a later critic commented.[109]

But he was now producing the kind of pictures which inspired a well-meaning visitor to the club's exhibition to write to him with a suggestion which he reported to Brett. 'She said she had been and seen my "New English" picture and that she thinks my eyes must be *wrong* to paint like that, and that I would do her a great favour if I would – at her expense – see an oculist!' (July 1913)

The result was that his pictures tended to be badly hung. 'Of course they've treated Gertler rotten,' commented Currie to Marsh after the autumn 1913 New English show. Currie thought the exhibition was appalling anyway: 'John's the chief attraction with a large impressive drawing. But to my mind it's humbug.'

* The amount of newspaper space given to his work at the May and November 1913 New English shows and the Friday Club the following February was negligible, though the *New Age* put in a good word for him at the May New English show – 'among the braver, younger throng by far the most interesting is Mark Gertler' – and the *Morning Post* had said he and Currie were 'among the ablest members' at the January 1913 Friday Club. One piece of encouragement came from the perceptive Marchant, of the Goupil Gallery, who wanted him to send work to their Autumn Salon of 1913.

Real danger signs had become visible when only one of Mark's pictures had been accepted for the November 1912 show. Secure until now in his membership of the New English he suddenly faced the imminent possibility that he might be cut off from their circle of buyers and be unable to get his work seen in the West End.

It was time to consider how the other progressive artists were faring. Roger Fry had tried to give a lead by organizing exhibitions for them (several had been included in his second Post-Impressionist Exhibition in October 1912), and his Omega workshops were started in the spring of 1913. The idea was to give young painters a chance to earn a little money by making designs for furniture and textiles in their spare time.

Among the Camden Town painters, Harold Gilman was emerging as a powerful personality and skilful leader. He had been the first to realize that the opposition of the New English Group to the new ideas was implacable. The Camden Town Group had failed to get a dealer really interested in them because of their small size and Gilman determined to gather all the advanced painters and merge them into one strong body. This he succeeded in doing. Though the support of Roger Fry and his friends was lost because of a quarrel between him and Wyndham Lewis, leader of the near-abstract group, all the other warring elements agreed to combine under Gilman in a society to be called the 'London Group'; it was obvious that, provided Gilman could hold them together, the group would act as a magnet for talent, and Marchant offered the use of the Goupil Gallery.

Mark put his name forward for election.

But he was in a dangerously isolated position. Few people really liked his work. Too advanced for the New English group, its realism yet made it suspect to the most advanced wing of semi-abstract painters such as Wyndham Lewis, Bomberg and Wadsworth.

Until now Mark had ignored art politics. He always went his own way, and, though far from unkind, and willing to help individuals, he was too obsessed with his own problems to work effectively with others, in groups.

Events now moved fast. On 15 November 1913 the new society formally designated its title as 'The London Group'. A week later it

was agreed to hold two exhibitions a year, and a meeting on 29
November the date of the first was fixed: March 1914. At this
meeting the prospects of further applicants for membership were
made worse by the choice of a stiff voting system for elections. It
was too tough: in an election on 6 December Mark and all thirteen
other applicants were rejected. The system was made more liberal
and on 3 January 1914 the group voted again. This time nine new
members were elected, but the losers included Currie and Mark.
With thirteen votes against him and only six in favour, Mark
hadn't had a chance.[110]

PART FIVE

Decisions

'Mark's attitude to friends is rather curious' – JOHN CURRIE

'In many ways I love Currie.'

MARK GERTLER TO CARRINGTON

CHAPTER 14

'Friendships are terribly difficult to manage'

Mark began to feel anxious about Currie. To outsiders, all seemed to be going well: 'I had a most delightful dinner at Raymond Buildings,' Marsh had told Rupert Brooke in the summer of 1913. The guests included 'John Currie and his mistress, an extremely pretty Irish girl with red hair called Dolly Henry, and Mark Gertler . . . they were tremendous fun.'[111] Currie was still working hard and by the end of August Marsh was buying his pictures. Many of them explored themes of common life,[112] a trend that reflected the influence of Mark who, over the last year, had been gaining an equal status artistically.*

In the autumn of 1913 Currie and Dolly found a charming little cottage in Hampstead – No. 3, Heath Passage, North End. 'I'm fixed up now in the cottage here,' Currie reported excitedly to Marsh on 7 October. 'Very delightful. Hope you'll come to see it sometime.'

One visitor wrote, 'I paid two visits to Currie at Hampstead. He was blazing with genius. All his nature was aflame. In this secluded house, in a passage near 'The Spaniards', I met two girls . . . Currie was reading Dostoievsky aloud to them. Photographs of a Cézanne

---

* When, in January 1914, Knewstub gave them another show at the Chenil Gallery, this was recognized by the critic of the *Sunday Times*: 'There is marked sympathy between the work of Mr Mark Gertler and Mr John Currie. It is characterized by an intense and often dramatic outlook. Of the two Mr Gertler is the stronger craftsman; but Mr Currie displays the more imaginative temperament . . . The drawings of Mr Gertler are worthy of serious attention and prove him a forceful and vigorous executant.'

Nevinson, too, had been following Mark's lead with subjects such as 'Liverpool Street' and 'Gasometer'.

landscape and of Italian primitives were pinned up in his little painting room. The fair-haired girl was evidently not highly educated, the darker girl was silent and intense.'[113] The fair girl was Dolly; the darker girl, Mary, was an Irish cousin of Dolly's who came to live with them with a position between guest and servant.

But beneath the surface happiness, tensions were building up. Dolly began to be afraid of his art, seeing it as a danger to herself. Later Edward Marsh maintained: 'There was no great harm in her, but she was extremely vain and quite empty-headed – and jealous of his work.' She struggled to understand it, but in a way this made matters worse. As Cannan put it in *Mendel*, her view was: 'I'm a woman and I stand for something in the world. A woman is more important than the biggest picture that was ever painted.' But she tried also to take part in the discussions about painting, and this annoyed Mark: 'It was bad enough when she kept quiet, but now that she gives herself airs and talks, I can't stand it.'[114]

The close links between Currie and Mark added further fuel to Dolly's irritation. She and Mark, underneath a pretended friend-ship, were rivals, with poor Currie in the middle. 'Mark's attitude to friends is rather curious – rather like mine to ladies,' Currie confessed ruefully to Marsh. 'A strange and tormented lot we are.' The stress began to affect Mark, who was further troubled by Carrington's attitude to Currie. On one occasion he had to write: 'My Dearest Friend Carrington. I shall certainly try and not ask Currie to come . . . You were very kind to me . . . How I *do* love you. P.S. I shall tell Currie that Brett asked *only* a certain number and you and Brett must keep that up to help me. It may be difficult.' In September 1913 he acknowledged to Brett: 'Currie and Henry sometimes amuse me terribly . . . but sometimes I feel I want to break that tie between us. Friendships are terribly difficult to manage; Henry is not intelligent at all, that's the trouble. Ties are a terrible nuisance and hindrance to an artist.'

It was soon evident to everyone that things were very wrong. Some put the blame on Dolly alone. 'She was lascivious and possessive to the last degree,' one friend said. 'Her lure for men was irresistible, and Currie was of course utterly enslaved to her physical attraction, a fact of which she was well aware. In her way she had a genuine love for him; but no glimmer of a notion that art could be of importance to anyone. Resenting his absorption in his work, determined herself to be his dominant preoccupation, she used her power to goad him from abject desire to baffled fury and then, suddenly complaisant, to win him back again. This dangerous cruelty led to violent quarrels and, I suspect, to blows.'[115] And Mark, as Cannan wrote in *Mendel*, came to hate Dolly 'with a pure simple unmovable passion.'

But Currie's violent temper made matters much worse.

At one point Mark made up his mind to break away. 'In many ways I love Currie, but there is something – something – that worries me and it must end,' he told Carrington. 'Of course it'll be difficult as he still likes me and as yet suspects nothing.'

Edward Marsh was sad to see the strife in his little circle of painters and Mark relented. 'I have not definitely broken from Currie. I merely wrote and told him that I want to be alone for a while. But do not think that Currie will be put out by my absence. I know him too well for that. Besides he has now many friends and above all a woman whom he loves! What more can he want?' (November 1913). By the end of 1931 Currie and Mark had made it up again.

In February 1914, Currie wrote to his wife, saying that he had 'quite done' with Dolly and would she go up and see him.[116] She went and found him in 'great distress of mind'. He broke down, and said that Dolly had told his fellow artists a lot of lies about him and had injured his reputation. Mrs Currie stayed with him for a few days and looked after him.

Currie had written also to Dolly's mother, who said later, 'He asked me to see him at a cottage he had at Hampstead. He there told me that Dolly had left him. I learned afterwards it was because he had knocked her about. He wanted me to patch it up between them. I saw her and she said she would not go back to him because he had knocked her about . . . There was a scratch across her throat, which she tried to hide. She said he had held a razor over her. Afterwards I got a letter from him apologizing, and saying that they were quite happy together.'[117]

Currie had lost his ability to concentrate on work, and a friend said: 'Currie told me he felt he was going mad. He said he had made a great failure of his artistic life and felt like ending it all.'[118]

Other friends wrote later that in revenge for Currie's ill treatment, Dolly 'slid from innate wantonness into defiant promis-
cuity,'[119] and one reported, 'A young Irish painter Flanagan was
said to have been the cause of flagrant faithless conduct.'[120]

Marsh had decided by January 1914 that the love affair was
doomed. 'I think Currie will be done for if he doesn't get Dolly out
of his head,' he told Mark.

As the winter gave way to the spring of 1914 the unhappy affair
see-sawed on.

In March Professor Sadler invited Currie to give a talk on
modern painting to his students at the University of Leeds. Currie
wrote from Leeds to Marsh. 'Dear Eddie, Before I go to bed here I
want to write and tell you that on Saturday I did not 'phone again
or do anything about the photograph as I became ill and had to
clear out. I went to Brighton of all places. The strain and worry of
the last three months or so seems to be getting too much for me.
And I wanted to do this lecture alright. I'm a trifle better and can
go through with it, I think.'

It was not a success. Sadler noted, 'Tho' he didn't show it at first,
he was in a very high state of tension. His lecture was a failure
... [It] only lasted twenty minutes. Afterwards, he told me he
had written a lot in the morning or afternoon before the lecture in
my study, but had forgotten to bring the MS with him to the
University. Under an appearance of calmness, he was nearly out of
his mind. That night, March 17, we had a very long and intimate
talk in my study. He told me of his anguish. The girl, the fair one,
was faithless to him. His life was a hell. But his love for her was
intense. I never came in contact with such fiery, consuming love.
He told me that he could hardly keep from suicide. The night
before, he had nearly killed himself in our house.'[121]

Currie realized his erratic behaviour was damaging his career and
upsetting his friends. He decided the only chance was to get away
from London, and make a supreme effort to pull himself together.
'Will you let me have Murry's address?' he asked Marsh on 19
March 1914. 'I want to go to Paris soon, and to talk to him about a
place to stay.'

On 25 March 1914 Marsh held a painters' evening at his flat for

Currie and Dolly, Mark, Gaudier-Brzeska and Stanley Spencer. They were all excited by the idea of a volume of reproductions of *Georgian Painters* to follow Marsh's *Georgian Poets*.[122]

Just before leaving London Currie wrote apologetically and hopefully, 'My dear Eddie, Your letter; you are very severe. I deserve all the reproach, but I cannot tell you how deeply I feel about hurting you so. I have behaved badly lately, but I am not really well. When I have been away, and am stronger, it will come to me more – my recent vagueness and inconsiderateness . . . But I seem lately to be drifting through a period of awful negation – without that force I have always had impelling me to go on . . . I shall come back well . . . Dolly is doing all that anyone could do to help. There is peace, but much is lost for the time. But it will return away from the Art group. I am thinking a good deal of the things I hope to do away. Brittany will do me good.'

CHAPTER 15

Rebel Grande Dame

During the early months of 1914, Mark faced the possibility – even the probability – of his work coming to a complete halt through lack of money for models and materials.

At the February Friday Club show his pictures were more or less ignored. He had put in 'Woman Resting' and 'Still Life with funny doll',[182] the latter being painted during January. 'I have suddenly got so fascinated by a funny doll belonging to my little niece that I have put everything aside in order to paint it, with some other objects. The whole makes a most interesting still life,' he had written to Carrington on 1 January 1914. He worked hard at it but the days were so short and dark that he could only do very little each day.

Progress reports to Carrington about his main project, 'The Fruit Sorters',[183] became increasingly gloomy: 'Today I spent the whole day painting the man's back. But of the two the model triumphed most, because he went away with my people's hard-earned seven shillings . . . I am working really hard and my picture is, I believe, coming along but very slowly. The more I do, the more there seems to do. What frightens me about it is when I think of the *money* it's going to cost!' (1 April 1914)

Later in the same month he wrote, 'I cannot work every day on my picture as my people can't afford the money for the models. I take care of every penny now, so that I should not have to lean too heavily on my people. My position as regards money seems rather hopeless at present, but something may turn up soon – I hope so. The worst of it is that the worry of having no money gets into one's head, and one cannot work so freely as when one could feel a little more settled in that way. I have reached a queer stage of my life now; I don't know how it will turn out. Some people say it is good for a young artist to be poor! I entirely disagree! Poverty makes one's mind sordid.'

In desperation Mark decided he would have to give up time from his painting and get a part-time job, and he applied for one as an art teacher at the Boys Foundation School in Whitechapel. He had to go back to his despised teachers and ask for help. Tonks, whom he had flippantly described not long before as 'that awful ghost', turned up trumps, and sent in a strong recommendation: 'He draws *very well* and has a very good manner. In fact he might do a great deal of good in spreading the knowledge of fine drawing.' Mark commented: 'Tonks has written me some very nice letters – most encouraging.' When he was interviewed by the Art Master and Headmaster of the school, it was all 'very frightening and very official and rather depressing.' They said they would let him know. The salary was very small, about twenty-eight shillings a week for three days; 'but I can't afford to grumble,' he reflected.

He failed to get the job.

If things got much worse he would have to give up painting altogether and take *any* kind of job. Replying to a suggestion of Carrington's he said, 'Thank you very much indeed for writing to me about that job. I wrote at once, but I am afraid that nothing will come of it. You see, it is practically clerk's work that they require and I really don't think I could do much as a clerk. Although I wouldn't mind trying it, if they took me on, but as it was too late even to get recommendations I stand no chance.'

Lady Ottoline Morrell, half-sister to the Duke of Portland, rebel *grande dame* and patron of the arts, enjoyed being a fairy god-mother. One of the many young writers she had taken up was Gilbert Cannan, who fired her curiosity with his tales of Mark. 'Cannan stayed with us from time to time and he and I had endless conversations about life,' she recalled in her memoirs. 'He was very anxious that we should know a friend of his, Mark Gertler. I went off to Liverpool Street Station and found my way from there to the mean, hot, stuffy, smelly little street where he lived. I felt very tall and large walking up the creaky little stairs.',[123]

Mark never forgot the sight of her as he waited in his studio with the Cannans, and she was gradually revealed as she came up the stairs to the top landing. A woman of forty, with extremely striking looks, she was to be described – and caricatured – by many writers. The most sympathetic was her lover, Bertrand Russell: 'Ottoline was very tall with a long thin face something like a horse, and very beautiful hair of an unusual colour, more or less like that of marmalade . . . kind ladies supposed it to be dyed but in this they were mistaken. She had a very beautiful gentle vibrant voice, indomitable courage and a will of iron.'[124] To a friend, David Garnett, she was 'extremely handsome' – 'Glacier blue-green eyes, a long straight nose, a proud mouth and a long jutting out chin made up her lovely haggard face.' Another summarized her as, 'a charac-ter of Elizabethan extravagance and force, at once mystical and possessive, quixotic and tempestuous.'[125]

When they became intimate friends Mark made her laugh at, and relish, the incongruity of the encounter: 'Gertler always says that the first sight he had of me was the crest of a purple feather: nearer and nearer it ascended, and at last the hat itself and then me, as if a large and odd bird had arrived. Indeed, I hardly believe that I was able to stand upright in the room, so tall and erect was the feather, so low was his room.'[126]

She was impressed by Mark, who she decided, 'with his small delicate frame and shock of dark curly hair, looked almost like a girl, but who was in reality passionate and ambitious and exceed-

ingly observant and sensitive.' And her flair for spotting talent came
into action: 'his pictures had an intense, tangible, ruthless hot
quality . . . There was the Jewish mark which gave them a fine,
intense, almost archaic quality.'[127]

Ottoline's formidable energies were at once devoted to getting
Mark launched.

First came a heart-to-heart talk over tea at her home in Bedford
Square, Bloomsbury. 'I tried to find out what he was really like . . .
I asked him if he didn't find it hard reconciling his home life with
the life he lived at the Slade, and with Mr Eddie Marsh . . . He
confessed that he could not but feel antagonistic to the smart and
the worldly, while at the same time he felt depressed by the want of
cultivation of his own people. I saw how intensely difficult it is to
understand each other's experiences . . . when I thought of [him]
being fed on any little herring that could be bought cheap of an
evening, and of the life in that dark hot East End Street . . .
Such a limited, almost walled in youth may give great intensity of
vision.'[128]

They liked each other, and Ottoline recalled, 'I admired the
persistence and resolution that dwelt in this apparently fragile
body.'

It was arranged that Mark should go to one of her Thursday
evening salons and show his work. Useful people such as Sickert
had been invited,* and the event made a deep impression on both
Mark and Ottoline. 'I see little Mark Gertler now, standing by his
picture, thin, erect and trembling internally, if not externally, at the
excitement of having his work looked at and discussed by anyone
like Sickert, whom he so respected,' Ottoline remembered. Mark
was given the entrée to Bedford Square, and so from this time he
could meet practically anybody in the progressive art circles of
London.

Soon life in the evenings became almost too full. Writing to
Carrington on 6 April Mark described the events of a few days. 'I
go to Gilbert Cannan next Sunday . . . I have seen the Edna Clarke
Hall show: it is rather good. Knewstub has sent my old kitchen
picture[171] to Leeds to a show there. Everybody likes that picture

* Another guest was the collector, Jasper Ridley.

10—MG * *

now. It is getting quite famous. Brett's brother and Zena [Dare] thought it wonderful. Last Thursday afternoon I painted Brett. Albert [Rutherston] came in to tea . . . I like Albert very much. After tea Brett and I had a walk in the park . . . Saturday afternoon Brett and I went to Shapiro's concert. It was rather dull and we both felt ill. After the concert we went to Albert's to tea. Many people were there. After that I had to meet Marsh. That evening was the opening night of the Crab Tree Club so we went. I think that club will fail. It seems just an inferior cabaret. John came in with his followers, he unusually drunk – very drunk. He came up to me and was very friendly but he behaved disgustingly and cheaply. I stayed until four o'clock and then went home to sleep at Mrs Hebbon's,* with Bomberg on one side of me and John Flanagan, the Slade painter, on the other. The next morning I was very annoyed with myself . . . Sunday I had tea with Brett's sister at Wimbledon. Captain Brett and Zena were there. I enjoyed it very much – they were so kind and nice to me. In the evening I dined with Marsh, Cathleen Nesbitt and Jeanette Ross Johnson; then we went on to a play by Frank Harris. The play was very bad. After the theatre Albert joined us and we had an excellent supper at the Waldorf. I had my black suit on and your other white shirt. I must have looked nice because Albert asked me to sit for him. I enjoyed that evening enormously. Everybody is being very nice to me just now. This makes me very happy.'

A few days later he went out with Brett and her sister, to dine at the Savoy. 'The richness of the place embarrassed me very much, and I did not feel at all at ease,' he wrote. 'There was a lot of footmen in grey plush coats and stockings. They all looked at me suspiciously. The dinner was excellent and with that at least I felt at home. I had pea soup, oysters, lamb and potatoes and then a baba with rum and coffee. When I came to my cigarette I had com- pletely forgotten all my worldly troubles. I don't suppose that the waiter there had any idea that I hadn't a penny in the world! After dinner we went to see a play.'

Ottoline made it clear that she was offering friendship as well as patronage: 'My dear Eddie,' Mark apologized to Marsh, 'Lady Ottoline wrote to me today and asked Carrington and myself to

* Mrs Patrick Hepburn, 'Anna Wickham', the poetess.

come with her to the Magic Flute on Monday 25th. Unfortunately
I think that falls on the same day as our opera. It's terrible but I feel
I can't refuse Lady Ottoline the very first appointment. Could you
possibly excuse me?'

The daylight hours were still sacred to painting in Elder Street
and Mark would rather get on with his work than show it to
visitors: 'Dear Eddie, Again I must put you off, about seeing my
picture. I am very sorry, but I really cannot get myself to show my
work to anybody. I showed it to Lady Ottoline simply because I
hoped she would buy it. As for Gilbert Cannan he came to see me
and it would have been silly to hide away my picture from him,
but in each case I hated showing it. I am very sensitive about my
work and if I had money, I wouldn't exhibit. Besides, at present my
work is very 'studentish' and really, I hardly think it would interest
you. Next Monday is sending-in day of the N.E.A.C. and if they
accept it, you will see it there. You must forgive these curious ways
of mine – I can't help it. I like to be friends with people, apart from
my work. I am your friend and yet I do not want to come down to
the Admiralty to see what you are doing! Please excuse this long
and serious letter. I know you prefer funny ones.' (May 1914)
He usually kept his nervousness and sensitivity well hidden, but
they showed in other ways as well: a suggestion by Marsh that they
go together to the private view of a coming exhibition in
Whitechapel which included some of Mark's pictures was refused –
'I never go to private views.'
When 'The Fruit Sorters' [141] was accepted and shown by
the New English in June, Sickert did his best for Mark. In a long
review in the *New Age* he wrote: 'The exhibition . . . may perhaps
fairly be said to belong to Mr Henry Lamb and Mr Mark Gertler,
[whose] "Fruit Sorters" is justified by a sort of intensity and
raciness.' The *Pall Mall Gazette* commented on its 'mixture of
arbitrary simplification with realistic detail', and most of the critics
had something to say about it. The simplification was too much for
some. 'The garment in which the central figure was draped . . .
would have passed for a fair representation of a green tree trunk,'
jibed the *Connoisseur*. What mattered from Mark's point of view

was that the picture was already sold before it went on exhibition. Ottoline bought it in her capacity as Purchaser, for a six-month period, of the Contemporary Art Society.

Things were looking up. The exhibition in Whitechapel was at the Whitechapel Art Gallery, which organized a show of twentieth-century art. Marsh and T. E. Harvey (Mark's friend from Toynbee Hall days who had become an M.P.) lent their pictures by Mark, which thus returned in symbolic triumph to the East End, and Golda had the opportunity of seeing her portrait on public exhibition in her own district. Reviewing the show, the *Star* thought that Mark was the best hope for realist painting.

But in a way the show only emphasized the remoteness of Whitechapel from the centres of art and Mark's isolation there. It seemed unlikely that advanced modern pictures would hang there again for the next dozen years.

He began to think about leaving.

His friends didn't like coming to see him in Whitechapel. When they followed his instructions and came to the turning off Bishopsgate they would hesitate before leaving the bright broad thoroughfare for the warren of dark little streets.

Students didn't mind too much – Carrington and Brett were used to it, and another, Barbara Hiles, was intrigued by her tea with Golda: 'a woman in black, who could only talk Yiddish. It was a dark slum house.' Nor did young painters such as Nina Hamnett: 'I found myself in a Jewish market where hardly anyone spoke English.' But it was unrealistic to expect many useful contacts to come and see his work there. Would there be many patrons with the enterprise of a Lady Ottoline?

Several visits to the country aroused a longing to escape from the East End. Since January he had been welcome at Gilbert Cannan's home at Cholesbury in Buckinghamshire, and the Nash brothers had invited him to their home at Iver. 'I enjoyed my visit to the Nashes very much indeed,' he wrote on 9 April. 'What a splendid way to live. What beautiful surroundings. It will be my ultimate aim to live in the country.'

In 'The Fruit Sorters' he had carried out a wish expressed in one letter: 'How I should love to bring into the backgrounds of my picture some buds of the springtime, little twigs, leaves and flowers! I would paint them very carefully and accurately.'

Mark's first decision to leave the East End was revealed on 1 April in a letter to Carrington: 'I have now *definitely* decided to move to Hampstead as soon as I can afford it. If only I could get a little money and settle myself at Hampstead I should be happy.'

But the issues were not so simple.

CHAPTER 16

'*I've learnt my place*'

The pleasure he took during his country stays in open spaces and fresh air was one of the factors behind Mark's decision to leave the East End. But another visit to the country – in the summer – made him reverse the decision and make up his mind that he would stay on in Whitechapel.

The Knewstubs had a house at Hastings and in July Mark found himself staying in a fisherman's cottage at Pett Level nearby. Writing to Carrington, he explained his new decision: 'I like this place enormously. I am not a bit lonely here, as I love the inhabitants. They are wonderful people. The people I am staying with are extraordinarily lovable. There is the old mother, monumental and big. She rules the house like some queen. Her dignity is splendid. When she walks she seems to sail along like a big ship. Then there are two rather beautiful daughters, healthy, big and brown, with simple unaffected minds. Then father and son. The father is very like Augustus John, but genuine. He drinks pints of beer. The son is a splendidly made young man, very, very strong. Amongst these people I am more at home and more happy than I've felt for a long time. They remind me so much of my own people, and, by the way, through them I love my own people more. Through them I see beauties in my own people which I never saw before. My place is by these sort of people. I belong to this class. I shall always be unhappy if I try to get away from this class to which I belong. There is a little inn a little way along in which the fishermen and sailors come to drink beer. They are wonderfully beautiful. It is a pleasure to look at them. Yes, it is a long time since I've so truly loved men and women as I do here. Well, from them I've learnt my place. It is a great thing to know which is our real place. I've also learnt that I must go on in the *East End*. There lies my work, sordid as it is.'

Mark wondered if he could find a compromise which would give him a chance to follow up his new interest in landscape. To Brett he said: 'I have a scheme. When I get back I am going to find a room or a small cottage in the country quite close to London to which I can run whenever I want to, to paint Landscapes, and for my health. That arrangement will allow me to combine the beauties of both the country and the East End. I am very happy with this plan. Knewstub has just sold my early kitchen picture [171] and he is going to give me some money so I shall be able all the more to carry this plan out.'

Sometimes the contrast between the treeless East End districts and his present surroundings was overwhelming. 'This place makes me hate London,' he reported to Carrington. 'I think London is a horrible place to live in and it is with sorrow that I look forward to going back. However it is as well to realize as soon as possible that we can't have everything as we should like it. I have a passionate desire now to live in the country, but I can't manage it for many reasons. So I *must* go back to my East End, where only God knows how many discomforts I suffer. However, if my plan works, about getting a place in the country, it would improve matters for me considerably.'

The simplicity of the village seemed even more pleasing when compared with the way of life of Epstein, who was staying at the other end of it. 'Epstein is the one fault in my holiday here,' Mark complained. 'Somehow he puts me off working . . . He has a filthy mind and he always has some girl living with him, *including* his wife. Now he has a horrible black girl. She tells me she's sat at the Slade. She's like a Gauguin. I hate her more and more every day!'

Though he enjoyed the country round Pett Level, Mark, who

always liked to get at close quarters with his subjects, found it too panoramic and 'scenic' to paint. But after a week his itch to paint landscape triumphed.

For his first serious landscape subject, Mark chose one of the little cottages.[184] 'It is a black and white cottage against a dull sky – silver and lead,' he wrote. 'The foreground consists of a golden elder seen through another plant, called pampas grass. The picture finishes up at the bottom with a dark green gate and fence. The scene, as it is in nature, is most beautiful. The pampas grass is a strikingly beautiful plant. It is made up of long, elastic and needle-like leaves which are most graceful. It looks most beautiful when it flirts with the wind – then it looks like a ruffled head of hair! I am trying my best to get the exquisite grace of this plant. No matter how the wind blows it about, it always retains the beautiful and graceful curves of its leaves! It is indeed wonderful. I have worked for many days on this plant alone, but it is as difficult as it is beautiful. I feel very tired after I have worked at it for a day, with mahl stick and sables. It needs a very steady hand.'

When he had finished he exulted, 'I loved painting landscape although I've done so little. It was fine painting things I've so long pined to paint. I should imagine the pleasure akin to that of a lover embracing, for the first time, the girl he for so long loved and longed to embrace. Just as he would passionately and lovingly linger over parts until then forbidden, so I lovingly lingered over those beautiful greens, greys and whites I knew so well but never before had the opportunity to paint.'

In the mood of the little picture Mark expressed a romantic dream, a melancholy stillness which contrasted strangely with the harshness of his East End pictures. As a later critic, was to put it, the picture had 'that sense of familiar things made strange . . . It is the work of an infinitely poetical artist.'[130]

As the holiday drew to an end he waited for news from Cannan. When they had first got to know each other Mark had been wary of accepting invitations from the writer, feeling that he might 'have to be engaged in intellectual conversation, which I hate so.' But it turned out that Cannan also disliked too much abstract philosophizing, and shared many of Mark's ideas about Whitechapel. 'Cannan thought I was extremely fortunate to live in the East End amongst *real* people,' Mark had written after a visit to him in January. 'He loves the Jewish theatre and agrees with me that it is far and away more vital than the English, in fact that there is no comparison. We discussed also the milk and water outlook of Roger Fry and his followers and most of the so-called "advanced" people.'

When developing his country cottage idea Mark's thoughts had turned to Cannan, and he had written asking if Cannan could help him to get something near his own home in Cholesbury, Buckinghamshire. 'If there was a country place that I could get to know, I am sure I would do very fine landscape', he wrote to Carrington. 'But you must get to know the country first. I was just beginning to see things in Gilbert Cannan's country, so it would be fine if I could get something there. What do you think? Do you know any better place near London? Let me know if you do.'

The holiday finished, it was time, as Mark said, to go back to his 'little den in the East End.'

This autumn there would be no evenings with Carrington. In the summer she had come to the end of her studies at the Slade. From now on she would be living away from London with her parents.

For nearly three years Mark had been helplessly in love with her. His subjection had been complete. 'I only hope that I am not a worry and nuisance to you. I will do my best *never* to worry you, if only you will agree to let me see and talk to you sometimes,' he had pleaded in October 1913. 'You cannot imagine how important you are to my work. You say you like my work, then will you be surprised if I tell you that I think of you in *every* stroke I do? That you have been a tremendous source of inspiration to me. Having told you this, you will not be surprised at my persistence in knowing you, in spite of your indifference and coldness towards me. There is only one thing – I feel that I am not worthy of your company. I feel that I am *far* too vulgar and rough for you. But I am hoping through my work to reach your level. The point is this – if you will *occasionally only* let me see and talk to you, you will be doing something that, apart from making myself happy, you will never regret. I mean the work you will make me produce . . . There is one thing more. If ever you have an appointment with me and something more interesting turns up, you can *always* put me off. Although I shall be unhappy, I shall understand.'

Carrington had been friendly, flattered by his ardour, and had been able to keep the friendship going on her own terms with little difficulty. Periodically, his desire overcoming his early resolve to respect her 'purity', he tried to make love to her, only to be rejected. When he found this too frustrating and tried to break free she would bring him back by calling his sincerity into question, or she would make him see how clumsy and bullying he sometimes was, when desperation drove out delicacy. 'Dear Carrington,' he had written on one occasion, 'There was no need in your letter to be so cruel. It hurt me more than I can tell you. You know that it is false. You know that I do love you. Why make me out a selfish liar?! I did not write to you because Friendship has become far too difficult with you. There can be no real friendship between us, as long as you allow that barrier – Sex – to stand between us . . . Remember I've tried to fight it for three years, without success. Now it cannot go on any longer. It is very very unfortunate . . . Please do not write to me any more letters. Just try and forget me. Under the circumstances letters from you only disturb my work. P.S. The above letter is very cruel I know, but it has the advantage of being really *honest* – the most *honest* letter I've ever written to you. P.S.S. I am not ashamed of my sexual passion for you. Passion of that sort in the case of Love, is *not* lustful, but *beautiful*!!'

'You English people are not so passionate,' he decided in another letter. 'You probably don't understand *real* sexual passion at all.'

In *Mendel* Cannan described Mark as saying to her, 'You want me to bend to your woman's will, for you know I cannot break away from you. You are with your soul like Dolly with her body; you are with your love like Dolly with her lust, and Currie and I are a pair – a miserable broken pair.'[131]

The attempt to break away had failed, but in Pett Level he determined again to end it. Before leaving London he had written, 'Dear Carrington, I can't help feeling very hurt and unhappy about last night. You seemed to think that I was vulgar and dirty and that I make "Rotten Remarks"! I don't think that we get on at all well together – we are very unsuited. I don't blame *you* a bit. I know it's all *my* fault – I know myself, that I am vulgar and disagreeable . . .

You must feel my inferiority. I thank you for having been able to put up with me.'

After this he had kept silent. When Carrington wrote sadly, he replied: 'You must not expect much to happen between us. I am afraid that our roads lie in different directions to a great extent. The difference of class will always be against our being real friends. You don't know, Carrington, what a difference there is between us . . . Please do *not* send me any photos of yourself, as they might disturb the peace of mind I enjoy here. Do not be annoyed at this, as I would very much like to have them, but they might awaken emotions in me that, for the sake of my work, I would rather keep under.' (July 1914)

But he was incapable of severing the link entirely. Wearily he wrote in late July: 'I shall try and be your friend if you want me to. Anyway it is always a pleasure for me to hear from you.'

CHAPTER 17

'I understand you'

When Mark got back to London everything was changed. The war had started. His reaction to the news that the major world powers had decided to fight it out amongst themselves was one of amazed disbelief. 'The war is indeed terrible,' he wrote, 'but how ludicrous! If it continues much longer, the working classes will starve . . . Isn't it strange that such a thing as war should still exist?'

For a time the war fever which gripped England, the patriotic ardour and zest for battle and victory which swept through the majority, including many artists, stirred him. Feeling it would be impossible to create in such an atmosphere he considered joining the services, where at least he would be fed. But he quickly drew back from the idea. He didn't feel the slightest personal involvement with the issues at stake. Even if it had been clear what they were, it would have made no difference: he intended to spend his time painting, not fighting, and he advised Carrington, 'Do not be unhappy about the war. The best way we can help is to *paint*.'

But it was impossible to think and work in the London of August 1914. When Cannan found a cottage for him at four shillings and sixpence a week and urged him to come to Cholesbury, he fled.

'I came back a week ago,' he wrote to Marsh, 'but London is so full of war that I am running away again . . . I am glad I am leaving London, for I love the country more and more now. I hope in the future to be able to live more among trees.' (17 August 1914)

But what was he to live on? The two props of his material existence – the fur business and the picture market – were both, as luxury trades, at once affected by the war. 'My father's little workshop is closed and soon he will be hard up,' he told Marsh. 'My own position is not very bright, but I shan't need much in the country.'

In the West End, art dealers waited in vain for buyers, and warned artists that no more advances would be forthcoming. Painters joined the armed forces, went home to their families or faced a bleak future. Even established artists were alarmed. Sickert, no worrier as a rule, lost his nerve, hastened back from Dieppe and installed himself in a teaching job with the London County Council.

Disaster was postponed by Brett, who had loaned Mark her studio and now said she would send him money each week. The cheap cottage had fallen through but Mark found another, where he would be fed and provided with sitting room and bedroom for £1 a week. 'I haven't the slightest idea when I shall return to London,' he wrote to Brett – 'Tell me when you want me to send you your studio key. Your offer of £1 a week during distress is extraordinarily generous. Thank you – I am afraid that I must accept. However I shall repay every farthing. I already owe you £15. In the meantime I still have money for some weeks. I will let you know when I shall need more.'

In the autumn the situation got desperate and Mark was back in the East End, writing miserably to Brett that the Chenil Gallery was abandoning him. 'Knewstub writes and tells me that he cannot let me have any more money. So my position is really terrible. I haven't a penny of my own and no prospects of earning any. This is after years of labour. Here in the East End it is considered a disgrace for a man of twenty-two to live on his people – I agree. Here am I *the* son. The son that my people placed all their hopes in, having to be kept by them! I hate doing "Pot Boiling". Besides even if I wanted to paint work that would sell, I wouldn't know what *does* sell!'

He was reduced to writing begging letters to Marsh. 'Dear Eddie, I hardly dare ask you so soon, but could you possibly let me have another £5? As I'm leaving "Chenils" I have to go back to Percy Young's for materials and unhappily I owe money there. I can't go back until I've paid my debt. If it is too difficult for you please don't trouble, as I shall then ask Brett to continue her £1 a week.' (October 1914)

The atmosphere in Spital Square and Elder Street sank to deep gloom. Everyone was worried. 'My brothers do not want to fight for Austria as they like England better,' Mark wrote to Carrington. 'But they do not, if they can help it, want to fight at all, as they are of a peaceful disposition.'

It was a bitter time to hear the dreadful news about Currie.

The reports during the summer from Brittany had been so encouraging. 'The country here is beautiful to enchantment,' Currie had told Marsh. Dolly had followed him there and all was well again. He wrote of 'a feeling of exaltation'. They were gay. 'Peasant ways are amusing. I suppose ours are to them . . . Strange to say, I've little difficulty in making myself understood; makes Dolly laugh at times – my mistakes. Food tastes intolerable at first; getting better. Of course the water is undrinkable, but I like the cider. Our landlady is a great Falstaff of a woman. We are nine miles from the town, where we rarely go but as this is a favourite inn, we see most of the natives. We have much dancing and Rabbilasian (how do you spell it?) humour.'

But the peasants' ideas of advanced behaviour fell a long way short of Dolly's own. 'Dolly has returned to London,' Currie reported. 'Difficult to tell you why. She has gone away friendly, but she was very much out of place here. Peasant life made her long for Cafés and clubs in Town. This is so much finer to my mind that I couldn't stand any mention of London. Then I saw that displays to

ragtime movements and town habits were objectionable to the
peasants, who prefer their own simple dances. But there were
certain other fooleries that made things rather intolerable and I
thought it best she should return . . .

'Baker⋆ disliked her talk of the "Art" Life in London and hurt
her by telling her he appreciated London in quite another way, as a
place to meet certain fine minds, and that the second-rate babble
that goes on between the "Artists" is of no account. Almost for the
first time she rubbed against a man without sex interest or flattery
and she didn't like it. I felt very deeply for her on leaving as I have
loved her until it has played the very devil with me. She enjoyed
herself here, and I have been generous to her, but I hope to God it is
the end of it. There are many good things in her, but all my recent
trouble in various ways might have been avoided had she better
sense. The emotional and sexual horror and beauty of the whole
damned thing – the months of torment and waste of energy, my
loss of control, seems like a hell to me now. But I'm infinitely
stronger and better now. A great change has set in. Fine walks, sun
and air and new ideas . . .

'I write this with a number of fine women in the room dressing a
child for her confirmation, a very beautiful sight. Outside a lovely
morning, the hillside alive with bird song. The exquisite purity of
the child as she holds an enormous candle. The sanctity of it all is
very beautiful. I feel there is great love and tenderness in everything.'

His mood of tranquillity grew. From Paris he wrote, 'Dolly is in
Cornwall working there. She was down in Dorset with John before
that. I think she is well and happy enough. She writes me very
tenderly. It is the sadness of the affair that is so distressing. We were
so wonderfully happy for three years until suddenly things went
wrong for some unaccountable reason, and sent my mind in a
whirlwind. But now all these things have happened, it is best it
should end. I think she will marry before I return to London. I am
asking her to accept an offer. So you will not think me unfair . . . I
feel a great relief already from my suffering. A very beautiful sense
of peace sets in to-day, and there is the sun and everything looks
better. You must forgive my sadness. I will be better soon.'

⋆ A painter friend of Currie's also staying in Britain.

From Cannes he wrote, with new determination and hope: 'I will get back on Saturday next, and do my best to get peacefully to work. No matter how good this is I weary of everything but work. The artificial, sensual, useless life of these people is appalling . . . My leaving unknown had a great effect on Dolly and she has written declaring her unceasing love, and looks to my return. The quarrel has all been a source of terrible suffering – loss of time, and great expense. I hope to God such a thing never occurs again in my life.'

Then he followed Dolly to Cornwall. Again they made it up, and Currie worked with something of his old zest. 'I'm in a very productive frame of mind,' he told Marsh. 'My large picture which I'm working on here also will be a summary, I hope it will, of my development up to now. I consider the things I'm doing better than what I have done up to now. I've had a long spell of chaos. I think its Nietzche, isn't it, who says something about one must have chaos to give birth to a dancing star. The Newlyn artists have given me quite a princely time. I seem to have stimulated them a little.'[132]

A special exhibition of Currie's paintings was planned for October 1914 at the Chenil Gallery and he looked forward to his return to London. 'I hope to meet you later in the year,' he wrote to Mark. 'I have much to say concerning work that will interest you. I always have the deepest feelings of friendship for you.'

Then to Spitalfields in October came news which was so confusing and so shocking that, two years later, Mark was impelled to set it all down, intending one day to write a complete biography of Currie. The fragment was headed 'The death of Currie':

'Although I had a studio to work in I very often, in my finer moments, preferred to work in my mother's kitchen. There I had painted my earliest pictures, simple and loveable little still lifes which expressed so directly my life, simple and clean as it was then. Now my life was complicated, hard, I lived in a maze, I was lost . . . So when things seemed unbearable I would take refuge in my mother's kitchen and there pretend to myself that all was as it used to be, simple and loveable. Yet all the time I knew it was not as it used to be . . . There was warmth in my mother's kitchen, true; it surrounded me but did not touch me, and between itself and myself there was a wall of ice which it was powerless to melt and so left me cold. It was dreary out, and the light in the kitchen was even worse than usual for painting. To get any light at all I had to drag the white lace curtains as far apart as possible.

'I was painting a portrait of my father. I sat him very near to one window while I sat near to the other a couple of yards away. Besides ourselves there was only my mother in the room. All was still. My father was sitting with his grey wistful little face slightly raised and was looking out of the window at nothing, thinking of nothing. My mother in the further dark end of the room was standing like a statue against the Cooking table beating some eggs in a white bowl with a wooden spoon. With one large wrinkled hand she gripped the bowl and with the other she splashed and beat, making a smacking noise and causing the thick yellow liquid to dance and splash against the white of the bowl. Only her beating hand moved. The rest of her was still as a statue. On her face she wore a smile, an endless smile, that meant nothing and everything and with her eyes she looked straight in front at nothing. The sound of the beating eggs only emphasized the oppressive stillness in the room and the dreariness outside and even the oppressive sadness that was weighing on my soul . . .

'Oh! My dear parents . . . you two have also had your share, I can see that, I can see that too well; Oh! the hardness of our lives, our three lives. So my thoughts ran on as I painted. To my people it must have seemed that I was lost in work and was only thinking of my painting. But in reality when I was painting I would have moments of intense suffering, especially at that dark period, when I was so lost in the maze of life.

'I was indeed just in the right mood that day to receive ugly news . . . and the ugly news came. I had been painting for about two hours when the telephone bell rang. So shrill and sharp did it sound that I almost jumped out of my chair . . . I dropped the receiver and was standing pale and helpless with tears in my eyes. "What's the matter?" gasped both my parents alarmed; "Currie has killed Henry and then shot himself. He is not quite dead. He is in hospital in Chelsea, dying. I am going to him."

'The journey to Chelsea I thought would never end. In the train I had difficulties in stopping my tears. I wanted to cry so much for pity and love of humanity, for hatred of the terrible demon that was, for no apparent reason, torturing us all. Yet I could not help noticing that some people were quite happy in the train, as if nothing had happened. I disliked and despised them for being happy and the fact destroyed the harmony of my thoughts. Then I felt really wretched and my body felt helpless with misery, but I did not want to cry any more. I was too wretched.

'On coming out of the train I became philosophic again and the tears came to my eyes once more, but I could not help smiling through my tears when I pictured Currie lying in a hospital dying, having at last done something real – a thing he had wanted to do all his life. I wondered if [he] would lie in a heroic attitude as he used to do formerly. What heroic words would he say to me! Ah! And what would I not say to him! Currie, I at any rate still love you! I understand you if nobody else does. Then he would squeeze my hand and turn away his head with emotion. My tears would fall on his face. What interesting stuff to tell my friends about; Heavens I am glad it happened. What a hero I am, what a wonderful person. What extraordinary things happen to me.

'I was just beginning to feel very happy and comforted when I remembered that it was all true and that I was nearing the beastly hospital. What a nuisance! Why did he do it, why did he kill her and then himself?! Have I not got enough trouble of my own. Is not my own life sufficiently sordid? But why should he have killed her? If he loved her why not live with her peacefully and if he could not live with her peacefully why not try really to break away from her? It would need strength of course. What a nuisance. What a nuisance. By that time I had reached the hospital. Why should I go in, I wondered. "Why you should go in, why you ask? Don't go to see your greatest friend dying," said a voice inside me. I somehow feel I know all about it, that I have already seen him. There was no need to go in. However I had already rung the bell and the door was opened and I was let in.'

Mark never knew exactly what had happened in the last few weeks of their lives. Newspaper accounts of the deaths were contradictory, but the inquest substantiated *The Times* report of 9 October: 'A young woman, whose name is said to be Dorothy or Eileen O'Henry, was found fatally shot in a house in Chelsea [50 Paulton Square] yesterday morning. A man who was with her was also found wounded. It is stated that the woman took rooms at

Paulton Square about five weeks ago. She was visited from time to time by a man whose name is now in the possession of the police. At a quarter to eight yesterday morning shots and screams were heard. The other occupants of the house ran upstairs and found the woman on the landing in her nightdress bleeding from wounds. In the bedroom a man partly dressed was discovered with wounds in the chest. He was taken to Chelsea infirmary but the woman died before the arrival of a doctor.'

Letters found in the room left many questions unanswered. One addressed to Dolly read: 'This crazy passion has wasted my strength and broken my will. I feel I can do nothing now. I am no longer master of myself, and what does it matter. You despise me. You are too harsh and too passionate to be kind to me; your bitter memories absorb you. My behaviour to you on Monday was nothing but a nervous attack, due to over-strain. You might have known it. A very fury of remorse and love and sorrow is raging in me. I blame myself for everything. I am over-whelmed with self-disgust. I see myself looking broken. You have had your revenge for all I have done. It is the work of some cruel monster who has driven us apart and destroyed us. I have lived with you day by day for these last few years and from the very beginning I created in you the image of my desire. As the days go on the feeling of all I have lost in you becomes so frightful I cannot breathe. I am looking for a place I can bury my heart and forget. Oh, how I want to forget it all. I will positively never write to you again, not from bitterness, but from utter hopelessness. I still believe the photographs were nude, to your dishonour.'

Another included the sentence: 'I believe in you, my dear Dolly, but the past can only be forgotten if the fellow is put out of the way.' A note in Currie's writing read: 'My motive is that Henry deserves death for her damaging untruths and the ruin of my career . . . Although it means my going too, I had rather that than this everlasting trouble with her.'

In a letter addressed to his wife he had written: 'I find she has done everything to degrade me. She has taken up with another fellow . . . In return for my sincere attachment she is making me a laughing stock . . . She has destroyed the greatest friendship I had . . . I still love her but her worthlessness makes life impossible

11—MG * *

. . . My work, whatever its distinction may be, will speak for me.'
    Many of his friends agreed with the view of one of them,
Michael Sadleir: 'Dolly drove Currie mad, and deprived the world
of a genuine artist and a devoted worker.' Mark knew that the truth
was much more complex, but he could only agree with Sadleir that
'Currie was a man who, had circumstances been a little kinder,
would have made a great reputation and lived a full and happy
life.'[133] Marsh wrote, 'I had hoped that this unhappy passion was
dying away . . . Currie made several attempts to break away, but he
really seems to have been unable to live without her, and she loved
him too in a way. I don't know that there is anything more to say.
Isn't it a dreadul wasteful business? I did think his love for his work
would keep him from what he has done. I am sure he would have
become a fine painter if he could have freed himself from that
disease of heart and will.'[134]

PART SIX

A new hope

'As you were so particularly husbandly on Thursday evening I will write you a wifely letter now.'
CARRINGTON TO MARK GERTLER

'Lady Cunard . . . says she *loves* my pictures, and carts me about in her motor car to Lords, Ladies and Baronesses who want to meet me.' – MARK GERTLER

CHAPTER 18

Writers in a mill

Currie's place in Mark's life was never filled. There were to be no more intimate friendships with painters, partnerships of work and mutual inspiration. Henceforth Mark coped in solitude with problems in his work and rarely discussed them with friends. In any case, after this it was as the only painter in a group of writers and other intellectuals that he was most often to be found.

Feeling more than ever a need to get away from London, he spent much of his time at Cholesbury for the last weeks of 1914.

Gilbert Cannan and his wife Mary lived in a converted mill house, and Gilbert's work room was at the top of the mill itself, looking over the fields towards Chesham.[184] There he spent every day writing.* He was twenty-nine – seven years older than Mark – and one of the best-known of the younger generation novelists. A tall and handsome young man, Cannan was compared by some of his friends to Hamlet, because he was 'so often lost in moody meditation, and because his expression, even when he smiled, was a sad one.'[185] He found Mark a stimulating companion: 'I do find with you a satisfaction that I get with neither the intellectuals on the one hand nor the sentimentalists on the other,' he told him.

Mark found Cannan 'soothing', grew very fond of him and looked forward to stays at Cholesbury. 'I am going off to the

---

* Gilbert Cannan, 1884–1955, born in Manchester, studied at Manchester and Cambridge universities, reading law. He became a barrister in 1908 but changed to acting, and then to writing, first as a dramatic critic and then as a novelist, starting with *Peter Homunculus* in 1909. He had also translated Romain Rolland's *Jean Christophe*. His wife Mary had left her previous husband, J. M. Barrie, for Cannan five years earlier and the only reminder of her previous life was the enormous Newfoundland Luath who had served as the original for Nana in Barrie's *Peter Pan*.

country. It will be a great relief to get away and a pleasure to see dear Gilbert and listen to his pianola,' he wrote on one occasion. And on arrival he affirmed: 'I am enjoying my stay here in a peaceful kind of way. But what I enjoy most here is the company of Gilbert Cannan and the talks with him. He is a true man. There are not many like him. I like him truly. In the evenings we sit in the dimly lit mill, where he plays Beethoven to me and then we talk and talk. Last night he read some of his poems to me. They sounded to me very good.'

When there was no room at the mill, Mark lodged in a little cottage nearby, which was rather less satisfactory: 'Mrs Gomm's rooms looked so hideous this time,' he protested once. 'Texts and pictures crammed all over the walls; "Simply to Thy Cross I Cling" – "Sweet Seventeen, Sweeter Seventy". Portraits of Queen Victoria, china and so on! Too bad. On all the chairs were pieces of intricate lace. Every time I sat down on my chair, my hair would entangle in the lace.'

At Cholesbury a little circle of writers had gathered. The previous year, at Cannan's suggestion, John Middleton Murry and Katherine Mansfield, who lived together, had joined with Gordon Campbell, a barrister, and his wife Beatrice, in renting a cottage. In 1914 D. H. Lawrence and Frieda had moved there to join them and Mark had met Lawrence by September. The others he had met the previous year in London, together with their friend S. S. Koteliansky. 'Kot', as he was called by his friends, was a Russian Jew working as a translator at the Russian Law Bureau in Holborn. He had also met Lawrence for the first time in the autumn of 1914, while on a walking tour.

Mark was to be one of the few people to gain, and retain, Lawrence's consistent approval. But he had to endure the initial Lawrentian onslaught of searching analysis carried out in Lawrence's own strange fashion: 'I partly agree about Gertler,' Lawrence wrote to Kot. 'It isn't potatoes, it's cooked onions: *come dice lui* – but Frieda is very fond of him, so take care.' (8 October 1914)

Mark entertained the others with imitations of Lawrence massaging his head with both hands and screaming, 'You lie! you lie!' or talking about Frieda: 'She's a *Baroness*, you know.' Lawrence observed Mark carefully and made use of him for the sculptor Loerke in his book *Women in Love*.

Soon all was friendship and Lawrence planned a visit to the East End, telling Kot: 'Gertler will ring up the Law Bureau tomorrow afternoon to tell us about going to see his studio . . . We'd like to go Sunday afternoon to tea.' (30 November 1914)

When Lawrence later moved away from London a steady flow of letters arrived for Mark. There were ideas for starting a colony overseas after the war with Mark, Kot, the Campbells and others as founder members of a 'new scene' and a new life. Other letters included tips about possible patrons ('there is nothing doing in the Bennett-Bibesco quarter'), thanks for Mark's offer of a loan and requests for books of reproductions ('What I would best like to do is Uccello; those hunting and fighting scenes'). He tried to lessen Mark's pessimism: 'You say, "it is life, life is like it." But that is mere sophistry. Life is what one wants in one's soul,' and gave good advice: 'Don't wear yourself down to the last thread without hope of relaxing!' His advice about Carrington was to urge Mark: 'if you could only give yourself up in love she would be much happier. You always want to dominate her, which is no good. One must learn to relinquish oneself, not to bother about oneself, but to love the other person. You hold too closely to yourself for her to be free to love you.'

They shared an intense dislike of officious patriotism: 'Write and say you are still alive and ready to have the last laugh of all these fleas and bugs of righteous militarism', Lawrence urged later in the war.

Beatrice Campbell described the endless discussions in the evenings at Cholesbury, with 'Gertler tossing his head backwards in laughter, Lawrence . . . thumping the back of a chair and denouncing everyone, including himself.'[136]

On one occasion in November 1914 when the young writer David Garnett was visiting the Lawrences' cottage, 'The door opened', he recalled, 'and two other visitors entered – a dark handsome young Jewish painter, called Mark Gertler, and a girl to whom I was at once powerfully attracted.' This was Carrington, who sat on the floor, 'stealing critical looks at each of the company in turn out of her forget-me-not-blue eyes . . . Gertler held forth amusingly about himself . . . Lawrence, who liked Gertler, cheered up considerably.'[137]

In a group which included two as volatile as Mark and Lawrence, gaiety naturally alternated with gloom. 'I've got a head that is so heavy,' Lawrence told Kot. (21 December) 'Gertler is here, very sad. We are going to tea with him.'

For the beautiful Katherine Mansfield, Mark felt liking and attraction. At a gay Christmas party at the mill they all acted a play dramatizing the strained situation between Murry and Katherine. Mark was cast as his successor. When they reached the point at which Katherine was supposed to leave Mark and return to Murry she departed from the script to stay with Mark instead. 'Katherine and myself – both very drunk – made passionate love to each other in front of everybody!' Mark reported to Carrington. 'And everybody was drunk too. No one knew whether to take it as a joke or scandal. Fortunately, the next day everybody decided to take it as a joke. The Lawrences were the last to come to this decision, as they were most anxious to weave a real romance out of it. Seeing that Katherine's man and myself were just as friendly afterwards, they *had* to take it as a joke. They were very disappointed. I like Katherine Mansfield.' 'It was just like Lawrence,' commented Carrington drily.

Mark's new friendships made life in Whitechapel seem a lot less interesting. Also the war and its consequent misery, and Currie's death, had all made him feel the need for a new start. When Marsh, in November, offered to pay him ten pounds a month while the war lasted in return for pictures, Mark determined to seize the opportunity to move to Hampstead. 'My dear Eddie, I can't tell you how thankful I feel to you,' he replied. 'It isn't the actual money that pleases me, but the generous and friendly feelings that prompted you to help me. I feel that you are a real friend and that makes me very happy. I do hope that some day I shall be able in some way to help you. I hope also to do such good work that you will feel that I was worthy of your help.'

It seemed as good a time as any to move. Harry and Jack had been naturalized and his family's fortunes had picked up a little; they had re-opened the workshop and seemed quite happy. At the end of the year Mark gave up his country-life idea. 'I have not been very happy here. It is very cold and I have been unable to work,' he wrote to Marsh from Cholesbury. 'It has decided me, that London is the place for me – at any rate for some time. When I get back I am going to look for a nice studio near the park. I should like to talk to you about it when I return. You and Brett are the only friends with whom I could talk about it.'

He was never again to seriously consider leaving London altogether. 'For some people it may be England my England,' he recalled later, 'but for me it is London, my London ... London where I have experienced so much, London that has become part of me to such an extent that I can almost imagine life more easily without the people I have known than its own embodiment and peculiarity.'

CHAPTER 19

'I shall be neither Jew nor Christian'

The choice of Hampstead was a natural one.* A great attraction was the height and the cleaner air, and Hampstead had pleasant associations for Mark: his visits to the homes of Rothenstein and Nevinson, his walks on the Heath with Carrington.

While Mark, with Brett as a constant companion, 'her little startled face quite white with exhaustion', searched for studios every day, Marsh gave him a key and a room in his own flat. 'I have never been so comfortable before in my life and never before had a bath every morning, for over a week,' Mark exulted. 'Every morning at nine o'clock Eddie comes and says, "Mark! Bath ready!" and helps me into a purple silk dressing gown! Oh! How good a thing is comfort!' (January 1915)

Finally they found 'Penn Studio' beside No. 13 Rudall Crescent, in Hampstead, and Mark moved in, the faithful Brett helping him

* Eventually Golda, Jack, Harry and their wives and families all moved to north-west London.

to get settled. Though their relationship always remained completely platonic, they had become very close. 'Brett, as usual, was a splendid help to me during moving time,' he said. 'I did not feel so lonely and lost as I would have done without her. She dusted all the books and did many things which I shouldn't have thought of myself. She is altogether a wonderful help. I don't know really how I should get on without her. However unhappy or unnerved I am she always brings peace and happiness to me with her presence – she has simply grown a part of me.' Mark decided: 'My two great friends are Marsh and Brett.'

Once he had moved, Mark felt an overwhelming sense of relief. 'Yes I am very glad', he reported to Albert Rutherston. 'I was getting so tired of the East End.' To another friend he commented, 'I feel both sad and immensely relieved at having to leave the East End and my parents. But the feeling of relief is greater than the feeling of sadness.' (27 January 1915)

Carrington, still living away from London, followed events. 'Gertler has moved from the East End and is going to live quite close to Hampstead Heath,' she wrote to a friend. 'He is so excited and happy – I hope he will not be disappointed later.' To Mark she said, 'It will be splendid to live near the Heath, won't it. Think of it in the Spring. You ought to be happy now . . . I am glad you are moving. I am sure Hampstead would be far healthier than Elder Street.'

Mark had a new sense of freedom: 'I shall be free and detached – shall belong to no parents. I shall be neither Jew nor Christian and shall belong to no class. I shall be just myself and be able to work out things according to my own tastes. I was beginning to feel stifled by everything in the East End, worried by the sordidness of my family, their aimlessness, their poverty and their general wretchedness. I used to get terribly depressed also by my father, in whose face there is always an expression of the sufferings and disappointments he has gone through. I keep wondering why they are alive and why they want to live and why nature treated them so cruelly. All this, you see, was depressing, and that is why I am relieved to get away. It'll be good to get all that change and yet be in London. Yes, I'm excited about it. It feels like the beginning of chapter one of the second book of my life. It is quite a change for me.' (January 1915)

In gratitude he wrote to Marsh, 'My studio looked so nice today that I got you these flowers as a thanksgiving. It was largely through you that I ventured on such a Studio.'

In January Mark had tried again to break with Carrington. He told Brett, 'I had since to write and tell her plainly that our friendship was over – she didn't seem to understand why I was silent. I wonder why life should be so ghastly. I mean why one should have to chuck the one person one really loves!' But Carrington held on. 'With loving,' she wrote, 'either you do, and then one goes on always, unless the person alters, or one alters, or else one *does not* love a person either when they are with you or away. Do you see what I mean. Only I won't bother you with writing letters if you don't want them and pester you for a friendship if you don't want it . . . Be kind Gertler and write to me sometimes, for I miss you badly.' (January 1915)

'Will you mind if I come to London anytime, if I come and see your "Eve"?'[186] she pleaded. 'I am so excited, now that it is finished. It makes me jealous that all these other people should see first. Barbara* wrote me a long letter yesterday all about Lady Ottoline's party. What fun you must have had. For a moment I had a bad pang inside to be back again. Do you miss my soups?'

Mark was willing to write, describing his wild life in the evenings: 'We are having very exciting times here in London just now. Last night we danced again at Brett's studio. There was Barbara, her friend and Brett and myself. Barbara was in fancy dress – trousers – she looked quite well. She is awfully good to dance with. I enjoy these hilarious evenings. We are trying to arrange to all suddenly appear tomorrow at Lady Ottoline's with masks and fancy dress. I don't know whether it'll come off. It'll be rather awful if we come upon them when they are rather in a quiet mood!' He avoided urging her to return to London: 'Of course if ever you come to London you can come and see my work. If you come in May you could see it in the New English, where I shall send it.'

* Barbara Hiles.

'What fun you all seem to be having in London', Carrington wrote wistfully. 'I am going to learn to make some puddings and good dishes to cook for you when I come back. As I am sure in time we will get tired of eggs on plates.' 'You certainly ought to learn something about cooking', was the callous reply. 'I should always prefer my girl friends to be better cooks than artists. Don't let this annoy you.' (January 1915)

She persevered. 'I am longing to come up, and see you in the new studio. How fine it will be, and to be able to go for walks after tea, instead of the bus from Bishopsgate! Think of it in the summer when the evenings are long. You are indeed leading the life of the idle rich at Eddie's. Does Eddie admire your legs from beneath the purple silk dressing gown at breakfast? You will become such an aristocrat in your new abode in Hampstead, and probably when I come to see you, I shall find you surrounded by the Lady Ottoline and nobility (and Winston, if the war is over), lounging in a silk dressing gown. And you will despise me, and reject me for my humble attire and because I have no title! Still I shall write your memoirs when you are old and toothless. The Chapter one of your life.

'Your picture of Faith* made me laugh and laugh. I nearly cried with joy! It recalled to my mind so vividly that endless chin, and bulging neck, and scornful indifference in her case as to whether one cares for her or not . . . I am being brave, and having great self control and am not being jealous of Barbara! But you must not forget me utterly! Because really it would grieve me so much if when I returned, I find you and Brett both entirely indifferent to my company. I am going to send you some ties next week . . . But I will learn to cook so that you will have no fault to find in me . . . I am afraid I miss you terribly, it is no use being reserved, so I confess. Write to me when you have time – as I love so much to get your letters, and hear your news.' (29 January 1915)

In return she got more descriptions of the exciting life going on without her: 'Last Thursday at Lady Ottoline's, was the wildest of all nights! I smashed Dodgen's glasses, kicked Miss Strachey so that her foot bled, and made a Belgian girl's arm black and blue!!! John was there. Tonight we danced at Brett's. That little German girl

* Faith Bagenal.

you drew nude, dances *excellently*. She has a lovely little figure to clasp. Barbara is going to sit nude to Brett and me! That will be useful as I can't afford a model. Dodgen, Chile,★ and young Spencer† all thought that my "Apples" was the best thing in the New English ... No, Eddie does not admire my legs. My legs are far too thin and hairy! He is used to the legs of Jim Barnes and Rupert Brooke, whose legs are as pink and plump as yours! I cut a very sorry figure after those people. However Eddie is very kind to me in spite of my figure ...'

When Carrington had left London the previous summer their relationship seemed at a dead end. Resigned to doing without her except as a friendly correspondent and very occasional visitor, Mark was trying hard to get her out of his mind. Reacting, as well, against the loss of Currie, he threw himself into social life in the evenings with a kind of frenzy.

'Gertler worked very hard during the day' recalled Beatrice Campbell 'but he seemed incapable of resting when he had finished painting. Socially he was a great success, for he seemed to know everyone and was invited everywhere. He was a great source of entertainment to us with his wonderful story telling. He loved to act his stories, imitating everyone. He loved music halls and would give imitations of the turns that he saw there. He called himself and Kot 'Beattie and Babs' after two famous music hall sisters who did a comic turn together ... Gertler was good looking but he seemed always to be saying "Don't touch me. Leave me alone." He was in need of sympathy and understanding, but unable to ask for it.'[138]

Mark was rediscovering his popularity with girls, though resulting affairs were brief sexual partnerships only. The relationship with Iris Tree seemed, at first, equally unpromising. The beautiful Iris, daughter of Sir Herbert Beerbohm Tree, was an ex-Slade student, intelligent and wayward. Mark's references to her were half-wary, half-contemptuous. 'Iris Tree would be better than this,' he had told a friend when describing the discomforts of his Cholesbury lodging. (23 December 1914) And, describing the Christmas parties there, he said, 'The parties left me so weak and dissipated that I feel as if I'd been to "Iris's Paradise" for a week on end! So I mean to lie low

★ Alvaro Guevara.
† Gilbert Spencer.

for a bit in order to recover . . . I don't think Iris Tree and myself will ever get on. She is so very different from me. I am afraid that we should have to come to blows. Besides, do you know, I've had enough of woman and love for a bit. I am going to rest from that.'

But a few months later he was becoming more involved. Writing to Carrington he said, 'Last night was another exciting Thursday. Brett had John, Iris Tree, Barbara and myself to supper in her studio! John arrived with two large bottles of wine. Of course we got drunk. Iris looked very beautiful in a pale-lemon coloured evening dress. She is so beautiful. I had a love scene with her, which I am afraid I must confess I enjoyed. I like Iris more than is good for me. I have come to the conclusion that it'll be better for me not to see her much. If she was like other girls it wouldn't matter, but she is so capricious and loves hurting one . . . Please, by the way, do not think me awful for getting drunk etc. last night. Do not think that I like that sort of thing. If you knew my nature you would be surprised how difficult it is for me, especially with women. I always suffer agonies the next morning – of remorse. As for Iris I shall not see her hardly at all. I am by no means trying to excuse myself to you. You can think of me exactly what you like. Only you are apt to misunderstand that sort of thing. Just because you are young and inexperienced and rather, if I may say so, cold or sexless. Anyway you are by Nature absolutely different to me or even Iris.' (3 March 1915)

But Iris's affection was to be more constant than he anticipated. 'I always think of you', she wrote in April, and whenever she was away letters would come for Mark.

It was a hectic time both in London and at Cholesbury where the Murrys and the Cannans gave parties. These often included plays in which Mark would take part, and one of the most popular entertainments was a piece by Cannan and Mark. 'They would act and dance a queer London East End Jewish play together, the refrains of which were the cry of that despised race, "I am only a Jew".'[139]

He made arrangements to take over a cottage at Cholesbury which the painter Ethel Walker was giving up. The final business discussion over supper in a Chelsea restaurant a few months later ended with them both drunk. She took a fancy to Mark: 'After supper we went back to her studio,' Mark wrote. 'There she dipped into her whole life story! All her love affairs and especially her great and first Fall! She was then 34 years of age. About this memorable event, she told me every detail. She gave me a minute description of her night shirt! How nice she looked. How she got into the bed and then etc. etc. etc!!!'

In London there were meetings with old friends: 'The other day I met Nevinson in uniform! He had come back from the Front! Told me in five minutes *all* about it, and you can imagine how ghastly it sounded in "Nevinsonian" language, God etc. etc.' (February 1915) and there were new encounters: 'This morning Eddie introduced me to Winston Churchill. He was coming out of St Paul's as we were going in. How plain he is – a cross between Clive Bell and Knewstub. He was quite nice though.'

Mark's work was held up until the new studio was ready in mid February. By then he was feeling the strain of too reckless a pursuit of pleasure and was only too eager to get to work during the day. 'I have been feeling very ill for some time,' he wrote on 12 February 1915, 'and today I realized that I had a bad cold, so I locked up my studio and came to my people here in the East End, where I mean to stay until I'm better. I have been suffering terrible pains in the head. I did not go to Lady Ottoline this Thursday, as somehow I felt for a time, I've had enough of that sort of thing . . . I feel now more anxious to settle down to work than anything. My studio is nearly ready and as soon as I get over this beastly cold, I shall start.'

He wrote to Carrington on the same theme: 'I am fed up with Lady Ottoline and her parties and dancing: I only want to get better and retire into my studio to work.'

At last he was able to start. Penn Studio was perfect. It was a separate little building consisting of one long studio and a small bedroom, and the studio ceiling was formed by a pitched roof with glass panes some thirty feet above the floor. 'Really it's like the country here,' Mark exulted. 'From the top lights of my studio I can see the bare black branches of trees against the sky, and the branches are always full of screaming birds. In my bedroom also there is a top light and from my bed I can see the moon, branches and the sky, also hear the birds. It is pleasant as I lie to look up through the branches and see the bellies and chests of the birds. Later on it'll be still better when the leaves are out.'

Installed in a comfortable studio, relieved by Marsh and Brett from pressing money worries, Mark was able to lose himself in work. During the next year or so his creative spirit began to reach its full power in a series of magnificent pictures.

His reputation was rising. 'Agapanthus'[187] at the February Friday Club drew some encouraging reviews. 'The technique is so much his own that no one would hesitate in recognizing his work,' commented the *Westminster Gazette*. The critic found 'unsympathetic qualities' and 'a certain hardness' but concluded nevertheless that 'he is the only English painter who will soon be usefully compared with Van Gogh for the passion with which he focuses on reality.' By the terms of their bargain under which Marsh had first refusal of pictures, it went to him.

Ottoline praised his work and introduced him to her brother, Lord Henry Bentinck, and other potential buyers.[140] Lady Hamilton bought the 'Black and White Cottage' for twelve pounds. Mark was pleased, though, as he said, 'it hurts me to part with those things . . . I loved them myself very much and should have liked to keep them.'

The London Group realized its error in excluding him: ' "The London Group" have at last thought it time to ask me to be a member. I got a formal letter from Wadsworth, who, it appears, is secretary, commencing with "Dear Sir". I accepted.' Mark was pleased, but with a spirit of independence added, 'whether I shall exhibit I don't know.' (February 1915) He decided instead for the time being to continue sending to the New English, who after all had given him his first start, in the hope that the hardening of its arteries was not too far advanced for it to show challenging work.

His 'Rabbi and Rabbitzin' [181] was accepted for the April exhibition, and again the perceptive critic of the *Westminster Gazette* praised the power of the young painter, recognizing, 'the knowledge of reality profound and passionately acquired, the astonishing force and sympathy . . . A man and a woman with all the history of an oppressed people behind them. The incisive and unflinching design to which these human elements are controlled without loss to their humanity . . . The picture proves he will be a great

artist . . . if he doesn't get cynical.' Mark showed again in this
picture that he had succeeded in his aim of creating pictures in a
twentieth-century idiom from his East End life.

But in his other exhibit – a 'Portrait of Brett' [188] – the *Westminster
Gazette* critic detected a different note in Mark's work: 'Power and
the surprising technical mastery are here again, but instead of
sympathy has crept in an element of caricature. The comprehension
has taken the form of cold, even cruel, dissection, rather than of
sympathetic intuition. It is a remarkable portrait, perhaps the most
remarkable in the exhibition (not excluding Mr Augustus John's
portrait of Bernard Shaw) but a distasteful one. Along this road
Mr Gertler cannot advance; to sneer at humanity is to close the
very gates of knowledge . . . his strong flood will be lost in the
deserts of cynicism and unfruitful formalism.' The *Observer* criticized the 'horrible distortion' of the features, which 'merely
suggests the twisted mirrors in a hall of laughter', and decided
that Mark 'worshipped at the shrine of ugliness'.

But the majority of other newspapers kept silent. Worst of all, his
'Eve'[186] was not on show at all. 'The N.E.A.C. have refused my
"Eve",' Mark had written. 'I was absolutely amazed and very
vexed because I had hopes of selling it there, and any extra money
would have been very useful just now. They refused it, I hear,
because the figure of Eve was considered indecent!' (23 May 1915)

It seemed like the end of the line for Mark's association with the
New English.

Yet he could, when he wished, produce charming visions of
conventional beauty. During the spring, for instance, he painted a
picture, 'Daffodils', which delighted Marsh. 'Gertler has painted the
most lovely picture I ever saw . . . it convinces me of his genius
more than anything he has done . . . (it's mine)' (20 March 1915)

Meanwhile Mark thought out his ideas for the next big step.
There was one similarity between Whitechapel High Street and
Hampstead. On weekends and public holidays the Heath was filled
with crowds of working people. From all over London – including
the East End – they journeyed for a day at the fairs and strolled
among the trees and ponds.

Watching them, Mark became excited. 'I wish painting wasn't
such a worry,' he wrote a few days after Easter. 'The strange part is

that I seem very often *most* worried when my picture goes most well'. The most difficult thing, I find, is to control my excitement. My ideas seem so wonderful and exciting that they make me feel wretched! They are too much to bear. I looked on to the Heath on Easter Monday. Wonderful ideas for pictures! Girls with brilliant feathers and youths swinging in coloured boats!!! The effect was like a rainbow!!! God! Give me patience and enough powers of control.'

With Carrington he went into more detail: 'I get amazing visions for pictures, some of them too complicated to paint, but wonderful as "ghosts". I got wonderful ideas here on Bank holidays. Multitudes of people. Bright feathers, swinging in and out of the clouds in coloured boats ... a blaze of whirling colour; the effect would be something like a rainbow. It would be wonderful if one could give the effect of the whirl and excitement, but it's too complicated an idea to paint yet.'

But were they really too complicated? After all, his powers were developing fast. 'I find myself growing very much in my work lately,' he wrote to Carrington. 'I hope very soon to paint you some very good things. The chief difficulty in painting I find now is to control my excitement. I get so excited. Over this last picture I got so excited that I thought I shouldn't be able to finish it.'

Art was never going to be an easy occupation. 'Painting to me becomes every day more difficult, more complicated, more wearing,' he told Carrington. He explained to Marsh: 'You shall have to have patience with my work. Although I get such little done, you must always know that I am working *extremely* hard and that I never stop working, it being the only thing I have to care for now. You see I am terribly sensitive about my work and I cannot leave a picture unless I feel that I have got it as near to my conception as is possible. With your present help I am able to carry this out. I have faith in myself and I hope to do really fine things some day, but in painting nothing can be hurried, at any rate I find I can't hurry with any success. And after all, quantity doesn't matter, you have only got to go to the N.E.A.C. to see that there are no lack of pictures!' (May 1915)

At least his surroundings were now healthy: 'After breakfast I go for a long walk on the Heath. That is fine! How different from the

12—MG

East End! Here I stand a much better chance of keeping healthy, as the air is good and the food regular. The Heath is magnificent really. Such good and varied ground. It is so good by the ponds. Sometimes for days on end I don't go into town at all.' And visits to doctors confirmed that physically, at any rate, there was nothing wrong: 'Oh! Eddie! I'm terribly happy! Tweedy tells me that there is no need at all to wear glasses in the street! If anything my eyes have improved since last he saw them. They have grown more together or something like that. All that was wrong was that my working glasses had to be changed.' He would be all right if he could control his nervous excitement: 'The other day I was so ill that Eddie sent me off to a specialist – Winston Churchill's doctor! He told me I was *extremely* strong! He gave me something for my nerves.'

By the end of the spring his 'Swing Boats'[189] was taking shape and another picture was well under way. 'I have the last two months been working very hard on my "Fruit Stall" picture,' he told Carrington[190]. 'At first the difficulty was tremendous, but after a hard fight and many illnesses and interruptions and despair, I've at last got it going now, so that the most difficult part is over. I think it is by far the best thing I've done.'

CHAPTER 20

'We have shared so much'

Perhaps, after all, there was a future for Mark and Carrington. Carrington was changing. She was growing up and with her physical maturity came hope for both of them: the chance for Mark to find the love and stability he needed and for Carrington to make a life with a fellow painter who loved her.

In April and in June 1915, during visits to Cholesbury, the barriers between them began to break down. Here and there in their many letters of the spring and summer they expressed what was happening:

Carrington (Andover, February 1915): As you were so particularly husbandly on Thursday evening I will write you a wifely letter now. I shall see you on Thursday evening at Brett's studio . . . Brett and I chose you a lovely shirt, some collars, and socks. What a gentleman you will look now! . . . I am bringing heaps of food back with me for our parties. I am getting excited about Thursday aren't you. I will bring you some clothes back to dress up in.

Carrington (Andover, February 1915): We have shared so much, nearly everything, for so long, that now I miss not having you here with me.

Carrington (Andover, February 1915): Today I have been suffering agonies because I am a woman. This makes me so angry and I despise myself so much . . .

Mark (London, 3 March 1915): I am sorry about your pains. I hope you are better now. Don't be angry and despise yourself for what is only natural.

Carrington (Andover, 2 April 1915): I did so love staying with the Cannans. It was the best time we have ever spent there. You are such a good comrade. And I love you also for painting those pictures . . . I wish you were with me . . . Miss Walker's cottage in August is a fine idea. I am excited over it . . . Do not forget to send me Gilbert's book on Butler and even more important the photo-graphs of your pictures. I will send you one of my still life, so mind pray do not forget to send me a photograph of yours. In return I will send you some flowers, and leaves. Write to me soon please and tell me what you are doing . . . I loved so much these last few days. Thank you again so much for being so good to me Gertler. It was quite the happiest time I have ever spent with you.

Mark (London, 5 April 1915): The stay at Gilbert's was certainly splendid. You seemed some how so much more sympathetic than usual . . .

Carrington (Andover, April 1915): I didn't quite realize until I saw you again how much I miss by not being with you more. My love to you.

Carrington (Andover, April 1915): Thank you so much for your letter. How happy it has made me: your friendship means so much to me. When you said that the artist's name didn't matter in a picture, and you did not want to be a big artist yourself, only a creator, I felt I loved you more than I ever have before. I will always come now once every month and see you . . . my love.

Carrington (Andover, May 1915) (after a quarrel had been made up): When I saw your hand writing on the envelope, I was so excited I hardly liked to open it. I am going to be perfectly honest in this letter, as I hope always in future to be with you, so I will not pretend to be reserved. I am so terribly happy now that I want to rush right up to London at once and see you . . . Do not be unhappy. Be very happy – already I am, far away, planning everything. Cannot I come and stay in Miss Walker's cottage? If what I write is badly expressed it is only because of my extreme joy, which I cannot contain . . . Do write me very long letters all about your work and what you are painting now . . . I find it impossible to write about these matter-of-fact things, when all the time I am only thinking, how good it all is . . .

Mark (London, May 1915): Thank you for your letter. Thank God we are friends again. Forgive me for having made you unhappy. I will now make up for it by trying to make you as happy as I can. Really I don't think it will ever happen again. I only try and leave you because you cannot give me as much of you as I want. But now I have definitely proved, that though what you give me is little in comparison to what I desire, yet that little I *must* have. I cannot live or paint without it. I suffered most when my work went well, because I would stop and say to myself, It's all very well, but *she* won't see it, *she* won't see it! Do you know, this used to make me stop work and waste time! I will not say that I'm happy. If I did, I should not be speaking the truth. But sorrow has become a second nature to me now and as long as it doesn't reach the point of horrible torture, I really do not grumble . . . I've seen very few people as I have been too depressed to speak – I just lost myself in work – I work from ten o'clock in the morning until seven o'clock. Now I shall go easier as you've come back to me. I need a rest badly.

Carrington (Andover, May 1915): I will bring some flowers when I come on Wednesday . . . I was miserable both the last times I was in London because every place I saw reminded me of you. We have been so much together in London.

Mark (London, May 1915): I am going to Cholesbury for the summer in July. I have now Miss Walker's cottage permanently. So come if possible before July. I shall be interested to see your landscapes. Will you bring them with you? . . . please do not try and improve for my sake or try to be 'less selfish or more honest'. That sounds to me rather silly – like a child who has been naughty and reproved . . . The effort would for me kill the beauty of the unselfishness and honesty when attained so please be natural as before at any rate with me . . . What I miss in you is something that is not in your nature to give me and is therefore out of the question. No amount of trying on your part can alter this . . . This friendship between us is not a pretty or pleasant thing to me, but a *necessity* like all great things – like painting itself. Is painting a pleasant or smooth occupation? Is life itself smooth? Why should our friendship be different.

Carrington (Andover, May 1915): When would you like to see me again? In about a fortnight?

Mark (London, June 1915) (after a stay together at Cholesbury): When the train took you away from me, I was stunned. Everything became unreal. I was hardly aware of Gilbert's presence, nor heard his voice . . . I was dazed and made vague answers to everything that was said to me . . . After supper of course Gilbert played the pianola, played so splendidly. I never wanted it to end. The whole time, I was with you, thinking with you, talking with you and listening with you. I dreaded an interruption; I wanted it to go on for ever, or if there must be an interruption it should be by you yourself – the reality, which is even always better than my imagin-ation. It ended and then . . . Gilbert and I talked. Again I woke up because we talked of you. I told him all. He thought our relations wonderful and worth much and he envied me, for knowing you. He appreciates you very much and I love him for liking you.

Now I am in London again and in my studio, I feel stunned again and unhappy and lonely. I don't know why you should not be with me always. Such a lot has happened the last two months. Every-thing has changed so. Especially you. You have completely altered . . . You seem to have suddenly grown up into a woman. I am almost frightened at the change.

Carrington (Hove, June 1915) (now living at Hove and doing a teaching job): It seems so like a dream last night and seeing you again that I find it is hard to believe it is quite true. I almost came round this morning to see if you had changed or were still, still there. But have I been rather stupid and selfish? I did like your work *so much*, and I never tell you lies now . . . Only you must help me. If we are absolutely candid then it cannot help being a fine relationship.

CHAPTER 21

'What you call a Passivist'

In the summer of 1915 Mark's friendships deepened with Kot, the Lawrences, Middleton Murry and Katherine Mansfield, as well as with Gilbert Cannan. 'I have seen Murry and his girl Katherine a good deal, also Koteliansky,' he reported to Carrington in May. 'I like these people very much . . . I envy Murry and Katherine the way they both live and work together.' And when he was away he would write to Kot: 'I think of you all sometimes in the evening, talking "plainly". Best wishes and remembrance to Katherine and Jack*'. (July 1915)

With these people Mark felt at ease. Each of the four men had had a difficult struggle. Lawrence, a miner's son, Murry, a poor scholarship boy, Cannan, an ex-board-school pupil and Kot, a penniless Russian, were all alien to the prosperous English middle-class society. They all suited each other in many ways, sharing a tendency to soulbaring discussions and emotional storms.

Mark's friendship with the Campbells continued, and he and Kot became frequent visitors at the Campbells' 'Sundays'.

In the spring of 1915 the Morrells had moved from London to an Elizabethan manor house at Garsington near Oxford,[141] where they quickly established a kind of Arcadia for intellectuals. Mark was invited and spent a weekend there with Gilbert Cannan in September. He was there again in October, with Duncan Grant and Clive Bell as fellow house guests. Ottoline's fondness for him increased, and he was always welcome at her house.

Nearly all Mark's friends were intense pacifists and Marsh began to be viewed with some disfavour in the circle: though not exactly militant he did spend all his working days helping to run the Government war machine. 'Gertler says all your work makes you

* John Middleton Murry.

happy,' Lawrence had written to him ominously. 'The war, of course, makes us very unhappy.' (13 September 1914)

Mark disapproved of the war as positively as any of them and he was troubled. Apart from anything else he had become very fond of Marsh. 'I really cannot express my thanks to you for your extraordinary goodness,' he had written in May. 'I must tell you that I feel that what you are doing for me is *far* more valuable to me than anybody else has ever done . . . If you find that you are hard up or that you do not feel inclined to continue your help during the war you must *immediately* tell me. I mean, supposing my work disappoints you or you get hard up or supposing the war lasts too long! Anyway you must not let me be a weight on you . . . I hope I may some day be able to do something for you.'

Even when joining in the popular pastime of making fun of Eddie, Mark's laughter was affectionate. 'This coalition business in Parliament had caused me great anxiety,' he wrote. 'Never was I so feverishly interested in a political move, simply because it was the only one that stood any chance of directly affecting me. What affects Churchill, affects Eddie Marsh and what affects Eddie Marsh affects me! However, although they have both been driven out like Adam and Eve from the Garden of Eden, all is not black yet. Anyhow it is not going to affect me, but poor Eddie is rather unhappy and I am sorry for him as his goodness to me has really made me love him. He hates Lord Fisher now and has burnt his photograph! He seems to think the other post they will get will be so dull; whilst at the Admiralty, "he did feel he was doing something for his country . . ." Poor dear Eddie!!!' (23 May 1915)

Through the summer his worry increased. 'Last night I stayed at Marsh's. Every time I see him I get depressed. I hate having to take this money from him.' (1 July 1915) In August, Harvey arranged a fifty-pound commission to paint Professor Sadler's portrait. This helped to give him a breathing space, although it also brought home the realities of his situation. From Leeds he wrote to Marsh, 'Really, commissioned portrait painting is a dreadful occupation. You can't think how this portrait is depressing me! Here I am, dragged away from my work that really means something to me, to paint a man whom I should never dream of choosing to paint. Just because I am paid a certain sum to do it. Never again will I accept a portrait *unless* the sitter interests or inspires me to paint him or her. I would rather starve. However, now I am in for it, I am doing my very best and I shall not leave it until I paint an honest likeness of the man and make as good a picture of it as I can.[191] I expect to be finished in about a week.'

Mark realized once and for all that portrait painting was closed to him. Not just the slick society portrait field but the more sincere work which brought in considerable sums to painters such as Augustus John. Seventeen years later he was to reaffirm this: 'I have never been able to "work to order", there is something about the conditions which paralyses my work and I can produce nothing I like that is any use that way.'[142]

The worst of it was that Marsh was so understanding. 'Your birth-pains over your pictures are quite torture enough for you,' he insisted. 'Don't worry yourself additionally about how you are to live . . . so long as you can manage on what I can do for you, and the extras that are quite certain to come in. Since the war, and still more since my friends died,* I don't care to spend money on myself, beyond just keeping up my life here. You know I believe you were born to be a great painter, and if that is true it will have been a proud thing in my life to have been able to help you, and leave you more or less free to develop yourself, unhampered. I can't imagine a worthier use of my money – and even suppose we were wrong about your painting, you are still my friend and I should hate to be "rolling" while you were in straits.' (18 August 1915)

If Mark gave up Marsh's help and failed to sell his pictures the situation could become desperate. He could no longer look for help from his family. Their troubles were increasing again. 'Last night I went home to see my people,' he reported to Carrington. 'They are all in a bad state. Ill and poor. My mother was in bed and my father was very angry with me, accusing me of not caring what becomes of them all. It depressed me very much. I owe them also £8!!

The last year had not been kind to the Gertlers. Louis had developed eye trouble. This was treated; but then he began to succumb to chronic bronchitis. 'My father's eyes are much better,

* Rupert Brooke had died in April 1915.

but his constitution seems to be breaking up rapidly.' Mark had written in January 1915.

Another worry was the possibility of deportation.

'Every day another poor little old Jew is being sent back to Austria,' he noted. 'These poor little people are quite unaware of the war and are no more Austrian in spirit than Hottentot.'

If Louis and Golda, as enemy aliens, were to be sent back to Przemysl they would find themselves in the middle of the fighting between Russia and Austria. As the papers had reported the previous autumn: 'further forts around Przemysl have fallen and the bombardment of the town has assumed huge proportions. The losses sustained by the garrison are enormous.' [143] In the spring the Russians had attacked again and the town fell in March 1915.

'Poor Mark is in a great taking about his parents,' one friend commented. 'They are not naturalized, aged sixty, infinitely poor etc. He fears they may be "repatriated" i.e. sent back to Austria.'

At least this threat receded in the spring: 'My people have now turned Poles! No more are we alien enemies,' Mark noted. 'There is a Polish Society that can officially turn all people that come from Galicia and that can speak Polish into Poles. So that's all right now.'

Mark was also worried about his own position and the possibility of being conscripted into the army. He rebelled fiercely against the idea, writing despairingly to Carrington, 'I expect I shall be dragged into this wretched war, before it's over, but I shall keep out of it as long as I possibly can. How hateful it would be to lose one's life, or even to be maimed for life, through a purpose in which one has no sort of belief.' Without his painting he felt he could not continue to live. 'All I have in life is my work. I have, underneath all, a certain undying impetus to paint and paint,' he wrote. 'It is inexplicable, yet the most living thing about me. At bottom I know that the most satisfactory thing in life is work – to work regardless of achievement or failure. Now, therefore, all I want is to be allowed to carry on my work; surely that is not much to ask for and quite harmless, yet I daresay this beastly War will succeed in disturbing me.'

In August he set out, in a fragment of a diary, a renewed exhortation to himself to pursue a life dedicated to art, living, if need be, simply and austerely:

'3 August 1915: You are now twenty three; you have fought your way through. That is, you have it in your power to do real pictures at last! Having realized this you have cut out all hindrances and unnecessary causes for endless torment and suffering. Having gained at last this power of painting real pictures, you start now life from the beginning as if new born, but equipped with this power.

'Paint your pictures; the satisfaction for you lies in the creation of them. There is no need to thrust them upon people more than will bring you in enough money to live. If you can manage to live and paint and be in good health that's enough. Master all nervous little bothers that crop up when working. They are only side issues and don't matter. They are in fact silly. You just work away. Life is worth living.'

But what *was* he to do about money? 'The future looks very black to me,' he wrote to Marsh, 'because the more I go on the less I can paint that which does not very forcibly move me to paint. It is *the idea, the idea* that matters to me. It is torture to me now to touch a canvas without a definite idea or conception, and my ideas are becoming more and more mystical. What I am driving at is that I shall not be able to do commissions and yet not sell my pictures! I think when I get to London I might try and get a teaching job in some art school; that would be better than commissions and I would not have to lean so heavily and constantly on you. I must above all try and arrange my life so that I can give birth one after the other to these pictures which are fighting in me to come out.'

Nevertheless Mark reached the decision that it was dishonest to go on accepting Marsh's help. After a preliminary hint – 'Mrs Lawrence tells me that she has written to you about your attitude towards the War. She seemed quite upset'–he wrote on 19 October 1915, cutting himself off from his only steady source of income:

'Dear Eddie, I have come to the conclusion that we two are too fundamentally different to continue to be friends. Since the war, you have gone in one direction, and I in another. All the time I

have been stifling my feelings, firstly because of your kindness to
me and secondly I did not want to hurt you. I am I believe what
you call a "Passivist". I don't know exactly what that means, but I
just hate this War and should really loathe to help in it. I wanted to
do some war work simply because the hateful atmosphere had got
into me and it seemed difficult to create at such a time. But now I've
changed my mind I shall paint as long as I can; as long as I am not
forced into this horrible atmosphere, I shall work away.

'Of course from this you will understand that we had better now
not meet any more and that I cannot any longer accept your help.
Forgive me for having been dishonest with you and for having
under such conditions accepted your money. I have been punished
enough for it. I stuck it so long, because it seemed hard to have to
give up this studio which I love. But now rather than be dishonest I
shall give it up and go to my cottage in the country. I have still a
little money of my own from the Sadler portrait; on this I shall
live. In the country I can live on £1 a week. I shall live there until
there is conscription or until my money is used up.

'Your kindness has been an extraordinary help to me. Since your
help I have done work far better than before. I shall therefore never
cease to be thankful to you. Also if I earn any money by painting I
shall return you what I owe you. I shall send you the latchkey and
please would you get Mrs Elgy to send me my pyjamas and
slippers.'

CHAPTER 22

Hunnish Indecency

In the autumn Mark faced the problem of where to send his work. It was unfortunate that as it was growing more personal and original, the public, whose attitudes were increasingly affected by the war, had less and less time for experimentation in art. This was true even of those critics who had been most kind to progressive work before the war. It began to dawn on artists that many of the reviewers had been in favour not so much because the new art was in any way understood, but because they felt it was good for young people to let off steam. The war revealed that, to many critics, art was a fundamentally frivolous and unimportant activity, and experimentation a kind of game which could not be allowed in serious times. One said, 'Less than ever do we feel inclined to look on with equanimity at these pranks, by which in piping times of peace, it was possible to be mildly interested – or at any rate amused.'

As far as the majority of the Press was concerned, 'Futurism and the other fashionable "isms" of the last few years, [as one paper put it], have been inserted in the casualty lists of the Great War.'

The Friday Club Spring Exhibition of 1915 had included many quite conservative pictures by artists such as Rothenstein, and the pictures which were most stylistically advanced – those of Nevinson and Roberts – attempted to deal seriously with war subjects. Yet one paper, *The Globe* had commented menacingly, 'This sort of art with its silly affectations and morbid extravagances has been killed by the war, and any attempt to revive it has happily no chance of success. People are in much too serious a mood nowadays to be amused by feebly vicious suggestions or by comic perversion of artistic principles.'

The dilemma that Mark faced was acute: he had to sell his pictures and the few collectors who were still buying modern work preferred to play safe and support the New English rather than the 'extremists' of the London Group. The New English exhibitions now appeared, as one critic put it, as 'the most respectable show in London'. These calm waters were not seriously disturbed, either by the revolution in art or the strife between nations. Another writer pointed out that 'peace reigns and not an echo of the world conflict is allowed to enter.'

The club had rejected one of Mark's pictures in the spring of 1915, but they had accepted two others and he still had some supporters there. The *Westminster Gazette* had picked him out as the only potential 'young guard' who might provide the future leadership the club would need.

Mark made up his mind. His three best pictures were sent to the London Group. To the New English he sent only a drawing and a still life. The latter was rejected, much to his annoyance; 'Aren't they an absurd crew? It's unbelievable really!' he declared. The drawing, 'Abraham and the Angels', passed more or less unnoticed by the critics, though the *Morning Post* called it 'impertinent mockery'.

But a storm broke over his exhibits in November at the London Group show, which was held at Marchant's Goupil Gallery. Deprived by the war of its most advanced members, the group's exhibition was a great deal quieter than previously: Wyndham Lewis, David Bomberg, Jacob Epstein and Frederick Etchells were all unrepresented, and the heart of the exhibition were the paintings of Harold Gilman, Charles Ginner and Robert Bevan. In this relatively quiet company, Mark's paintings looked spectacular. When he went to the private view with Gilbert Cannan[144] he felt no doubt that his was the most challenging work in the exhibition, remarking brutally, 'What a rubbishy show! all the pictures, except my own, were composed of washed out purples and greens, and they matched so well that it seemed almost as if the artists all collaborated to create harmony at the show. In reality it means simply that they all paint alike and equally badly!'

Mark's work met the fate to be expected by solitary challengers. The pictures were fastened on by the critics as the most provocative in what was professedly the most advanced group in London.

It was only to be expected that authorities such as Sir Claude

Phillips of the *Daily Telegraph*, who had come down firmly against the new ideas in art, should go into the attack: 'Remembering the character of the exhibition held last year by the society . . . we could not but dread another infection of the same kind, and it was with something like dread that we approached the present show. Our fears were justified . . . We do not propose to offer any detailed criticism of Mr Mark Gertler's vast and glaring still-life piece "Fruit Stall"[190] or of his "Creation of Eve"[186], a deliberate piece of eccentricity which does not greatly amuse or interest us.'

But Mark's pictures were too advanced even for the more progressive critics. 'He enters with a tremendous flourish of trumpets,' said the *Pall Mall Gazette*. 'But unfortunately the trumpets are horribly out of tune. They make a piercing and offensive noise, and the notes they utter have nothing to do with music. To put it in plain words: Mr Gertler's "Creation of Eve" is merely a piece of impertinence with a slight seasoning of blasphemy, and his "Fruit Stall" looks like a caricature.'

The *Observer* commented, 'The unpleasantly sensational side of art is represented by Mr M. Gertler alone. No one will take his "Creation of Eve" and "Fruit Stall" seriously. Both pictures are obviously intended to shock, to offend and arouse discussion. Their crudeness of colour puts to shame the most extravagant "orchestration" of a coster girl's feather hat.'

The only two effective voices raised in Mark's defence were those of Sickert and Frank Rutter, and though neither really understood what he was trying to do, they defended his right to experiment. Chiding the New English Group for rejecting his pictures, Sickert, with his usual wit, wrote in the *Burlington*, 'The London Group is certainly the Newer English art club of the two. Here is Mr Gertler, legitimate and sturdy child of the Slade School though he be, left like a foundling in a copy of *The Times* on Mr Marchant's doorstep. Has the old New English reached the critical age when she is no longer able to suckle her own offspring? For Mr Gertler has passed master painter and no jury of painters has the right, it seems to me, to reject him.'

In the *Sunday Times* Rutter said, 'Mr Mark Gertler breaks altogether new ground in his paintings, which are curiously unusual in colour. His most important contribution, the "Fruit Stall", is a very striking and original painting.'[145]

At the exhibition itself an unpleasant event reminded Mark of a new danger which was looming up. There were even more alarming things than having his work derided and misunderstood.

Mark had been especially proud of his 'Creation of Eve'[186] This lovely, imaginative conception was the last picture he had painted in Elder Street the previous winter: 'My Eve is finished,' he had written exultantly to Carrington in January 1915. A little tea party of friends, including Iris Tree, had been summoned to see it. Then the Morrells had inspected it, the perceptive Ottoline finding it 'quite beautiful'. The new security of Marsh's protection had allowed Mark to hope for a time that there was no need to sell it quickly: 'It is nice to feel that I shall be able to keep my "Eve" for some time, as that is the best of all,' Mark wrote to Carrington in February.

After the opening of the London Group show Mark recorded: 'Some people in a rage stuck a label on the belly of my poor little "Eve" with "Made in Germany" on it.'

The war news was bad: the Gallipoli venture had failed, Zeppelins were raiding London. Asquith's Government had fallen. While hundreds of thousands of men slaughtered each other on the battlefields hysteria was mounting among the people at home: anything German was beastly, even German music was frowned upon. Mark was not only a pacifist and a close friend of Lawrence, the Morrells and other leading pacifists, but seemed, as near as made no difference, an enemy alien. His British nationality would not have existed had he been born a year or two earlier – before Louis and Golda left Przemysl – or a year or two later, when they had returned.

A further hint of trouble ahead was the review in the *Morning Post*. It included no detailed discussion of Mark's pictures, but the critic referred to the 'Hunnish indecency' of 'Creation of Eve'.

It was an extremely opportune moment for new supporters to appear. In the conception and style of his pictures Mark had taken a long stride forward. While still drawing ideas for subjects mainly

'The Fruit Sorters'; while painting this picture in Whitechapel in 1914 Mark got his first chance to see much of the country outside London. He wrote, 'How I should love to bring to the backgrounds of my picture some buds of the spring-time, little twigs, leaves and flowers! I would paint them very carefully and accurately'. And the picture is much brighter in colour and lighter in mood than most of his work of this time. **(16)**

Golda Gertler. (17)

Mark (*left*) and his brother Jack in
1910 when Mark was eighteen. (18)

Louis and Golda Gertler. (19)

Mark at thirteen, after his Barmitzvah. (20)

When Mark had finished this large and ambitious picture 'The Return of Jephtha', a friend photographed him with it on the back roof of his house. (21)

'Class of 1912' at the Slade School of Art; front row, left to right: Carrington, unknown student, Nevinson, Mark Gertler, unknown student, Adrian Allinson, Stanley Spencer, unknown student; Dorothy Brett is seated directly behind Mark and Nevinson, Isaac Rosenberg is behind Carrington on one knee. Professor Brown is third from the right at the back. (22)

'Creation of Eve', 1914; the last picture painted before Mark left Whitechapel. It was at first considered too indecent for exhibition, and when it was shown, during the First World War, a critic referred to its 'Hunnish indecency'. Mark noted, 'Some people in a rage stuck a label on the belly of my poor little Eve with "made in Germany" on it'. **(23)**

'Black and White Cottage', 1914. 'No matter how the wind blows it [the pampas grass] about, it always retains the beautiful and graceful curves of its leaves! It is indeed wonderful. I have worked for many days on this plant alone, but it is as difficult as it is beautiful.' The picture was acquired by Lady Hamilton and given to Violet Asquith as a wedding present. (24)

'Self Portrait'; painted in the months after the symptoms of tuberculosis had begun to develop in 1920. **(25)**

'The Merry-go-Round', 1916; D. H. Lawrence wrote, 'It is the best *modern* picture I have ever seen: I think it is great and true. But it is horrible and terrifying. . . . The outer life means nothing to you, really . . . I have for you, in your work, reverence. . . . Take care. . . . You seem to me to be flying like a moth into a fire'. **(26)**

Above 'The Boxers'. **(27)**

Below 'Swing Boats'; one of his most successful pictures, it later disappeared, like many other important works, and was forgotten until this photograph came to light. **(28)**

Above 'Ballet Dancers' (detail). **(29**

In the years 1915 to 1918 Mark Gertler developed several new ideas in technique and style:

Below 'Acrobats'; Mark wanted to continue wit sculpture but no one took it seriously, and he wa forced by lack of money to abandon his plans. **(3**

'The Manor House, Garsington', with the pool in the foreground. (31)

'The Bathers', 1917-18; Mark wrote, 'a day's work on it makes no more impression than a flea bite on an elephant's back! So I can see myself going on forever at it'. (32)

John Currie, Mark Gertler and Dolly Henry at Ostende in 1912.
(33, 34)

Carrington when she began at the Slade School. (35)

John Currie and Mark Gertler. (36)

'Agapanthus', 1914. **(37)**

Gilbert Cannan in front of his mill house, where Mark often stayed from 1914-16. When the picture was exhibited a critic said, 'It seems to be a caricature both of nature and of man, but one cannot quite see the joke of it.' **(38)**

'Golda Gertler', 1924; Mark wrote, 'I was so anxious to keep the picture for myself that I stipulated that I would only let it go for £200, and he [the dealer] sold it for that price, the largest sum I have ever received for a picture'. **(39)**

'Gipsy at her Toilet', 1924. **(42)**

from the life of the common people, his new, severely stylized, semi-geometrical forms had left straightforward representation well behind. Although if alienated many, his work now attracted the serious attention of the group which was to dominate art criticism after the war. The originality of the pictures was recognized by both Clive Bell and Roger Fry.

'Dear Gertler,' Bell wrote, 'I saw your big picture – the coster and fruit* – admired it immensely, and meant to write and tell you so. Roger Fry and I had been making a round of the galleries, clockwise, and coming on yours at last were very much impressed. I don't know when last I saw an English picture that seemed to me so much the real thing. It was a queer sensation being really fixed and fastened by a picture at Goupil's.'[146, 190]

Duncan Grant also sent his support: 'Dear Gertler, I must write to tell you that I think your big picture at the London Group very remarkably good. It is much the most serious picture there and to my mind much the best work of yours I have seen. I should like to talk to you about it one day – perhaps I can come to tea one day soon?'

Carrington had watched with enthusiasm as the new pictures were created. 'I *do* appreciate the "Swing Boats",' she had written in June. She consoled him about the attitude of the New English Group, pointing out, 'You cannot expect men whose whole aim in life you disagree with to like your work. Do not be depressed about it. For when you go and see Miss Walker's work hung in a prominent place, why then I guess you must be glad they don't like yours. I think it would be rather a vile insult to be popular with the New English Art Club.' Writing in December 1915, she wondered if another reason for the New English Group's attitude might be 'a personal dislike for you, because you do not pander, and pay them homage.' She agreed with Mark's criticism of some contemporary work. 'As you say nicely matched mauves and greens. So artistic so as not to hurt the eye, or wake people up, like a draper's shop "soft" coloured materials. And such bad drawing. Everything rotten.'

While it seemed that he would lose the support of the more cautious collectors, the attacks of the critics at least made him talked

* 'Fruit Stall.'

13—MG * *

about: 'I am having an exciting time,' he reported to Carrington. 'My pictures, apparently, have created a tremendous uproar! The critics are quite mad with rage. God knows what they are wild about. One paper said that I had done them simply to shock and create sensation! However, those criticisms seem to have done me more good than harm, for I have several offers for both the "Eve" and the "Fruit Stall"!!! This is to me very encouraging. Lady Cunard in the meantime is furiously excited, says she "*loves*" my pictures, and carts me about in her motor car to Lords, Ladies and Baronesses who want to meet me; and would you believe it, all these people pretend that they like my pictures! On Friday I lunched with a Baroness and this Baroness is coming here this afternoon for tea!'

Mark watched with an ironical eye as it became almost the mode for a fashionable revolutionary to support him. 'So you see for the moment I am famous! I expect my fame to last quite four days, but these four days may be long enough for me to get some money out of these titled wretches, so that I can go on quietly again for a while and paint what I want to. Lady Cunard assures me that I am "the talk of London". Also my little picture the "Black and White Cottage"[184] was given as a wedding present to Violet Asquith by Lady Hamilton. It hung among the presents at Downing Street "where it was much admired". "What Fame! What success!" After this my people concluded that I am the bosom friend of the Premier and that before long the Queen will kiss me on both cheeks and say, "How do you do Mr Gertler." '

Carrington was pleased and impressed. 'Your letters of course excited me terribly. I am still always excited about motor cars and duchesses!! So you are famous, and *also* infamous to judge by the critics! I hope you will sell your pictures. That is most important when one has to do with these idle rich . . . I wonder who all the Baronesses are who you are meeting? . . . How pleased your people must be with you at last!'

Who's Who, following up an earlier recommendation of Eddie Marsh, included an entry for Mark from the 1916 edition onwards.

The overall result of the *succès de scandale* was that many people saw the pictures. Perceptive judges admired them, and henceforth it

was to be increasingly difficult for critics to avoid giving serious
consideration to Mark's work, or to dismiss the view that he was
one of the leaders in the new kind of painting.

Other young artists wrote in praise of his pictures: 'Wadsworth
sent me a card to say that he liked very much my "Fruit Stall", and
thought it the best thing I'd done,' Mark wrote. 'This rather pleased
me, as I am myself still thrilled about the "Fruit Stall" and am
convinced of its value. Some day people will recognize its value; at
present it's too "hot from the oven." '

But a piece of bad luck lay in the future.

When the next generation of critics came to assess Mark's work
they would not know about or be able to see these pictures. 'The
Fruit Stall' and 'Swing boats'* and the much praised 'Apples'[192]
were to disappear from view, like earlier important works.

* The picture is known only from a single bad photograph.

PART SEVEN

The Merry-Go-Round

'Take care, or you will burn your flame so fast, it will suddenly go out.' – D. H. LAWRENCE TO MARK GERTLER

'If only the torment would end. It is like a terrible disease and incurable. We both put our heads together to try and end it, but we can't.'

MARK GERTLER TO S. S. KOTELIANSKY

CHAPTER 23

Pursuits

Mark had met Lytton Strachey in 1914 at Ottoline's, where the thirty-five-year-old writer was a frequent guest, often dominating the conversation with his brilliance. His urbanity and learning were impressive and Mark willingly agreed to further meetings.

Like Eddie Marsh, Strachey was much more interested in young men than girls; but whereas Marsh's feelings had taken the form of a sentimental, low-key affection with no physical intentions, Mark now found himself the object of a full-scale emotional assault.

It had begun very quietly, with Strachey meekly receiving his East End navigational instructions: 'I shall be very pleased if you could come and have tea with me next Friday at about four o'clock,' Mark wrote. 'Make for Liverpool Street Station and then continue for about three minutes along Bishopsgate Street on the Right, until you come to White Lion Street. Elder Street is 2nd on the left of that . . .' (30 November 1914)

Soon they were seeing each other quite often. 'I have become great friends with Lytton Strachey,' Mark told Carrington. 'We carry on a correspondence. He is a very intellectual man – I mean in the right sense. I should think he ought to do good work. He writes such good poetry. He mentions me in one of his poems . . . He is splendid to talk to.' (3 March 1915)

In appearance Strachey seemed unprepossessing to Mark: a long cadaverous face, spectacles and beard reared over thin spidery limbs, and when they walked on the Heath together boys were liable to shout mocking remarks. Mark was amused and entertained his friends with imitations of the comic figure, talking with a high squeaky voice while running his hand over his beard.

Strachey wooed him with tact and charm, had him to stay at his parents' home in Belsize Park and his own cottage in Wiltshire, sent him books – *Hamlet*, Hardy's poems, Virgil, Dostoievsky, and his own work. The last included a pornographic piece about two girls. Mark replied, 'Thanks very much for the work you sent me; "Ermyntrude and Esmeralda" I thought extremely amusing. But the poems I thought were fine. I wonder if you have any more work you could let me read? I should like to.'

He was flattered by the older man's interest and tried to cope with the Strachey brand of sophistication: 'No, I shouldn't be a bit surprised if, in the story of Susanna and the Elders, Daniel himself was all the time the young man in the garden – as you say. Anyway I am altogether on the side of poor old "Elders".' (2 March 1915) Mark also hastened to agree that pretentious artists who merely followed fashion were not nearly as useful as ploughboys – '*Of course* the Ploughboys are better, *much* more beautiful and simple minds, *much* more useful and I bet you far more beautiful' – though sometimes he felt he hadn't quite grasped the true point of Strachey's witty sallies.

When the real nature of Strachey's interest in him became clear Mark was embarrassed. But he was anxious to be as sophisticated as the next man, and though the friendship did not develop any further, it remained in existence. As he put it to Carrington: 'I like Lytton . . . I was only put off since that event – you know which I mean – Since then I feel uncomfortable when I am with him – that's all. You can't think how uncomfortable it is for a *man* to feel that he is attracting another *man* that way . . . to any decent man to attract another physically is simply revolting! Hence my difficulty with Lytton Strachey.'

Strachey was disappointed but ever hopeful, and throughout 1916 letters and visits continued. When he heard that Mark was in desperate straits for money, although he was hard up himself he hastened to help, writing with his usual delicacy: 'I have long wanted to possess a work by you, so will you put aside for me either a drawing or some other small piece, which is in your judgement the equivalent of the enclosed [£10]. And I'll carry it off when next I'm in London. I only wish I could get one of your larger pictures – what idiots the rich are! And how I loathe the thought of them swilling about in their motors with their tens of thousands, when people like you are in difficulties. What makes it

so particularly monstrous is that the wants of artists are so very
moderate – just for the mere decencies of life. All the same, though
I'm very sorry that you're not even half as well off as an ordinary
Civil Servant, you may be sure that I don't pity you, because you
are an artist, and being that is worth more than all the balances at all
the banks in London.' (12 May 1916)

Strachey tried to get his friends to help Mark. 'I've just heard
from Gertler, who says he's on the brink of ruin,' he told Clive
Bell. 'Do you think anything can be done? I'm sure £10 would
make a great difference to him and I thought perhaps you might be
able to invest some such sum in a minor picture or some drawings;
or perhaps you could whip up somebody else. If you do anything,
of course don't mention me, as his remarks about his finances were
quite incidental, with no idea of begging.' (12 May 1916)

But sometimes, in spite of Strachey's kindness, Mark would
weary of his attentions. 'Strachey came today,' he wrote once to
Carrington. 'But I peered through the door and didn't let him in.'

Even had he been able to contemplate the idea of returning a
homosexual emotion Mark was far too deeply committed to
Carrington to become seriously involved elsewhere.

A new problem had destroyed their mutual happiness of the
spring and early summer of 1915, and turned them once more into
pursuer and pursued. With her increasing maturity Carrington had
given Mark permission to make physical love to her, but then had
found herself quite unable to allow him to do so, and she remained
a virgin. It became evident that she had a fundamental dislike of her
femininity, and a fear of sex.

She had grown up in a household in which 'any mention of sex
or the common bodily functions was unthinkable,' her brother
Noel later recalled. 'We were not even expected to know that a
woman was pregnant. Even a word like "confined" was kept to a
whisper.'

Mark tried to understand, but the more urgent his entreaties, the
more Carrington shrank away.

Mark (London, 1915): I want *all* of you or nothing. I want you to
love me, to love me properly, or not at all . . . I want your body as

well as your mind. Whenever I've said anything else, I've been insincere or hysterical . . . The desire for the body in the case of real love is not low, but beautiful, and something quite different to the ordinary desire one has for a well made person . . . Words cannot express love, just as words cannot express painting. Each has its own medium. Painting expresses art and Physical contact love . . . Think about it and you will understand. When you realize that physical contact is the expression of love, you will then understand how people can marry people who seem to others so physically ugly. Because it is not the outward form that they are embracing, but all that goes to make up that which they love . . . You have never really told me why you don't want physical contact. Why is it? Write to me plainly. Am I repulsive to you? But surely in that case you can't love me . . . Is it simply perhaps because you don't want children? Then we should not have them like many other couples?

Carrington (Andover, 1915): When you talked to me about it at Gilberts, and said you loved my friendship, were you hysterical and insincere? Yes I know that your real love is "beautiful and not low". Do not think I ever doubted that. Only I *cannot* love you as you want me to. You must know one could not do, what you ask, sexual intercourse, unless one does love a man's body. I have never felt any desire for that in my life . . . I do love you, but not in the way you want. You made love to me in your studio . . . one thing I can never forget, it made me inside feel ashamed, unclean. Can I help it? I wish to God I could. Do not think I rejoice in being sexless, and am happy over this. It gives me pain also. Whenever you feel you want my friendship and company, it will *always* be here. You know that. This is all I can say . . . You said, 'remember that I would sacrifice all for you, my very life, if you asked it of me.' You write this and yet you cannot sacrifice something less than your life for me. I do not ask it of you. But it would make me happy if you could. Do not be angry with me for having written as I have. And please do not write back. There can be nothing more to say. Unless you can make this one sacrifice for me. I will do everything I can to be worthy of it.

Mark (London, 1 July 1915): How dreadfully disappointing and inconsiderate you are very often. You are a sort of person with

whom one never gets beyond a certain point of intimacy, or if one
for a moment oversteps the boundary line, one finds that you have
immediately rushed back, leaving one alone gaping. You are in
some ways amazingly inhuman.

Mark (Cholesbury, July 1915): I cannot bear the thought of only
looking forward to seeing you occasionally. Therefore you must
live with me or promise to do so, or I must free myself from
you ... If by any chance, I get weak again and want you to take
me back, you *must not* do so. Please, for my sake. Let this at last be
the real end ... You can come and see my work whenever you
want to. I shall always be pleased to show it you. *Don't* write
anything back now; *unless* you can make up your mind to live with
me some time. I could wait any time if you promised. Also we
could live together *without sex*. Oh! What do I care for sex. It's
your constant companionship that I want so frightfully. Forgive me,
I am terribly sorry, I have struggled my hardest for your sake. I shall
never come back to you now as before. If the desire to come back
as before, masters me, I shall kill myself rather than give way to it.

Carrington (1 November 1915): Be happy, little onion.

Mark (London, 27 February 1916): Try to help me out of myself,
out of my petty vulgar mean little self.

Carrington (London, April 1916): You are too possessive – and I too
free. That is why we could never live together.

Carrington met Lytton Strachey in November 1915. At first she
found him distinctly unappealing – 'a horrid old man with a beard'
– and having no idea what a homosexual could be, was shocked
when a friend explained. But her initial disapproval of 'a man so
contemptible as that' quickly gave way to admiration and liking
and then gradually to love. His mind was packed with all kinds of
fascinating learning and his ideas and comments on life and literature
were exciting and stimulating; as one of the inner circle of the
brilliant group, the 'Bloomsburys', whom she had hitherto
admired at a distance, he brought her into close contact with
people such as Leonard and Virginia Woolf, Clive and Vanessa
Bell, Roger Fry and Maynard Keynes. Above all he was a delightful
and amusing companion, kind, witty and gay. Although he was
not particularly affectionate, being cool and astringent rather than

warm, his very detachment was a relief after the storms of her relationship with Mark; with Strachey she felt she could forget her sexual inadequacies and lavish affection upon him without fear of invoking any problems.

As she slowly, and almost without realizing it, fell in love with him she found herself able to confide in him, and Strachey thus received detailed accounts of the events between herself and Mark, and the attitude of others to the affair, as when she wrote from Garsington: 'I was dismal enough about Mark and then suddenly without any warning Philip* after dinner asked me to walk round the pond with him and started without any preface, to say, how disappointed he had been to hear I was a virgin. How wrong I was in my attitude to Mark, and then proceeded to give me a lecture for quarter of an hour! Winding up by a gloomy story of his brother who committed suicide. Ottoline then seized me on my return to the house and talked for one hour and a half in the asparagrass bed, on the subject, far into the dark night.'

For his part Strachey, not realizing how strong her attachment to him was growing, was at first amused by his new disciple and passively willing to be adored.

* Philip Morrell.

CHAPTER 24

'A claw with dreadful long nails'

To Mark, Carrington's behaviour became more and more and more unaccountable. She said she loved him, yet saw him seldom and took holidays with others. Nothing could be less alarming to him than her friendship with Strachey, a homosexual twice her age, but Mark missed her, and, himself incapable of deceit, was tormented by the contradictions between her loving letters and her evasive actions.

As 1916 wore on, this torment grew worse. When, in November, they began to have sexual intercourse it was already too late for them to find happiness together. Although Mark could not know it, Carrington had been seduced, not by desire for him, but by her feelings for Strachey, and by the sophisticated ideas and outlook of his circle of friends. Difficulties of adjustment, problems of contraception, which wholehearted love and desire on Carrington's part could have made light of, became disgusting and crippling.

Throughout this miserable year the confusions and contradictions of the affair were indicated in their letters, which they exchanged every few days.*

Carrington to Strachey (Andover, 20 April 1916) (arranging a meeting with him): Perhaps on Euston platform at ten o'clock on Saturday. Incredible internal excitement.
Carrington to Mark (Andover, 22 April 1916): How good it is that everything is alright again. I am longing to see you again. Like a hungry person who has been waiting for a meal a long time. I went a long walk Thursday onto the wild common. It was such a perfect evening. What a rotten system it is that you should not be here with me . . . We will see a great deal of each other now.
Mark to Carrington (London, April 1916): It will give me the *greatest*

* This chapter contains a small selection of passages.

pleasure to keep the relationship as *you* want it, as then I shall have an opportunity of showing how great my love for you is!

Carrington to Mark (London, 16 May 1916): We are going to be so happy next week. If it's fine I will spend a long day at Kew with you. You will not love me in vain. I shall not disappoint you in the end. But I wish I could see some things more clearly.

Carrington to Mark (Garsington, 19 May 1916) (after a quarrel following a flirtatious kiss between Carrington and Cannan): I care so little for anything except making you happy that I will promise not to kiss anyone since it causes you pain . . . but do you not see that you cast a cloud of doubt on our trust in each other by thinking for one moment that anything else or anyone could interrupt it? We shall always live in one sense apart. But I feel we will always come back to each other. There is nothing, absolutely nothing which can affect us now . . . You must cease being miserable at once, and believe me. What do I care for anyone else? . . . I feel so happy now things are clear again. So that we can really get on. It has felt like a lock on the river, with our two boats up against the lock. Now, it is open, and we can rush so swiftly down the river.

Carrington to Mark (Garsington, May 1916): Are you happy now because I love you? . . . tell me what you are doing and how you feel towards me. Even although I am certain and love you also.

Mark to Carrington (London, 20 May 1916): I am depressed just now because I am feeling all over again the isolation of my spirit. I cannot make people understand me or my work, neither can I understand them. The best thing that happens is between us . . . You ask me if I am happy now you love . . . Your Love is so unusual and difficult to understand; . . . You ask me how I feel towards you. Well, I will tell you. As always I love you . . . You are not able to return me an equal love and for that I hate life. What is the good of having this depth of feeling if no one wants or understands it! I paint pictures that seem to me wonderful but no one understands them; I love but no one wants my love! Forgive me again please; perhaps I exaggerate in your case.

Mark to Carrington (30 May 1916): If only I could believe in you more, all would be different, but I can't. You do and say things which disprove the whole. One small detail can upset the whole for me. Besides, physically I am no use to you – you would hate me. I have a small wretched skinny knotty stringy body, worn out by continual nervous strain. All my limbs speak of my wretched life. You alone have tormented me for five years and now after all that time I find you unsatisfactory. Please leave me, I cannot bear any more. *I have a reason for writing this letter.* It is not just out of my head. I feel now so tired and ill that I can't think how I will go on living.

Carrington to Mark (Garsington, 31 May 1916): Do you not see an island in the middle of a big lake? Many islands of adventures which one must swim across to? But one will always return to the mainland. You are that mainland to me. I will leave you sometimes perhaps, but always I shall come back . . . This world is so big and full of surprises but the great thing is an implicit faith in you, and a greater love for you than mankind. Do you never feel the excitement of this big world, and ships, and many people? . . . I will not fail you. Do not fear. But I am human also. You have had phases and moods. I also am mortal and am like unto you. I may have had phases also. You must never be surprised or distressed because you know I shall come through and we are in the whole part together.

Mark to Carrington (2 June 1916): I am miserable because in trying to help you out of your wretchedness last night, I feel that I only succeeded in being nasty to you. I did not know how to help you, I only felt with all my being a desire to help you. I shall in future study your moods.

Mark to Koteliansky (London, 11 June 1916): I hope you have not been miserable much. I of course have gone through my usual wretchedness. But I am sick of complaining. Life has been to me like a claw with dreadful long nails. When I was a child and first became conscious, the claw only touched my flesh with its pointed nails. As I grew older, it dug its nails deeper into me and as I grow older still, it digs its nails deeper and deeper into my flesh.

Mark to Koteliansky (Garsington, 20 June 1916): But I am tired, tired of speaking of my eternal worry. You know what it is. It gets more and more complicated with C. I am so tired and worn out some moments I can scarcely stand. And I have to pretend I am happy here. If only the torment would end. It is like a terrible disease and incurable. We both put our heads together to try to end it, but we can't. It goes on in spite of our both being tired and worn out. But I will not write about it any more, because it has neither beginning nor end.

Carrington to Strachey (London, 5 August 1916): We had tea at Eleanor [Wittering,] and swam in the warm sea. Even Mark came in. Looking very absurd, in a bathing dress.

Carrington to Mark (Andover, August 1916): I *have* been happy with you. Wittering was a very wonderful time for me, and all through you . . . how much I loved being with you in those fields, and for showing me so much . . . What a long time it seems already since I saw you! No sentimental phrases but you know what I do not write.

Lady Ottoline Morrell to Mark (Garsington, 8 August 1916): Carrington is like some strange wild beast – greedy of life and of tasting all the different 'worms' that she can find without giving herself to any mate. Sometimes I wonder if she ever will find a mate that fulfils all she desires. I wish she would concentrate more on her work. But I hope she will soon – for after all nothing is so important as that. It would get her proportions straight . . . I love Carrington too and you. I hope you will always tell me anything you feel like and when you feel like it.

Carrington to Mark (August 1916, on holiday in North Wales with Strachey and two friends): I am most happy here. Just Lytton, Barbara [Hiles] and Nicholas [Bagenal] . . . What a perfect time we had at Wittering. It amazed me afterwards when I thought it over . . . I miss you. The intimacy we got at lately makes other relationships with people strangely vacant, and dull . . . How annoying it is to be able to write so little of what I want to you. But it always seems rather false directly I put it down. But you must believe much more now by what I have felt with you.

Carrington to Mark (North Wales, August 1916): Lytton sends his love. You must like him, because I do, so very much.

Mark to Carrington (Cholesbury, 15 August 1916): What you say is so true, about how all other relationships besides our own intimacy seem lifeless. How well I feel that. But you must be happy and enjoy yourself where you are, as I am always with you in spirit – I never leave you for a moment. I am always talking to you and I have never loved you more and felt more thankful to you or more happy. I daren't say how happy I am and my happiness is solely due to our wonderful friendship. Nothing else matters, everything else is subsidiary to it and could not exist without it . . . The country sounds wonderful . . . My *love* to Lytton.

Carrington to Mark (North Wales, August 1916): I do feel that you do not appreciate Lytton very much. Probably as you say because that other objection comes so much always before you. I have altered my views about that, and think one always has to put up with something.

Mark to Carrington (London, *circa* 1916): I am deeply disappointed to find that you are still as casual as ever about engagements, unable to keep them. I really could not face another engagement with you for the present, to be uncertain all day and then to be left alone with eggs and fruit!

Carrington to Strachey (Andover, 1 September 1916) (after their return from Wales and Bath): I did enjoy myself so much with you, you do not know how happy I have been, everywhere, each day so crowded with wonders . . . dear Lytton. I have been so happy, incredibly happy! Quelque fois je voudrais être un garcon de moulin! votre niece Carrington.

Mark to Carrington (London, 1 September 1916): Thanks very much for the Donne poem. I like it very much, but there are some others I like even better. I read all Donne and Marvell at the Mill, also Shakespeare's sonnets. I like them all. But Donne impressed me immensely. But how wonderful Marvell's 'To His Coy Mistress' is. It nearly made me weep . . . If you have it . . . you *must* read it carefully . . . It is only given to lovers to experience that most ecstatic of emotions, the exchange of souls, or to make two souls into one, for one moment of ecstasy by love! I am a lover myself, so I know that ecstasy from perception. I have never actually felt it myself, because I am a lover without a partner. I, like Moses, have only been shown the "promised land". But that was a torture rather than a pleasure, for having seen that wonderful country, I long to live in it. All else, friendship, seems cold in comparison. But enough of that! . . . I find you such an inspiring person to know. Without you all my life would collapse – like a punctured balloon.

Carrington to Mark (Andover, 3 September 1916): Could you

possibly get me a Marvell? I should like one so much!... I am excited over everything lately. The fullness of life. So many people alive whom one doesn't know, so many wonders past which one finds everyday and then the things to come. Oh the wonder of it all!

Mark (London, 4 September 1916) (unsent letter): Who are you that I love? I don't know. Ought I not rather to hate than love a creature that tortures me so?... I hate and love you terribly. You are furthest from me and nearest to me of all living creatures.

God, I ask only one thing of you – one little tiny prayer. Let me love and be loved. Create an inseparable bond between some being and myself. God, I am lonely – so lonely... Help me to break down the hard granite of my prison. Then I will sharpen my axe and do likewise to my neighbour's prison...

Carrington... oh! you are an artful Devil! How cleverly you evade all the important Questions in my letters... Cold, Cold Girl!... When I kiss you so lovingly, so tenderly, you are still cold, you even speak at the moment of my love making in a dry intellectual manner. Oh! How can you...

God save me from this Hell that I have been living in for so long. Save me soon, I can't bear it much longer! Your body seems most beautiful to me. Most painfully I long for it. In the spring I once asked you suddenly, 'When are we going to be lovers?' – You said in the Summer! But later again you looked at the idea as some impossibly far off thing...

Ugh! Ugh! How I hate the coldness of life! It is not your fault Carrington. Life is so arranged. Life has made you cold... Your ego has never been surpassed! You are frightened – frightened always, of soiling yourself! You are always writing to me of the bigness of the world, the many people – freedom – many ships on the sea – etc; etc;... But my poor virgin. You have known *no* man yet!... What's the good of your cherishing these 'modern' ideas of many men etc., if you have not had one yet! Know *one* first. Know me – Love me, then if you want many more go to them afterwards. How could I keep you!

Carrington to Mark (Andover, September 1916): Thank you indeed for the Marvell books! How glad I am to have them... It seemed so long since I had heard from you. I love that poem

14—MG * *

'To His Coy Mistress'. It is difficult to stand up against such poetic persuasion! Donne and Marvell together may bring about my fall. Who knows? . . .

[At Garsington] I went out into the garden . . . Katherine [Mansfield] and I wore trousers. It was wonderful being alone in the garden. Hearing the music inside, and lighted windows, and feeling like two young boys – very eager. The moon shining on the pond, fermenting, covered with warm slime.

How I hate being a girl. I must tell you for I have felt it so much lately. More than usual. And that night I forgot for almost half an hour in the garden. And felt other pleasures, strange, and so exciting, a feeling of all the world being below me to choose from. Not tied – with female encumbrances, and hanging flesh.

Write to me soon again. If I find many more poems by Donne urging me to forsake my virginity I may fall by next spring, when the sun is hot once more.

I think he is a man of such rare wisdom that I take his words very seriously. Far more so, than Philip and Ottoline and all these worthies with good intentions. But I ought not to write this to you. As my moods vary like a sky of clouds! But my love. May I have a . . . photograph?

Mark to Carrington (London, 2 November 1916): What wonderful times we've had, more wonderful than ever! . . . Our love has been and is nothing less than a classic, so wonderful is it. What a book it really could make! How can people ever know what goes on between us on Mondays! Heavens! how wonderful it all is!! . . . we ought in fact rejoice in having found each other . . . But above all do not be afraid of hurting me. You cannot now – I love you too much. So let yourself be free – do everything you want to. What we have between us no person or thing can touch. It does not matter when we start – tomorrow or next year – or never! It does not interest me! What a fool I was to think all these years that that was what I wanted! I have lost all interest in it except as a natural physical necessity.

Carrington to Mark (London, *circa* November 1916) (after they have begun, for the first time, to have sexual intercourse): I do care so much now, as you know . . . You must get that other thing as well – or I will not . . .

Carrington to Strachey (London, 10 December 1916): Next week I am going to stay with the Jew at Cholesbury. Gilbert has lent him his castle for a week. He is going to ask you to come down on Wednesday or Thursday for a day or so. You will come?

Carrington to Mark (London, *circa* December 1916): If you come tomorrow evening . . . please do not make love to me. Leave it all until we go to the country. As it distresses me sometimes rather.

Carrington to Mark (London, December 1916): Do you miss me very much already? . . . I read Marloe again last night and knew what one thing meant more than I did last week! It certainly is a necessity if one wants to understand the best poets.

Carrington to Mark (London, December 1916): I only like sugar* sometimes, not every week and every day in my coffee . . . I think you would like it so much and take it so often in your coffee that you wouldn't taste anything in time, and miss the taste of the coffee. But darling I shall look after that alright, and only allow you three lumps a month. You've had more than three for this month, So no more till next year.

Carrington to Mark (Andover, December 1916): I am sorry if I have annoyed you lately about that business, and making such a fuss. It is only my inability to really get interested I am afraid. And really I did try that thing, only it was much too big, and wouldn't go inside no matter what way I used it!

Mark to Carrington (London, December 1916): My dearest and most beautiful girl, How happy I was to get your letter this morning! . . . I never quite knew how very beautiful you were! . . . I must see you *very* often. I shan't worry you for much 'sugar' if only I can see you and talk – I must, I must.

Mark to Carrington (London, December 1916): How I hate your 'advanced' philosopher self! . . . you have lately added hateful parts to yourself . . . A person really in love is *not* advanced. I loathe your many ships idea. I may yet tear myself away from you – then you can have your beastly ships . . . Those ideas of yours – got from people who never loved . . . Some moments I wish one of us dead! Also you would not call love-making 'vulgar' if you were in love. You would not arrange for it only to happen three times a month. You would want to see me more. But all these things – my

* Code word for sexual intercourse.

undisturbed beauty – you don't understand. I hate you for three things:

1. Because you can't love passionately.
2. Because of your advanced ideas.
3. I hate you because I love you and am therefore in the power of your cruel, advanced and unpassionate self! But please remember dearest that I love you far more than before.

Carrington to Mark (London, December 1916) (he was spending a few days at Swanage): I have missed not seeing you ... Darling I do want you to come back again. We will have such good times. And I will be so much better to you ... I want so much there to be a very decent relationship between us, and so honest. It's not really quite sometimes is it?

You are good to me Mark – I am sure I would not be to anyone who had been so cruel and vile all these years. Lovingly yours.

CHAPTER 25

The Merry-Go-Round

In the early months of 1916, with no money from Marsh, no regular income, and suffering from severe headaches, Mark had pushed on with his painting in a kind of reckless despair, 'working hard on a large and very unsaleable picture of a Merry-Go-Round,' as he put it. His forebodings about its saleability were to prove only too well-founded, although years later many critics were to believe that it was his finest work. Reaching over six feet in height, the picture[193] was far larger than anything he had attempted before. To design on this scale was a real challenge, and Mark set out with great excitement to develop his theme – soldiers, sailors and civilians at the fair on Hampstead Heath.

'I feel this last year or so much surer with my work,' he wrote on 4 April to Rothenstein. 'I have never felt quite like it before. I live in a constant state of over-excitement, so much do my work and conception thrill me. It is almost too much for me and I am always feeling rather ill. Sometimes after a day's work I can hardly walk! One seems to work at the expense of one's body and there is no other way, apparently, of doing it. At any rate I can't find an easy way of working. However it is worth the sacrifice.' But his money was steadily running out; collectors were increasingly wary of advanced work. Augustus John, who advised several, had moved from indifference to disapproval: 'Mark Gertler's work has gone to buggery and I can't stand it,' he advised the rich American collector John Quinn. 'Not that he hasn't ability of a sort and all the cheek of a Yid, but the spirit of his work is false and affected.' (16 February 1916)

Even to the uncompromising Lawrence, Mark's rejection of Marsh's help now seemed over-scrupulous. 'You had better make your peace with Eddie,' he advised. (10 February 1916) But there was no going back to the old terms of intimacy and the regular allowance, and relations remained distant, though not unfriendly; Marsh sent five pounds for a picture and Mark tried to pay off his outstanding debt by sending more pictures. 'You should have received the painting and the drawing . . . I now owe you £39,' he wrote in April 1916, and asked Marsh to intercede for him with another potential buyer. Lawrence wrote, 'It amuses me that Eddie is beginning to rake in his debts.'

In May Mark told Strachey: 'Yesterday I drew my last £2; in about a week I shall be penniless. I hate with all my being the idea that money should so be able to influence my freedom. It is terrible to think that the more interesting my work becomes, the more difficult it becomes to sell it and to live! I only ask of life to be allowed to paint, to be allowed to dip deeper and deeper into the wonderful mysteries of art. But if one has no money the purity of one's art studies are spoilt, because one can't help thinking of what the *stupid* buyers would like, as one *must* live. That is *my* trouble. To be a good artist one must have an income. Believe me that is true. The starving artist in the garret is a thing of the past. To paint good pictures one must have a comfortable studio and *good* food – a garret and crust of bread isn't good enough. Let no person come and tell me that poverty is good for an artist! If an artist is poor he simply has to please, if not always then sometimes, the public, and the public doesn't know a picture from a broomstick! That's my experience anyhow.

'Please forgive me for thrusting my troubles at you and please don't be sorry for me. I shall get along somehow and what's more paint my pictures too! I shall paint what *I* like . . . I am *so* excited about the "Merry-Go-Round". It will be finished in a few weeks.'

Mark was more convinced than ever that, as he wrote, 'If I am to get something satisfactory out of life, it has to be from my work;' he assured Kot: 'The best thing I have found so far is *work*. I can bear anything as long as I am working.'

But unless he could get some money it would be impossible to go on. Already he was being forced to paint pot-boilers, he disclosed: 'I have hardly touched a brush for a fortnight. This for various reasons. Firstly I am almost penniless again, so that I had to leave my big picture in order to paint some small saleable things, and so trying to paint these I found that I really could not paint anything I don't want to paint with all my being. Besides my heart is in my "Merry-Go-Round".' (3 May 1916)*

He had sent six pictures to the March Friday Club. One or two were praised† but his financial plight had not been relieved.

To the June 1916 London Group exhibition he sent a picture of Cannan standing in front of his mill at Cholesbury.[185] By now the more progressive critics were accepting the idea of pictures making use of elements in nature to create a vision which need not actually look like the real world at all, and the *Westminster Gazette* critic

---

* Letter to Richard Carline. He added, 'However, yesterday, after a fortnight's delay I managed to start a picture of daffodils, and have got really interested in it, which means, probably that it will be too good to sell! It is an experiment. This lovely spring sunshine has given me new notions for colour, and in this flower picture I shall be able to try them.'

† 'For a life that is more vivid than any reality, for colour articulate and lyrical one turns to Mr Gertler's Still Life', said the *Westminster Gazette*. 'A piece of audacious fantasy, it is at the same time a texture completely realized and resolutely executed, a texture of solid forms and singing colours. In this remarkable picture he has taken theory in his stride and plunged serenely into feeling. Nothing else in the exhibition, though there is plenty of good work, has much interest beside it.'

recognized that 'Mr Gertler's picture is closely related to nature though it does not resemble it. With its personal style and emotion deeply felt, it is nature imaginatively realized in terms of the painter's feeling for colour and forms.'

The Times spotted a new element in Mark's work: 'It seems to be a caricature both of nature and man, but one cannot quite see the joke of it.' As a later critic, Sir John Rothenstein, was to point out, there was 'something of the character of a sophisticated and express-ive folk art' in the 'Mill' and 'Merry-Go-Round' pictures. 'It was as though life presented itself . . . less as a kind of reality perceptible to the ordinary eye than as a kind of puppet show at a fair.' In 'Cannan at his 'Mill' 'the odd man, beside his strange home, the upright converging Gothic forms, [were] all treated with a robust-ness, almost, one might say, a heartiness, that makes sinister over-tones.'[147] In fact, Gilbert Cannan was already beginning to suffer from the insanity which was soon to overcome him.

By the autumn, 'Merry-Go-Round' was finished.

The theme, like 'Swing Boats', had been inspired by the fair on the Heath which had given Mark such pleasure when he had started his new Hampstead life. But now the painting had nothing of the pleasure of life in it. The figures were reduced to puppets, little metal machines held in the harsh swirling design. As Sir John Rothenstein was to point out, 'The folk art figures express, although in a more sophisticated fashion, the brutality that the boisterous jollity of the traditional Punch scarcely masks.'

Mark had succeeded overwhelmingly in his effort to combine a realistic approach with new ideas of picture making. The 'Merry-Go-Round' was a far more compelling work of art despite its uncompromising ugliness and shrieking colours, than a typical 'New English' picture with its charm and beauty. With its harsh, flickering restlessness the painting seemed to be a comment on Mark's life in the various scenes through which he had passed – Whitechapel slum, young artist's Bohemia, fashionable society, the Garsington intelligentsia. It was impossible, too, to look at these mechanized soldiers going round and round without recalling the horrors of the deadlocked Western Front, where the war engine was now voraci-ously consuming men but getting nowhere. 'Lately the whole horror of the war has come freshly upon me,' Mark had written to Carrington.

'Oh Lord, Oh Lord, have mercy upon us!' Strachey wrote to Ottoline after seeing the picture. 'It is a devastating affair, isn't it? I felt that if I were to look at it for any length of time, I should be carried away suffering from shell shock. I admired it of course, but as for liking it, one might as well think of liking a machine-gun.'

Lawrence, to whom Mark sent a photograph, was deeply stirred: 'Your terrible and dreadful picture has just come,' he wrote. 'This is the first picture you have ever painted: it is the best *modern* picture I have seen: I think it is great, and true. But it is horrible and terrifying. I'm not sure I wouldn't be too frightened to come and look at the original. If they tell you it is obscene, they will say truly. I believe there was something in Pompeian art, of this terrible and soul-tearing obscenity. But then, since obscenity is the truth of our passion today, it is the only stuff of art – or almost the only stuff.

'I won't say what I, as a man of words and ideas, read in the picture. But I *do* think that in this combination of blaze, and violent mechanized rotation . . . and ghastly, utterly mindless human intensity of sensational extremity, you have made a real and ultimate reve-lation. I think this picture is your arrival – it marks a great arrival.

'Also I could sit down and howl beneath it like Kot's dog, in soul-lacerating despair. I realize *how* superficial your human rela-tionships must be, what a violent maelstrom of destruction and horror your inner soul must be. It is true, the outer life means nothing to you, really. You are all absorbed in the violent and lurid processes of inner decompositions: the same thing that makes leaves go scarlet and copper-green at this time of year. It is a terrifying coloured flame of decomposition, your inner flame. But dear God, it is a real flame enough, undeniable in heaven and earth . . .

'It would take a Jew to paint this picture. It would need your national history to get you here, without disintegrating you first. You are of an older race than I, and in these ultimate processes, you are beyond me, older than I am. But I think I am sufficiently the same, to be able to understand.

'This all reads awkward – but I feel there ought to be some other language than English, to say it in. And I don't want to translate you into ideas, because I can see you must, in your art, be mindless and in an ecstasy of destructive sensation. It is wrong to be conscious, for you: at any rate, to be too conscious. "By the waters of Babylon I sat me down and wept, remembering Jerusalem." At last your race is at an end – these pictures are its death-cry. And it will be left for the Jews to utter the final and great death cry of this epoch: the Christians are not reduced sufficiently. I must say, I have, for you, in your work, reverence, the reverence for the great articulate extremity of art.'

But Lawrence was worried about the violence and total commitment of Mark's assault upon life and work: 'Take care, or you will burn your flame so fast, it will suddenly go out. It is all spending and no getting of strength. And yet some of us must fling ourselves in the fire of ultimate expression, like an immolation. Yet one cannot assist at this auto-da-fé without suffering. But do try to save yourself as well. You must have periods of proper rest also. Come down here and stay with us, when you want a change. You seem to me to be flying like a moth into a fire. I beg you, don't let the current of work carry you on so strongly, that it will destroy you oversoon.

'You are twenty-five, and have painted this picture – I tell you, it takes three thousand years to get where your picture is – and we Christians haven't got two thousand years behind us yet.

'I feel I write stupidly and stiltedly, but I am upset, and language is no medium between us. With love from Frieda and me.

'P.S. I am amazed how the picture exceeds anything I had expected. Tell me what people *say* – Epstein, for instance. Get somebody to suggest that the picture be bought *by the nation* – it ought to be – I'd buy it if I had any money. How much is it? I want to know – how much do you want for it?' (9 October 1916)

Only Lawrence could have thought there was a chance of the picture being bought by the nation. For someone in Mark's position to depict soldiers in so unheroic and unpleasant a fashion was asking for trouble. His friends were alarmed.

St John Hutchinson, the barrister, who had experience of helping writers in conflict with the authorities, urged him not to show the painting publicly: 'I have been thinking over matters and I want to ask you whether you think you are quite wise in exhibiting the "Merry-Go-Round" at the London Group? It will of course raise a tremendous outcry; the old, the wise, the professional critic will go mad with anger and righteous indignation and what strikes me is that these symptoms may drive them to write all sorts of rubbish about German art or German artists in their papers and may raise the question acutely and publicly as to your position under conscription. I think if matters remain quiet you are quite safe, but I am rather afraid of what might happen if the matters got into the papers and were taken up by the public at large. I don't want to advise you, that would be impudent on my part – and of course nothing of what I imagine may take place – but I thought I might draw your attention to the question as it strikes me, so that whatever you may decide you will do after full judgement. Monty Shearman* and I thought that perhaps it would be rather fun to have a sort of little exhibition of your work at his room. We could of course ask all sorts and conditions of people – It might be worth thinking of?'

While Mark digested the advice that his pictures should be hidden and shown only in a hole-and-corner fashion to a selected few, another problem arose.

It looked as though he wouldn't have the choice of exhibiting the painting at the London Group anyway. 'Marchant, the owner of the Goupil Galleries where we held our annual shows, sent an ultimatum to the Group,' Allinson recorded. 'No enemy aliens, conscientious objectors or sympathizers with the enemy were permitted to exhibit in his galleries and should the Group contain any of these his walls would be closed to them. At a special meeting it was unanimously agreed that politics should be kept out of the domain of Art and the Group rejected Marchant's terms. Fortunately Mr Heal (now Sir Ambrose), whose premises offered the public a large selection of applied art from Central Europe, was less susceptible to passions raised by the war. He offered us the hospitality of his Mansard Gallery, which thus became our home for some years to come.'[148]

No work of Mark's was to hang in the London Group again until

*Montague Shearman, the barrister and picture collector.

the series of exhibitions at Heal's started in May 1917, but Mark then sent in the 'Merry-Go-Round'.

In the autumn of 1916 Monty Shearman, who had become very friendly and interested in Mark's pictures, stepped in with an offer of support: 'Dear Mark, Money is a horrible thing. I should like you to feel however that you can always have what you want from me if you like. But it must be as between friends and there must be no feelings of patronage or obligation whatever. I don't want to be a Conway or an Eddie Marsh, not that I am saying a word against Eddie Marsh who I am sure meant to be kind. But I am not, as you know, the sort of person who would give money and expect to take pictures instead. If I want a picture I would buy it outright. So if you would like me at any time to guarantee the extra room or rooms out, or the studio itself or any other thing you like, let me know. I am sure you would not ask for more than was necessary and I hope you would not mind accepting it, if it is necessary. If it isn't, so much the better, but if it is I can easily afford a bit and I think it would help your work, if you felt more comfortable.' (12 October 1916)

Shearman's admiration for Mark had been growing for some time. Later in the autumn he wrote, 'Your absolute independence and contempt of all fleeting and material things in life is always a source of admiration to me . . . I think you are infinitely greater and deeper in your moods than any Englishman I have met and when there is a contrast I prefer you to them.' (22 November 1916)

CHAPTER 26

'Why doesn't he paint?'

The completion of the 'Merry-Go-Round' left Mark in an unstable, restless state of mind.

While at Garsington in the summer he had started a painting of the pond which showed a change of mood from the harshness of 'Merry-Go-Round'. 'The Pond', quiet, poetic, was, as a critic of *The Times* put it, 'as vivid as something seen in a dream'.[194]

His efforts to find a point of balance between materialism and spirituality, ugliness and beauty, led him to formulate his ideas in a journal entry:

True Spirituality – 5 July 1916: 'True Spirituality does not come from Heaven; it grows from the earth heavenwards like a tree, and in order to live it must be rooted in the earth also like a tree. I do not believe in a person's spirituality, who has not some time or other sat firmly with his or her bum on the earth. The more spiritual a man is, the stronger must this backbone be. The spirituality of a man without backbone is like a cut flower, or a bubble; nice to look at but empty inside. When we look at a tree in blossom, and wonder at its loveliness, we must not forget that it springs from strong, ugly serpentlike roots, hidden from our sight in the earth, and that the lovely blossom could not exist without these ugly, ropy serpents, grovelling in the earth among the worms. It is the rose, and not the root of the rose, that smells so beautiful. Yet without the root, the rose could not be. And so it is with everything that matters in life, like Art and Love; primarily, they are strongly rooted in the earth.'

In August 1916 Mark arrived at Cholesbury for a fortnight's visit. There, for the first time, he began seriously wondering whether he could find a way of expressing himself in other arts besides painting. 'I don't understand the art of literature or poetry as I should like to,' he confessed to Carrington. 'I feel everything more and more through form and colour. Although I understand and feel music quite as much as my own art, when I come to literature I immediately feel it *not* as art but as *thought*. . .*

'Of course I get a *great, great* deal from literature and poetry; the *thought*, the psychology of the people in Dostoievsky's books interest and excite me enormously. I may yet get hold of the *art* of literature and as you know I have great desire to write myself, but I shan't do so until I discover for myself the art of it.

'As for my philosophy, I am excited about it and believe what I have written absolutely. I would like to tell you now that I feel, if I live long enough, I shall do not only important painting but also sculpture and writing! I even sometimes get ideas in sound!!!... Every now and then a vision of a huge and wonderfully coloured piece of sculpture comes before me. It dazzles me and makes my blood run cold . . . My inspirations are dear to me, though painful! I must stop. I can't write any more – I am full to a bursting point. I must control myself or I shall destroy myself, through mere abundance of feeling.' (15 August 1916)

A few days later he was writing: 'Some moments I long for London and work. I find it very hard to go idle. When I am not working hard at my art, I begin to be critical about life and sure enough there is much to be critical about. I then get very, very miserable. There have been times here even when I have been un-utterably bored! If I hadn't my art, I could not possibly go on living. However, I have it and therefore I must not grumble . . .

'My feelings for Dostoievsky grow stronger and stronger. I have taken up 'The Idiot' again. Heavens, how wonderful it is. What a great man he was to write such books. I get so excited when reading him that my heart beats with a thud and I feel my flesh fall away from my bones. I can read nothing after him . . . He is my Shakespeare. I worship him.

---

* 'It's the *thought*, the *idea* that matters to me,' he added, 'but I don't feel satisfied because I know there *must* be something else – *the* 'something' that I feel so well in plastic art and in music. The *only* time I've ever felt it in literature was in the Song of Solomon and even in other parts of the Old Testament, but in no other literature. You see, I can't even feel the art of Shakespeare. But I suppose it is difficult, too much to expect almost, to understand all three arts?'

'I read my philosophy to Gilbert. He liked it very much and also a poem I've written – some time ago – in a light-hearted mood.' (20 August 1916)

But he refused to send it to Carrington: 'I am sorry but I can't send you my poem; I am too sensitive about it. I only read what I have written to Gilbert, because I wanted to see what kind of effect it would have on a literary man. Otherwise what I write is really only for myself, especially this poem, which is only a light sort of thing and not worth troubling about, I assure you. I may read it to you some time in the future.' (24 August)

A little later he told her he had begun to write down the impact which had been made on him by Currie's death and had completed another poem; 'It was so exciting and painful to do. Last night it kept me awake all night; at last I had to get out of bed and write a verse of it that kept singing in my head! Today, therefore I am feeling worn out, but I am pleased to have expressed a thought in writing. In fact I am excited and pleased with my poem! I dare say it's technically all wrong and bad poetry, but I don't care as long as I have expressed a thought of *my own* and that I know I *have* done.

'I have read parts of my diary and the beginning of my 'Currie' chapter to Gilbert. He was impressed and certain bits he said "were very good bits of writing".'

The 'light' poem which Mark wouldn't send Carrington was called simply 'Poem, August 1916':

> If my love were not impassioned,
>   or could with will be moderate,
> I could bask, in pleasant friendships'
>   lukewarm sun, contentedly:
> But Love's beauty once perceived,
>   mere friendship can no longer satiate:
> So when I saw your love's immensity,
>   iron-coffined by virginity,
> Pain turned my love into hate.
>
> Hatred sprung from too great love,
>   From perception, then desire,
> Of your great love's intensity:

From possessor's greed, from your alcove,
that shrouded you from all embracing love's eternity:
    From your bolted door, virginity,
Ever mocking, mocking from above.

From too great love I hated you,
    I hated your virginity:
And hatred soon, my devillish lips
    began to screw,
Artfully, to kill all incongruity,
    Into a butterfly of blood red hue.

Then hovered it revengefully,
    Oh! disguised devil,
Above your flower, and then around,
    then lower, lower, its circles made,
Until on level;
    Alighting then, as if innocently
a pretty rose had found,
    Not honey then, but your blood
it sucked, that my virgin rooted devil.

So did your cherished virginity,
    Turn God into Devil,
Love to Hate, Desire to Pain, by futility:
So was Love forged into Hate,
    on coy virginity's anvil;
So murdered cruel virginity,
    all embracing love's immensity!

In the autumn Mark started a play, and in a letter to Kot on 29 December, he confided his intention of taking up writing in earnest: 'I now seriously mean to express a great many of my thoughts in writing. Some of my feelings cannot be expressed in painting. So I will write also. It is so exciting and so relieving. What does it matter after all if I do it badly as long as I express a little bit of what I feel. Besides it is just a safety valve – a relief. Well I must stop now as Gilbert is walking up and down as 'a lost fart', as we say in Yiddish, and he is getting on my nerves.'

Mark returned to London on 1 September, with several burning questions: Should he write, paint, or do sculpture? Was his experimental mood a new beginning, or was his talent failing? 'Now I am back I really don't know what sort of work I am going to do,' he told Carrington. 'My sculptural conceptions have thrown me into a chaos and painting into the background.' (1 September)

There were formidable difficulties with sculpture: he had no technical training, and even should he succeed, and create anything worth while, would people take him seriously as a sculptor? The signs were not promising. Lawrence wrote: 'Perhaps you are right about sculpture – I don't know – probably you are, since you feel so strongly. Only, somehow, it seems to me to be going too far – over the edge of endurance into a form of incoherent, less poignant shouting. I say this, trying to imagine what this picture will be like, in sculpture. But you know best.' (9 October 1916)

Nevertheless Mark decided to go ahead with an idea for a group of acrobats, modelled in clay.[195] 'I am doing a small model in plasticine for my "Acrobats",' he said in September. 'So far it goes well, although the technical difficulties are most worrisome. There are hundreds of little things I don't know which I ought to know.' Help and advice came from two friends – Miss Berry and Mary Randolf Craig – and later in the month he wrote 'I have done my small model and am now about to start the full sized one in clay,' and talked about his 'most exciting world of sculpture.'

Another idea was for a sculpture inspired by his 'Merry-Go-Round.' This time he decided to try carving rather than modelling. On 30 November he sent an account of his aim to Carrington: 'Sculpture is certainly a great art – but it needs almost more patience than we "moderns" have got, and a badly finished statue is much worse than a sketchy painting. I am now working on my carving of the "Merry-Go-Round"; if it goes well it will be a beautiful thing, but it is a greater job than I thought and will take a long time.'

Still Lawrence lacked enthusiasm: 'Looking in a dictionary the other day I saw, "*Sculpture*: the lowest of the arts." That surprised me very much – but I think perhaps it is true. Sculpture, it seems to me, is truly a part of architecture. In my novel there is a man – not you, I reassure you – who does a great granite frieze for the top of a factory, and the frieze is a fair, of which your whirligig, for example, is part . . . Painting is so much subtler than sculpture, that I am sure it is a finer medium. But one wants the unsubtle, the obvious, like sculpture, as well as the subtle . . .' (5 December 1916)

Yet Mark's vision intensified. In December, while staying with Monty Shearman at Swanage, he found that all the different coloured rocks kept suggesting sculpture to him. On the 29th he talked about 'huge rocks and quarries, chunks of beautiful stone everywhere. I wish I could carry a lump of stone home with me for carving in . . . I am doing at home a drawing for a wood carving which, if I am not hindered by lack of craft from carrying it out, ought to be very wonderful.'

It was clear, however, that sculpture would be even more difficult to sell than large paintings like the 'Merry-Go-round'. 'Nobody wants to buy my sculpture and I have nearly come to the end of my £60,' he told Carrington on 31 December. 'So soon, I shall be hard up myself and it will be very difficult for me to get money as long as I do sculpture . . .' In the New Year the pace of his work quickened. Progress was reported in letters to Carrington during January.*

'I have at last managed to get the wood I want and am just off to the East End to get it cut in a neighbouring saw mill. They will cut off for me all the unnecessary chunks, which will save me time and trouble.'

* In odd moments, new ideas for painting were also born: 'I have been overcome with my "Nude" idea, which has suddenly become clear to me' he wrote. 'I have started a small design for it in pencil. It is to be a good old fashioned "Cézannish" Bathing scene, but I am very excited about it – the opportunities are immense for drawing and colour; I shall revel in the drawing of the nudes. The background is to be based on my "Pond" picture. So now I am full of these two things, the carving and the Bathing Scene. How I should love to make studies of *you* for my picture instead of having models! But you are so busy aren't you? . . . My biggest trouble just now is *money* – I have practically no money!'

15—MG * *

'Yesterday I came tearing back here from the East End with my log of wood, which was so heavy that I nearly collapsed on the way! But I bore the burden bravely! and proudly! I started work on it immediately and worked till bedtime! Oh! the excitement! the muscles of my arms ached so when I finished. I had to saw out middle bits and the plank is four inches thick.[149] Still I don't know if I shall be able to carry it out, through ignorance of the craft of wood carving. How I wish I could, because my conception is such a good one – about the best thing I have done. If I fail I shall turn sadly towards my picture,[150] but I shall feel like a defeated man. God! You can't think how hard it is to carve a subtle thing, out of a large rough square piece of wood! Especially when one is ignorant of the craft . . . But I love it in spite of all the difficulties, because it is the only thing that is keeping me going through all this wretched period that I have been passing lately.'

But defeat lay ahead, and Mark could see it coming: 'My money is coming to an end,' he told Carline, 'and people, even some of my best friends, think my sculpture only a *phase*, which they would be glad to see the end of! You can't think how this irritates me! "Why doesn't he paint", they say! They will not understand that it is a *natural* and *necessary* development and that it is a *real passion* that makes me do it. So in my sculpture I am even more isolated than before in my painting.' (22 January 1917)

'Acrobats' was finished and painted blue and yellow. But when Mark exhibited it in the Spring 1917 London Group show, the general opinion of the critics was that it was just a toy. 'Quaint' decided the *Globe*; an 'Entertaining and Amusing [toy]' thought *Colour* magazine. As a last effort Mark later spent twenty-two pounds on getting it cast in bronze: 'the expense will ruin me, but I *must* have it in bronze,' he wrote. (July 1917) Then he had to admit defeat, and gave up the idea of going on seriously with sculpture.

The carving of the 'Merry-Go-Round' disappeared. But 'Acrobats' was to find a place in the Tate Gallery, and a future critic, Professor Quentin Bell, was to describe it as 'a superb piece of sculpture', and say that as a sculptor Mark had 'astonishing gifts'.

CHAPTER 27

Louis

'We have always felt an artistic temperament must be an uncomfortable possession,' said *Outlook* on 16 December 1916, 'but never has the belief been quite so irresistibly forced upon us as after reading Gilbert Cannan's odd, brilliant study of a Jewish artist.'

Mendel had finally appeared and instantly became famous. Henceforth Mark was to be constantly irritated by reviews of his work which began, 'Mark Gertler, who of course is the hero of *Mendel*.' So much of the book was true that it was difficult to deny the distortions. Cannan had listened carefully to Mark's witty caricatures and flights of fancy about his friends and patrons, and then set down, in some cases, only the most unflattering characteristics, with some of his own inventions thrown in. Rothenstein, for example, emerged as a most unpleasant figure – yet Mark had only the previous year written to this now rather neglected artist saying, 'My dear Rothenstein . . . I always appreciate the help I received from you during the early part of my career. I have never ceased to be grateful to you.'*

When Rothenstein protested about the book Mark reassured him that his early help had been 'one of the most wonderful experiences of my life', and that the book was 'cheap trash . . . an awful and distorted affair' that he had 'never ceased to blush over'.

But some of the descriptions were shrewd. Carrington was 'Just an English girl with all the raw feeling bred out of her . . . True to type: impulsive without being sensual, kind without being affectionate.'

Everyone was annoyed. 'How angry I am over Gilbert's book!'

* The letter began, 'I have been meaning to write to you ever since our conversation at the Grafton Galleries – apropos of the younger generation of artists not writing to their elders. All I want to say on our behalf is that if we do not write it does not mean that we do not appreciate older artists . . . If ever you feel like it, I should be very pleased if you would come to tea.'

Carrington wrote. 'Everywhere this confounded gossip, and servant-like curiosity. It's ugly, and so damned vulgar. People cannot be vulgar over a work of art, so it *is* Gilbert's fault for writing as he did. . . .' (1 November 1916) Shearman found it fascinating and disgusting. Only Lawrence, who had lost so many friends by putting them into books, was tolerant: 'We had *Mendel*,' he told a friend, 'Gertler lent us his copy . . . Gertler, Jew-like, has told every detail of his life to Gilbert – Gilbert has a lawyer's memory and has put it all down – and so ridiculously when it comes to the love affair. We never recognized ourselves – or Frieda – but now I remember she must be Mrs Lupton – or whatever it was – wife of an artist. I only glanced through the book.' (2 December 1916)

Lawrence agreed with Mark that the book was bad as a work of art: 'I looked into *Mendel*,' he said to Kot. 'It is, as Gertler says, journalism; statement without creation. This is very sickening. if Gilbert had taken Gertler's story and recreated it into art, good. But to set down all these statements is a vulgarizing of life itself.'

But the main outline of Mark's life came through and gave some parts of the book a compelling power. *New Witness* wrote, 'Throughout the story of the young painter's struggles, one is conscious that at the back of all his attempts there lies a blank; he is a man without roots, the child of a race without a country, whose aspirations, shorn of that loyalty which we call patriotism, can find no outlet in the Ghetto, and is yet unable to accept or understand the ideals which actuate the Christian people among whom he lives . . . A tragic portrait of the young Jew, for whom the law and the prophets are barren, but who cannot discover the fount of the waters of life.'

'Louis', said the reviewer in the *New Witness*, 'ranges far and wide in his search for money, and voyages to America; but he always returns to Golda, the wife of his youth, and his fidelity redeems the sordidness of his outlook, the rank materialism of his philosophy. Golda was his wife; in her he was bound more firmly to his race and his faith, and there was no need to look beyond: he was rooted . . .'

Outlook was also impressed by the character of Louis, 'with his fierce pride and his appalling poverty, and his fanatical belief in his own faith.'

Gilbert Cannan himself had been behaving oddly for some time. In January 1917 came the first signs of serious trouble. 'Gilbert is ill and is at present in a nursing home,' Mark told Carrington. 'I went to see him last Saturday and am going again tomorrow. He has had a bad nervous collapse.' Later he sent another report: 'Gilbert is worse and Mary terribly upset and I am very sorry for both of them.' (January 1917)

Cannan's letters grew more and more incoherent: 'My dear old Mark . . . I'm in a very queer condition, terribly weak physically, but with such a mental and spiritual clarity as I never had, and the terrible unceasing effort to get it has produced the growing indifference to anything else which looks to outsiders like sheer madness . . . Poor little Mary has lost her head in her turn, but it will all work itself out in time.' Another letter pleaded, 'Don't be worried over the bursting of the cloud of insanity that has been growing and growing in me until now when I have emerged sane and in my right mind. The facts are appalling but they simply are not open to moral judgement. I have been right through the whole Hell of it and the story is more mysterious and terrible than anyone can guess, and I want to tell you, for I am only just now in possession of the facts of my life.'

In *Mendel* Cannan had described Louis and Golda as 'eternally together, in an affection that never found any expression, harsh and bitter but strongly savoured, like everything else in their lives.'

Louis was unaware that his life and character were being dissected in public: he was dying. His former strength, sapped by a life of privation, had finally collapsed under the combined effects of several ailments. Efforts to move to healthier surroundings outside London had been forestalled by Government restrictions: to his adopted country he was still an alien. When the end came on 5 February the doctor hazarded a conjecture on the cause of death as (1) chronic bronchitis, three years, and (2) heart failure. He was sixty years old.

'My father died last Monday at six o'clock – a few hours after I left him', Mark told Carrington. 'He was buried yesterday in the Jewish burial ground at East Ham. It is the custom among Jews, for the family of deceased to sit "Shiva" in the house where the person died. This means, that the family sit on low stools for a week, say special prayers, and also the men are not allowed to shave for a month. I shall have to keep this up to some extent for the sake of my mother and also because I somehow want to. I shall not shave, probably for a week, and shall be going down to my people every day for that time to mourn with them.'

The letters of condolence took the usual tone, except for Lawrence's, which urged Mark to think of himself: 'Take care not to be knocked up. These things do one a good deal of damage inside. To think of oneself, and cherish one's flame of life, is very necessary.' Mark's reply was such that Lawrence said to Kot later, 'I *do* hope Gertler is better. His letter was so painful I couldn't write about it.'

To Carrington Mark explained, 'Your letter this morning gave me new life ... To see my mother, whom I love so much, in such misery, crying and wailing aloud, over the coffin that contained my father and her companion for over forty years, was a sight that nearly broke my spirits for ever. However I am glad to say that I comforted her quite a lot; as hard as she clung to the coffin, so hard did I cling to her, declaring my passionate love to her and kissing her with all my might. But Dear Carrington it was terrible; never shall I forget this moment and certain other moments of this black week. The thought of my mother upsets me to the core – I can't bear it: And my brothers – they suffered silently, but awfully. I tell you these terrible things so that you may know why I am so unhappy. But how good it was to see your dear self again on Thursday. You bring with you such sunshine for me; my greatest troubles melt away as soon as I see your beautiful person. Thank you so much for saying that you will see a lot of me next week.'

Louis's death marked the end of the house in Spital Square as a centre for family life. Only Jack and Golda were left, and after a while Jack took a flat in the West End where he spent much of his time, while Golda began to circulate uneasily among her other children. Now that he was without this line of retreat Mark's intimacy with Carrington assumed for him an even greater significance: the close relationship with his family in the East End had been replaced by an equally intense one with Carrington in his new life.

CHAPTER 28

'This wretched rigmarole we call life'

During the early months of 1917 the difficulties which beset Carrington and Mark grew worse. Nothing remained of their early freshness and spontaneity, and both understood that the best response to his ardent love-making that Mark could hope for was one of amiable indifference; often he received only a grudging permission, of which, nevertheless, he would avail himself.

But he could not give up hope. He brought to their love affair not only his desperate need, but the same tenacity which had carried him out of the slums, the same ardour and devotion which he expended on the development of his art, and he could not afford to admit to himself that he had failed.

An ending was inevitable, but the actual outcome was more shocking to Mark than anything he could have foreseen: one which seemed to him an obscene, tragic and ludicrous waste.

Carrington to Mark (circa December 1916): Will you not ask me to live with you often when I come back. I don't like it very much. I like it better when we are just friends. I think it makes me rather upset. But sometimes, since you care for it, I do not mind.
Carrington to Strachey (5 January 1917): What a peace to be with you, and how happy I was today.
Carrington to Mark (London, 5 January 1917): I could hardly sleep last night through wretchedness because I am so miserable at making you unhappy. And how to explain it? . . . I want frightfully

to get on with you but I feel so wretched when I am with you now . . . It's something in between us that is hateful. Really inside me . . . Dear, please for heaven's sake forgive me this wrong I am doing you.

Mark to Carrington (London, January 1917): In future I shall control myself more and not ask you to live with me often, although control is hardly necessary to prevent that often, because what with your moods and our quarrels and country goings, we, in any case only meet about once a month on the average . . . *Please* do not be afraid to tell me in future when you do not want 'that'!

Carrington to Mark (Asheham House, 5 February 1917): Dear, I want you to forgive me for the many wrongs I've done you. I am going to [be] less selfish and make you happier.

Mark to Carrington (London 2 March 1917): I shan't pester you very much, only now and then.

Mark to Carrington (London, March 1917): You *must not* resist me physically . . . By entering into it with more lightness, even humour, you will do away with half the trouble at once and I will only appreciate your kindness and sacrifice, and love you with a beautiful love; also I will not abuse your kindness for I *quite* understand your difficulty. In doing this you will *not* be dishonest but *kind*. I will not be mislead; I never was in fact. But I shall be happy through gratitude . . . Do you understand? Don't let us withdraw from each other in spirit for a single moment. Let us always understand . . . think of the spring evenings in the woods! . . . Oh how different to all my other springs! This time *at last* you will be *with me*. Oh! almost altogether!! I shall love you in front of trees in Blossom! Yes that has been my ambition for years! How tenderly I shall kiss you in front of such a tree, at last, at last. Oh! my beautiful girl!

Carrington to Strachey (London, 22 March 1917): I missed you horribly today, and felt slightly angry for having confessed to you that I did care so much. How loveable you are sometimes.

Strachey to Carrington (23 March 1917): I miss you too, you know. That was such a divine hour – why regret any of it?

Carrington to Mark (Andover, 25 March 1917): I want you to meet my friends and share my interests more, not be cynical about them and make me keep them inside myself. This is rather my sin as I seldom take you with me, or tell you what I think and do. But I will in the future; only you must be very honest and not pretend to care and then go and say to Monty: "They are no good, they don't really feel things. How I dislike these people who only want life to be amusing."

Carrington to Mark (Marlow, Bucks, April 1917): I am sorry you are not happy with Monty. Also over Evan [Morgan]. But it is no use arguing with you over that, if you don't delight at all in a man's body and if you do feel it is wrong so definitely.

Mark to Carrington (Cholesbury, April 1917) (she is staying with the Stracheys): Oh! But I am happy now, and I hope you are too. I hope your friendship with Lytton is a happy one. I shouldn't like to feel that you are unhappy there. The woods remind me of you.

Carrington (diary entry, April 1917) (after confessing to Mark that she had fallen in love with Strachey): His calmness amazed me and his complete unselfishness and generosity. I became more and more wretched and wept. It seemed like leaving the warm sun in the fields and going into a dark and cold wood surrounded by trees which were strangers. I suddenly looked back at the long life we had had between us of mixed emotions. But always warm because of his intense love and now I had to leave it all and go away. Then suddenly he saw it also: the end of all this closeness, the final goodbye, the separation of two brothers, with a life between them, and he broke down and sobbed, and then it was agony. For he wanted to die and I thought how much this love mattered to him, and yet in spite of its greatness I could not keep it, and must leave. His loneliness was awful. We left the studio and had tea in a Suisse café in a dark back room. He didn't talk much, hardly at all about Lytton; only – 'Will you live with him?' 'No.' 'But he may love you.' 'No he will not.' That I thought made it easier a little.

> *Strachey:* But it's too incongruous. I'm so old and diseased. I wish I was more able.
> *Carrington:* That doesn't matter.
> *Strachey:* What do you mean. What do you think we had better do about the physical?
> *Carrington:* Oh I don't mind about that!

Carrington (diary entry, April 1917) (after explaining to Strachey that she has told Mark).

Carrington (diary entry, April 1917): I went at 7.30 . . . to meet
Mark. He was a little late. For a brief moment we talked of
pleasantries. Then suddenly I said 'We had better now I think not
see each other any more.' Mark said, 'Yes I had come to that
conclusion also . . . To think after all these years in three months
you should love a man like Strachey, twice your age and emaciated
and old. As I always said life is a crooked business.'

Mark to Carrington (London, 18 April 1917): I in no way blame you
for anything that's happened. We have done well to part at last, and
this time it does seem the end of that long and terrible struggle. I
shall commence right away to build up my future life, brick by
brick, and I have hopes. My work will be the basis. From now
onwards my life will be a more decent and spiritual thing than it's
ever had a chance to be before. I hope you too will find yourself
soon on your feet and with a better knowledge of your mind and
feelings.

Mark to Carrington (April 1917) (after he had begged her to go on
seeing him): I cannot help writing to thank you for bringing me
back to life, by giving me again your friendship . . . One must
be sooner or later absolutely self-contained. This is what I am
struggling for.

You have been wonderful lately. Really there is no one I care
more for as a person than you. I can't tell you how much you've
moved me these last few days. I must confess, I never knew how
splendid you were. And do forgive me for all the suffering I caused
you. The shock was too great for me. Now I am thankful for what
has happened, and if you will be able to go on giving me the tiniest
bit of friendship for some time yet, I shall be quite happy. As yet I
cannot do without that tiny bit. So be kind and let me have it a
while longer. Perhaps quite soon I shall be able to release you
altogether. I can't as yet, as I am not quite fully reborn or
self-contained, so I must perhaps prey on your kindness.

Carrington to Mark (28 April 1917) (distressed by Strachey's relative indifference to her, she had attempted to strengthen her new relationship
with Mark, writing him affectionate letters and again allowing him to
have sexual intercourse with her): It was good seeing you again today –
I've only just woken up from this nightmare; and today it seemed we
were back again together at last with our foolishness and comic jokes.

Carrington to Mark (May 1917): I am sorry to have made such a commotion about it. But what really upset me was (1) That you had not been *quite* honest in not telling me, everything. (2) That seeing that you did not know whether it might not by chance have gone right up that you took any risk. Through (I still maintain) selfish and lazy motives. That was really what upset me so much. I care so much for living, that the prospect of that [pregnancy] fills me with for a moment even, with absolute horror . . . But talk about it no more. I will come tomorrow at five!

Carrington to Mark (Warsash, Hants., May 1917): You have been slightly brutal not to write to me when you said you would. But I am overlooking it and writing to you.

Carrington to Mark (London, May 1917): I *don't* want to live with him [Strachey].

Carrington to Mark: You never write to me. I wonder why . . . Do write to me soon please again . . . You see how contradictory it all is. But I love seeing you so much more now.

Carrington to Mark (London, July 1917): Yes I say it frankly, Lytton will be away for two months. So you will have no more reason to curse him or me. For you will have me every night you want. What confessions we honest people make!

Carrington to Mark (summer 1917) (after visiting Duncan Grant and Vanessa Bell): It was so good to be with artists who talked about painting . . . Do not leave me, Mark!

Carrington to Mark (London, July 1917): When anyone runs Lytton down you ought rather to say, 'he must be better than we think since Carrington loves him.' Do you not see that if you love me, you *must* believe in what I love, and not agree with the public who are stupid and prejudiced in saying it is illsorted, and I am misled . . . Mark, your friendship really does mean so much to me now . . . You know I love seeing you so much.

Mark (draft of projected letter): I am afraid that I cannot support you over your love for Lytton, and because I love *you* I need *not* necessarily believe in what *you* love. I'd believe in *you*, but nothing on earth will make me believe in Lytton as a fit object for your love. I am sorry Carrington, but nothing will ever make me change my mind. But believe me, whenever the subject arises I always uphold you and always shall, to other people . . . I feel that I must

once and for ever tell you fully what I think of your love for L.S. I
have not told you before, because I felt it was useless. If you had
come and told me that you thought L.S. was a wonderful man and
that you had an admiration for him, I should have tried to dissuade
you because I do not think that he is. I think very much to the
contrary in fact. But you came and told me that you *loved* him.
Then I knew I was powerless and that it would only be a waist of
breath to be critical. However now that we are on the subject, I
must tell you that I regard your relationship with L.S. with
abhorrence and I shall never change my mind. You have by your
love for that man poisoned my belief in love, life and everything;
you by that love turned everything that I once believed in and
thought beautiful into ridicule. I laugh bitterly the whole time now
at this wretched rigmarole we call life. You could not have grasped
that which I as a being stand for, in the least, to have turned so
suddenly after all these years of devotion and love for you, aside to
love a man like that. For years I wanted you – you only tortured
me; then suddenly you give your love to such a creature; and you
yourself said had he wanted your body you would without hesitation have given it to that emaciated withered being. I, young and
full of life, you refused. Tell me, Carrington, what am I to think of
life now?

'You say you are happy, yes you are. *But I am not.* I long to fly
very often to another country where I shan't smell the stench that
fills my nostrils constantly from the combination of your fresh
young self with that half dead creature who is not even man
enough to take your body – your beautiful body. But thank God he
cannot, because if that happened, I should be sick all day. I do not
believe in L.S.'s mind; his atmosphere is as thin as his body; he is
merely learned and scholarly but fundamentally empty. By himself
I can accept him; but by no means in combination with you. He
will deaden you in time, and that is what hurts me so. You are
absolutely at his feet; you follow him about like a puppy; you have
lost all self respect; I shudder to think of it. No, I shall always hate
it. I only hope soon, the nausea of this wretched relationship of
yours will poison the spirit of my love for you and so diminish the
stink of it all. But never as long as I live will I ever get over it.
Never could I have contemplated such a nauseating thing.

Mark to Carrington: Please do not write to me. I really mean to have done with you – You spoil my life – always have, and always shall as long as I shall know you. So I don't want to know. You think by holding my hand or giving me an occasional kiss you have a relationship with me. But there is no relationship . . . If you write to me I shall return your letter unopened. So don't write as I want to forget you quickly.

Carrington to Mark (Cornwall, October 1917): May I come and see your paintings when I come back? Please, Mark. Do not think of me vilely and try and forgive me.

Mark to Carrington (London, 4 October 1917): It has been difficult for me to write because honestly, I do not feel the prospect of returning to you as at all enticing . . . You have treated me abominably, Carrington – always until the last moment, and it is hard not to hate you for it. Your attitude to me has been most unhuman, and brutal; your selfishness appals me – it is terrifying. And you will be just the same in the future – you can't help it. You are made like that, and I don't like you for it. By your treatment of me you have done me ever so much harm. You have sown seeds of bitterness inside me, by your brutality. I have to spend all my time now undoing what you have done to me . . . However in spite of all this I will try not to hate you and to forgive you. I will even see you sometimes if you wish it. Yes you can come and see my work whenever you like.

PART EIGHT

Collapse

'I am passing through terrible changes. I don't know what awaits me the other side ... Veil after veil I keep tearing off my eyes and the disclosures are more and more terrible. What I see is ghastly, almost too much to bear.'

MARK GERTLER TO S. S. KOTELIANSKY, APRIL 1917

CHAPTER 29

The only chance

Hitherto Mark had been able to control the violent and unstable elements in his character, and there had seemed little danger of their overwhelming him, as Lightfoot, Currie and Cannan had been overwhelmed. But now things were different.

The restraining influence of his early home background with its strong customs and beliefs had diminished after he left the East End; with the death of Louis the home had broken up altogether. Although love remained, and Golda was eager to help him, he had moved beyond her reach and changed too much. 'Coming into contact with one's family is always *most* distressing. Even if one loves them as I do,' he wrote. 'I think it is because one has become so very different and yet, somehow, one can't help feeling that there is after all some ghastly link. A link which one cannot shake off altogether, and so one feels it would have been better either not to have changed from them at all, or having changed, the link should automatically have broken itself; but no a sort of link *does* persist in remaining.' (1 January 1919)

The hope of a future with Carrington had gone, leaving instead loneliness, cynicism and rage.

Even his ardour for work seemed to be faltering, after the depressing reaction to his sculpture and his recent pictures. He had shown the 'Merry-Go-Round' at the London Group in April 1917, and although personal attacks on him by the critics had been milder than his friends had expected, they had been quite sufficient to put off prospective buyers, and this, his most ambitious picture, remained unsold. For many years henceforth it was to remain in his studio unwanted.

'Lately have I been unable to work much,' he wrote in April 1917. I have been far too preoccupied with life itself and the problems of life . . .

The spells of depression grew worse: 'I get these fits – like a disease,' he wrote once. 'Yesterday morning it was at its height and it was terrible – it is a sort of nervous depression. When in such a state I lose all control and my harmony. It's a sort of madness.' (5 December 1918)

He knew that his work offered the only chance of survival, and, as in past crises, he worked at it, as much from need as from ambition: 'The older I get the more necessary does painting become to me, necessary to my very constitution. If I don't paint I become restless, bored and even ill.'

It was a dangerous time to be exposed to a fresh blast of new ideas.

Roger Fry, who had been watching his work with increasing interest, now made friendly approaches, inviting Mark to take part in an exhibition of 'copies' at his Omega workshops in April 1917, and in shows of modern art which he organized at Birmingham in July and at Heal's, London, in October.

At the Birmingham show Mark's pictures looked particularly uncompromising among the others. 'Except for Gertler we are fearfully tasteful,' Fry reflected in a letter to Vanessa Bell.

Fry rather liked to disturb people – after all if artists weren't willing to change and develop they could never scale the heights. Mark entirely agreed; the last thing he wanted was to go on repeating himself, as he now believed that Augustus John, for example, was doing. He was very encouraged by Fry's appreciation and understanding of his work 'especially my statue which so few people can make anything of.'

Fry's understanding of art was profound, and his knowledge of the French Post-Impressionist painters far surpassed that of any other English critic. In his company Mark experienced again the shock of his first contact, several years before, with modern French art. This time his understanding was greater and the shock correspondingly more intense. Fry appreciated in particular the

16—MG * *

importance of Cézanne and his revolutionary discoveries, and showed Mark the profound significance of these ideas.

The friendship developed, and in October 1917 Fry invited Mark home for a weekend and was still further impressed. 'Really, artists are a different race,' Fry wrote to Virginia Woolf after it. 'He is really passionately an artist – a most rare and refreshing thing.' A year later Fry again encouraged Mark by acquiring one of his drawings and included him with Duncan Grant and others in a small exhibition at the Omega Workshops in December 1918.

Henceforth contact with Fry's lively mind was a constant challenge for Mark. 'We had much interesting and feverish discussion about painting,' he wrote after Fry visited his studio one afternoon. (5 December 1918)

During Mark's visits to Garsington, Ottoline's constant enthusiasm for modern French art kept the ferment going and he pored over the books she bought or borrowed, particularly ones on Cézanne. He again took up the study of French and worked at it for half an hour every day, though with limited success.

But whereas in the past he had been able to change his ideas and still develop successfully, this time he could not find the way forward. 'Marvellous new and wonderful things have passed through my brain, but actually I have managed only to spoil a number of canvases!' he confessed on 12 September 1917. 'Oh! Real painting is so wonderful, but so hard – so devastating. I suffer headaches – I have worked terribly hard – my eyes ache – and nothing to show! My friends will be bored with me in the future, because I have got into the habit of painting the same thing over and over again. Yes it's all exercise – study, experimenting – wonderful internally, but no external results – and this will go on for how long? I don't know, I don't care. I am furiously interested in still-life again – wonderful exercise; I shall do thousands! How dull, everybody will say, but I don't care. I may even do everything I've ever done again!'

For two years, on and off, he toiled at his ambitious, large picture of 'Bathers'[196] – nearly as big as 'Merry-Go-Round' – but could not bring it to a really satisfactory conclusion. Bright colours almost vanished from his work, to be replaced by subdued and rather sombre schemes.

At times, some of his experiments, for example the almost abstract elements in 'Bathers', represented new peaks of adventurousness, but there was no steady development, and at other times his artistic personality weakened too much to hold its own against the influence of Cézanne and the other Paris painters, and the style of his work was too close to theirs. A critic, Konody of the *Observer*, complained irritably in 1918 that he was 'still groping about and jumping from extreme to extreme,' and the following year it was commented that his work was 'neither representation, nor interpretation, nor decoration.'

As the months, and years, passed, matters did not really improve. Instead his work went by fits and starts, and there were periods of idleness darkened by depressions:

'My dear Kot,' he wrote once, 'I am suffering altogether from a melancholia of such a nature, as I think even I have not experienced before. It seems this time so permanent. These last few weeks I seem to have really aged by years and years. Life now does seem irremediably horrid. What I hate are the little mean things of life which in spite of their littleness are just sufficient to be constantly soiling one's spirit and imprisoning it, so that one can hardly ever feel freely and beautifully and above the material. But really I cannot express exactly what I mean in writing. I am rather sorry I tried to now.' (15 August 1919)

To add to his troubles conscription into the army became an imminent possibility. When the problem had first come up Mark's friends had hoped that contacts of Ottoline's such as Asquith, then Prime Minister, might help to keep him out. But even Asquith had lost much of his power to help minor friends. The war had become much grimmer and attitudes had hardened. On 27 February 1918 Mark was served with call-up papers.

The summons came when for once he was in the middle of a burst of hard work: 'You can't imagine what important discoveries I have been making for myself lately,' he wrote, 'and now I have to leave it all in the middle and go and do God knows what! And come before tribunals, and talk to asses of men.'

Shearman and Hutchinson set to work to help him: appeals were sent in using the grounds of Austrian parentage, and Mark's conscientious objection, and the issue was once more averted.

During the summer of 1917 Mark had not replied to Carrington's letters. But, 'like a child, she found it hateful to choose; and after breaking off a relationship for ever she would immediately set about starting it again.'[151] She persisted, and during the autumn they began once more to exchange letters frequently.

Carrington had another childish characteristic: 'She would tell lies which were bound to be found out and her life was complicated by continual deceptions and imbroglios.'[152] In 1917, at Christmas she moved in with Strachey and henceforward they lived together. She tried at first to hide this from Mark but it soon became too well known to all their friends. Despairingly Mark wrote to Kot, 'I sometimes think that my real life will not commence before my passion for Carrington ends. But God only knows when it will end. This passion of mine may yet ruin me. It makes life so hateful to me – so ugly – and crooked. I hate life at present with a bitter hatred.' In February 1918 he was writing, 'Really until that relationship has in some way worked itself out I am a lost wretched creature. Over and over again I feel that I shall *not* survive it.'

One night the same month – on Saint Valentine's day – Mark came upon Carrington and Strachey together at a party of the Hutchinsons at Hammersmith. His self-control broke, and in the street after the party, as Strachey, was walking away with Carrington Mark followed and attacked him. The two were separated by friends. The following day, seeing Strachey in a restaurant, Mark made himself go over and apologize.

On another occasion he wrote (but kept to himself) a bitter and obscene letter to Strachey about the strange triangular affair:

Long shanks, long shanks, how do you do today?
Long shanks, long shanks, tickle your weapon to play,
For she waits, she waits, alas, she waits for you
So sharpen your blade, Her oil stove is wet
    And let there be some to do.

For years and years has my sword been unsheathed
Upright and glistening and full charged.
But for your pointless dagger, your rusty blade
Gapes her virgin sheath, so subtle and beautifully made.

So long shanks, long shanks trundle your bows and try,
Tickle it, shake it, but never say die,
For you can taste, which I a boy
Pined many a long year to enjoy.

Still the correspondence with Carrington persisted. She would often hint that they might one day come together again, even if by then he was grey-haired and she a bent old lady. But neither of them was to live that long

Mark's mind seemed to be sliding into chaos.

To many of his acquaintances he had always seemed as wild a character as any in the Russian novels they were all reading. 'What can I tell you that will interest so violent a character as yourself?' wrote Mary Hutchinson once. Often he was nearly overcome with irrational, absurd impulses. On one visit to Cholesbury he had written: 'My cottage here is very nice, but sometimes I get a curious desire to chop it up and burn it and watch it burning until there is nothing left but a small heap of ashes!'

In April 1917 he admitted to Kot: 'Never have I been more out-of-love with life and its cruel mechanism. Never have I laughed more sardonically. I frighten Shearman with my new Ideas... good brings forth good, evil brings forth evil. Life feeds me with evil. Therefore I am becoming evil – a scoundrel.'

Kot, though a source of moral strength in most things, had himself a streak of violence. One night Mark and he called on Monty Shearman, and using the key Shearman had given Mark, entered his beautiful room at the Adelphi. He was out, but the place was arranged for a supper party on his return. As they looked round the elegant interior of their friend and benefactor, an illogical, savage animus seized them both: 'they dashed at the bottles and liqueurs, drinking everything and eating all the sandwiches, holding them madly in both hands. They threw the flowers and cushions all

over the place and Kot took a painted wooden tray made by Roger
Fry at the Omega workshops and smashed it down with both hands
over Gertler's head . . . Gertler leaped about over the furniture
shaking the eau-de-cologne everywhere.'[153]

When they left the room was in a shambles.

Letters from Lawrence tended to feed the springs of violence. He
was now living in the country alone with Frieda, in great poverty
and missing his friends ('there is nobody to quarrel with,' he told
Mark). A constant tension underlay invitations to stay with him and
in his letters were disturbing passages: 'It is bound to come, the
great smash-up in this country – and Oh God, if it would only
come quickly,' he had written on 5 December 1916. In 1918 there
were a number of desperate statements: 'I feel like a wild cat in a
cage,' (March); 'My soul, or whatever it is, feels charged and
surcharged with the blackest and most monstrous "temper", a sort
of hellish electricity – and I hope soon it will either dissipate or
break into some sort of thunder and lightning, for I am no more a
man, but a walking phenomenon of suspended fury.' (April); 'I am
very restless and at the end of *everything*. I don't work – don't try to
– only just endure the days. There will either have to come a break
outside or inside – in the world or in oneself.' (26 June); '[I have] no
money and no hope.' (2 October)

Lawrence felt that Mark, almost alone of his friends, would
understand his mood. When proposing a visit to London he wrote
to Kot, 'I don't want to see anybody at all – don't want to let
anybody know I am there – save perhaps Catherine Carswell and
Gertler.' (30 April 1919)

Carrington was alarmed by rumours of dissipation and excess. 'I
heard from four different sources accidentally that you had been
leading a gay life and when I saw you I thought you looked ill and
you must admit you were rather drunk.' In January 1919 she wrote:
'I beg you to take care of your health.'

But an insatiable appetite for drink, parties and sex now possessed
Mark. Most of his new relationships with women were casual and
basically unsatisfactory, and the accounts of them that he gave his
friends were cynical. Writing to Kot, for instance, after one encounter, he declared: 'To be made love to by Mrs Goff is like
placing one's head into a beehive – she bites so – curse her – my lips

are still sore, and other places too! What a cat!' On another occasion he told Kot, 'I dined with Mrs Goff and had a horrid and debauched night.' (June 1918)

In his work Mark's breach with the N.E.A.C. and its buyers had become more or less final. 'It is rather a good sign than otherwise that the New English did not accept your picture', he advised Brett on one occasion. 'I really don't think one ought to send there at all. I don't think I shall ever send again.' (January 1918) The following May he declared, 'I have long ceased to send there or even to go to its shows.'

Although Shearman did what he could, money was even more of a problem and in the end Mark had to acknowledge that he could not survive as an artist without finding other outside help or giving up his cherished integrity and painting to please potential buyers.

Harry tried to come to the rescue. He had built up the furrier's business again and was willing to help Mark indefinitely with small loans, but by mid 1918 Mark's debt to him was over a hundred pounds and the central issue could no longer be disguised.

Sadly he painted pot-boilers.

'I hope by the time I return to have a few saleable things done and so straighten myself financially,' he once wrote to Kot from Garsington: 'Lack of money gives the finishing touch to life in making it absolutely fifth-rate, tedious and altogether a bad tasteless joke. If I had the money, I could go on at any rate experimenting in different ways, but as it is, I must be covering canvas with paint because in that way alone I can get enough money to live. After all it is not pleasant to sponge on people.' (17 July 1918)

'The most hateful thing to me now is that I must keep producing – for money', he asserted. (July 1918) Even then it was not easy: 'I sell and sell and still it's not enough,' he wrote. (December 23, 1918)

CHAPTER 30

A sort of family

During this wretched period the support of two people gave Mark his best chance of making a new start. Ottoline offered him the hospitality of Garsington Manor whenever he chose, and more and more often he slipped away from London for a few days to find refuge there. Every summer from 1917 he stayed for many weeks at a time and at Christmas would be there again.

While other guests came and went, he and Brett, who had become a close friend of Ottoline's, were the 'painters in residence.'

'I love working all day here and then the pleasant meal in the evening, with either the pianola or reading afterwards,' Mark declared. They would lounge in 'incredibly comfortable' armchairs in front of the enormous log fire. The walls of the living room were Tudor panelled and Ottoline had had them painted Chinese red with the grooves in gold. When the servants brought in the oil lamps the specially made paper shades would make an enchanting effect on the rich yellow curtains, the maize-gold Samarkand carpets, and the black-and-gold Chinese cupboards.

In the day time, if Mark's work went wrong, he could seize upon someone to walk with at any moment or join in a game of croquet.

Brett was a great comfort. 'She is invaluable, she is so good. She understands me and my work and what I want to do better than anyone – I do love her for this,' he announced. 'How much she helps me, even to domestic details – such as washing my hair. Once she even came on her own account to scrub my back in the bath! This place has spoilt me! How shall I live without all this now! Brett has real talent too.' (12 September 1917) Brett had supported all his experiments, being 'frightfully excited' about his sculpture and 'very pleased' that he was writing.

After the long summer stay in 1917 Mark realized that it was at Garsington, not in London, that he now felt most at home. Writing to Brett he said, 'Last night there was no raid, so I will wait a bit longer before deciding about staying here or running back to you all at Garsington. These raids fill me with the utmost depression. The sight of a tube station crambed full of poor panic stricken people is enough. I assure you that my stay at Garsington will not fade away like a dream. No, it was too real and valuable for that. Also you have no idea how comforting it feels, to have a sort of family and home now at Garsington. There have been moments since I returned, when I sunk to the lowest pit of depression. At such moments the thought of Garsington was my only consolation . . . You must try and impress upon Ottoline how thankful I feel and how much I like her, also Philip. I find it difficult to tell people to their face, so I leave it to you.' (3 October 1917)

'This morning I had a letter from Ottoline, a good letter; it rather moved me,' he affirmed on 15 November. 'I really like her very much and value her friendship, and the idea of Garsington means quite a lot to me now.'

When Ottoline came to London they would go out together to ballets and concerts. 'She is better to meet in the evenings than most people,' he commented. (October 1918)

In time he came to see Ottoline almost as a second mother. There could be no embarrassments about class – she was simply beyond such considerations: at Garsington it was almost an advantage to be of humble origins.

Although she was not exempted from his mimicry, and he used to give very funny imitations of the way she spoke, 'a sort of cooing, moaning noise', he disapproved of the rather malicious intrigues and caricatures circulated about Ottoline by others.

For her part she appreciated his directness and loyalty, and sympathy for her ill health. 'You don't know *how* much *I* value your friendship,' she wrote. 'It means so much to me to be able to get in *contact* with anyone that I like – and I feel I really *do* get into communion with you – and that we have an "understanding" together – you know what I mean – and really can understand each other without explanations. I have such awful health and feel so ill so often that it makes it very difficult for me to talk as much as I would. Today and yesterday I feel so well and I realize what a nightmare I have to fight through most days, for this last three months my head has nearly driven me crazy. I don't want to worry you with all this, only I feel I am often very dull. Really life and friendship, and the world and nature, and buttercups and poetry, and spiritual and concrete images, their impact is so tremendous and great and vivid. Even when sometimes one sees it all too clearly and one is almost frightened by the truth.'

The other person on whom Mark depended more and more was Kot, who became his closest companion. In this relationship Mark returned to the kind of people he had grown up with. Kot's stern integrity and authority were as great as that of Louis. 'If you knew Kot well you understood what a major Hebrew prophet must have been like,' commented Leonard Woolf. 'If Jeremiah had been born in a ghetto village of the Ukraine in 1882 he would have been Kot . . . He was not a comfortable man . . . [with his] passionate approval of what he thought good, particularly in people, his intense hatred of what he thought bad, the directness and vehemence of his speech, his inability to tell a lie . . . If you said to Kot "Do you like such and such a book?" and he did not, he would say: "It is hor–r–r–ible", and the roll of the r's was like the thunder from Mount Sinai.'[154]

Mark admired Kot's insistence on an ideal of a life of artistic and intellectual integrity. Kot was drawn to the mixture of fierce independence and vulnerability in Mark.

Kot shared with Mark a passion for Dostoievsky and other Russian authors, and made translation of their works into English his main interest in life.

As part of a circle of writers – Lawrence, Katherine Mansfield and Middleton Murry – they developed further mutual friendships.

With Kot Mark was at home and at peace. They understood each other and viewed the world with similar values: in both a ghetto upbringing had been followed by isolation from their own race and religion. Their pessimism, violence, depressions and ill health were shared. 'I wonder who is more wretched, you or I?' Mark asked once. To a friend he confessed, 'Some moments Kot's life oppresses me terribly, and God knows I am not a very happy person myself.'

Kot's mind was often deep in memories of the Pogroms, Russian politics, or new dangers to his relatives. Even his humour emphasized his difference from his London literary friends: for example his ability to give a howl so melancholy, convincing and penetrating that dogs half a mile away would answer, had been acquired as a young man. Walking the miles back to his village after seeing a girl home to another one he would howl into the darkness. The replies of the dogs from distant villages would lessen his fears and loneliness.

The bond between Mark and Kot had been quickly formed: 'You are so necessary to me', Mark had written soon after their meeting. By August 1917 he was saying, 'You are the one person I can in my inmost being without hesitation call a friend.'

It was a bond based on total frankness and pitiless candour. When Lawrence had received a photograph of Mark's 1916 painting of Kot,[197] he had objected. 'The portrait has really something of you – quite true. But is has indeed none of your good looks. It makes you uglier. It is you in your bad and hopeless moods. I don't really like it. But don't tell Gertler. There is still a youthful and foolish warmth about you, which is perhaps the nicest part, and this is left out on the photo. You are here the old, old, old *Jew* who ought to hasten into oblivion. But there is a young and clumsy uncouth human being, not a Jew at all, a sort of heavy colt, which I should paint if I painted your portrait.'

Of Mark's other friends the closest and most helpful was another Jew – Monty Shearman. He became devoted to Mark: 'I know perfectly well that what I feel for you, you will only feel for a woman', he wrote, 'but I am now quite contented in our relation-ship . . . I have a deeper feeling for you than for any other living person . . . You need never feel in the least uneasy with me because I really couldn't and wouldn't want to be ever gross or horrible.' (15 April 1917)

Shearman's rooms were a rendezvous for the little circle, and Mark had the additional pleasure of seeing on the walls the pictures of his which Shearman had bought. 'I have a great deal to thank Monty for', Mark wrote. 'He and his room have been a blessing to me and still are – there I can always go and find a friend.'

Shearman bought some pictures, and his friends, the Hutchinsons, were kind. 'They are helping me to sell my pictures', Mark wrote.

He was sometimes critical of Mary: 'You must not be like Mary Hutchinson who judges one by little parts, and turns her back on one, because one "doesn't always carry one's soul on one's nose," ' he advised Carrington. (February 20, 1918) But he appreciated their hospitality and was a regular attender at their parties.

Iris Tree was as affectionate as ever. When she left for America she wrote, 'Yes, it is you almost most that I wish for in London. You were the nicest in many ways; because you loved your art better than others, loved life more, as a thing to look at and laugh with, as a place to enjoy and step away from; because you were serious and friendly with me, and did not regard me as a curious yellow bird in a golden cage; because I liked your paintings best of all, and it was sweet to come to your studio on the top of its hill, and drink tea restfully in happiness after irritation, boredom and intellectual iniquity with the epicures of echoes and mirrors . . . Miss me please when you get this letter.' (25 July 1919) In another she said, 'I never forget you and never will forget you.'

Mark made a new friend, Madame Suggia. They went to dances or spent evenings in his studio: 'She is beautiful and she plays Bach on the cello – the cello is my favourite instrument and Bach my favourite composer.' (January 1918) And an important new friend was Valentine Dobrée. 'I miss you quite a lot sometimes,' she wrote when she was away in 1919.

One friendship was over. Gilbert Cannan appeared for a time to have recovered from his breakdown, but the former intimacy between Mark and him had gone. Others also found the change in Cannan distressing. When Middleton Murry ran into him in the street early in 1918 he was struck by Cannan's' childish self absorption and vacant insouciance,' he said. 'I fled, miserably, from the stare of that wild unseeing eye, with the certainty that I should never encounter it again.'[155] Another critical account of Cannan was given in a letter of Carrington's to her brother, finishing: 'Also a murky past has been disclosed . . . he was a dirtee liar and raper of young females.'

Cannan had now left his wife and was friends with Gwen Wilson,* whom Mark nicknamed 'Pluck'. Mark found him totally changed and rather unpleasant. 'So Gilbert is really, after all, a

* Later Gwendoline, Lady Melchett.

blown-out eggshell,' he reflected. 'I am not surprised.' (19 July 1918) And he soon gave them both up. 'Gilbert and Pluck gave a party last Wednesday,' he wrote on 22 December 1918. 'Much dancing and drink, but depressing. It decided me finally against Gilbert and Pluck. It is good to feel so definite and final about anything as I feel about them – that is – that they are not worth seeing.'

CHAPTER 31

Like a drunken wasp in an apple

Mark struggled on, fortified by his friends and finding in Garsington a haven where he could collect his feelings and thoughts. Often he would take a book and walk to a favourite vantage point: 'It is a beautiful spot, high up with endless fields of different colours and a few haystacks looking like half lemons on the sun against the intense blue of the sky. I won't say I feel happy at such moments, but it *does* feel good.'

Towards the end of the war and during the years after it the moods of hope became more frequent, the periods of idleness shorter. He explained to Kot that though all his efforts came to nothing, 'This is simply because my mind has leapt into a higher consciousness, and I am not yet able to paint up to it. I might repeat the old song "My heart is good, but my hands won't let me." Only hands instead of feet, and it expresses absolutely my present state. I assure you however that my present failures are far more interesting than my past finished pictures.' 'The old things will not do any longer,' he told Brett. 'I feel curiously reborn, fresh, yet unhappy. But I feel that once I find myself again it will be a much better, stronger, find than ever before. I am only temporarily thrown off my balance'.

'I am starting from the ABC again,' he noted on 12 December 1918. 'Right from the beginning as though I have never painted before . . . The whole business meanwhile is a very painful struggle and terribly exhausting. I am ill and worn out with it all. Why

should it be so painful and difficult? I don't know – sometimes I feel
that perhaps one ought to paint more lightly, gaily, but if this is
possible to some people it is not to me. *I* can't work without
desperate seriousness.'

'You see I do want so much to paint . . .' he had written to Kot
from Garsington in February 1918. 'Work is my only salvation but
I mean to be saved, somehow . . . We are thinking of having a part
of Brett's studio here partitioned off, for my use, so that I can
come here anytime, and immediately work . . . I feel hopeful
because I know that the trouble that comes from Carrington *is*
working itself out. I don't know exactly in which direction, but I
know it will not last much longer. But whatever way it will end I
know it *will* end and *soon*.' They hardly ever met now, though
letters were still exchanged, but sometimes, when together, their
former feeling for each other would kindle again.

Although Mark really preferred Garsington when he and the
Morrells were there alone, it had also the advantage of being a place
where he could meet people without effort after his day's work.
Ottoline's taste in people was catholic: a bewildering succession
of visitors included – beside Bertrand Russell and the various
'Bloomsburies' – Simon Bussy (the French painter married to
Dorothy Strachey; 'a nice comic little chap with an enormous;
stage laugh'), the MacCarthys, Aldous and Julian Huxley (who
became lifelong friends of the Morrells), T. S. Eliot, Picasso, the
Asquiths ('I don't like them, they distress me. Elizabeth is awful'),
Mrs A. P. Herbert, Lady G. Churchill, old Professor Brown of the
Slade, the Bishop of Oxford and Lord Harcourt ('he asked me at
once to come over to see his "pictures"! I declined – hateful man').

Several friends of the Morrells, having been allowed as conscientious objectors to do agricultural work instead of military service,
worked on their farm, and the evenings were enlivened by the
presence of these brilliant intellectual labourers, who would come
into the house to 'puff churchwarden pipes by the fire, and talk
cleverly in cultured and earnest tones about significant form in the
arts and the misdeeds of the militants,' as Siegfried Sassoon noted.
Sassoon himself was a frequent caller ('The Captain, as we call him,'
said Mark. 'I can never look at him without wanting to slap my
calves with an imaginary whip in a-hunting we will go style'). An

old friend reappeared – Middleton Murry, now 'a string in the wind – shifty, back-boneless, fearful, ill, but rather nice and pathetic'.

Much of the conversation centred on the work of friends who were beginning to enjoy public acclaim: Katherine Mansfield's *Preludes* for example, and Sassoon's *Poems*, out in 1918. Some of the successes aroused mixed feelings in Mark, whose work and reputation had progressed little in the past two years. In the summer of 1918 Strachey leapt to fame with *Eminent Victorians*. 'The conversations and discussions are still raging round Lytton Strachey's book,' Mark observed to Kot. 'Personally I've lost all sense of judgement. I am dazed into apathy by all the wonderful and "exquisite" books and other kinds of masterpieces that seem to come out every day like mushrooms in season – I am stunned like a drunken wasp in an apple with the immensity of modern production.'

When he found the company too overwhelming he would bury himself in a book or quietly slip away. Sometimes he offended Ottoline by an irreverent attitude to her guests, as when Yeats came. 'Worst of all, Sunday for tea time came, ssh, YEATS! The great Irish poet,' Mark told Kot. 'I was sent for to come and hear "the *interesting* conversation". (I had hidden, because there were so many people.) When I entered the room there was the Great Man. He seemed to be sitting on a chair much higher than anyone else's and holding forth. Everyone sat with rapt faces listening. The funniest part was Bussy who, as ill luck would have it, sat next to Yeats. The higher up Yeats sat, the lower little Bussy seemed to sink. The contrast was well worth seeing. I have never met a more pompous and theatrical humbug of an Irishman than Yeats. I escaped from the room as quick as I could.' (31 August 1920)

At other times the press of visitors interfered with his work: 'I've been as happy here as I can be, but I find now that, from a serious working point of view, it has its drawbacks. Until now I have been painting on the edge of the pond and really it was like trying to paint in some market place, or rather pleasure ground.' (22 July 1919)

Occasionally the endless gossip and intrigues irritated Mark. 'All this sickens me, *so so very much*, I long to fly away,' he told Carrington. 'It is all so petty, malicious, vicious, and disgusting. Your "Bloomsburies" as they are called, are the most capricious and vicious – I know more than I can tell you, but they all back-bite their supposed long and best friends! It is all so small – so hateful'.

'Clive [Bell] has made mischief between Jack [Hutchinson], Mary and myself,' he noted once. 'He is a dreadful fellow. I should really have nothing more to do with him!' Nearly two years later he was telling Kot, 'Virginia [Woolf] received me rather coldly. Later I learned that Clive Bell has been at work again – mischief about Mary, the usual boring stuff, not worth talking about. It is a pity though, because Virginia is really so interesting a person.' Mark felt that Bell disliked him. 'Clive Bell distresses us all here,' he wrote on another occasion, 'such a mischief maker, so loud, so bumptious. His voice gets on my nerves. But I must say we have had good painting talks together. In spite of which he dislikes me intensely. I know this to be a fact.'

Clive Bell's attitude to Mark's work was less consistent than Roger Fry's, and included some stiff criticism as well as praise. One review included the statement: 'Gertler's artistic gift, one inclines to suppose, is precisely that irreducible minimum of talent without which an artist cannot exist . . . he has only two or three notes and they are neither "rich nor rare".'[156]

In these years Mark was known more for his gaiety and ability to entertain than for his depressions, which were hidden from most people. Beatrice Campbell recalled a party at the Russian Ballet (then the rage of London) when everyone went round Lopokova's dressing-room after the show. 'Gertler would go out of the room and return as Lady Ottoline Morrell, then as one of the Stracheys or Sitwells or Maynard Keynes or some other, making himself fat or tall, short or thin, while we all laughed helplessly.'[157]

If no other subject was at hand he would burlesque himself. After dinner with Lady Tredegar he wrote: 'We both got slightly tipsy, and Lady Tredegar found her words rather difficult. I began to imagine myself the son of a Lord, and stood and talked in a special way, very dignified and well bred, at any rate so it seemed to me. I was somehow particularly anxious to impress the servant with the idea that I was the son of a Lord, and that my cheque trousers was but a Lordly Caprice – that I was just tired of evening clothes! – Well – Well.'

CHAPTER 32

Collapse

Mark was used to feeling slightly ill, with his 'nervous anxious tremulous life, influenza, headaches, eyeache, indigestion, stomach ache, love ache mental despair every other day'. But after the war the warning signs increased.

He knew that overwork was just as likely to bring trouble as excesses in social life. 'How I wish I had a stronger nervous system,' he told Brett. 'The mere excitement of conceiving a picture makes me positively ill.' But it was unthinkable to allow his life – at least his life as an artist – to be ruled by this consideration. 'I feel that for me it is worth while always to be rather run down and get the best out of myself than to be well and robust at the cost of my work and spiritual life,' he had told Carrington. 'Of course if I could manage to keep quite fit and to live my nervous spiritual life at the same time it would be ideal, but I am afraid that is impossible, in fact they don't go together somehow. Finally, I am happier at work though worried and ill in London than when I am feeling lazy and well and unproductive in the country – I soon get bored. No, I must live this nervous strained life always, always, and always. I must feel worried and ill – that is my fate. Therefore never feel worried when I look pale and haggard, it is part of me.' (June 1917)

When the war ended the chance came to see what the new generation of French painters were up to.

In August 1919 Mark wrote from Garsington to Kot: 'We suddenly got a wire from Ottoline, who was in London, asking us all to come up at once to go to the ballet and see a show of French pictures which were being hung at Heals. So we rushed up.'

The show revived his old distrust of French 'prettiness', and also of painting which gave little importance to subject matter, but he responded enthusiastically to the new ideas and obvious talent of the
17—MG

artists. 'At present I am not working, because a change is going on in my mind again, perhaps caused by the French pictures,' he admitted to Kot. 'They are all very nice and fine and clever, but I am *not* a Frenchman. Anyhow, what I mean is that they made me want to paint as differently from them as possible, and not, as one would think, like them . . . Do you know what a Jew says to a "shatchan" when the proposed bride is unsuitable? He says, "Very nice, very fine, but not for me". That's what I feel about the French pictures.'

The following March a visit to Paris with the Dobrées raised him to a frenzy of excitement. 'We went to see the Pellerin Collection', he reported to Brett. 'All those Cézannes that we know the reproductions of for years and years. Heavens! what a sensation it was, seeing them in the "flesh" at last! So Queer – so Queer! Some disappointing – some very fine. Oh, but the sensation! How Queer! . . . All these people's work by the way are cracking badly! And I am sure a knife placed under any of the cracks – and —!!!' A week or so later he wrote, 'There are many Cézannes which I find disappointing, not so good and suggestive as their photographs. Others quite fulfil one's expectations and are superb. But Renoir has made an enormous impression on me. In fact I am not sure that I do not like him best! I have seen a magnificent one, done only two years ago, when he was seventy-eight! One of the finest things I've ever seen. About the more modern stuff I am really not at all sure; there is nothing that takes one's breath away like those giants.'

Paris was full of English artists, and they greeted Epstein, Nina Hamnett, Roger Fry, Duncan Grant and Vanessa Bell. All the French looked artistic, 'even the bootmakers'. They met André Derain and other painters; and Mark commented: 'most of the younger artists here are *not* French, but different kinds of Jews. They talk Yiddish to me.'

But all Mark wanted to do now was get back to work. He assured Brett: 'I long to paint – only to paint. But I must wait until I get back to London, because my bedroom is a tiny dark hole and in the whole of Paris there isn't a single room to be got even if I wanted to work here, which I don't.'

On his return he set to work immediately, still grappling with his old problem: could he develop his new ideas inspired by the French painters without losing his own essentially realistic emphasis on subject matter? At any rate he decided 'to paint only from nature' and think things out again.

'Yesterday I saw Murry,' he noted on 22 May 1920. 'We talked of my Paris trip and of Cézanne and Renoir. I told him *my* way of understanding these great men and how terribly misled one has been all along by the "wizards and intellectuals" interpretations of them. I mean Roger Fry and Co.'

Painting only from nature was no problem when doing still lifes, but he was soon 'panting' to paint people, which meant difficulties in finding models. 'I am working hard and with much trouble, chiefly on account of my sitters,' he wrote in May. 'I am full of a new motive and feverish to express it. Yesterday another model came – an old hag of forty-five. You should see her! But still I started a nude of her! I *must* be painting someone! But by leaving out the wrinkles and the crumpled skin I shall, I hope, turn her into a rather fascinating and plump woman of thirty. Younger I *cannot* make her – but you know even *she* is full up and can't come again until next Sunday! Painting in the way I am doing now one is simply almost completely in the hands of one's sitters and this is an awful thought. Yet I can't paint any other way *just now*, as it is just *that* which is my *idea*.'

Everything seemed to be turning out well. Critics were becoming more enthusiastic. The previous year Clive Bell had praised him in the *Athenaeum*, and Frank Rutter, commenting on his 'Bathers' at the Friday Club, had said: 'Mr Gertler in "Bathers" must be taken seriously ... He reveals a capacity for expressing plastic form in paint possessed by no other artist exhibiting in London today.'

In pictures of 1920 Mark's colours were growing stronger and richer again and he was developing his mature style. Marchant was so impressed with his work that in July he offered a one-man show – Mark's first – at the Goupil Gallery for March 1921. This, with its great suite of galleries and red velvet walls in Lower Regent Street, was a much more important gallery than the little Chenil in Chelsea, where Mark had shown with Currie.

For the rest of the spring he worked hard in London, then in July moved to Garsington for the summer, where he found the now overwhelmingly French atmosphere rather hard to take. 'Of course there was a great deal of French spoken,' he wrote to Kot on one occasion André Gide and 'a *supposed* nephew, a boy of eighteen', were there. 'I hate the sound of French more and more, also French men. Why will they say that everything is Horrible! Ces Magnifique! Ces Terrible! Ces Exquise!! Oh, ces formidables!!! They all make me feel as if I were on the stage. We walked round the pond by moonlight reciting Verlaine in the above melodramatic manner. Sometimes I dislike poetry as much as I dislike French!' (31 August 1920)

By late August he already had fifteen pictures ready towards his show, 'which is exactly half of what I should like to get done for it.'

Mark tried to put out of his mind an ominous event in April: one day in a fit of coughing he had spat blood. After various medical examinations and tests he noted in August: 'My chest is weak, they tell me, and I am to take great care of myself and all that.' His general reaction was one of impatient bravado: 'It's all boring and I don't care either way.'

But he was scared: 'I never before realized what an evil disease was. The thought that I *might* be *really* ill took all the life out of me, and made me reflect, more than before, on the horror of it . . . and if I am not ill, others are, and I think now that disease is the greatest evil on earth!' (22 July 1920)

In November Mark collapsed.

The illness was tuberculosis, and he was sent to a sanatorium in Scotland. He was still there in February and did not see his one-man show. It was only moderately successful.

PART NINE

Achievement

'Dependence on people – on love – brings disaster . . .
Gradually I shall grow more and more into myself till at
last I shall be free.' – MARK GERTLER TO CARRINGTON

CHAPTER 33

The mental traveller

When Mark left the sanatorium in May 1921 his chances of developing further as an artist were severely limited: for the foreseeable future he would have to exist in a prison made up of a rigid routine of careful living – the walk every morning, the hour's rest before each meal, the fixed times for painting. Extensive travel, with its opportunities to study deeply the art of France and other countries, was out of the question. Even short holidays made him ill: ships and trains upset him, and it was difficult to get the right food overseas. He would arrive home in a state of collapse and have to take a rest to recuperate. His social life was limited: evening outings had to be rationed. To new acquaintances he seemed at times to be over-fussy always worried about his health, living in fear of the violent attacks of migraine which would incapacitate him for days at a time.

He dared not relax his regime. Every few years would come a grim reminder – collapse followed by weeks or months in a sanatorium: in 1925, 1929 and 1936. Tuberculosis, which killed his friends Katherine Mansfield in 1923 at the age of thirty-five, and Lawrence in 1930 at forty-four, was the worst danger, but in fact the disease remained more or less quiescent, and Mark's breakdowns were usually nervous in origin.

Yet in the decade which followed 1921 he developed his talent to the full. A sustained effort of creative activity produced pictures which included his finest works, and earned him a permanent place in history as one of the most important British artists of the time.

He achieved this by submerging the man almost entirely in the artist. After all, his early ideal and desire had been for a life dedicated to art, and the events of the previous decade had removed any hopes of personal happiness which his original pessimism might have allowed him to nurse.

While he was in the sanatorium in 1921, Carrington had written rather sentimentally. Mark had replied: 'I confess that your recalling of memories saddened me rather. It might have been so much better – I loved you so . . . I wonder if you ever realized how much I loved you! What agony and suffering I went through on your account! How terrible it was when you turned to L.S. . . . I used to start up in bed at night – all in a sweat – from sheer agonies of jealousy. Ugh!' (13 April 1921) A fortnight later he reassured her: 'You are not old my dear – that is a fable – and you are as beautiful – both internally and externally. I at any rate shall always think you so and love you. To me your presence is always beautiful and stimulating – like champagne – only the excitement is of a more spiritual and intellectual nature. I think of you when I paint.'

But Carrington's nostalgia was caused by a decision to marry. She was still living with Strachey, and though their relationship was more or less platonic, he provided fatherly affection and a safe retreat when her attempts at sexual relationships with others failed, as they always had. He had become very fond of a friend of her brother's, Ralph Partridge, who had come to live with them, but the stability of the household had been upset when Partridge fell desperately in love with Carrington. In the end she reluctantly agreed to marry him, with Strachey's blessing, to keep them all living together. The wedding ended the correspondence between Carrington and Mark and their occasional meetings. To him it had a finality which made him act decisively to break contact; his letters ceased and he sought Ottoline's understanding: Garsington was barred to Carrington. When she protested Mark wrote, 'I have told Ottoline my difficulty about seeing you so that she will not expect you and will understand your not coming. I thought it best to do so.' (14 July 1921)

Carrington's marriage did not last and time gradually revealed how hopeless Mark's affair with her had been, and why. Even without the advent of Strachey they had virtually no chance. After her marriage Carrington fell in love again, with her husband's friend Gerald Brenan, and, as her friend David Garnett put it, 'her affairs with Mark Gertler and Gerald Brenan follow a curiously

similar pattern: almost the same deceptions, excuses and self accu-
sation are repeated in each relationship. And in each it was the hatred
of being a woman which poisoned it ... The greatest of her, or
perhaps I should say of our, misfortunes was that the men she
loved and lived with after her breach with Mark Gertler cared little
for painting ... There was nobody to work with her ... It is
possible that if there had been such a companionship, her psychological blockage would have been overcome. But in her isolation it
increased.'[158]

She never achieved a stable, happy sexual relationship with a
man, and in later years found herself increasingly drawn to other
women.

Mark had already found advantages in having a routine: 'You
wonder how I can "harness" myself down to rules," he had said to
Kot. 'Well, I find it good for my temperament to harness and
regulate myself. Strange as it may seem, I wish I could do so more.'
(19 July 1918)

Henceforth the core of his life consisted of the long solitary hours
of painting in the quiet high-walled studio. With or without a
model he worked in silence. Working hours were as regular as a
bank's – 10.30 a.m. to 12.30 p.m., and 2 p.m. to 4.30 p.m. Callers
were barred until 4.30 p.m. on six days a week. The time before
this was sacred to painting or thinking about painting, and he left
the studio only for the morning walk on the Heath or to go to his
rooms nearby for a solitary lunch.

When he returned to his studio after an absence he would exult:
'It is so good to be here once more, between these tall, silent walls.
Here I can do what I please – no one can interrupt me or get on my
nerves.'

Many of the factors which limited Mark's personal life could be
turned to advantage in organizing his work. Travel could be
unsettling and distracting as well as stimulating. So could strong
emotional attachments, or a varied social life. 'Travelling would
only throw me into a chaos,' he had told Kot years before. 'It
would be destructive to my temperament and to my art. The
greatest traveller is the mental traveller and the mental traveller
travels round the world in a backyard.' (20 June 1916)

Time had confirmed this belief. 'I *have* got enthusiasm for travel,' he wrote. 'Only there is just one thing I have even a greater enthusiasm for and that is painting – and I swear that moving about is bad for one's work. When I was young I felt that instinctively and now I know it consciously. Also travelling always exhausts me so much that the pleasure becomes doubtful.' (21 March 1921)

The domestic background necessary to this ordered existence was provided by a landlady, Mrs Bruce, who made no fuss, no demands, and offered no challenge to his peace. An ex-housekeeper, she had taken No. 19 Worsley Road, near Mark's studio, and he rented a simply furnished bedroom and sitting-room on the first floor. She cooked for him, and provided surprisingly good meals when he had friends in to dinner. He regarded her as his greatest piece of good fortune. 'Goodness only knows what I should do if I hadn't those rooms to go to,' he wrote from a sanatorium in 1925. He thought that they and his landlady were 'The one bright spot, the one bit of luck in my life.' When discussing money matters he told Kot, 'All I want is enough somehow to keep my rooms. They make all the difference to my life. I shall have to stay in a certain amount in the future for the sake of my health, and if I hadn't a fairly decent place to stay in, I don't know what I should do.' (29 September 1925)

Both his landlady and the woman who cleaned his studio became close friends. When the latter died in 1924 he wrote to Kot, 'I heard today that my little old lady from Hampstead died. I am sad about it. She was a loveable old thing and I shall miss her creeping about the studio, always anxious, pessimistic, and suspicious. She thought, I am sure, that she and I were the only decent people in the world, that the rest of the world were conspiring their utmost to ruin and destroy us, that we must fight our hardest against them to survive. Even her brother-in-law, old May and his family, she was mistrustful of. She used to refer to him merely by a sarcastic nod of her little head and say "him". She used to look carefully at me every morning, with a condoling look, as if to say: "Hm, the world *has* done it on you *this* morning to be sure." She very often would know before I did if I was going to be ill. I therefore used to dread her careful scrutiny, and would often try to avoid it by looking away. Her smile was worth seeing – I loved it – but if I sympathized with her over any little grievances her eyes would immediately grow red and be on the point of tears. I am sure she loved me and I her. I am so unhappy that some flowers I sent her will have arrived too late, as I know they would have made a difference to her. I am also sorry that I was away and so unable to see her before the end.' (8 August 1924)

CHAPTER 34

'I thought I always was serious'

Almost everyone who knew Mark considered that he was more dedicated to his art than anyone else they had met. In the twenties all friendships were subordinate to it: as long as the light lasted and he had the strength, he worked. Yet his friends were important to him. As he explained to Richard Carline once, 'I must read Goethe after what you say, but there is so little time for reading. I long to read more, but I simply can't find the time. The more I go on, the more does my painting absorb me. Really in order to paint at all, one must give oneself altogether and sacrifice everything. So it seems to me. Yet it is hard to give up some other things – reading especially. You see, I work all day, and in the evening one must see a human being.'

His social life was organized on a system nearly as constant as his working day. On Thursday evenings he entertained Kot and a group of men friends at his lodgings in Worsley Road, one other day he would have people in to tea, and another evening would be spent mainly alone with Kot. They would dine at a Jewish restaurant (Ross's in the Tottenham Court Road) and perhaps later see their mutual friends, the Russian-Jewish writer Michael Farbman and his wife. On Fridays Mark would often go to Golda and his brothers to see the Sabbath in. Though religion was left far behind him he was always moved by Golda's piety, and he liked to see the Friday candles lit.

On the other evenings he might go to a party, or to friends for a meal, and sometimes to concerts and plays. He liked to have friends in the studio: 'I love my studio at night . . . we have scrambled eggs and ham, fruit, coffee, later tea and buns.'

At first, the regularity of many of his leisure meetings was designed to reduce the bother of making engagements, but soon he enjoyed the ordered, ceremonious rhythm for its own sake. The days were never varied: if he returned to London on a Saturday it didn't occur to him to bring the group meeting forward in order to see his friends sooner. He made new friends only slowly, and over more than a decade the members of his circle hardly changed.*

When Mark did find time for reading, the books were often biographies. Ever since the story of the Victorian artist Frith had started him on the road to becoming a painter he had never lost his youthful love of literature about great men: 'They somehow stimulate me,' he said. Apart from an occasional adventure story he liked thick, serious books and filled in the gaps in his education by reading his way steadily through English literature, as well as the Russians, whom he still enjoyed so much. 'He used to speak of his three gods: Cézanne, Dostoievsky and Bach,' a friend recalled.

The friends who came to see him on Thursday evenings had a variety of occupations. There was Herbert Milne, a classical scholar on the staff of the British Museum, John Mavrogordato, later Professor of Modern Greek at Oxford, the scientist J. W. N. Sullivan, the poets Ralph Hodgson and James Stephens, and the poet and music critic Walter Turner, whom he had met at Garsington. Later additions were Dr A. S. Fulton, Keeper of the department of Oriental Books and Manuscripts at the British Museum, Dr Stewart Mackie, an ophthalmologist at Moorfields Hospital, Sydney Waterlow, and Dr Andrew Morland, whom Mark met when ill in a sanatorium.

But the circle was mainly literary – between one and two dozen

* Friendly relations with Carrington were resumed when she wrote to him in 1925, hearing that he was ill, and thereafter occasional letters were exchanged though they hardly ever actually met. She and Strachey continued to live together.

of the books on his shelves were presented by the authors. In some, such as Aldous Huxley's 'Chrome Yellow', he was able to recognize himself in one of the characters.★ Although he was on friendly terms with painters such as Nevinson, Richard Carline and Bernard Meninsky, the only really close friend interested in painting was Marjorie Hodgkinson, an ex-Slade student some ten years younger than himself, whom he met in the mid twenties.

Sometimes the group of men friends would have supper first at the Café Royal before going back to Mark's lodgings to drink tea and talk. Conversation was serious but not particularly erudite, and intuitive rather than rational: Kot might talk of events in Russia, the poets and scholars might discuss seventeenth-century literature, or Hodgson might expound on boxing, for which he had a passion.

Women were rarely admitted to the Thursday meetings, but on other occasions the men would bring their wives, and Mark got on particularly well with three of them: Delphine Turner, Christine Mavrogordato and Dorothy Morland. Other close female friends included Valentine Dobrée, Brett's sister, Sylvia, who was Ranee of Sarawak, Lydia Sherwood and Norah Meninsky.

Mark was very attractive to women and had a number of affairs, many of them with models. These friendships were easy going, sensual and gay, but none of them touched him deeply. He liked them to be on a footing of civilized equality: 'I don't want a good wife nor a good mistress,' he told Kot once. 'I like women to be my friends and equals, or superiors, as the case may be. Not half mistress and half slave . . . I hate that state of affairs.'

Many of his early companions had left England. Iris Tree spent much of her time overseas, but he heard from her from time to time. Brett went off to join Lawrence and Frieda in their travels in America and Europe.

Mark was not entirely unhappy at Lawrence's absence. 'At one time I used to blame myself for fearing to be disturbed by him,' he admitted. 'I put it down to a sort of cowardice. But now I have altered my mind because I think the kind of disturbance he creates is of the wrong sort, and does one only harm.' (8 October 1925)

★ The painter Gombauld.

He found Lawrence's attitude to some of their mutual acquaintances hard to understand. 'He seems always to prefer hurling himself back into relationships with people even when they have long since become rotten,' Mark pointed out. But he was worried by reports of Lawrence's condition, suspected that he had tuberculosis, and sent details of regimes which might help. Lawrence refused to see doctors and it was Mark's own doctor who, at his instigation, finally managed to visit Lawrence in Italy – but too late.*

Gilbert Cannan had written several more books, but as his friend the critic Frank Swinnerton put it, 'although verbosity increased, the talent remained stationary, and was covered over at last with a kind of rank growth of words ... but the talent had been real enough.' After several breakdowns from 1918 onwards Cannan was admitted in 1924 to The Priory mental hospital at Roehampton and there remained for the rest of his life.

Until Beatrice Campbell left London Kot and Mark ('them Roosshians', as her cook called them) still went often to her 'Sunday evenings'.

Some of the hours which Mark enjoyed most were spent in Kot's hous at No. 5 Acacia Road, Swiss Cottage; it was 'scrubbed and polished, with a special place for every cup, plate and book or piece of paper', and evenings would often end with the two of them sitting there, drinking Russian tea.

When Mark left London it was usually either to stay at Garsington, until Ottoline sold it in 1928,† or with Walter Taylor or other friends, never alone. But he needed a room of his own as a retreat, and would refuse an invitation if it meant sharing sleeping accommodation.

In the summer of 1921, Ottoline had fitted out a little cottage for him at Garsington and provided most of the furniture. Ottoline's daughter Julian, now growing up ('to my senses very beautiful, I love her solidity and bigness'), was an added attraction. 'I really love her,' Mark averred. But her playfulness added to the difficulty

* Dr Andrew Morland.
† The Morrells then moved to London; Mark continued to see Ottoline regularly until her death in 1938.

of concentrating on work in that 'pleasure ground'. 'She ought to wear a placard with "Please remember I'm only fifteen" on it,' he grumbled wryly. (June 1921)

Taylor, elderly, elegant and rich, had entered his life when he bought a picture in 1919. An amateur painter himself, Taylor had a good eye for pictures and had built up a fine collection. He was witty and amusing, and the two became firm friends. They could often be seen together at hotels in England, and sometimes overseas at Paris or St Tropez, or at Taylor's home in Brighton.

Mark liked Brighton, with its 'sea full of plump Jewesses of all ages. The language of Brighton is Yiddish so thank God I can make myself understood.' There was always plenty to see and do. He thought of writing a book about it one day, 'a sort of eulogy, to show we have a gay little Paris in our midst.' (August 1926)

On their travels he was usually Taylor's guest. The hotels were always good and comfortable, and Mark grew accustomed to periods of ease alternating with his frugal existence at home.

Doctors advised him to move out of England altogether and settle in a better climate. It would have been cheaper as well as healthier, and occasionally he was tempted. The beauty of St Tropez 'made my heart ache' he said. But he clung to the few roots he had. 'I should be bored to death living all alone abroad, he once told Kot; (29 September 1925) 'one must have roots somewhere and headquarters, don't you think?' He felt that his work lay in London: 'I am drawn to it as if by a magnetic power. In London is my true life.' Periods abroad usually ended in homesickness: 'I couldn't live out of England – it doesn't belong to one. Oh I am pining for Hampstead.' (9 April 1930)

Mark became almost happy. After all his troubles he had achieved a productive and more or less stable existence. 'I am fairly happy – I have a number of good friends', he wrote to Brett in June 1928. 'My health, as long as I take care, keeps fairly good. Materially I am comfortable – no financial worries. Mrs Bruce, my landlady, and my room continue to be a great comfort to me. As to my appearance – people tell me I still look young . . . I don't quite know what Juliette [Huxley] means by saying that I have grown very serious – I thought I always was serious.'

Life was a serious business, and his objection to people who 'only wanted it to be amusing' was as strong as ever. As far as he was concerned it could only be made tolerable by achievement. 'As long as I work I feel somehow that I am really *functioning*, to use one of your words,' he told Kot. His attitude was that of the professional, and amateur painters who met him found him arrogant and disparaging if they ventured their opinions on art with any persistence. Because the taste of life, to Mark, had something fundamentally 'unsatisfactory and sour' about it, he reacted impatiently against light disputation on its philosophy. Once Carrington, describing discussion at a weekend with some Bloomsbury friends, had said 'everyone agreed that Pleasure was certain, but argued over Good and Evil and Beauty.' Mark's reply was heavily crushing: 'I think that of all those uncertainties, Pleasure is the *most uncertain*.'

Yet his talent for humour was undiminished. 'Even when he was depressed he would sometimes flare up with something funny – he was a delightful companion,' recalled Juliette Huxley.

Like most artists Mark was used to the fact that many of the people he saw were potential buyers of his work; almost all his friends had bought a picture at one time or another; even Carrington had wanted to buy a drawing, but he had insisted on giving it to her – 'your money would choke me,' he said; and he appreciated the importance of keeping up a good front. As a result many thought him vainglorious. 'He considered himself a cut above most of his contemporaries,' an acquaintance observed; and Lytton Strachey, describing to Ottoline in 1916 how he had visited Gertler, seen the 'Merry Go Round' and found himself unable to like it, had added, 'fortunately he does all that for himself – one needn't bother with one's appreciations.' The feeling that it was necessary to put on a show, coupled with a desire to entertain people, would lead him to hold the floor at a gathering with seemingly absolute assurance. With head held high and a brilliant, lively look in his dark eyes he would tell story after story in his fast, clipped, amused voice. 'His humour was boundless and completely irreverent,' wrote Sylvia Lynd. 'It depended for its effects not on any verbal jest, but on accurate observation and aptness of mimicry. Mark describing an altercation in a restaurant, an incensed neighbour in a cinema, a Spaniard explaining to another Spaniard the difficulties that Mark was having with the water supply in his house, a friend missing train after train at a railway station because he had left his overcoat behind in the hotel and could not remember the French word *surtout*, and a friend uncertain what to pack for an elopement, a blind beggar, a man in uncomfortable boots walking along a road – with two words, two gestures, the person, the situation suddenly was there. His gentle low-pitched voice retained some of the Cockney vowels that were a legacy from Whitechapel, but it was a marvellous instrument for catching a tone or a phrase.'

Another friend recalled that Mark would mimic a Frenchman arguing, using nonsense words but catching the right cadence. 'And once he imitated an Italian singing outside a pub so well that we thought he must really have a fine singing voice which we didn't know about.'

'Not least often he made himself the butt of his own stories,' said Sylvia Lynd. 'His account of his confusion in foreign cities, of his social solecisms in England, of his adventures with over robust or excitable people, were hilariously funny. I have never heard him repeat himself in the seventeen years of our acquaintance. Whatever befell him he turned into a fantasia of absurdity, and it is this running commentary of laughter that will be most missed by his friends... His stories were not edifying, but they were the stories of a man ... whose experience passed through the whole scale of living.'[159]

Beatrice Campbell recalled, 'He used to make funny stories out of his most tragic moments.'

When he had heard in 1921 that Carrington was going to marry someone else, Beatrice Campbell wrote, 'He was so shattered that he felt that nothing but a revolver could end his pain. He went out to buy one, but found it was Saturday afternoon and all the shops were shut ... He could laugh at his sufferings.'[160]

Many of Mark's stories were about his family and the brothers' slightly eccentric business methods. Although the fur business brought in money steadily its official status had kept changing: in 1910 it had been 'Gerty Gertler, furrier', in 1914 'Henry Gertler', and so on. In 1924 Harry and Jack went bankrupt, as their brother-

in-law Atelson had done earlier, but within a year or two they had
recovered. There were several fires: when, from the heights of
Hampstead, any of Mark's friends saw a fire in the East End they
would wonder if this was another Gertler business on fire. Mark used
to describe his brothers' bewilderment when he rejected their offer
to insure his studio heavily and arrange one of these conflagrations
there.

Sometimes the various members of Mark's world would converge
in odd meetings, as when Taylor went to the East End, took a fancy
to the Gertlers and thereafter became very friendly with them; or
when Brett, before her departure from England, decided to
'educate' one of Mark's nieces and he disapproved: 'Dear Brett, I
somehow can't see my niece talking Chekov, Michael Angelo or
Dostoievski etc. Neither do I desire her to. Why should you try and
educate her? How queer you are about such matters. I should advise
you to leave her alone, and not fill her mind with badly digested
stuff. A Spanish picture or a Chekov story will never mean any
more to her than the paper I am writing on means to me. She'll
only, in consequence of your teaching, go about talking a lot of
nonsense; whilst on the subject of getting a rich husband she is at
least sincere and the desire is genuine. You must realize there are
different kinds of people in the world and each kind gravitates
automatically towards the thing it has most need of for sustenance.'
(11 December 1920)

Once there was an encounter at Brighton. 'Julian Morrell longed
to dance, and dragged us to the "Metropole", a beastly vulgar hotel
filled with Jews and Americans of the very worst type,' he told
Valentine Dobrée. 'My brother Jack of course was staying there
with a "smart chap" and "girls". And so we all got mixed up.
Julian adored it . . . What with that and a most incredible dinner at
Marchant's, who has a large family with two tall young sons, to
whose charms Julian immediately fell – And Taylor's adopted
daughter who also appeared on the scene, it turned out to be
something between a cinema film depicting "Smart Life" (because we
were all constantly getting into evening dress) and a scene out of the
"Possessed" . . . At the "Metropole", they have invented a life based
entirely on the Cinema. Words cannot describe it.' (August 1923)

18—MG   *   *

CHAPTER 35

A world of wonder

In the twenties Mark's work was appreciated, and it brought in a sufficient income to live quietly, barring emergencies. Harry and Jack played a vital role because if Mark got into serious difficulties he knew they would come to the rescue. He had to call on them when he became really ill, and each time he emerged from the sanatorium they would help him to get started again.

At the sanatorium in 1921, as soon as he began to recover, Mark had started painting again, in defiance of doctors' orders. It had been a strange experience: 'Painting today seriously for the first time since three months had an extraordinary effect on me,' he told Kot. 'I don't know how to describe it. My old paint box, my brushes so well known to me, the very same with which I struggled at Penn Studio and Garsington; it was so extraordinary and for some reason so sad. I really don't know why it affected me so much, but I wanted to cry. My poor old paint box in a sanatorium . . . but really I can't describe it. The only sensation I can liken it to is – supposing you loved a person very much, but whom you saw only occasionally and then only among other people – always in a bustle – and suddenly one day you and your beloved are shipwrecked on a deserted island. Just you two . . .' (28 November 1920)

By the time he came out, after six months there, he had finished nine paintings. Marchant was so impressed with them that in May he promised to pay Mark a regular advance of three hundred pounds a year against sales. Marchant held shows of his pictures every year at the Goupil Gallery, and when he died and his gallery failed the Leicester Galleries stepped in after a short interval with a similar arrangement. Thanks to these two galleries Mark worked from 1921 to 1932 with no pressing financial worries.

He remained faithful to the London Group, and their exhibitions also led to occasional sales. It was only necessary to sell a few paintings a year: a sale price of £50 or so for one picture would alone pay the rent of his studio for most of a year.

Roger Fry's support, though intermittent, was crucial. Of Mark's show in 1921 he wrote: 'In each fresh series of pictures Mr Gertler sets to work to acquire some new quality. It looks now as though he would arrive at sensibility by a sheer process of exhaustion. By pushing everything he does to its furthest limit he learns exactly what not to do next time . . . he never hides behind an evasive statement . . . throughout the whole process of his self-education Mr Gertler has stuck grimly and determinedly to the whole plastic vision . . . it is this that gives to his art its compelling quality.

'One might dislike his vision; one could never altogether pass it by. It was always realized with full conviction. His work has often been ugly, repellent, brutal; it has never been irrelevant or insignificant, and above all never insincere or facile.'[161] For an important exhibition in 1928 he again wrote a long review in the *New Statesman*.

'Fry wrote a very good article on my pictures Mark said once. 'What a relief and comfort it was to read what he had to say, after all the usual "favourable" meaningless bosh of the average critic. Thank goodness we have at least *one* critic in the country.'

In the twenties Mark painted mostly still lifes and single figures, the latter including a series of female nudes, which are among his finest works. His pictures showed little of the strong interest in character and personality which had been such an important feature of his early work: now he concentrated on the more sensual aspects of people, or simply on their purely visual qualities. Often he preferred to paint humanity at one remove from reality by including pictures of Staffordshire figures in his work, focusing an intense scrutiny on these and other inanimate objects. He collected objects such as plaster busts, Benin heads, China parrots and artificial silk flowers. He never tired of painting these props and they were used over and over again, built into closely organized, brilliantly patterned designs.

Behind Mark's work seemed to lie a need for something stable and enduring. After his death, Valentine Dobrée maintained that he put in his pictures all the things that he loved: 'And as is so often the way, the things that he loved were the things of his youth: the interior, the lace-veiled front room, with its ornaments, the bright ruched cushions, the slightly dusty artificial flowers, all a little crowded, and presided over by the monumental figure of his mother. The grandeur, the scale, were those a child sees. Anyone, who knew him at the time, will remember his delighted discovery, when he felt that he could discard the unpractical, because fleeting, real flower for the artificial one, which would always be there . . . One feels, here is a man who loved permanence: permanence in the way a Victorian would have understood it; the permanence achieved by making as complete a statement as possible. Nearly all his pictures are highly wrought. "Genius is an infinite capacity for taking pains", comes into one's mind, and with it all the mockery that has been aimed at the first-rate swotter. Yet, if the taking of pains is fortified by a constant and enduring passion, this is certainly the right description.'[162]

In Mark's pictures there were other qualities which seemed to be understood most by people who knew Mark himself, and which drew them closer to him. Writing of a painting of a teapot at an exhibition, Beatrice Campbell was moved by 'the profundity and mystery, the beauty of the paint, the queer sense of eternity that it contained!' About another picture, a Staffordshire man on a horse, she said, 'It was so final a statement, so completely realized and understood, that it made everything else in the gallery look like tinsel.'[163]

Yet in spite of the permanent appearance of the full, clearly defined forms, there was something in Mark's painting which suggested the gypsy – a rich, exotic, almost gaudy quality.

Although Mark had a wide circle of acquaintances and a handful of close friends, his life in the twenties was essentially solitary; he had learnt how to be less vulnerable only by not letting people be close enough to have the power to hurt him. But his work brought him immeasurable delight.

Beatrice Campbell recalled: 'Gertler said that every emotion he felt in ordinary life was amplified a hundred fold in painting – every anguish, every ecstasy, every sort of pain and suffering, every kind of joy and contentment.'[164] The disappointments could not cancel out the delights. As Mark wrote once, 'The inspiration inside me still goes on – nothing now can harm that world of wonder that I contain inside me and which has become as if fixed there.'

To Kot he declared, 'It is wonderful to create and to feel, as I do, able to create wonderful things. You can't think how wonderful I feel sometimes. I wish I could tell you of my wonderful inner experiences. I would like you to know.'

PART TEN

The purpose

'My work was my faith, my purpose.' – MARK GERTLER

CHAPTER 36

Golda

Mark's need to develop as an artist was fundamental to his character. A combination of extreme integrity and self doubting humility
forced him always to keep up the pace of experimentation. Constantly on his guard against the danger of empty repetition of styles
and techniques, he painted each picture as if it were his first, and his last.

Towards the end of the twenties his doubts intensified, although
the critics were happy enough. When his 1930 exhibition opened at
the Leicester Galleries the *Nation* said, 'It dispels any doubt, if doubt
there was, that he is one of the most important of English painters
at the present day.' The *New Statesman* commented, 'Mr Gertler has
found a completely personal expression, and though the word
genius is not one to be bandied lightly, it is something like the
liberation of a genius which is to be witnessed at the Leicester
Galleries at present.' The following year Roger Fry wrote in the
same paper: 'Gertler's intensely individual style isolates him curiously
from all his colleagues. He is I suspect the most ambitious artist of
the modern British school. The kind of persevering courage that
impels him to squeeze the last drop of significance from his subject
is rare in this country where we tend to admire the man who succeeds
without taking too much trouble.'

But Mark's obsessive vision was unsatisfied. In his notebook he
expressed his doubts and tried to sort out his ideas:

'What is the matter with me? Well it is something serious – the
greatest crisis of my life. In fact, for the time being I see no solution.
The trouble is my work. What is my value as an artist? What have
I in me? Is there anything there worth while after all? That is the
point. I doubt myself, I doubt myself terribly – after all these years
of labour. And how I worked – so so hard, and I have lived and fed
up my work. My work was my faith, my purpose. But, as I find

now to my acute discomfort, an essential part of that faith and that purpose was not just to work alone, but the hope that I will, some day at least, produce pictures that will *stand*, that will have some place among work that counts. Well have I achieved anything of the sort so far? I doubt it very much. Do I stand a chance of succeeding in the future? *That* is the point!'

His veneration for the great moderns, while still a continual spur, was also a reminder of his own limitations.

'Today I set up a new little still life,' he wrote on 20 November 1929. 'Pomegranates in a basket with a yellow bow. Yes, beautiful, and I saw before me my vision. How *I* see it. And I get a fit of depression. How different to the vision of a Matisse, a Picasso! Ah! those aristocrats! Moving so high above me. What a rough, clumsy peasant they make me feel! What an everyday vision is mine compared with theirs! How strongly do I feel the height of men who really *achieve* and my own lowness. My past work keeps floating through my mind's eye, awful ghosts that torture me. I cannot bear to go to a house that contains any of my pictures, for at once I am flooded with misery and despair! Seeing any good picture or reproduction does the same thing to me. I feel inferior, inferior to all . . . Of course I contemplate death, over and over again. Sometimes it even seems the logical solution, for I frankly confess it, I cannot live without that *purpose – to create real work*. It seems to me that it is either one of two things: either I regain sufficient faith for my 'purpose' or I die . . .

'Sometimes I think of finding something else to do. But what? To kill myself; there is the dreadful selfishness of it! Think of my mother . . . and perhaps a few others! . . . I am putting up a strong fight. I feel hopeful at times that there will be a sort of rebirth – a new sort of adjustment – something I don't know of what nature. But I am doing my best to treat this dreadful period as a sort of pause, giving myself the time to be reborn . . .

'A few days after my last note I went down to Leicester Square to buy a revolver. I felt I ought to have one, so that I had in my possession an easy means of ending my life. When I got near the shop my tongue went dry with horror. I felt that by getting an 'easy means' I should not be giving myself a chance. Anyway I felt cheap and degraded, and I turned away in disgust.'

The thought of the shock it would be to Golda always prevented an actual attempt at suicide. Such an act would in a sense be robbing her. His life and his success were the tangible results of her own sacrifices in the early years of privation. To throw his life away would render pointless the fight she had made for it.

Besides, she now needed him, more than ever. With age her relationships with her other children were becoming increasingly strained. She took Jack for granted and criticized Harry because she didn't like his wife. Moving from one to the other she grew tired of living with each, and they, in turn, found her more and more difficult.

Only with Mark was she really happy, listening by the hour to his stories, discussing his affairs, and offering him shrewd advice. Though she could not comprehend his problems with painting, she was acute and understanding about people, and always anxious to help. He hid nothing from her, and through his talk she knew all the people he knew. They were patient with each other. In spite of a charming geniality of manner, neither found it easy to maintain close relationships with other people, but their own had an un-breakable resilience.

In essentials she had changed little with the years, and Mark still drew from her the same strength and reassurance as in the days in Spital Square when she sat in her dusty black dress in the dark kitchen or outside the front door watching the life of the East End.

At the end of the twenties, after living some years in a Jewish hotel in the East End, (the Central Hotel), she moved into a top flat with Jack at Number seven Christchurch Avenue, Kilburn, about a mile and a half from Mark; Harry and his family, and Mark's eldest sister Deborah and her family, all lived nearby. The road was tree-lined and the houses, red brick semi-detached, were spacious and pleasant.

Often Golda and Jack, accompanied by Mark, would go over to Harry's or Deborah's house for a huge meal and a family evening of games with the children, and gossip; this consisted mostly of reminiscences or humorous stories by Mark and Jack, who would vie with each other while the others laughed helplessly. The talk was in a mixture of languages: Mark and his brothers spoke English to the children and to each other, Yiddish to Golda. To her they were still Harrish, Jankel and Max; she was never at ease with English.

Although she accepted the fact that these cheerful households had discarded much of the rigid orthodoxy of her training, and although she didn't appear to mind her children's loss of interest in religion, she herself scrupulously observed all the fasts and ceremonies of her faith, and on the Day of Atonement she would pray to the end. If she ever stayed at a hotel it had to be a kosher house and her own life was as simple as ever, devoid of cinemas, theatres or even books.

In 1929 Golda fell and broke a hip. The injury was wrongly diagnosed and she was advised to exercise it. The resulting pain and complications were so severe, and the deterioration in her condition so rapid, that the doctors advised there was no hope of recovery. She was saved by another doctor – found by Mark – who correctly diagnosed her trouble in time for treatment. From this time she could move only slowly, taking an hour or more to dress each morning, walking with a stick and always using a stool for her leg when she sat down.

Mark had himself been in hospital in the summer of 1929. He had collapsed, and the doctors feared a fresh attack of tuberculosis. On this occasion his friend Marjorie Hodgkinson accompanied him, staying near the sanatorium, at Mundesley, Norfolk.

Over the previous five years they had been seeing each other more and more frequently and writing to each other between meetings. Mark had come to miss her when she was away from London. 'First I feel conscious of a sort of blank, then I realise it is your absence,' he had written the year before. 'We are, I think, a real support to each other.' She had become devoted to him, and after his troubles of 1929 – the spell at the sanatorium and his mother's illness – he turned to her for comfort.

He was now forty. When his friends asked him why he hadn't married he used to tell them that he had plenty of affairs, hadn't the money to support a wife, and didn't really want children. 'If I marry at all,' he said, 'it will only be to please my mother and then I must marry a Jewish girl.' Once he had actually become engaged

to a Jewess – Phyllis Wilkinson – who was related to one of his
brothers-in-law. She was not particularly well-off, but Mark felt
that a life with her would give him a place among his own people
and would please Golda. He had broken off the engagement soon
after, seeing it as the result of an impractical dream of security and
happiness.

Although Marjorie was not Jewish, Mark found himself in 1930
discussing with her the idea of getting married. At the time, they
were on holiday together, in Paris. They had plenty of interests and
friends in common – for instance, Marjorie got on well with
Ottoline and Kot. An aunt of Marjorie's had died the previous
autumn, leaving her an income of two or three hundred pounds a
year, not large, but enough to pay her share of living expenses, so
that it seemed they could manage financially together.

Both wanted to keep their independence and guard their privacy,
even to the extent of having separate bedrooms. It could be a
flexible kind of marriage, an alliance for mutual companionship
and support.

Mark was rather nervous of his family's reaction if he married a
Gentile, but he decided to go ahead, and on 3 April they were
married quietly, with no friends or relations present, by the British
Consul in Paris. The family, informed at the last minute, were
staggered. 'My people object strongly; just what I expected,' Mark
told Kot. But their objections sprang from concern and doubts
about the wisdom of his action, and were quickly put aside. A small
comedy typical of the family ensued. Jack had himself married a
few months earlier and raised no serious objection when his wife
Dorothy, braving Golda's expected disapproval, sent a telegram of
congratulation, though he grumbled, 'I don't know what's going to
happen. The family will be annoyed at your sending it.' Dorothy's
next step was to telephone Mark's hotel in Paris, and put Golda on
the line. After ten minutes agitated conversation all was well: she
gave her blessing. 'My mother is pleased!' Mark wrote excitedly to
Kot. Golda, putting the phone down, told Dorothy not to tell 'the
family' about the call, as they might be angry with *her*. But Harry
and the sisters soon accepted the situation as well.

For their honeymoon Mark and Marjorie went to Bandol, joining Aldous and Maria Huxley there. In the autumn, back in

London, Mark gave up his lodgings and they moved into a two-roomed flat nearby at 22 Kemplay Road.

Golda was living with Jack and his wife in a house they had taken about a mile away, and Mark took Marjorie round. On her previous visits Marjorie had felt that Golda was rather suspicious of Mark's women friends, and though Golda now made an effort to be pleasant, it was difficult for her to hide the belief that Mark had made a mistake; alone of her five children, he had not married in a synagogue; cordialities were exchanged but there were fewer than half a dozen meetings between the two women.

Although Golda had been tough enough to make a surprisingly good recovery from her illness she was left with a number of disabilities which made her a semi-invalid; a further complication was a fear of treatment of any kind. She had always been wary of doctors, and the memory of the pain from exercising the broken hip, besides causing nightmares, made her refuse any further medical treatment. Her condition was not improved by remedies such as keeping a small hot water bottle inside her dress to alleviate pain and cold, together with a tight scarf round the neck to cover the hot flushes caused by the heat of the bottle.

After a year or so Golda moved out of Jack's house into Harry's. A few months later both she and Harry felt a change was desirable and Golda moved again, this time to a friend's house nearby, where she rented a room, going over the road to Deborah's house for meals.

Early in 1932 came her last accident. This time she broke bones in both shoulders. After three weeks in hospital she again made a remarkable recovery and was discharged, but within two days of returning home she caught pneumonia and died, quite suddenly, on 22 February.

For the second time Mark and his brothers and sisters sat shivah together. Over the previous three years they had become acclimatized to the thought that she would die soon, and the actual event took place and slipped into the past with surprisingly little pain at first. The effects of her death began with a gradual disintegration of the group of households: within a few years they had scattered, Jack to North-east London and Harry to Middlesex, leaving Deborah in Kilburn. Soon Mark began to forget his Yiddish.

CHAPTER 37

Marjorie

For many years Mark had had little contact with any of the 'Bloomsbury' group except the Morrells, although he liked Roger Fry (and after he died in 1933 Mark produced a picture called 'Homage to Roger Fry'). If he ran into Lytton Strachey they would pass the time of day, but their old friendship had never been renewed, and he was little moved by the news of Strachey's death from cancer in February 1932. Then, a month after Golda's death, came another sad event which shocked him deeply.

He had written sympathetically to Carrington about Strachey's death, but she was inconsolable and her moods grew sadder and more strange. She sent him a wedding present – two years after his marriage – and took out his old love letters to her and read them all. When she told Mark of this he replied that by a curious coincidence he had come across hers in a drawer some months earlier and had read them again. 'We were both very young – and probably unsuited,' Mark wrote. 'And it is over now and nobody's fault.' On 11 March Carrington shot herself. 'She felt unable to live without Strachey,' Mark reported to Brett. 'It was a terrible shock.'

With the death of Golda Mark was even more grateful for Marjorie's love. They were happier than he had expected, and their little flat became the centre for a wide circle of friends. On Saturdays they would hold open house, and though the hospitality consisted only of lemon tea and talk so many people came that some were unable to get into the flat at all and had to stand and talk on the stairs.* On holiday they made more friends, such as Sidney Bernstein, the theatrical producer, and at a little country inn in Fontainebleau Mark became so gay with the local peasants – and

---

* New friends included A. P. Herbert and his wife, T. S. Eliot, J. B. Priestley, V. S. Pritchett and Henry Moore. Both Pritchett and Moore later recalled that they were very impressed by Mark's daily routine of hard work.

so drunk – that he demonstrated a skill of his youth by dancing for them on a table.

They kept their independence, occasionally going away separately.

In August 1932 their son Luke was born, and the following year they took a pleasant, dilapidated early Victorian house at 53 Haverstock Hill, in Hampstead.

All might have continued well if they had both had good health. But Marjorie's was also uncertain, and the impression of vigour and strength which she gave was deceptive. She became very ill with a kidney complaint just before Luke's birth – which was premature – and she proved to be as liable to colds and influenza as Mark. Sometimes they were both ill at once: 'We have a nurse, the flat is like a hospital,' Mark wrote in January 1933. Irregular meals and hours began to take their toll of Mark's health.

The following year Marjorie became pregnant again. There seemed to be nothing for it but to find a doctor willing to operate. 'In the first place it might have been serious for her to have another baby and we decidedly didn't want another anyhow,' Mark wrote. He was forced to borrow the money from a friend.

Still they were happy. In 1934 they took a house for the summer in Castelltersol, near Barcelona, and shared it with an aunt of Marjorie's and a friend of Mark's – the publisher and picture collector Tom Balston, whom he was teaching to paint. Mark took pleasure in the 'good, quiet, simple life' ('as Freda Lawrence would say,' he wrote, 'the country is so Real, the landscape is so *Real* and the people are so REAL!') and he enjoyed watching Luke developing. 'In the village he is a great favourite,' Mark told Kot. 'We took him to some open-air dancing (there has been a fiesta here); he caused a great sensation. He ran about laughing and excited during the intervals and the people threw confetti at him. As he ran the confetti showered from his head like golden rain.' It was a 'wonderful holiday,' Mark remembered.

In the autumn the Leicester Galleries were putting on another show of his work.

'I feel the usual anxieties etc. but if it was anything like last time I shall be alright,' Mark said to Sidney Bernstein. 'I have confidence in this collection and I can't help feeling they are the best lot I have so far produced. I should like you particularly to notice the pastels, I think I've struck something new there. I like the actual texture of the medium so much, it is like Fresco. I hope people will be encouraging about them as I should like to work a lot in Pastel.'

The depression of 1930 and its aftermath had made it much more difficult for artists to sell their work: 'These are terrible times for painters,' Mark had written. Though his 1930 show had gone 'fairly well', in the following year he had to begin teaching art at the Westminster Technical Institute in Vincent Square on two evenings a week. 'It's rather dreadful and precarious,' he told Sidney Bernstein.

The 1934 exhibition was not a success.[165] A few days after its opening Mark wrote to Marjorie, who had stayed on in Spain for an extra month: 'Dearest Marjorie, it would be a great blessing if you could get back on the 26th, as I badly need someone to have a word with. I am going through a very bad time. My show looks like a complete failure and the pictures generally very unpopular. There is not much chance of my receiving any more cheques from the Leicester Galleries.' (11 October 1934.)

The failure was all the more worrying because he could no longer ask his brothers for help. In 1930, another bankruptcy petition had been filed against Harry and Jack. This time it was serious: the brothers had never been particularly good at organizing a business but for a while the terms of trade had favoured them. Now the fur trade had declined considerably since the boom of the early 1920's, and the 1930 depression brought the collapse of many small firms. Two years later Mark was saying, 'My brothers' business has gone down to nothing and they are starving!' (19 April 1932)

An important prop to Mark's existence had been removed. From now on there was no falling back on the family if he was in difficulty. On the contrary it was now his turn to do what he could for them. Harry had been able to earn a living as a fur cutter, but Jack had been reduced to extremes, and Mark asked Sidney Bernstein if he could help: 'Could you possibly find some sort of job for my brother – the poor one? He is in an awful state again – quite destitute. He has, poor chap, tried so many things – electric

'The Doll', 1914; 'I have suddenly got so fascinated by a funny doll belonging to my little niece that I have put everything aside in order to paint it'. **(43)**

'Young Girlhood', 1923; one of the best of Mark's series of pictures of girls and women in the 1920s. (44)

'Young Girlhood—II'; another picture of Alice Edwards two years after 'Young Girlhood'. **(45)**

A painting of the Manor House, Garsington, where Mark spent many summers from 1916 to 1927 when Lady Ottoline Morrell and her family lived in it. The picture is now owned by Ottoline's daughter, Mrs Julian Vinogradoff. **(46)**

'The Coster Woman', 1923. **(47)**

'Coster Family on Hampstead Heath'; the girl on
the left modelled for 'The Servant Girl'; the girl
on the right is Alice Edwards. **(48)**

'After Bathing', 1924; another picture of Alice Edwards. (49)

Left 'Supper', a portrait of Miss Natalie Denny, 1928; a contemporary critic said, 'It epitomizes this warm luxuriant aspect of life which is peculiar to Gertler'. **(50)**

Below 'Reclining Nude', 1928; Alice Edwards is here painted in a close-knit design of sweeping curves. **(51)**

Opposite page Mark liked to collect objects such as china parrots and Staffordshire figures, and the ones he was most fond of were painted over and over again in various elaborate arrangements. *Above* 'The Basket of Fruit', 1925. **(52)** *Below* 'Still Life with Aspidistria', 1926. **(53)**

Mark as a young man. (54)

Edward Marsh 1912. (55)

Marjorie Hodgkinson; she married Mark Gertler in 1930. (56)

John Middleton Murry. (57)

Mark as a young man, in 1926. (58)

Katherine Mansfield. **(59)**

Mark as a young man. **(60)**

Mark at forty-five. **(61)**

S. S. Koteliansky. **(62)**

St John Hutchinson, a portrait by Mark Gertler. **(63)**

Aldous Huxley, Brett and Mark at Garsington. **(64)**

Back row left to right: Delphine Turner, J. Mavrogordato, Mark, W. Turner; *front:* Christine Mavrogordato, Kate Foster, Jason Wood, Marjorie, Richard Carline. **(65)**

Mark Gertler and Ottoline Morrell. **(66)**

...tting left to right: Ralph Hodgson,
S. Koteliansky, J. W. N. Sullivan.
...anding left to right: Mark Gertler,
W. Turner, Professor H. Hugh,
H. Milne. **(67)**

'The Sisters', 1929; two of Mark's nieces. **(68)**

'The Song', 1932. (69)

ndol'; painted during Mark's
neymoon in Spain in 1930. (70)

Opposite page: Above 'Homa
Roger Fry', 1934; one of a
of pictures for which he
pastel. **(73)**

Below 'The Spanish Fan',
(74)

After 1930 Mark gave up the
very successful manner in which
he had painted for ten years to
try to develop new ideas. *Above*
'Still Life with Head', 1935. **(71)**

Right 'The Mandolinist', 1934.
(72)

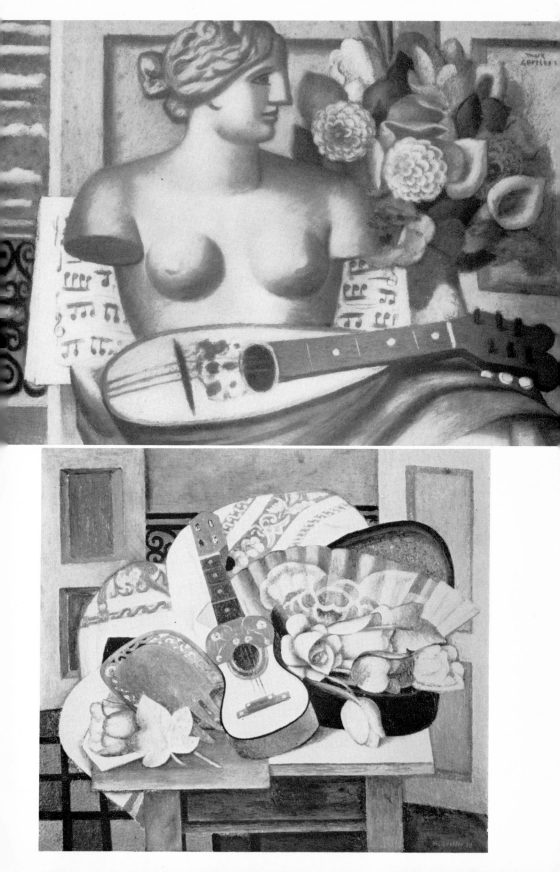

bulbs – stockings – but no success. Now he is longing for some *regular* work. He doesn't mind *what* it is as long as he could earn about £2 a week. My family suggest that you might be able to employ him in one of your theatres – commissionaire or something.' When Jack applied to the Jewish Board of Guardians in the following year for help in opening a shop it was Mark who provided all three of the necessary backers: Walter Taylor, Thomas Balston and Sidney Bernstein, to whom Mark wrote about his guarantee: 'If necessary I promise to pay the £50 myself.'

Not all the unpopularity of Mark's pictures could be put down to the depression, or even to the fact that he was struggling to develop a new kind of picture and many of his former admirers were 'shocked and puzzled'. He was uneasily aware that his work was far less consistent in quality than it had been. A large part of his energies had been diverted from painting to grappling with domestic difficulties – bills, accounts and servant problems. While on holiday, instead of longing to get back to London as a peaceful working place, he now shrank from it. 'I am really reluctant to return to London with all its complexity and servant problems and telephone calls,' he had written from Spain (29 August 1934).

The peace and stability in which his work of the twenties was conceived had been replaced by constant movement. In 1932 the owner of Penn Studio died and he had to leave. 'I have been pushed out of my studio where I functioned for nearly eighteen years,' he told Sidney Bernstein. 'I cannot get over the tragedy of leaving. When I am on holiday it will come over me . . . that for the first time in history I shall not have my studio – a real workshop – to go back to?' After a few uneasy months of trying to work in a room at home he took another studio in spite of the expense. When they moved to Haverstock Hill, he gave this up and worked in a room at home. In 1936 the lease of the house was due to expire and soon they had to begin house hunting again.

By early 1935 he was feeling 'half dead and very depressed.' To their other worries had been added concern over Luke's health. It was found that a series of delicate operations was necessary. In March he wrote to Balston: 'I have just come from the hospital, where poor little Luke went through his operation. Unfortunately I

19—MG

arrived at a bad moment; he was having his first dressing changed. His screams have completely unnerved me . . . Don't get married and have children. Life is quite hard enough without the two extra lots of worries and complexities that a wife and child provide. At the moment I feel that I shall never paint in peace again. I feel trapped and hate like poison the least little pain that Luke must suffer – and I always shall!'

The cost of the treatment for Luke increased their worry about money, which grew worse with problems about Marjorie's income: 'For some long time before the holidays I had to pay for everything to do with housekeeping because Marjorie's overdraft was so impossible – she now owes me £50,' Mark wrote on one occasion.*

In the summer of 1935 they went again to Castelltersol, but the harmony of the previous year had gone, leaving friction and strains between them. Mark, suffering from headaches and depression, grumbled about the house and criticized the friends of Marjorie's who were staying with them. 'Marjorie is in an ecstasy of happiness and loves being here. She has staying with her Greville† and a man called Hiller,' he told Kot, adding disparagingly, 'Both the sort of people she loves living with.' Mark was uneasy about Marjorie's relationship with Hiller, and there were rows and 'talks'. After they got back to London, Mark wrote, 'My life seems to have got into a complete mess, caused chiefly by Marjorie. I don't know how it will end. Sometimes my nerves seem at snapping point. Although her intentions and behaviour are alright, there is obviously something very wrong underneath, and the atmosphere is pretty strained. Yet there seems nothing we can do about it. Our lives are really very much involved and mixed up together, and an immediate parting is really very difficult. So there is nothing to do but to struggle on and hope for some change to happen.' (1 October 1935)

They both tried to mend matters. 'Marjorie is being very nice lately and so perhaps things may go better as time passes,' Mark told Balston in January 1936. 'But I really cannot make out what

* An investment which provided part of her income had failed.
† Greville Foster the dancer, who was married to a Spaniard.

her real feelings are just now – We don't discuss it any more as it is obviously best to let things drift for the time being.'

Mark's depressions and attacks of migraine grew worse, and he began to cough again, 'a cough that makes me feel more nervous than anything else,' he noted in June. 'Of course my ill health is partly due to my relations with Marjorie, which are not right even now. We had another 'talk' in fact, but arrived nowhere as usual. She swears the change has nothing to do with her feelings for Hiller, yet there's no doubt her feelings have become dulled towards me; and it is that which is somehow exasperating. She admits this detachment but still says there would be "no life" for her without me.'

Inevitably he ended up again in the sanatorium. This time it was almost a relief. 'I arrived last night,' he wrote on 2 July 1936. 'I have been in a way longing to get here – though dreading it too. I have been so unhappy at home that I longed for *any* change; when I got here I went through the usual fit of depression this place always gives me on arrival, but I soon got over it, and now feel thankful for the peace and rest, which I have not been able to enjoy for months and months . . . I hope to paint as soon as I feel up to it . . . Marjorie came with me and is staying in a hotel near by; she leaves tomorrow and then we do not meet for well over three months. I think this is a good thing for both of us. I don't know what our future relationship will be like, but a rest from each other for a time has become absolutely essential. Anyway it will give me time to get strong enough to face more trouble if necessary – at the side of her I felt I could not rest.'

The doctors could find no evidence that the tuberculosis had started up again, but the general breakdown in his health was more extensive than had at first appeared. After a week or so his condition worsened: 'I am running very high temperatures, 104! Horrible headaches and life isn't worth living . . . They don't quite know if it is the lung or what. Whatever it is it is horrible.' (10 July 1936) Every day he grew worse: 'It's like being on fire with terrible headaches.' One day, unable to bear the pain any longer, he yielded to an overwhelming impulse and slashed open one of his wrists. But the will to live and paint was still strong; he rallied and rang for the nurse in time.

CHAPTER 38

Last Try

By the end of August 1936 Mark was rapidly getting better. The view through the window of his room at the sanatorium excited him and he began to paint again. Finding himself still too weak to stand he worked sitting down, trying to finish the picture before the flowers faded.

In his previous spells at sanatoria Mark had never allowed friends to visit him, unwilling to allow himself to be seen until he recovered. This time he raised no objections. They found him increasingly cheerful, making light of his suicide attempt and turning it into amusing stories. Describing one of these, Beatrice Campbell wrote that on the night afterwards, when he was not to be left alone, 'the only person who could be found to stay with him was the night porter. On the table of Gertler's room was a large book of reproductions of Picasso's drawings and paintings, and to pass the long hours the porter looked through this book. Gertler pretended to be asleep. He watched the man slowly turning the pages, then turning the book upside down and from side to side. When he came to the end he went back to the beginning again and so the night passed. Gertler said afterwards, "That night porter was never the same man again".'[166]

In October Mark was ready to come out of the sanatorium and rallied his strength for a supreme effort.

For a while it seemed he might succeed.

As he had no money and no hope of earning any until he could work, Phillip Morrell tried to organise a whip-round among wealthy acquaintances. He had little success, but some of Mark's friends helped him to make a new start. Sidney Bernstein paid the first month's bill at the sanatorium – an enormous £72; Shearman helped, and Mavrogordato sent £10, saying he was unable to afford more. 'I am afraid "Plucky Little Gwen" has ignored my appeal for money; on the other hand I received £40 from

Hutchinson's daughter and £10 from himself,' Mark told Balston. 'They heard from Shearman of my illness and sent me the money. Very nice of them indeed.'

While Mark was in the sanatorium Marjorie had worked at the task of preparing a new home for them – a house at No. 5 Grove Terrace, near Hampstead Heath, which had been bought with a mortgage raised by her father. Mark looked forward to joining her there. 'Well, perhaps I shall see you next Saturday,' he wrote. 'Meanwhile all my love and let me tell you that I feel proud to be 'linked' to a woman as beautiful, as exceptional and of such good taste as you. Why say all this? Well, because I just feel that way about you . . . I am longing to see Luke again,' he avowed. 'I've almost forgotten what he looks like.'

There were still severe problems to be faced in their relationship: 'That something which has gone out of her feelings for me has not returned,' he wrote after getting home. 'This shows itself mainly in our physical relations. I expect this happens in most married relations. The only difference here, is the suddenness with which it happened, so that I have still not yet had time to get used to it. When these things happen slowly over a period of years one would, I suppose, hardly notice it. As it is – as it is – I still find it depressing and irritating.' But Marjorie was affectionate and solicitous, 'being very nice and doing her best,' Mark wrote, and he started work in his new studio, a small building at the bottom of the garden. 'I must make that studio and my work my chief refuge,' he resolved.

A new dealer was found, the Lefevre Galleries; they did not have quite the prestige of the Leicester Galleries but were progressive in outlook. Mark worked hard for an exhibition the following April, and Aldous Huxley wrote a preface for his catalogue. When the show opened there were some encouraging reviews. *The Times* said, 'Mark Gertler seems to have arrived at the form of picture which best suits his remarkable talent' and *The Observer* found the exhibits 'of outstanding interest'. In the summer of 1937 he painted for some weeks at Balston's house in the country (near Newbury), and by August was feeling almost healthy, saying, 'Everybody tells me I'm looking well . . . one headache in five weeks is not so bad for me.'

In September 1937 he took a trip to Paris, and saw an exhibition at the Petit Palais: 'One has never before had so good a chance of studying contemporary French painting. It was extremely stimulating,' he wrote. His ambition was fired anew. 'I've got the fever for work just now,' he reported. 'I have been working very hard, perhaps a bit too hard . . . I have still not got over the impetus received in Paris.' In November he saw Lefevre's and fixed up a show for May 1939.

But the old problems were still there.

'Marjorie's overdraft is being more than ever a worry – it reached £229 last month,' Mark told Balston on 12 January 1938. 'My having done a bit better doesn't help matters much as I am not well off enough to pay *both* halfs of the bills – however I've taken all her money matters in hand and am gradually reducing the overdraft.'

In this month the nurse they had employed to look after Luke decided to leave. She had been almost in complete charge of him, sometimes taking him away altogether to stay in the country, which had made life a lot easier for both Mark and Marjorie. Nevertheless, to save money, they determined not to replace her; soon they did without a part-time maid as well, and Marjorie struggled on unaided. Luke needed a great deal of attention; he was still delicate, suffering from various minor complaints besides the series of operations which seemed to go on for ever, swallowing up money and making all their lives 'a horror that has been hanging over us for so long,' as Mark put it. There had been complications and Mark felt that the surgeon was 'rather a brutal young man' with no idea of how to calm a child's fears. 'Every time Luke has to undergo an operation he is absolutely beside himself with terror and this does him a great deal of harm,' Mark reported to Balston.

The money from Mark's 1937 exhibition was fast vanishing, and he was forced to take time from his painting to do more teaching. But with the domestic turmoil and the strain of eking out insufficient money his health worsened rapidly; the attacks of disabling migraine headache became frequent, causing him to lose more painting time and miss teaching periods (and thus lose the money). 'Every time I get a bit run down I get nervous and wonder how long I shall be able to go on with the teaching,' he wrote. For a long time he had been 'so tired of this poverty and having to ask people for money like a beggar,' yet nevertheless he had again to ask Balston's help: 'I wonder if you could possibly double your guarantee at my bank. It is £50 at present... On account of Marjorie's difficulties I had to bury £50 of my savings from the show in her bank as security... I now have £200 there but can't touch it! In fact it is that loss of Marjorie's £50 which has put me out – I think we could just have got through the summer.' (27 May 1938)*

In the summer, at Cassis in the South of France, matters grew worse: 'My habitual depressions are worse here – probably due to crowds etc. and the close confinement 'en famille'... in London I have means of distracting myself a bit.'

Mark's instinct urged him to concentrate on his work to the exclusion of all else. He needed Marjorie's love and companionship, but if necessary he was prepared to be solitary. His best pictures had all been produced when he was 'working and thinking in that peaceful way one can only do when one is quite alone.' By 11 August he was saying to Balston: 'I long nowadays to be alone – *quite* alone. I do enjoy painting so much when I am living alone. I have never been more full of new ideas than now, and how I long for a year of bachelorhood, to work them out. But I'm afraid it is not possible as, ironically enough, Marjorie is again very much attached to me and dislikes being away from me; she gets quite miserable – whereas before she would not have minded so much. So for the time being I must do the best under the circumstances.'

To Marjorie he explained, 'For the most part I get irritable and depressed by things that disturb my life as a painter. Family life

* In a later letter he explained: 'Her money seems to be dwindling away completely – Now – this quarter – one of her most staple investments hasn't paid... One can't tell if it is all gone west. If that happened she would be left with an income of £100 a year. I teach more and more, but with her money dwindling it seems no use. It's no good asking the old fox [Marjorie's father, Mr. Hodgkinson] about it, one can get nothing out of him, and his clerk seems just as foxy. I can never make out what he is talking about. What is so bad is that we are never *told* when anything goes wrong – I only discover it through threatening letters from her bank. Then I look into the pass book and find that some large sum of money has not come in at all; and so it goes on. All our struggles to live cheaply seem of no avail; it is most disturbing.' In January 1939 he noted 'the whole of Marjorie's income during 1938 was £262 minus her income tax.'

... prevents me so often from getting just that detachment and isolation I need for my work and, by God, how I do enjoy it when for a little while I get it! What grieves me also is that these moods prevent me from expressing the fullness of my love for you. I don't believe you've ever realised how much I love you!' (10 September 1938)

But what was to be done? 'The desire to be undomesticated has by now become a sort of obsession – just to be left alone with my work – and so it is all very difficult,' he wrote a fortnight later to Balston. 'It is probably temporary, and adjustment to my circumstances would be best. However, I've talked it all over with Marjorie and we agreed that, if my mood continues, some kind of more separate life might be preferable. We both know that the trouble is not fundamental, as we do really love one another. But there are two creatures in me – the painter and the man. It is the painter in me that causes difficulties. Unfortunately most ideas for living more detached cost more money. Anyway it would be a great upheaval so we are leaving things for the time being.'

At the end of the year Marjorie decided to go to Paris for a few months to take up her painting studies again, first leaving Luke at a school in Davos, Switzerland. In January 1939 they departed.

Mark worked with desperate determination. 'Macdonald (of the Lefevre Galleries) came here about a week ago and was very pleased and excited with the work he saw, and thinks the next show ought to be even better than the last,' he had remarked on 20 November. 'But I need another four or five more pictures. So I hope my headaches and general debility won't last long.'

In his pocket diary for 1938, apart from noting a few engagements and keeping a record of Marjorie's overdraft, Mark showed his overriding concern with three problems: his falling weight, the fits of depression and the violent prolonged headaches. The last two sometimes lasted for days at a time, making work impossible.

At Cassis he had noted:

14 August More or less continuous bouts of depression xx* Very bad. Surely this must end?

* A symbol for migraine.

15 August   Coughing with sputum most of the time here.

18 August   Another *very* bad attack. No special reason.

And since then he had had little relief. For the last weeks of the year he wrote:

13 November   Very bad depression, sort of settled though absolutely no fresh reasons – just chronic.

17 November   Awful headache all day and night.

19 November   Awful head day and night. Bad week as usual.

26 November   Horrible week, usual depression, much heads and sickness – hardly able to work.

3 December   Still more horrible week, bad cold. Bad heads and bad xx – unable to work.

10 December   Fearful headache all day.

15 December   Horrible day as usual remarkable only for sudden change to calm towards evening.

31 December   Awful year due almost entirely to xx, specially since Cassis.

Mark's last show of pictures – twenty-nine of them – opened at the Lefevre Galleries in May.

His work during the thirties had shown an increasing adventurousness in colour schemes. Highly spiced and glowing, they were always brave and sometimes risky, as when he combined crimson with tawny orange. He now painted most pictures with a palette knife rather than a brush, and had developed a new treatment of forms in a series of solid hieratic figures. In contrast with these, another new direction was indicated by pictures in which the space appeared so shallow that objects were flattened to two dimensional shapes.

Mark was never to resolve these contradictions and develop his vision further.

Historians are divided about the value of this work. Many thought it showed a falling off. But others disagreed. Denys Sutton considered that 'his final still life pictures show that he was on the verge of resolving some of his difficulties, blending his innate lyricism with a sense of structure,' and Professor Quentin Bell wrote, 'In his last years Gertler does recover. The 'Mandolist' ot 1934 is at once massive and psychologically right . . . Gertler's death at this moment, just when he . . . might have had another twenty years of superb achievement before him, is one of the great tragedies of British Art.'[167]

Clive Bell said: 'During the two or three final years he had so enriched his experience and strengthened his gift of expression that he had it in his power to achieve things beyond any he had yet conceived . . . Gertler's death . . . just when he seemed to be coming into his own, was a tragedy . . . The extinction of an artist before he has given what he and he alone could give is tragic; it is a loss to civilisation that can never be repaired.'[168, 198]

Some of the reviews of the Lefevre exhibitions were favourable. *The Times* said: 'Mr. Gertler has long passed the stage when his rank or kind as an artist could be questioned and the interest of the present exhibition is mainly in seeing how he is developing.' The *News Chronicle* critic wrote later: 'The show was surprising because it included several successful experiments in landscape painting quieter in colour and gentler in design than anything he had done before. It seemed that one of the ablest and most promising of English painters had found new inspiration and power.'

But others were lukewarm, and Roger Fry's sympathetic voice was gone (he had died in 1933).

Mark desperately needed encouragement. Even a moderate success might make all the difference to his spirits. But potential buyers were already inhibited by the shadow of war. 'I'm afraid I am very depressed about my show,' he told Eddie Marsh. 'I've sold only one so far! . . . That show represents two years' hard work and there is all the expense, frames, etc. attached to it. It's very disheartening.' (8 May 1939)

But even Marsh found the pictures difficult. 'My Dear Eddie,' Mark wrote a few days later. 'Of course I am not angry with you for writing what you think; you are much too old a friend, and have done so much for me in the past that you have a *right* to say what you think. Besides, what you say is I suppose true in a sense, as obviously a number of other people feel as you do about my recent works. The trouble is that I can never *set out* to paint to please. My greatest *spiritual* pleasure in life is to paint just as I feel *impelled* to do *at the time*.

'Each time I get a change of conception I am thrilled; and it is such changes which make painting worth while and prevent monotony. Of course I love it when people like my pictures. But to *set out* to please would ruin my process, and you know me well enough to realise that I am sincere. To paint to the best of my capacity is and has always been my primary aim in Life – I have sacrificed much by doing so. Also there *are* a number of people, whose taste I trust, that find some of the others as attractive as the 'Flowers' – even more.

'You must remember that many works by artists of the past were considered unattractive during their life time. There is just a chance that some of my works may be more appreciated in the future.' (11 May 1939)

It had been intended that Marjorie should return with Luke at Easter, but when the time came she had decided to stay on in Paris. Luke seemed to be happy at school in Switzerland.

'Both Marjorie and Luke seem well,' Mark told Balston on 13 May. 'I've arranged to go to Paris over Whitsun to see Marjorie. But now I wish I hadn't, as I ought to save every penny for the summer.'

But when Mark returned, Balston recorded, 'I had tea with Mark at Stewart's . . . He said that at Whitsuntide (i.e. May 28) when he went to Paris . . . Marjorie told [him] she was never going to return.'

Mark began what was to be the last month of his life in solitude. He had wanted peace and quiet in which to work. Now, paradoxically, he started to feel lonely. The house was to be sold, and when the Fosters, who rented the ground floor and basement, moved out, Mark, on the upper floors, was left alone in the house, except for a stray cat. A charwoman prepared breakfast and lunch for him, and he ate supper at a local café.

The number of friends with whom he could discuss his problems or simply relax had grown fewer. Ottoline had died the year before; it was 'a great shock and a great loss,' Mark wrote. The members of his little group of men friends were gradually drifting away and he was making no new friends to replace them. Once a week he still prepared for them but only Kot was coming with any regularity. When he failed to arrive, Mark was left alone waiting. Finally he had written to Kot: 'I have decided to stop the evenings . . . nobody seems to turn up.'

At times loneliness became oppressive and his thoughts wandered incoherently. 'Some afternoons I get panicky,' he wrote, starting another fragment of autobiography. 'How silent the house is. Marjorie has been away nearly five months, and poor little Luke without either of us – at some school in Switzerland – 'very good for him' said Marjorie. I am suddenly frightened, I don't even know how to get through the next 3 hours till my teaching. The cat is mooching about, looking at me, meowing. Poor little Luke, just as old as I was forty years ago in Zion Square; a different sort of 'home' this – instead of one room and a corner, a large house; instead of one room for seven people, a large house all empty, save for one lonely man and a cat!

'Hell! What shall I do? I look at the shelves and take down Lawrence's "Kangaroo". It bores me, but I *must* go on reading just a bit longer. Damn! The cat is getting on my nerves. Alright! alright! We'll have tea. Heavens, there's no milk! Only a drop at the bottom of the jug and gone sour. The cat is still meowing and looking me straight in the eye; I can stand it no longer. I *kick* him down the stairs! Yes I kicked him. This morning the man came with the brown basket; Good-bye cat.'

In the empty house, Mark gave up trying to paint and took stock of his situation. Money was desperately short. 'What is going to happen? I don't know', he wrote. 'I have now arranged to do the maximum amount of teaching – two days and three evenings – but even that is going to make it difficult for me to pay for materials, models and frames. However, I can just live on it. But my immediate worry is the summer. I only get one more payment until about the end of October! And unless I sell another two medium-sized pictures I shall be in a real hole.'

World events added their contribution to his fears. In Germany Jews were being persecuted, and the country was growing every day more menacing and threatening to the rest of Europe. 'We may all be blown to bits any moment,' Mark observed. 'I heard the

voice of the brute pouring poison into the hearts of his country-
men on the wireless – it was awful – like wild beasts.'

For the second time he faced the prospect of years of war, in
which artists would be among the most expendable members of the
community. He felt that no one would buy his pictures and he
would also lose the teaching job. 'We were told that in the event of
war the school would be closed instantly – and no salaries,' he
wrote to Balston. One way or another, it seemed clear that he
would not have enough money both to live and buy materials to go
on with his painting.

When the First World War had come he was a young prodigy in
process of being discovered and taken up by patrons, such as Eddie
Marsh, who had saved the situation. But patrons didn't adopt
forty-seven year old artists. Their attention, like that of the critics,
had shifted to the generations coming along behind. The very
earliness of Mark's youthful success told against him; to the young
he seemed already a part of history, and their interest was focused
on the artists who had made their name after the war.

Perhaps some of the more savage criticisms of his recent work
were justified. Mark had long since made up his mind that he
would not continue to live once his creative power was exhausted,
and it seemed that this might now have happened. There was less
need, now that Golda was dead and his marriage disintegrating, to
worry about the 'dreadful selfishness' of killing himself. There
would be few to suffer or even to mourn. Most of the friends with
whom he had experienced the most exciting, and perhaps the best,
years of his life were dead, all before their time: Lightfoot, Currie,
Katherine Mansfield, Carrington, D. H. Lawrence.

They had been lucky at any rate to be spared the process of
growing old. Mark's view of the pleasures of old age, coloured by
the pain which his body had already caused him, was very pessimistic. As he had once said to Kot, 'One's youth is spent unhappily
through over-ardent seeking for happiness. But at least one is
hopeful. When youth has gone, there comes to take its place,
gradually but surely, the ever-increasing horror of approaching old
age and the realisation of that awful and inevitable final, death. So
how can we be happy? No, there is no such thing as true happiness.

There is only its make belief – forgetfulness – and to forget is a form of cowardice.'

Some critics had said that Mark had never bettered the work which he had done in his youth before leaving the East End. About a year earlier, he had taken Marjorie to Whitechapel to see the scenes of his early successes, and his thoughts now turned again to this visit. 'We followed the whole length of Brick Lane,' he wrote, 'and found ourselves in Whitechapel, a rather fine broad Road. Almost facing us, a little to the left, was 'Gardiners', the shop I thought so grand on my first day in London; Still more to the Left could be seen the steeple of Whitechapel Church, to the right of which, I knew, was Zion Square.

'A few minutes later, we were standing in a deserted square, where I had lived nearly forty years ago. I looked about me trying to find number two. Suddenly a voice broke the silence: it came from somewhere high up. "What are yer looking for?" I looked up, and saw the bust of a woman resting on a window sill. Rather like a Despiau in a frame. I didn't quite know how to explain, so murmured something vague, but she persisted. "What number d'yer want?" – "Oh, er, Number 2." – "Who d'yer want to see?" she persisted. – "Oh! er, no one. You see, I lived here, a long time ago." – "*How* long ago?" – I really felt I couldn't tell her what a long time it was, so I said, "Oh, a *long* time." "What is yer name," she asked. I told her rather impatiently. To my great surprise she said, "How's yer sister Sophie?" So this woman had been living here, all these years. "Did you know her?" I asked. "Yerse, we played about, we were awful pals – give her my best respects . . ."''

Mark and Marjorie had walked over to look at Spital Square. Though his sisters had left the East End many years earlier, it was only eight years since his brothers had moved. For most of Mark's adult life the furriers' business at number fourteen had provided him with an essential underpinning of financial security; the final bankruptcy in January 1930 had been one of the first of a series of events which had destroyed his stable way of life of the twenties.

In the course of their exploration he and Marjorie visited the Machzike Hadass, the synagogue whose worshippers had inspired some of his finest early work. 'When we reached the main entrance, the 'Shammas', or keeper, was just about to enter,' Mark wrote. 'I

addressed him in Yiddish – and suddenly felt extremely uncomfortable – I found myself hardly able to talk it! My mother had been
dead some years and since then I had not practised it. Heavens, he'll
think I'm an impostor – a Christian. But all was well; he understood . . . And so we entered. Yes, it was impressive – the same as
ever . . . the old men. They looked magnificent, but I didn't want
to paint them. Lucky old Rembrandt, to have lived when it was
right to paint such things . . . One praying man, near me, pushed a
prayer book into my hand, and looking down at its opened pages, I
found that I had even more completely forgotten my Hebrew than
my Yiddish . . . After a while we slipped out.'

The district had changed a great deal, but Mark could still sense
the vitality which had inspired his early pictures – and the noise, the
smells, the dirt and the poverty which had ruined his constitution.
The contrast between the decaying buildings, the sterility of the
sour earth in the little back yards where nothing would grow, and
the vitality of the surging crowds was as startling as ever. Once he
had been one of the most determined and vital of these people,
working hard to learn the techniques to express, in paint, the
intensity of his feelings about life.

Was it true, as some critics maintained, that while his powers of
expression and skill at design had increased as he tried to make his
art become more cosmopolitan, moving nearer to the mainstream
of European painting, the vitality and intensity of his earlier work
had been lost?

His admiration for the leaders of the school of Paris had been
constant, his humility profound. 'I would never dare to show in
Paris,' he had said once. 'I paint because I *must* paint: because it is as
natural for me to paint as it is for a bird to fly, but that does not
necessarily mean I *must* paint great works. For although it is natural
for all birds to fly, some fly higher than others.' His efforts to give
of his best had been prodigious, but some were saying that the
influence of modern European masters such as Picasso and Matisse,
whose greatness he had been one of the first painters in London to
recognise, was too strong in his later work, that he had failed in the
struggle to maintain his individuality while absorbing from them as
much as he could learn. Had he lost the battle which every artist
fights all his life – the struggle to find and preserve his own identity

and prevent it from being submerged by the artistic personalities of the painters he most venerates? Certainly it was true that in some of his pictures of the thirties the influence of the Paris painters was too obvious. But did these pictures constitute a significant proportion of his work?

Mark saw few people during his last month, but two or three of them recalled later that he was suffering from repeated attacks of terrible migraine headache, was worried about his health and a possible recurrence of the tuberculosis, and seemed also to have lost confidence in his work. At the end of May he had written to Balston, 'I felt so disgusted and disheartened that I really did not feel able to paint.'

Early in June, Mark took 45 grains of Medinal and turned on the gas. Then he turned it off again and called Dr Morland.

On 22 June he wrote to Balston, 'I am struggling along, but things on the whole feel bad still – I've also had some bad health. The worst part, almost, is being so unsettled as to where and how to live. Marjorie's father is sending an agent here to value the house, and then we shall talk business. I don't really know what to do.'

The brothers had drifted apart a little and Mark had not seen Harry for three years. He telephoned to try and arrange a meeting for Friday the 23rd. They could not manage this, but it was decided that Harry, Jack and Mark would meet a week later.

On that Friday 23 June Mark arranged instead to meet a friend, Maria Donska, in the evening.

In the morning at 11.30 the agent came to value the house. He said later that Mark showed him round, but that although he asked three times to see the studio in the garden, Mark avoided the question and did not answer. After he had gone Mark locked the door of his studio and placed a mattress near a gas ring and a gas stove. When he was found in the evening both were turned full on and he had been dead for some hours.

The post mortem verified that death was due to gas poisoning, and showed that the old tuberculosis had healed completely.

Mark was buried in Willesden Jewish Cemetery, as Golda had been. At the funeral the service was short and the Rabbi explained that the family could not sit shiva, as he was a suicide.

Epilogue

In the years immediately following Mark Gertler's death there were a number of exhibitions of his work, beginning with the Leicester Galleries (1941) and the Ben Uri Gallery (1944). In 1949 the Whitechapel Art Gallery put on a large memorial show. But it was not until the late 1960s that his pictures became widely appreciated and sought after by museums and collectors.

Mark's generation was the last to be severely affected by tuberculosis. Within a few years of his death the drugs which provided a straightforward cure were discovered, and the sanatoriums were closed or converted to other uses.

A Note on the Development of Gertler's Painting

Mark Gertler's subject matter and style, and his professional life (membership of groups, exhibitions, etc.) are discussed in the main text, and the following detailed notes on some aspects are intended to supplement, but not replace, these discussions.

Many of Gertler's numerous early portraits of his family, such as 'Artist's Mother' (1909)[199] recall William Rothenstein's work, which Gertler admired and paid special attention to: Rothenstein was a Jew, a famous painter, the man who had got him into the Slade and an artist who had made fine pictures from Jewish subjects in Spitalfields. One or two others, such as 'May Berlinsky',[200] show his admiration for Corot.

Gertler concentrated for the next several years on Jewish subjects, including his family.

During his four years at the Slade, he absorbed all that his teachers could show him. He developed the ability to manage complicated figure paintings in depth, such as 'A Playful Scene'[172] and delighted his teacher, Tonks, with his powers of draughtsmanship. 'Artist's Mother' (pencil) (Tate)[201] shows why he was regarded as the best draughtsman since Augustus John. And the painting of his mother in 1911,[169] established an enduring characteristic of his art: his interest in clear, solid forms.

Gertler's generation was well placed to take advantage of French Post-Impressionist and twentieth-century art when it was first shown in quantity in London by Roger Fry, at his two Post-Impressionist Exhibitions, in November 1910 and October 1912. There is no doubt that Gertler and friends such as Nevinson, Roberts and Wadsworth were keenly interested. They watched the

reactions of the generation before them to these events and would
have been very impressed by pioneering English pictures of 1911
such as Wyndham Lewis's simplified, angular figure drawings, (e.g.
'Girl asleep' [1911] [Manchester], 'Head of a woman' [1911] [Quinn
coll.]), Henry Lamb's paintings of Breton peasants, Roger Fry's
figure paintings (e.g. 'The Tramp' [Rieff coll.], 'E. M. Forster'
[Barger] and 'Canal and Lock gates' [1910] [pte. coll. London]) and
series of Turkish landscapes, and Innes's Fauve landscapes. Of
particular interest to Gertler would have been exciting work by his
fellow Jew, Epstein, dating even earlier than this. Painters developing a Post-Impressionist style included Duncan Grant, Vanessa Bell,
Frederick Etchells and some of the Camden Town painters such as
Spencer Gore, Harold Gilman, Charles Ginner and Robert Bevan.
This was actually Bevan's second reaction to French painting; his
first had taken place many years before when he was friendly with
Gauguin in the 1890s.

In general, Gertler wanted to be associated with the new movement and keep in close touch with what was going on.* His first
showing in the West End was at the February 1911 Friday Club,
and this exhibition was probably the first at which signs of the new
movement among the English painters could be seen by the public.
The leading members were Fry, Grant and Vanessa Bell. Frank
Rutter commented: 'Mr Roger Fry leads the extreme left, and
contributes to a wall chiefly composed of pictures almost certain to
be labelled as post-impressionist.' His painting was compared to
Vlaminck, that of Bell to Van Gogh, and Grant to Maurice Denis.
Gertler's picture 'Jews Arguing'[202] was singled out for praise. As
there were thirty-eight exhibitors in all, Gertler must have felt well
pleased with his first appearance.

At the much larger New English Art Club exhibition, where he
got his chance to show in the autumn of 1911, his 'Artist's Mother'
went more or less unnoticed among about three hundred exhibits.

Gertler showed half a dozen drawings and pictures in February
1912 at the Friday Club, which was to be a regular exhibiting place
of his for some years. Here he and his friends Nevinson,
Wadsworth and Currie found themselves in the van of the Post-

* 'Artist's Mother' 1911 (Tate), is evidence of his interest in Cézanne.

Impressionist battle. The Bloomsbury contingent was seen as dominating the Club, which was compared by the *Morning Post* to 'a constellation in the midst of which Mr Roger Fry is the sun. P. G. Konody called it 'a very Witches Sabbath of Fauvism and Post-Impressionsism'; and the *Pall Mall Gazette* felt it was 'like a nursery where a lot of naughty children are playing at Red Indians and shouting at the top of their voices.'

Gertler thought of himself as a progressive artist, but he also intended to try and make a living by his pictures, and he may have found all this rather alarming. His conservative pictures had really nothing in common with advanced efforts such as Etchell's 'Hip Bath' (Courtauld Institute), and 'Three Figures' described by the *Pall Mall Gazette* as 'a downright insult to visitors to the Gallery.' Gertler may not have been altogether disappointed when the Bloomsbury painters moved away from the Friday Club and formed their own group. Gertler's pictures were picked out by several reviewers who were looking for a more moderate element to praise.

Gertler's views at this point, and his search for a way of assimilating the new ideas without departing too far from his original realism, may be deduced from an interview in the *Jewish Chronicle* early in February in which he said, 'I have always held that brilliance can never be an excuse for slipshod painting. One should never forget the primary function of art – the music and rhythm of colour. Characterization and psychology, so important in the novel, are quite of secondary importance in the picture. To be really great, I hold that a picture should be able to thrill us by its harmony of tones, just as a harmony of notes in music might thrill us. Take Piero Della Francesca's "Nativity", assuredly one of the finest pictures in the world, or Giovanni Bellini's "Circumcision", and see if you cannot feel the music and rhythm of their colour. Botticelli, too, I feel, has helped me a great deal to see clearly in that direction. I strongly doubt whether the old masters are ever likely to be approached in this respect. There is too much visualism, and not enough brain, in modern art. People do not think enough before they put brush to canvas, and then we are not such keen craftsmen as they were in the old days. The old masters made colour mixing a science, and painted in the finest of mediums-tempera – which we do not, and again, we give too much attention to mere subject, when all that really matters is the treatment of the thing. I can find all the beauty I want in a simple head by Holbein. Because of that, people have accused me of belonging to the morbid realistic school – of being philistine in my outlook, but I think I have been misunderstood. Though I am by no means a romanticist, I am not unsusceptible to the allegory as a means of expressing the beautiful, though I hold that one can get all the achievement of the allegory in a simple portrait if one is only really successful. Painted with the master-touch of a Chardin, even the commonplace onion does not lack beauty. To me, there always seems more credit attached to the beautifying of what might be drab in Nature, than in actually imitating the beauty as it exists in Nature.'

'What are your views, then, on modern art?' asked a reporter.

'Decided and not flattering. I have no "parrot" veneration for the old masters, but I say this, that until we begin to paint in the same sincere spirit that they did, we have no chance of approaching them as painters. Of modern painters, I think John really great, and as far as Jewish art is concerned, I do not think we have yet distinguished ourselves as much as we could do.'

Like Augustus John, Currie and Gertler became interested in tempera and painted a number of pictures in this medium in 1912. Gertler got some advice from John and started on a 'Coster Family' and two religious themes, a 'Hager' and an 'Adam and Eve'. He adopted the practice of painting a picture first in oils, then copying it in tempera.

The Chenil Gallery exhibition in December 1912 (where pictures by Gertler and Currie shared the first floor, with a whole room upstairs filled with paintings by John, and another room containing the work of Innes, Derwent Lees, Wadsworth and Nevinson) showed how, inspired by the modern French artists, John, Gertler and Currie were reacting against three hundred years of increasingly faithful representation of the visible world by first looking back to archaic and primitive work such as that of the Italian fourteenth-century artists Duccio and Cimabue and of the Italian painters of the fifteenth century. Partly because they had worked in tempera, Gertler was trying it as well.

The interest in tempera had been stimulated by some lectures at the Slade by Mrs Sargant Florence. Gertler painted Carrington in the new medium, her vivacity making her an awkward sitter: 'You shouldn't jump about so much when I'm struggling with tempera.' (September 1912) The style of this painting and of others at the time such as 'The Violinist'[203] and portraits of his friends the Harveys,[204,205] recalls that of quattrocent artists such as Botticelli.

The critics spotted that the artists on show at the Chenil Gallery were making 'a swing back to early Italian art for inspiration.' (*Daily Chronicle*). The *Observer* stated 'when their modernity is closely investigated it seems to belong more to the fifteenth century than to the twentieth century. Indeed the most "advanced" of the exhibits take us back to the days of Giotto.' But the paper thought it was 'praiseworthy to attempt the rescue of art from the dullness of realistic *trompe l'oeil* imitation of Nature,' and *The Star*, noticing that Gertler and Currie were 'forming their styles on a close study of the early Florentine work', thought it interesting and pleasing 'to apply its principles to subjects drawn from the life of today.' Less pleasing to Gertler was the emphasis laid by some critics on the remaining traces of John's influence. 'L'ecole de John,' the *Saturday Review* jibed, 'cleverly reproduces the mannerisms, but of course misses the spirit, of the master.' *Truth* considered Gertler's 'Coster Woman and Child'[206] at the Chenil a cross between John and Cimabue. But all the same it was 'the most striking work' in the whole show; other critics noticed, and complained, that Gertler's work showed greater distortion of natural shapes than the others. 'What is really surprising is that his painted heads, with the exception of "The Violinist" give little evidence of his really remarkable powers of draughtsmanship,' said the *Observer*. 'They are, perhaps deliberately, misshapen.'

Currie had led the way in the interest in primitive art with his exhibits in the summer of 1912 at the New English. Now the *Observer* said, 'Mr Currie shows that he has the power to treat a modern subject in terms of primitive art without doing violence to truth and probability . . . his pictures have a haunting beauty of pure colour and of bold patterning. They are like brilliant medieval illuminations on a large scale.' The *Daily Chronicle* observed: 'Currie's "Workers' Wives" are types from Mr Arnold Bennett's "Five Towns" all dipped in a Florentine bath and emerging precisely primitive in radiant colours.' Alan Gwynne-Jones, who went to the Currie-Gertler show, later wrote this note[91]: 'To my eye their great impact (after the John show) was that they tended to be much simplified, chunky, very strong, often crude in colours and decorative and static in design . . . the Gertlers I thought the better, and the better drawn, but the "influence" I felt to be Currie's.'

Gertler's next important work was 'Rabbi and his Grandchild',[179] which took several months. It started as a portrait of an old Jew. Then, perhaps inspired by Ghirlandaio's picture of 'The Old Man And His Grandson', Gertler conceived the idea of adding a little girl's head, so that the final scheme was of two figures, one larger than the other, as in 'Apple Woman And Her Husband.'[173] But now the contrast was not one of light and shadow, but of old and young. This theme had been treated several times by Cranach, one of Gertler's favourite painters. The actual painting of the child's face, however, is closer to the sytle of Rogier Van der Weyden and may be compared this with artist's 'Portrait Of A Lady' (National Gallery).

The little girl later recalled[108]: 'The first works he did were pencil drawings, head and shoulders, three-quarter face. I think he did several pencil drawings of me before doing any painting. In fact I am sure I never actually saw him use paints, though I went to the studio to sit for him for a period of about a year. When I saw a picture of myself sitting on the knee of a Rabbi, I recall running home and asking my mother how Gertler could possibly have painted this picture. I had never met or seen the old man.' He exhibited the picture at the summer 1913 exhibition of the N.E.A.C. and it was well received by the critics.

Looking at Gertler's work as a whole in the years after 1912, how did he respond to the Post-Impressionist challenge?

At the Slade his work, like that of most of the other students, showed references to Augustus John. 'Portrait Of A Girl' (1912) (Tate) recalls John, and John's friend Henry Lamb, and 'Apple Woman And Her Husband' has links with Lamb and with Currie.

The work of all these painters was much influenced by Gauguin at this time, and there is a reminder of this kind of painting in the interest in silhouettes, pattern making and tone contrasts in the two figures in profile shown in 'Apple Woman And Her Husband'. It is recalled also in 'Vanity'[207] and 'Rabbi and his Grandchild' by the emphasis on the continuous silhouette uniting the figures, the simplification of forms, especially that of the child, and the clear contours. In contrast to 'Apple Woman And Her Husband', Gertler here shows no attempt to convey a consistent lighting with shadows.

The branch of French Post-Impressionist painting represented by Gauguin, Serusier and Maurice Denis was the first to gain acceptance in London and had been included in several exhibitions from 1910-12.

Gertler's interest in pattern and rhythmic design grew. In 'The Fruit Sorters',[183] and 'Rabbi and Rabbitzin',[181] the space became more shallow, with an increasing emphasis on the picture plane. The emphasis on all-over design also increased. From an involved pattern of arms in 'Rabbi and Rabbitzin' we come to the complicated design of 'Gilbert Cannan at his Mill'[185] with its patterns of parallels in the trees and the mill and the Vs of the figures' legs, the mill, and the branches. In 'Daffodils in a Blue Bottle'[208] of 1916, Gertler makes a complicated pattern with flowers, and the figures in 'Merry-Go-Round' are tightly bound into a geometrical design.

In 'The Fruit Sorters' (1914) Gertler is still following the general type established by Augustus John in pictures such as 'Way Down To The Sea' and 'Decorative Group' (Johannesburg). The figures in Gertler's painting are disposed against a landscape in a rather frieze-like effect and the picture is designed as a pattern of figures and limbs. It relates to Post-Impressionism in its Gauguinesque patterning of figures and landscape, and in the simplification of the figures.

Other artists who had painted this kind of picture were Henry Lamb ('Fisherfolk' of 1914) and Duncan Grant. Gertler probably owed the idea of painting women with baskets on their heads to Grant's 'Lemon Gatherers' (Tate). Grant's picture of 'Dancers' – also a pattern of linked figures against a sky – was bought by Marsh.

Elements in Gertler's style which place him beyond Post-Impressionism and in twentieth-century art appear in 1913. In 'Still Life' (King's College, Newcastle),[209] 'Head Of A Young Girl' (Manchester)[210] and 'Jewish Family'[177] his previously rather Gauguinesque curves have changed to more geometrical shapes.

This links Gertler with the kind of work associated in England with Epstein, Gaudier-Brzeska, Wyndham Lewis, Roberts,

Wadsworth and Bomberg. Epstein and Bomberg returned in June 1913 from a three-month trip to Paris where they had met important modern artists such as Picasso and Derain. It was Epstein who had fired Gertler's enthusiasm for the hieratic, rigid, simplified forms of the Egyptian figures in the British Museum in July 1912 ('Egyptian art is by far by far by far the greatest of all art', he decided), and Gertler would certainly have known of works by Epstein such as the geometrical 'Sunflowers'. He often visited Bomberg's studio, and had given this artist the use of his own at one period. Gaudier-Brzeska was another personal friend. But the similarities in form between Gertler and all these artists are only superficial.

This geometricization of forms derived ultimately from post-Cézanne work in Paris. We can compare the still life in Gertler's 'The Artist's Mother' (1913)[178] with Picasso's painting of *circa* 1908, for example 'Nature Morte' exhibited at the second Post-Impressionist exhibition (No. 60) and illustrated in the catalogue.

Gertler was interested in Picasso's work and his own shows the effect, first of early Picasso (in such pictures as 'Family Group'[180] and 'Jewish Family') and then of Picasso's post-1906 work (for example, the treatment of the eyes in 'Rabbi and Rabbitzin'), but Gertler's work is still closer to the Picasso-inspired art of Jean Marchand or André Derain. These two artists are also recalled by the polyhedral apples in 'Still Life' (King's College, Newcastle), and the general air of 'The Fruit Sorters', 'Agapanthus',[187] 'Gilbert Cannan at his Mill' and others. Both were becoming very much admired as a progressive alternative to Cubism by Roger Fry and Clive Bell, whose ideas strongly influenced the young English painters.

Like the French painters, Gertler became very interested in Negro carvings. 'The only thing that pleases me just now', he wrote on 2 February 1915, 'is a little piece of African woodcarving "Husband And Wife" that I picked up for 10s. 0d. It has in it qualities that I'm always trying to get. The strange part is that the man has a hat on, something like a bowler! Just like I've got in my "Husband And Wife" ["Rabbi and Rabbitzin"].' In another letter he wrote that it was 'like they have in the British Museum . . . it is like my work.'

The faceting of 'Still Life' (King's College, Newcastle) soon disappears. With one or two isolated exceptions it is not found in

Gertler's work from now on, and in general, rounded forms, rather than angular ones, predominate throughout his career.

But it is evident that Gertler was interested in Cubism: the space in some pictures is very arbitrary, and in 'Rabbi and Rabbitzin' (1914) cups and teapot, table and bench are seen from different viewpoints. His style developed rapidly in 1915–16 and 'Merry-Go-Round' is a post-Cubist picture. Forms such as the clouds and the horses' features are not derived from nature by simplification or distortion: they are conceptual signs for the things represented. Some of the details in the picture are purely abstract elements, included for compositional reasons. Naturalistic space is disregarded: the top and bottom of the roundabout are seen from different viewpoints, and the scale and position of the horses and riders is purely schematic – the horses on the far side of the roundabout are on *our* side of the front supports, and no 'real' space is provided for the groups of riders such as the one in the right foreground.

Some of the above features occurred in the important picture 'Swing Boats'[189] 1915 (whereabouts unknown). From a photograph it can be seen that, like 'Gilbert Cannan and his Mill' and 'Merry-Go-Round,' the picture is based on a piece of rotating machinery. It is similar to both in its use of repeated shapes in patterns, and the boats, the couples in them, and surrounding clouds are reduced to diagrammatic form.

But Gertler did not follow up the new kinds of picture suggested by Cubism. If we consider the mood of his work in this period it is evident that Gertler is making use of the new formal language of French painting to paint pictures which are basically Northern in character and a comment upon life. He was never entirely happy with the emotional coolness of French painting.

He had started in the realist tradition with an admiration for artists such as Holbein and Dürer, as seen for example in 'The Artist's Mother' (1911) (Tate) 'Rabbi and Grandchild' (1913). We can see two threads after this, both Northern in type.

The first might be termed a kind of naive primitivism of approach with expressive distortion in style which relates him in England to Stanley Spencer. Spencer's country village and Gertler's

Whitechapel were both isolated, intense communities, and there are similarities between the two artists' conceptions in, for example, Gertler's 'Head of a Girl' (blacklead 1912) (Leeds)[211] and Stanley Spencer's drawing of 'Gilbert Spencer' (1909) (coll. Mrs. C. Gardener). Formal similarities between the two artists occur in the block-like treatment of the figures in Gertler's 'Jewish Family' and Spencer's 'John Donne Arriving In Heaven' and 'Visitation'.

In both artists this kind of angularity was temporary and is evidently in the main a reaction to common stimuli, but there may well have been an interaction in their work. The patterns of arms in Gertler's 'The Fruit Sorters' (1914) recalls Spencer's 'Apple Gatherers' (1912–13), for example. While Gertler was engaged in painting 'The Artist's Mother' (1913) (Swansea), his friend Marsh acquired Stanley Spencer's 'Apple Gatherers'. It is interesting to compare the distortion of the limbs and hands in the two pictures. In both cases the distortions are for other than purely pictorial reasons: the artists enlarged parts of the figures which they wished to emphasize, after the manner of primitive art. (There are traces of this also in Gaudier-Brzeska's work, for example the hands of 'The Wrestler' of 1912.)

The work of Spencer also comes to mind when one sees in Gertler's 'Jewish Family' (1913) the exaggeration of the features such as heads and hands, and a kind of naive primitivism in the treatment. This kind of distortion had probably begun in Gertler's work early in 1913. In February, he exhibited a picture entitled 'Woman Resting'.[212] Its whereabouts are now unknown, but a contemporary critic described the woman as having 'enormously fat hands' and 'elephantine body'. Another wrote: 'The figure is depicted with phenomenal arms and hands. The picture might possibly be the embodiment of the mental vision which a small boy, undergoing corporal punishment, conceives regarding the weight and strength of the limbs of his castigator.'

But it is the general mood of some of Gertler's pictures rather than particular details which recall Stanley Spencer, and the combination of arbitrary simplification, realistic detail and an almost naive and rather dreamy atmosphere seen, for example, in 'Black and White Cottage',[184] 'Creation of Eve'[186] and 'Cannan at his Mill'. These pictures also recall aspects of the pre-Raphaelites and earlier English painting such as Blake, as well as the Italian primitives. All these were, of course, common sources for both Gertler and Spencer.

Gertler may be indebted to Spencer for the narrative element found in some of his pictures after 1914.

Gertler and his friend Currie admired Stanley Spencer more than any of their English contemporaries in 1913. The relationship cooled later when Gertler became a great admirer of Cézanne's work. Richard Carline, a friend of both, recalls that the difference in views caused a personal quarrel.

The contrast between the two painters is clearly seen in the much harsher mood of Gertler's 'The Artist's Mother' of 1913 (Swansea) compared with Spencer's portraits, and this illustrates the other Northern strain in Gertler's work from about 1913.

It is the underlying barbaric, expressionistic note in Gertler which makes his work of this period hang together in spite of its frequent changes in style.

This note can be seen in the expressive distortion and the grotesqueness of the figures in 'Jewish Family' and 'The Artist's Mother' of 1913, in the expressions on the faces in 'Rabbi and Rabbitzin', in the violence and clashing colours of many of Gertler's pictures (for example 'The Merry-Go-Round'). Though we can see, behind the 1913 'The Artist's Mother', a memory of Cézanne's portraits of his wife, it has more of the intensity of a Van Gogh portrait.

Gertler himself felt that his first attempts in 1912 to assimilate Post-Impressionism, (for example 'Vanity') were leading him away from his basic aim of realism. As Currie put it in a letter to Marsh, Gertler thought that 'the earlier work was more essentially personal . . . the present work [21 October 1913] is a return to, and a fuller expression, of the earlier.'

Gertler's work is, in many ways, nearer to German than English art, and essentially linked with his racial origins.

There is no reason to believe that Gertler was directly influenced by contemporary German art. It is possible that a memory of Franz Marc's semi-legendary animals in landscapes might be behind the deer and the bird in 'Creation of Eve', but such comparisons are hard to find. Modern German painting was then almost unknown in London, though five of Marc's works (graphics and oils) were exhibited at the Twenty One gallery in February 1914.

Gertler had curiously little contact with the avowed realists among contemporary English painters. The aims of Gilman and Ginner, members of the Camden Town Group, were set out by Ginner in an article entitled 'Neo-Realism', published at this time. And this is a term which might fairly be applied to Gertler's 'The Artist's Mother' of 1913. But if we compare it with pictures by Gilman and Ginner, though there are similarities in style and in the purple-green colour scheme, we can see that these are at a much lower emotional temperature.

The nearest to Gertler in mood among contemporary artists in England were perhaps Epstein and Nevinson. There are no strong formal similarities with Epstein, though we might compare Gertler's 'The Artist's Mother' of 1913 with Epstein's 'Maternity' of about 1911, or 'Rabbi and Rabbitzin' with Epstein's 'Female Figure In Flenite' of 1913. But 'The Merry-Go-Round' and Epstein's 'Rock Drill' have a great deal in common, both in feeling and in the reduction of forms to machine elements.

A similarity between Gertler's figures and machines had grown since the doll-like figures of the 1913 'Jewish Family'. In 1914, 'The Doll'[182] is another sign of this approach.

Nevinson had been getting a lot of publicity as the 'English Futurist' and a painter of topical subjects. The heavy, rather violent atmosphere of 'The Merry-Go-Round', the mechanization of figures, and the harsh tone contrasts may well owe a debt to similar features in Nevinson's work such as 'The Arrival' (exhibited at the London Group March 1914 [39]) and 'La Patrie' (on show in the London Group Exhibition summer 1916, while Gertler was working on 'The Merry-Go-Round'), and others such as 'Belgian Refugees' of 1914 and 'La Mitrailleuse' of 1915.

In the broadest terms we can view Gertler's work of this period as the expression of a passionate temperament which, as we can see by the increasing rigidity of his designs, was under the strong control of a disciplined, rational intellect.

There is a striking contrast between his temperament and his method of execution, which was slow and laborious, and consisted of painting in small exact touches. 'The most difficult thing . . . is to control my excitement . . . my ideas seem so wonderful and exciting,' he wrote. 'God give me patience and enough powers of control.' In company, Gertler was often stimulating and light-hearted: in his work he was always deadly serious.

Another enduring characteristic was the long and careful study of the motif before he began to paint.

After 'The Merry-Go-Round', in 1916, Gertler turned for a few months to sculpture, and then went back to painting in 1917.

The 'Acrobats' (Tate)[195] was not only Gertler's first piece of sculpture but the first figure composition in which the figures were not more or less upright. It is a very well worked-out design, though perhaps with less force and tension than his paintings. In his big picture of 'Bathers',[196] which he worked on intermittently for the next two years, he built a composition of divers in mid-air in the same pose as one of his acrobats, watched by standing and reclining nude figures. It is a very ambitious pattern of continuous rhythms, and an audacious design, painted with great skill. Figure compositions, on themes of contemporary life, formed the most important part of his work in the period 1917–20: 'Boxers',[213] 1918 shows two simplified featureless forms in a very schematic representation of a ring, he started a picture of footballers,[214] did a painting of two ballet dancers, and his interest in fairs and circuses, first seen in 'Merry-Go-Round', is taken up again in several pictures.

Some of the pictures of 1917–19 represent his furthest advance in the direction of abstraction. Examples are the abstract elements in 'Bathers', the extreme distortion of the figures in 'Ballet Dancers'[215] and the bold schematization of 'Boxers'.

Behind most of the work of this period lies the figure of Cézanne, who now, years after the first Post-Impressionist Exhibition of 1910, came to dominate his work. 'A Still Life' (Manchester)[216] showing fruit with a tipped-up plate on a crumpled napkin, is almost a copy of Cézanne; he is the source for themes such as 'Bathers', for compositions such as 'The Tea Set' (1918)[217] (in which the saucers and the tops of the cups are tipped up towards the picture plane), and 'Geranium' (1919)[218] (in which the plant is shown in front of a window frame making a pattern of angles, and after disappearing behind the pot, emerges at a different level). The simplification of figures in pictures of this period such as 'Bathers', and the actual painting, for example, in 'Bathers', in 'The Tea Pot' (Tate)[219] and in 'The Bokhara Coat' 1920,[219] also recalls the work of Cézanne.

In the autumn of 1917, Roger Fry organized a show of modern art at the Mansard Gallery in London. Gertler was invited to exhibit. There he had the opportunity of studying afresh pictures by Marchand, Vlaminck, Friesz and Derain (all artists much influenced by Cézanne) and the French artists most admired by Roger Fry. From 1915 onwards he had the opportunity of studying books on Van Gogh and Cézanne at Garsington, and he became enthusiastic about one on Cézanne which contained many reproductions. In 1918, he was able to study a Cézanne painting bought by Maynard Keynes and at the end of the year visited Prince Bibesco in order to study the two Cézannes in his collection. 'Imagine my excitement when I heard of these at Garsington,' he wrote. 'But the Cézannes somewhat disappointed me! Yet they were typical. Do you know I fear that I may miss something in the originals that I get from the reproductions! In reproduction Cézanne stands quite alone. He doesn't somehow quite so much in the originals, at any rate those that I have seen. However, they *were* good and I have really not seen enough originals to judge.' (31 December 1918)

On 5 January 1919 he wrote: 'About the Cézannes, I liked the Maynard [Keynes] one more than the Bibesco's and, so far, more than any original Cézannes I have yet seen. In that tiny one there is that plasticity and construction one likes so much in him in reproductions.'

The two most knowledgeable and enthusiastic people in England on the subject of Cézanne were Roger Fry and Clive Bell. Gertler's relationship with them was at first rather distant. 'I am surprised to hear that you have stayed with the Clive Bells and that crew', he wrote to Carrington in December 1915. But Gertler later much appreciated the interest and encouragement of Roger Fry. In April

1917 Fry invited him to show at an Omega workshop exhibition of copies (he chose a Cézanne as his model) and Gertler went in October 1917 to stay for the weekend at Fry's home, where he enthusiastically studied Fry's collection of photographs of paintings.

Roger Fry had a wonderful sensitivity to art and was a most persuasive man. With their closer association he would have been able to explain more fully the theory of significant form which Gertler may have found too abstruse when it was first published in Clive Bell's 1914 book.

With the ending of the war, the invasion of ideas from France became irresistible. André Derain came to London in 1919; Gertler went to see a show of Modern French Pictures at Heal's in August, and at the end of the year the Leicester Galleries put on an exhibition of Matisse and Maillol. With the new decade, modern French painting was on show at several West End galleries.

Gertler made a trip to Paris and his enthusiasm now embraced Renoir as well as Cézanne. The work of the younger French painters made relatively little impact on him and at this critical moment he reacted against the more advanced art by making up his mind to concentrate on direct painting from the model. This feeling remained with him. In December 1920 he said that he had lost all interest in work which was not done directly from nature.

In the 1920s, apart from a 'Coster Family'[221] (1924) in which he carried out an idea first planned more than ten years earlier, and 'The Sisters',[222] Gertler gave up multi-figure subjects.

Some of the most important of Gertler's pictures of the twenties were of single nude figures. He had painted an occasional nude before this (exhibiting two studies at the 1916 Friday Club, a seated nude at the Omega workshops in November 1918, another nude at the May 1918 London Group, and his big 'Bathers' in May 1919) and now produced a series which recall his new favourite French artist Renoir. The figure of Derain also lay behind much work of this period, such as 'Young Girlhood – II',[223] and 'Gipsy at her Toilet',[224] which also has reminiscences of Matisse. Gertler, like Derain, was 'looking for something fixed, eternal and complex' in his work. Apart from the general similarity to Renoir and Derain,

21—MG * *

references to Cézanne continued to occur, for example in 'China and Roses'[225] of 1922, and 'Basket of Fruit'[226] (1925) (Tate).

After the mid twenties, Gertler's designs become even more solidly textured and there is an increasing emphasis on all-overness, instead of figure-against-ground treatment, as we can see in 'Supper' (1928)[227] (R. A. Bevan), 'The Sisters' (1929)[222] and 'Homage to Roger Fry'[228] (1934) (Peyton Skipworth). He felt himself that there were parallels between his closely organised designs and music – in 1916, for example, he had told Lytton Strachey that 'Merry-Go-Round' reminded him of Bach.

During the thirties, the neo-classicism of Picasso, added to that of Renoir, inspired a series of massive, monumental female figures such as 'Nude with Mandolin',[198] and 'The Red Shawl'[229] (1938) (Mrs René Diamond). One or two of these figures, such as 'Standing Nude' (reproduced *Studio*, October 1946) recall the work of Henry Moore. They had become friends after Gertler had bought one of Moore's drawings and sought him out. In parallel with these is a contrasting trend to a flattening of objects. An example of this is 'Still Life' (1939)[230] (Mrs Blundell), which recalls the late work of Juan Gris. And another innovation of this period was the extensive use of the palette knife.

Gertler's closest relationships with modern Continental artists were indicated by the books on his shelves. Among many on the Old Masters were several on Renoir, and copies of the following: *Cézanne*, by Julius Meier-Graefe (1913); *Cézanne*, by Fry (1927); *Derain*, by Daniel Henry Kahnweiler (Leipzig, 1920): *Matisse*, by Elie Faure et al (Cahiers d'Aujourdhui, Paris, 1923); *Matisse*, by F. Fels (1929); *Picasso*, by M. Reynal (Munich, 1921); and *Picasso*, (Cahiers d'Art, 1923).

His attitudes to these painters is expressed in a number of letters.

The admiration for Renoir was undiminished in the 1920s: 'No, no works of Matisse, Picasso or Lhote or Derain have ever given me that hard blow of satisfaction that one gets from a real pic- ture... I don't get that from anyone after Renoir in France.' (November 1920) 'Thank you [Carrington] for the magazine on Renoir... how massive and grand. I am struggling also with the text, but I find I can understand very little French.' (March 1921)

In 1921 Gertler wrote to Richard Carline: 'Brett tells me you had a model, female, fat and rather Renoiresque. I am looking for a model of that description. [Also] do you know of any child models?'

And in July 1929 he wrote of a picture by Renoir: 'It was magnificent. How many painters are capable of painting a picture which one might almost describe as "pretty pretty" and which is at the same time a masterpiece? A picture that could be appreciated from a servant girl to a Roger Fry.'

But Gertler's own approach was basically quite different: 'Renoir is exquisite – delicious', he said in April 1924, 'but that is also his fault – I prefer him in reproductions. He is really too 'tasty'. It is too refined for us – too sweet. We must have something more brutal today . . . I felt the same about [Cézanne]; far too *precious*.'

This ambivalent attitude carried over into his opinion of Roger Fry's criticism: 'I had a nice letter from Roger Fry . . . I can't help feeling that my work is really not for him, that he and I are too fundamentally different for my work ever to really appeal to him or his kind. Also he is altogether too hopelessly French just now for my work to be really understood by him.' (February 1921)

Yet Gertler watched developments in French painting and visited Paris every two or three years:

'The Picasso show interested me as his work always does. But frankly I don't know what I really think of it. He has *such* a lot of talent, yet sometimes it seems to me that as results his are too much *made up*. I wonder if he has anything moving to express – but I don't know . . . I was somehow more moved this time by the happy, gay, decorative colours of Dufy! He is doing a beautiful screen, and now keeps a sort of workshop with young men assistants, like the old days, and full of work. Making money too! Also Matisse is nice, with his bright spontaneous colours.' (April 1924)

'There is a wonderful show of French pictures at Knoedlers'. I have been twice – Matisse, Bonnard, Derain, Picasso, Vuillard, Marchand, Segonzac, etc. All good examples. But they have there the Bonnard you told me of – 'The Girl in the Bath'. It is a masterpiece. He is a very fine artist. There is also a show of his work at the Independent Gallery – all very exciting . . .' (10 February 1928)

I have been recently to Paris and there are some first-rate things being done there . . . the new work of Derain, Matisse, Picasso and some of the younger men is as fine as ever, full of life and promise.' (September 1932 interview in *Studio*)

The importance of the subject matter in Gertler's pictures diminished after his early work. On 1 January 1921 he was writing about his studio: 'I could work for hours and hours with a 'gris clair' light. I love painting in a good, large, convenient studio with a steady light, where things look the same for ever. To me, comfort is more important than subject. I mean that I infinitely prefer painting a dull subject under comfortable conditions than something thrilling under conditions that are constantly changing. Then it's questionable if there is such a thing as a dull subject.'

His subject matter was not adventurous, but this sprang rather from a wish to explore fully the potential of conventional material than an indifference to the choice of theme.

'Apples are always inspiring,' he asserted in November 1918; 'I have found them so all my life and always shall.' But in 1921 he commented: 'There are certain subjects I have set my heart on, and which cannot be done here such as large life-size portraits, nudes, nudes with still lifes, compositions of several nudes done from nature and so on.'

A central characteristic of Gertler's view of art was his respect for the craft of the Old Masters. In January 1921 he wrote, 'It seems almost as if they used different materials, so superior is their craft – and I love craft; beautiful paint – that kind of paint that makes you say, "What lovely stuff." Since Goya there's only been Cézanne, sometimes Renoir. No one else has that *sense of paint*. I have never yet loved a picture wholeheartedly unless it has that *sense of paint*.' A week or two later he said to the same friend: 'I'm glad you agree with me about the paint of the old masters . . . we should be original enough for the mere trying, because as far as I can see, no one else seems to care about it.'

Gertler was suspicious of movements: 'As for Surrealism, I don't know anything about it, but I am becoming more and more suspicious of "movements", with intricate and startling ways of painting and writing etc. I am more and more convinced that the best methods are after all the simplest and the traditional – and at the moment they are even the newest – because to attempt to be new and unusual for its own sake is so common now that the only possible newness and freshness left is in the simple and traditional. If a man is a bore he'll be a bore even under the most startling and "original" of methods. If on the other hand he really has got something personal to say, he will say it all right without having to attach himself to any of the innumerable new "isms" that have sprung and are apparently still springing up like mushrooms everywhere.' (20 September 1927)

Yet he was essentially an adventurous painter with the will and the stamina to go on developing. A note in his journal read: 'There is a certain kind of studiousness, which is absolutely necessary in a work of art, a hesitating, groping, quality. Every new work must be a new and further struggle; a new work ought not merely to be one done with the conventions discovered in the last work. Every work should be done as if one had never done a work before; one should forget all one's past work or, if remembering, remembering only to repeat oneself. It is almost more important to forget one's own work than other people's. Influences from other artists or suggestions received from them is in fact a good thing, but to be influenced by one's own work is to repeat oneself merely.'

Fry, writing in the *New Statesman* (21 November 1931) wished that there were more artists as ambitious as Gertler. 'In Peaches and a Green Bottle',[231] commented Fry, 'he tries to do an extremely difficult thing. He tries to keep the surface organization of his picture, its flat pattern, at the utmost strength and yet to realize the spatial and plastic relations of his objects just as vigorously.'

He experimented ceaselessly, making careful notes of aims and technical devices. For example, in February 1928 he wrote, 'I really believe I am acquiring something that my work needed – my experiments in working higher in key, brighter in colour, and more fluid in the contour are, I think, repaying me.'

A note of 24 August 1928 recorded: 'Latest system and its advantages: Contours more varied and lost – working right across and not at any stage defined, advantage – a greater flow and continuation – no stoppage.' Other heads were: 'More colour in shadows and more air generally . . . freshness and light . . . unity and general realizations . . . Form and design realized by light and shade seems a deep unalterable characteristic – why try and alter it?' And this kind of technical note continued until the end of his life, often showing very elaborate experiments with supports, grounds and media.

In his last recorded affirmation of his aims, Gertler said, 'What my forms represent is of secondary importance . . . I am a classical painter . . . studying nature is necessary but most important is to study the great paintings of the past.' (*World of Art Illustrated*, 17 May 1939)

Biographical Summary

1891	9 December	Born at No. 16 Gun Street, Spitalfields, London.
1893		Family returns to Austria.
1896		Family again emigrates to England.
1897	20 October	Starts at Settles Street School, London.
1900		Starts at Deal Street School; living at No. 8 Bacon Street, Spitalfields.
1905	January	Family moves into No. 56 Leman Street, and starts furriers' business there.
1906	January	Leaves school.
1907		Passes Polytechnic examinations in three art subjects in the summer.
	30 December	Starts at Clayton and Bell, glass painters.
1908	February	Family moves to No. 14 Spital Square.
	Summer	Wins Bronze Medal.
	October	William Rothenstein helps him to get to the Slade.
1911		Exhibits at the Friday Club in February and the New English Art Club in November; wins a British Institute Scholarship.
1912	February	Leaves Slade.
	April	Moves into studio at No. 32 Elder Street.
	Summer	Elected member N.E.A.C.
	December	Exhibition with J. Currie at Chenil Gallery.
1913		Meets Edward Marsh; meets Gilbert Cannan.
	December	Chenil Gallery exhibition.
1914	January	Begins visits to Cannan's home in Cholesbury.
	Spring	Meets Lady Ottoline Morrell.
	April	Included in mixed exhibition at Leeds Art Gallery.
	May	Contemporary Art Society buys 'Fruit Sorters'.
	May	Included in Whitechapel Gallery Exhibition of Twentieth-century Art.
	9 October	Death of Currie.
	Autumn	Meets S. S. Koteliansky, D. H. and Frieda Lawrence, J. Middleton Murry, Katherine Mansfield, the Campbells and Lytton Strachey; Marsh starts to make him an allowance. Lives at Cholesbury.

1915	January	Moves to Penn Studio, No. 13 Rudall Crescent, Hampstead, and works there until 1932, living later at 19 Worsley Road, nearby.
	Spring	Elected to London Group. N.E.A.C. rejects 'Eve'. Meets M. Shearman.
	11–13 September	First visit to Garsington Manor.
	October	Gives up Marsh allowance.
	November	Exhibits at London Group; Carrington meets Strachey.
1916		First entry in *Who's Who*; Summer: Cholesbury, two weeks at Garsington, stay with Hutchinsons at Wittering.
	Autumn	*Mendel* published, Shearman offers support, last exhibit for some years at the N.E.A.C.; starts sculpture and writing.
	November	Becomes Carrington's lover.
1917	5 February	Father, Louis, dies.
	April	Carrington declares her love for Strachey.
	May	Exhibits London Group, and most years henceforth.
	August and September	Spent at Garsington (and henceforth until 1927 most summers and several Christmases spent there).
	October	Weekend with Fry; exhibits at Heals 'Modern Movement'.
	Christmas	Carrington and Strachey start to live together.
1918	18 February	Attacks Strachey; considered for war picture commission.
	November	Included in Omega Workshops exhibition of paintings. Fry buys a drawing.
1919		Included in Goupil Gallery autumn salon.
1920	January	Included with modern French in New Art Salon.
	Spring	Visits Paris. Goupil offers show and makes an advance on March 21.
	13 November	Sanatorium at Banchory, Scotland, until the following May.
1921		One-man exhibition at Goupil Gallery (makes £140 net) (the Gallery shows his work each spring until 1926); included in 'Nameless' exhibition at Grosvenor Gallery; Carrington marries.
1922	August	Exhibits several paintings of pottery figures; paints landscapes on a visit to Dobrées at Larrau, France.
1923	August	Visit to Lyme Regis.
	Autumn	Meets Marjorie Hodgkinson.
1924	February	At Café Royal party for D. H. Lawrence.
	April	Paris and St Tropez with Walter Taylor; becomes engaged, then breaks it off.
1925	January	Spends a month with Taylor at St Tropez, then Paris for a week to see 'a very important picture show'.
	August	Fortnight with Taylor at John Fothergill's 'Spread Eagle',

Thane, then joins Mavrogordatos and Turners at Frinton on Sea, Essex.

September   Has haemorrhage while dining with Morrells in Gower Street, then sanatorium at Mundesley, Norfolk, until December; Morrells and Taylor donate £30 each.

1926   Correspondences with Thomas Balston and Marjorie Hodgkinson start.

August   Stays at Lyme Regis with Turners, then with Taylor in Brighton.

Autumn and Winter   Payments from Goupil Gallery stop; Leicester Galleries start payments of £30 per month.

1927   Spring   Stays at Stratford-on-Avon some weeks to see Lydia Sherwood.

August   Cornwall with Mavrogordatos.

1928   March   Debt to Leicester Galleries is £480; then first exhibition there is very successful (£700 taken in first three days); contract renewed for two years.

1929   April   In Paris.

Mid July until August 24   Mundesley Sanatorium (doctors say TB cured; 'My breakdown this time was entirely mental strain.')

1930   January   Visits Charmouth, Dorset·

9 January   Brothers go bankrupt.

3 April   Gets married in Paris to Marjorie Hodgkinson; honeymoon in Bandol, where Lawrence and Huxleys had stayed; paints landscapes.

August   Stays with Valentine Dobrée at Harleston, Norfolk, then with the Mavrogordatos at Charmouth, Dorset, then with wife to the Morlands at Mundesley.

September   Takes two-room flat at No. 22 Kemplay Road, Hampstead.

November   Leicester galleries exhibition and contract renewed for two years.

December   Holiday with wife at Fontainbleau.

1931   Visits Charmouth, wife visits Switzerland.

April   Both at Fontainbleau.

August   To Hastings with Taylor while wife stays South of France with friend Dick Cotton.

October   Starts to teach on Tuesday and Friday evenings at Westminster Technical Institute in Vincent Square.

1932   22 February   Mother, Golda, dies.

February   Strachey dies; then Carrington kills herself.

March   Visit to Paris with Balston.

Spring   Moves out of Penn Studio.

16 August   Son Luke born.

	October	Takes No. 1 Well Mount Studios, Well Road; Leicester Galleries exhibition.
	December	Visits Dobrées.
1933		Meets Henry Moore.
	March	Visits Paris with Balston.
19 May		Moves with family into No. 53 Haverstock Hill.
	Summer	Wife holidays in Spain.
	August	Stays at Hastings.
1934	Summer	Castelltersol, Spain with family.
	October	Leicester Galleries show failure.
1935	February	Exhibition of drawings at Agnews.
	Summer	Castelltersol with family and Balston visits them there.
1936	January	Stays at St Leonards with Taylor.
	July	Mundesley Sanatorium; suicide attempt.
18 October		Leaves sanatorium and moves with family into No. 5 Grove Terrace, Hampstead.
1937	April	Exhibition at Lefevre galleries.
	July	Stays at Balston's home in Holt End, near Newbury, while wife visits France, and son and nurse stay in the country.
	September	Visits Paris; son starts in resident nursery school.
1938	April	Stays with Balston at Holt End.
	July to September	Cassis with wife and son.
	December	Visits Taylor at St Leonards, Morlands at Mundesley, Balston at Holt End.
1939	January	Wife goes to Paris and takes studio there; son in Switzerland.
	May	Exhibition at Lefevre Galleries is a failure; visits wife in Paris.
23 June		Commits suicide.

POSTHUMOUS

1941 Memorial exhibition, Leicester Galleries.

1944 Memorial exhibition Ben Uri Gallery.

1949 Exhibition at the Whitechapel Art Gallery.

1971 Exhibition at Morley College, London, The Minories, Colchester, the Ashmolean Museum, Oxford, and the Graves Art Gallery, Sheffield.

A Catalogue of the Work of Mark Gertler

The owner of each work is given in brackets after the title; where the name of a town is listed the picture is the property of the municipality and is normally kept in the appropriate public art gallery. Unless otherwise stated the medium of the picture is oil on canvas.

Abbreviations

c. = circa
d. = dated
n.d. = not dated
exh. = exhibited
lit. = literature
repro. = reproduced
coll. = collection(s)
G = Gallery
Leic. G. = Leicester Galleries
Letters = *Mark Gertler, Selected Letters*, 1965
N.E.A.C. = New English Art Club
Whitechapel = Whitechapel Art Gallery
Colchester 1971 = exhibition in 1971 at The Minories, Colchester, The Ashmolean Museum, Oxford, Morley College, London, and Graves Art Gallery, Sheffield.

'Greek Head' (Mrs Blundell) Charcoal; 15″ × 12″; d. July 1906; *exh.* Whitechapel 1949 (**D 1**)

'Still Life with Apples' (Mrs Blundell) 9″ × 12″; d. 1907; *exh.* Ben Uri 1957 (**1**); Colchester 1971 (**1**). The artist refused offers for this picture and kept it until his death

'Sea Shells' (Fitzwilliam Museum, Cambridge) 11″ × 15″; d. 1907;
    coll. Howard Bliss
'Fruit and Flask' (Marsh Coll.) 12″ × 18″; n.d. *c.* 1907; *exh.*
    Whitechapel 1949 (**1**)
'Man, Woman and Child' (Mrs Blundell) 20″ × 16″; *c.* 1908
'Still Life with Bottle of Benedictine' (L. J. Morris) 16″ × 19″; d.
    1908
'The Artist's Mother' (Lionel Jacobson) 22″ × 17″; d. 1908; coll. S.
    Samuels; *exh.* Ben Uri 1944 (**43**); Whitechapel 1949 (**3**)
'Still Life with Melon' (Mrs Blundell) 17″ × 21″; *exh.* Ben Uri 1944
    (**48**); Ben Uri 1959 (**2**); Colchester 1971 (**2**). The painting gained
    a Bronze Medal in the Board of Education National Competition
    for 1908. Gertler entered as a Regent Street Polytechnic pupil.
    See p. 48.
'The Artist's Mother' (Mrs Blundell) 36″ × 32″; n.d. *c.* 1909
'Portrait of a Woman' (P. Anthony) 26″ × 20″; n.d. *c.* 1909
'Portrait of a Man' (P. Anthony) 24″ × 20″; n.d. *c.* 1909
'Landscape with Trees' (Mrs Leonie Lyons) 11″ × 15″; d. 1909
'The Artist's Mother' (Mrs Blundell) 23″ × 18″; d. 1909; *exh.*
    Colchester 1971 (**3**). Relates quite closely to William
    Rothenstein's work. *See* p. 333
'Self-Portrait with Fishing Cap' (unknown) *c.* 1909. Plate **2**
'Onions' (coll. Mr Lesser) 1909; *see* p. 58
'Self-Portrait' (K. Preston) Pencil; 10″ × 8″; d. 1909; repro. *Selected
    Letters* fac. p. 32. Quentin Bell (Intro. to *Selected Letters*): 'Here
    was a young man who could do anything. He had taken some-
    thing from . . . Rossetti (he never quite forgot Rossetti) and at
    the same time he had acquired a bold sharp decisive use of line
    (observe the treatment of the nose) which comes from France via
    the N.E.A.C. It is precise yet free, intelligent but nevertheless a
    little sentimental, in short it is all that a Slade drawing was
    supposed to be.'
'The Artist's Parents' (Mrs Blundell) 18″ × 20″; n.d. *c.* 1909–10
'Portrait of a Woman' (Mrs Blundell) 24″ × 20″; n.d. *c.* 1909–10
"The Artist's Brother Jack' (Mrs Blundell) 13″ × 9″; n.d. (un-
    finished) *c.* 1909–10
'Jews Arguing' (unknown) *c.* 1909–10. *Exh.* Friday Club Feb. 1911
    (**125**) (*Sunday Times*: 'He is to be congratulated on having

approached this Will Rothenstein subject in a way which is
anything but that of Mr Rothenstein and he shows a great
capacity which, sooner or later, will force him to choose between
being either a popular Academy exhibitor or a superior person in
the New English Art Club.'); *see* pp. 67, 334

'Head of a Girl' (sold Christies 19 Jan. 1971 (**74**)) Red Chalk;
19¼″ × 11½″; d. 5 Sep. 1910; coll. Paul Nash

'The Artist's Mother' (Victoria & Albert Museum) Sanguine;
21″ × 15″; d. 1910; *exh.* Whitechapel 1949 (**D 2**)

'May Berlinsky' (David Burleigh) 30″ × 24″; d. 1910; *see* pp. 74, 333

'May Berlinsky' (unknown) 24″ × 16″; n.d. *c.* 1910; *see* p. 74

'A Playful Scene' (The artist's family) (Birmingham) 30″ × 40″;
n.d. *c.* 1911; *exh.* Leic. G. 1941 (**7**); Ben Uri 1944 (**42**);
Whitechapel 1949 (**4**); Colchester 1971 (**5**). Painted for a Slade
summer composition on 'Leisure'. From left to right: The artist's
mother, his sister Sophie, his brothers Jack and Harry, in their
home at No. 14 Spital Square, Whitechapel. *See* pp. 78, 333 and
Plate **3**

'The Artist's Mother' (Tate Gallery) 26″ × 22″; d. July 1911; *exh.*
Nov. 1911 N.E.A.C. (**25**); Leic. G. 1941 (**18**); Whitechapel 1949
(**5**); Colchester 1971 (**6**); repro. *Apollo*, Jan. 1944, p. 1; *Selected
Letters* fac. p. 33; The picture clearly relates to Cézanne's 'La
Vieille au Chapelet' (National Gallery) which was at the November
1910 Post Impressionist exhibition; *see* pp. 2, 72, 333, 334, 341
and Plate **4**

'The Artist's Mother in her Kitchen' (Tatham Art Gallery,
Pietermaritsburg) 27″ × 30″; n.d. *c.* 1911; *exh.* Leeds Apr. 1914
(**133**) (£40) as 'The Housekeeper'; repro. Whitworth and General
Catalogue. *See* pp. 71,139,144, and Plate **6**

'The Artist's Sister Deborah' (Swindon) 40″ × 30″; n.d. *c.* 1911;
coll. T. Balston; *exh.* Whitechapel 1949 (**6**); Ben Uri 1957 (**4**);
Colchester 1971 (**4**); repro: *Selected Letters* fac. p. 48

'The Artist's Brother Harry' (Miss Celia Gertler) 24″ × 20″; n.d.
c. 1911; *exh.* Whitechapel 1949 (**7**); Ben Uri 1957 (**5**)

'Mrs Harry Gertler' (Miss Celia Gertler) 36″ × 24″; d. 1911; *exh.*
Ben Uri 1957 (**6**)

'The Artist's Sister Sophie' (Mrs Blundell) 24″ × 11″; n.d. *c.* 1911

'The Artist's Sister Sophie' (L. J. Morris) 24″ × 20″ n.d. *c.* 1911

'Winter Cherries' (Leslie Morris) 20″ × 16″ *c.* 1911

'The Artist's Mother' (Tate Gallery) Pencil 14¾″ × 10″; d. Dec. 1911; *exh.* Whitechapel 1949 (**D 3**). *See* p. 333

'The Return of Jeptha' (Frank Foster) 43½″ × 59½″ n.d. *c.* 1910–12; coll. Edward Troy. *See* Plate **21**

'Jacob Offering up his Son' (Mavrogordato) 12″ × 18″; n.d. *c.* 1910–12 coll. Leonard Atelson

'Mrs T. E. Harvey' (R. S. Rowntree) 24″ × 19½″; Jan. 1912; painted at her home in Hutton-le-Hole. *See* p. 337 and Plate **10**

'Mr T. E. Harvey' (R. S. Rowntree) 24″ × 19½″; n.d. *c.* 1912–14. *See* p. 337

'Portrait of a Girl' (The artist's sister Sophie) (Tate Gallery) 20″ × 16″; d. Feb. 1912; *see* pp. 81, 338

'The Apple Woman and her Husband' (The artist's father and mother) (Melbourne); d. May 1912; coll. A. M. Daniel; *exh.* N.E.A.C. May 1912 (**142**); repro. '30 years of British Art' (*Studio* 1930) p. 135; *see* pp. 79, 338, 339 and Plate **5**

'Sir George Howard Darwin' (National Portrait Gallery) 35½ × 23½″; d. May 1912; *see* p. 79

'Coster Woman and Child' (unknown) *Exh.* Chenil Gallery Dec. 1912. (*Truth*: 'I am quite sure that Gertler's Sienese-cum-John Coster Woman and Child with the little black straw hat to point the moral, is the most striking work shown.') *See* p. 337

'Vanity' (private coll. London) 48″ × 18″; d. 1912; *exh.* N.E.A.C. Nov. 1912 (**178**). (*Architect & Contract Reptr*: 'Here is depicted an unbeautiful mis-drawn nude female, afflicted with the jaundice, and seated in an armchair upholstered in emerald green, with a right-minded clothed figure in the background.'); Ben Uri 1957 (**7**) as 'Two Women and Lampshade'. *See* pp. 338, 343 and Plate **11**

'The Artist's Mother' (unknown). Lit. *Letters* p. 49. Nearly complete Dec. 1912: 'This is really the very best thing I have done. Although I am sure everyone will disagree with me. They will say "it is not as *carefully* finished as usual." I do not care what anybody says. It was done in fever heat. Never was I so inspired as when I painted this. It is quite different in technique to anything I have done. You see I sacrificed *everything* to the spirit.

I know that, had I gone on and finished it, it would have died a horrible death. So I was content to get a little of something into it, rather than finish and please the foolish buyers. But that little that I have got is surely there.'

'Carrington' (Dr F. H. Kroch) 19" × 15½"; *exh*. Chenil G. Dec. 1912 (**2**) (*Star*: 'Shows a close study of the early Florentines . . . the precision of modelling and the fresh bright colour are admirable'.) *See* p. 88 and Plate **7**

'The Violinist' Fine Art Society on panel 15" × 11"; d. 15 July 1912; *exh*. Chenil G. Dec. 1912; *see* p. 337 and Plate **9**

'Head of a Girl' (Leeds) Blacklead; 8" × 7½"; d. 1912; *exh*. Colchester 1971 (**52**)

'Head of an Old Man' (Adelaide) Drawing d. 1912; coll. E. Marsh

'The Violinist' (unknown) *Exh*. Friday Club Feb. 1913. (*Star*: 'The Violinist is a little disappointing. It is a second version of a painting which I admired very much a short time ago at the Chenil Gallery. The present version is much flatter and emptier than the first.') *See* p. 400

'Woman Resting' (unknown) *exh*. Friday Club Feb. 1913 (**4**) (*Connoisseur*: 'Depicted with phenomenal arms and hands.') *See* pp.136, 342, 400

'The Furrier' (unknown) *Exh*. Friday Club Feb. 1913 (**6**); *see* p. 400 n. 107

'Rabbi and his Grandchild' (Southampton) 19" × 18"; d. May 1913; coll. S. Samuels; *exh*. N.E.A.C. May 1913 (**174**); Leic. G. 1941 (**8**); Ben Uri 1944 (**47**); Whitechapel 1949 (**10**); Colchester 1971 (**7**). The model for the little girl was Dora Plaskowsky, later Mrs Silver. The theme recalls Ghirlandaio's 'Portrait of an Old Man and Child' in the Louvre, and the style that of paintings such as Rogier van der Weyden's 'Portrait of a Lady' in the National Gallery, although there is a strong influence of contemporary French painters such as Gauguin. At one stage in the painting Gertler added another girl's head, but then painted it out. *See* pp. 127, 338, 341, 400 n. 108 and Plate **12**

'Family Group' (Southampton) 36" × 24"; coll. Denys Sutton; *exh*. N.E.A.C. Nov. 1913 (**54**); Whitechapel 1949 (**2**). Lit: *Apollo* Nov. 1953, p. 133 (repro): 'All the naive charm of Rousseau. The forms, slightly angular, somewhat in the manner of stained glass, are designed on straight lines. The figures are nearly flat, and look as though they were cut out in thick paper and stuck on to the canvas like silhouettes ... the clothes, primitive in simplicity, are of varying shades of green and red, the scheme being carried from one to the other, with a pearly wall incorporating the same hues. The bareness, eloquent and intimate, speaks of poverty, and stresses the human aspect of the little family. The mood of the picture recalls Picasso's early work.' *See* pp. 127, 340 and Plate **8**

'A Jewish Family' (Tate Gallery) 26″ × 20″; d. 1 Sept. 1913; coll. E. Marsh; *exh.* Whitechapel May 1914 (**270**) (*Star*: 'In Mr Mark Gertler's Jewish Family (270) so much emphasis is placed upon certain characteristics of the sitters that representation is occasionally pushed to the point of caricature. The seated old man in this picture is as monstrously grotesque as a gargoyle or some of the figures in medieval wood-carvings. But this kind of wilful exaggeration and emphasis belongs to a different world from that of abstract geometrical diagrams. It belongs to the world of flesh and blood and therefore stirs our imagination and our sympathies. It seems on the whole the only proper development of the realistic art of the nineteenth century, as it brings back vitality and vivid personal expression and interest to an art which had become too scientific and impersonal.'); Ben Uri 1944 (**51**); Whitechapel 1949 (**8**); Colchester 1971 (**8**). Repro. *Selected Letters*, fac. p. 49. A number of relations may be seen in this picture: to pictures by Picasso, and the English painters Henry Lamb and Stanley Spencer ('The Visitation'). The same old man was painted in 'Rabbi and his Grandchild.' *See* pp. 108, 127, 339, 342–4, 400 n. 107 and Plate **14**

'The Artist's Mother' (Swansea) 17½ × 16½″; d. Dec. 1913; coll. E. Marsh; *exh.* Whitechapel 1949 (**9**); Colchester 1971 (**9**). *See* pp. 114, 127, 340–4 and Plate **13**

'The Artist's Brother Harry Holding an Apple' (Mrs Blundell) 20″ × 14″; *c.* 1913

'Still Life' (Bowl, spoon and apples) (Hatton Gall. King's Coll., Newcastle) 16″ × 12″; d. 1913; coll. E. Marsh; *exh.* Whitechapel 1949 (**11**); Colchester 1971 (**10**). *See* pp. 339, 340

'Head of a Young Girl' (Manchester) Black chalk; d. 1913. *See* p. 339

'Seated Nude' (British Council) Chalk and water colours; 14″ × 9″; d. 1913

'Portrait of John Currie' (J. Isaacs) Pencil; 13½″ × 10″; d. 1913; *exh.* Whitechapel 1949 (**D 6**)

'Head of a Child' (Miss M. Parker) Drawing; *c.* 1913; *exh.* Leic. G. 1941 (**5**)

'Old Man with Beard' (Luke Gertler) Drawing; 11½″ × 8½″; d. 1913; *exh.* Colchester 1971 (**53**)

'Standing Nude' (unknown) Charcoal; 18¼″ × 8″; d. Dec. 1913; coll. E. Marsh; *exh.* Whitechapel 1949 (**D 5**)

'Head of a Woman' (Sir John Chadwick) Drawing; *c.* 1913; *exh.* Leic. G. 1941 (**4**)

'The Doll' (private coll. London) 29½″ × 19½″; n.d.; *exh.* Friday Club Feb. 1914 (**16**); Whitechapel 1949 (**16**); Colchester 1971 (**14**); *see* pp. 136, 344 and Plate **43**

'The Fruit Sorters' (Leicester) 30″ × 25″; d. 1914; *exh.* N.E.A.C. May 1914 (**271**). *New Age* (W. Sickert): 'The picture is important because it is a masterly piece of painting in well-supported and consistent illumination, and the work of a colourist at the same time rich and sober. The Contemporary Art Society have made an excellent choice in buying a work which painters will agree to consider exemplary.' *Pall Mall Gazette*: 'The design is primitive Egyptian, eked out by a sky and a landscape spaced in the manner of . . . John.' Colchester 1971 (**13**). In August 1916 Gertler wrote of his 'inner life before I painted my Fruit Sorters, when I was all confusion'. The model for the girl on the left was his sister Sophie. *See* pp. 136, 141, 142, 339, 340, 342 and Plate **16**.

'Mother and Baby' (unknown) *exh.* Whitechapel May 1914 (**261**) (*Sunday Times*: 'Decorative.' *Daily Telegraph*: 'Design of some breadth but of little vital force or distinction.')

'Great Grandmother's Dress' (unknown) *Exh.* Whitechapel May 1914 (**272**) as coll. T. E. Harvey

'Still Life' (unknown) *Exh.* Whitechapel May 1914 (**275**) as coll. T. E. Harvey

'Rabbi' (unknown) Charcoal; 19″ × 11½″; d. June 1914; coll. E· Marsh who bought it for £6 in 1915; *exh.* Ben Uri 1944 (**44**); Whitechapel 1949 (**D 8**). 'The drawing of the Old Jew is I think

one of the best things I've done. Eddie Marsh now has it.'
(Gertler, Feb. 1915)

'Black and White Cottage' (Mrs F. C. O. Speyer) 19½″ × 13½″; d.
1914; Painted in July 1914. 'One of the best things I've done.'
(Gertler, Feb. 1915) *exh.* N.E.A.C. Nov. 1914 (**110**); Whitechapel
1949 (**21**); Colchester 1971 (**12**). Bought for £12 by Lady
Hamilton in 1915 who later gave it to Violet Asquith as a
wedding present and it hung among the presents at Downing
Street. Repro. *Selected Letters*, p. 64. The combination of a
'dreamy' mood with precision of detail recalls pre-Raphaelite
pictures such as Arthur Hughes' 'The Long Engagement' and
'April Love'. These pictures were included in exhibitions of pre-
Raphaelite work at the Tate Gallery in Dec. 1911 and July 1913
respectively. The picture relates also to Stanley Spencer's work.
See pp. 145, 169, 204, 342 and Plate **24**

'Agapanthus' (Melbourne) 24″ × 20″; d. Sept. 1914; coll. E. Marsh
who bought it for £25 in 1915. *Exh.* Friday Club Feb. 1915 as
'Blue Flowers'; Ben Uri 1944 (**50**); Whitechapel 1949 (**13**).
Repro. *Colour Magazine*, March 1915 (in colour). Lit. C.
Marriott *Modern Movements* (1920): 'Interesting as an attempt to
intensify reality by simplification and a slight formality of treat-
ment.' The treatment of the plant recalls the Douanier Rousseau.
See pp. 169, 340 and Plate **37**

'Torso' (unknown) Sanguine; 15″ × 11½″; d. Oct. 1914; coll. E.
Marsh; *exh.* Ben Uri 1944 (**46**); Whitechapel 1949 (**D 9**)

'Apples' (unknown) *Exh.* N.E.A.C. Nov. 1914 (**105**). *Observer:*
'Truth in the rendering of surface texture can go no further than
in this highly accomplished, precise and yet free painting of
"Apples".' 'Chile [Guevara] and young Spencer [Gilbert] all
thought that my "Apples" was the best thing in the New
English . . . I think [it is] one of the best things I've done.'
(Gertler, Feb. 1915). 'I think your Apples were one of the best
things you have ever done.' (Carrington, May 1915). *See* p. 205

'The Creation of Eve' (private coll.) 33″ × 26″; d. 1914; coll. Lady
Ridley; *exh.* London Group Nov. 1915 (**76**); Leic. G. 1941 (**9**);
Whitechapel 1949 (**12**); Colchester 1971 (**11**); repro. *Selected
Letters*, fac. p. 80. Finished in No. 32 Elder Street, Spitalfields in
Jan. 1915. The picture recalls Blake, who was the subject of an

exhibition at the Tate Gallery in Oct. 1913. It is curiously similar in colour and conception to Franz Marc, though there is no indication that his work was known in London as early as 1914. *See* pp. 164, 170, 185, 186, 204, 342–3, 403n, 145 and Plate **23**

'Rabbi and Rabbitzin' (private coll. London) Pencil, ink and brown wash on paper, squared up 19″ × 15″; d. 1914; *exh.* N.E.A.C. Apr. 1915 (**59**); Vienna Gallery of Secession 1927 (**36**); Leic. G. 1941 (**1**); Whitechapel 1949 (**D 7**); Colchester 1971 (**54**). Repro. *Selected Letters*, fac. p. 65. Completed by Feb. 1915. Bought by Sir Thomas Beecham and Lady Cunard in Nov. 1915 for £10. Shows the influence of Picasso, for example in the treatment of the man's eyes. Lit: John Rothenstein, *Modern English Painters*: 'Extraordinary insight . . . precisely focused intensity that gives the best of his early work a glowing actuality in the company of which most others seem the lifeless products of indifference.' Quentin Bell, Intro. to *Selected Letters*: 'The harsh, bold post-Impressionist . . . tough, uncompromising . . . has looked, not only at Cézanne, but at the Vorticists, and probably at William Roberts. A hint of what the century was to experience in the way of ruthless metallic form and fierce sculptural statement. The sentiment . . . is strictly confined by the austerely calculated design.' Mark Gertler: 'The other day Lady Ottoline came to see my "Eve" with her husband. She thought it "quite beautiful" but what delighted me was that she liked very much my "Husband and Wife", the one nobody liked. You know, the one in which you didn't like the stomach. She is thinking of buying it!' (Jan. 1915 to Carrington, referring either to this picture or to 'The Apple Woman and her Husband' 1912). *See* pp. 127, 169, 184, 339–4 and Plate **15**

'Head of an Old Man' (Ernest Franklin) Sanguine; $10\frac{1}{2}″ \times 8\frac{1}{2}″$; 1914? *Exh.* Whitechapel 1949 (**D 10**)

'Daffodils' (Stalybridge) 24″ × 18″; n.d. Ex coll. E. Marsh who bought it for £20 in 1915, exercising his right of first refusal (S. Schiff had also wanted the picture). *Exh.* Ben Uri 1944 (**41**); Whitechapel 1949 (**14**). Completed by 20 March 1915. *See* p. 170

'Abraham and the Angels' Charcoal; *exh.* N.E.A.C. Nov. 1915 (**68**). *Morning Post*: 'Impertinent Mockery.' 'Cannan liked my charcoal study of Abraham and the Angels.' (Gertler, March 1915).

'Portrait of Dorothy Brett' (unknown) Bought by Prof. F. Brown for £20 in May 1915; *exh.* N.E.A.C. May 1915 (**7**). *See* p. 170

'The Fruit Stall' (unknown) *Exh.* London Group Nov. 1915 (**75**). A big picture of costers and fruit, finished by Apr. 1915. Sold in the autumn of 1916. 'My Fruit Stall" commenced one period . . .' (Gertler, Mar. 1917). *See* pp. 172, 185–6, 203–5, 403n, 145 and n.146

'Sir Michael Sadler' (Leeds) Painted in Aug. 1915. *See* p. 179

'Swing Boats' (unknown) *Exh.* London Group Nov. 1915 (**11**); Heal's Gallery Oct. 1917 'The New Movement' (**30**). Painted in the autumn of 1915 in London. A preliminary oil study was painted in the summer at Leeds. *See* pp. 171–2, 203, 205, 225, 341 and Plate **28**

'Acrobats' (unknown) Sepia wash on grey paper; 14″ × 9¾″; d. 1915; sold at Sotheby's, 15 Dec. 1971 (**75**)

'Studies of Heads' (J. Isaacs) Sanguine; 19″ × 16″; d. 1915; *exh.* Whitechapel 1949 (**D 11**)

'Penn Studio' (unknown) 24″ × 20″; n.d. *c* 1915 coll: E. Marsh; *exh.* Ben Uri 1944 (**53**); Whitechapel 1949 (**17**)

'Gilbert Cannan at his Mill' (Ashmolean Museum, Oxford) 40″ × 28″; coll. Montague Sherman, T. Balston; *exh.* London Group June 1916 (**93**); Heal's Oct. 1917 (**32**); Leic. G. 1941 (**11**); Whitechapel 1949 (**15**); Colchester 1971 (**15**). Repro. *Selected Letters*, p. 81. Painted at Cholesbury, Herts., during visits from June 1915 to spring 1916. At one stage a three-inch strip of canvas was added at the bottom. 'I have for the moment put aside the "Mill" in order to do some studies for it and some studies, in general, from nature. I found water colour did not quite suit my purpose, so I am doing my studies in oil and on very small panels . . . today I started a small painting of one of those chestnut trees and tomorrow I hope to start a largish study – carefully done – of the same tree. I shall carry these two on together. When they are finished I shall come back to the Mill which I think is going to be a good thing.' (Gertler, July 1915 at Cholesbury.) The work of Andre Derain, such as his 'Window at Vers' (exhibited Second Post-Impressionist Exhibition) is recalled, especially in the treatment of the tree. *See* pp. 158, 224–5, 339–42 and Plate **38**

'Daffodils in a Blue Bottle' (Richard Carline) 27" × 22"; n.d. *exh.*
Friday Club Apr. 1917; Colchester 1971 (**16**). Started on 2 May
1916. *See* p. 339

'Merry-Go-Round' (Ben Uri Gallery) 76" × 56"; n.d.; *exh.* London Group Apr. 1917 (**52**) (*Sunday Times* 29 Apr. 1917: 'Mr Max
Gertler is at his brazen best in "Merry-go-Round" (**52**), a joyous
clash of metallic blues and shrill orange yellows, a riot we almost
hear as we enter the gallery. It is the apotheosis of the steam
organ in paint, and a style of decoration admirably fitted for the
adornment of a popular restaurant.' *Observer*: 'The undeniable
talent of Mr Mark Gertler is wasted upon performances of
incredible eccentricity, like the painting "Merry-go-Round",
with its crude clashing of unbroken blue, red, orange, and black
on figures as wooden as those of the carved animals, and the
sculptural and equally crudely coloured group of contortionist
acrobats. All this is sheer sensationalism.' *Westminster Gazette* 23
June 1917: 'The colour scheme . . . is appropriate to the blare and
heavy swirl of the subject, and Mr Gertler's success in suggesting
the movement and character of the scene is remarkable. The
picture is however a product of intellectual rather than sensual
reaction.'); Leic. G. 1941 (**14**); Ben Uri 1944 (**52**); Whitechapel
1949 (**18**); Ben Uri 1957 (**8**); Colchester 1971 (**17**). Repro. *Selected
Letters*, fac. p. 129. Painted in the spring and summer of 1916 in
London. *See* pp. 222, 225, 226, 235, 250, 339, 331, 343–5, 348
and Plate **26**

'The Pond: Garsington' (Leeds) 25" × 25"; d. 1916; *exh.* Friday
Club Apr. 1917; Heal's Oct. 1917 (**33**); Leic. G. 1941 (**15**).
Painted in the summer of 1916. *See* pp. 230, 235, 267

'Portrait of Koteliansky' (Michael Campbell) 36" × 25½"; 1916;
coll. Lady Glenavy. Repro. *Selected Letters*, fac. p. 144; 'M.
Gertler' Fleuron pl. 3. *See* p. 261 and Plate **26**

'The Straw Hat' (Mrs V. S. Pritchett) Charcoal; 25" × 20"; d.
1916; *exh.* Whitechapel 1949 (**D 12**)

'Flowers' (unknown) 16" × 21"; d. 1916; coll. Mrs Violet Schiff;
exh. Whitechapel 1949 (**19**)

'Portrait of Gilbert Cannan' (Gwendoline, Lady Melchett) 1916?

'The Acrobats' (Tate Gallery) 23½" × 16½" × 12½"; Bronze; *exh.*
London Group April 1917 (**94**); Colchester 1971 (**51**). Repro.

Selected Letters, fac. p. 145. Started in Sept. 1916, completed by Apr. 1917. In its simplification and hardness of form and in its tight design of interlocked limbs, it recalls 'Merry-Go-Round', and also reminds one of Gaudier-Brzeska's relief 'Wrestlers'. Gertler's 1914 drawing 'Acrobats' shows a different design on the same theme and also recalls Gaudier's work. *See* pp. 234–6, 345 and Plate **30**

'Still Life' (J. Wood) 20″ × 24″; d. Aug. 1917

'Still Life' (Manchester) 25″ × 30″; d. 1917; coll. Lord H. Bentinck; *exh.* London Group Nov. 1917; Colchester 1971 (**19**). *See* p. 345

'Two Female Nudes' (unknown) Black crayon on brown paper; d. 1917; coll. Abbott & Holder

'The Pond Garsington' (Dept. of the Environment) 1917? Plate **31**

'The Bathers' (Gwendoline, Lady Melchett) 45″ × 56″; d. 1917–18; coll. artist at death; *exh.* Friday Club May 1919 (**104**) (*Westminster Gazette*: 'an ambitious but rather laboured composition of continuous rhythms'); Colchester 1971 (**18**). Painted in London. 'I have been overcome with my "nude" idea ... I have started a small design for it in pencil – it is to be a good old-fashioned "Cézannish" bathing scene, but I am very excited about it. The opportunities are immense for drawing and colour. I shall revel in the drawing of the Nudes. The background is to be based on my "Pond" picture.' (Gertler, Leeds, Jan. 1917.) 'I am working hard on my "Bathing" ... in this picture I intend to take a definite step forward ... I want to step right forward now on all that I have discovered these last 2 years. My "Fruit Stall" commenced one period and this "Bathing" commences another.' (Gertler, May 1917) ' "Bathing" is giving me more trouble than anything I've ever worked on before ... not only because the subject is a more difficult one, but because I feel that I simply *must* get something new and better into this picture, even as it stands I believe it to be the best thing I've done.' (Gertler, July 1917) 'My "Bathers" ... impressed me with its fine composition and endless possibilities, but I still can't see it, even in my imagination, as a completed thing. I have worked on it all day, but a day's work on it makes no more impression than a flea-bite on an elephant's back. So I can see myself going on forever at it. In fact I shall have to work at other smaller things either before or in between, and use it as a sort of permanent study. I see no other way at present.' (Gertler, 3 Oct. 1917). *See* pp. 235, 236, 252, 253, 269, 345-7, Plate **32**

'Nude' (unknown) unfinished? 'I am painting a "Nude" of a little girl of eleven, a model I've got hold of. I might make something of it – But it's too early to tell yet.' (Gertler, Jan. 1819)

'Montague Shearman' (unknown) Completed in London, March 1918

'Shop Window' (unknown) Drawing; *exh.* Friday Club Apr. 1918 (**72**). *Times*: 'Remarkable.'

'Still Life with Self-Portrait' (Leeds) 20″ × 16″; d. 1918; *exh.* Colchester 1971 (**22**). Given by Miss H. G. Thompson in memory of the late T. E. Harvey 1956

'The Teapot' (Tate Gallery) 16″ × 20″; d. July 1918; *exh.* London Group Nov. 1918 (**9**); Whitechapel 1949 (**20**). Painted at Garsington. *See* p. 346

'The Pool Garsington' (Dept. of the Environment) d. 1918

'Trees at Garsington' (Gwendoline, Lady Melchett) 20″ × 18″; n.d. *c.* 1918; sold at Christie's 21 Jan. 1972 (**83**) to Leicester Galleries as 'Trees'

'Boxers' (Private coll. London) 55″ × 40″; d. 1918; *exh.* Leic. G. 1941 (**32**); Ben Uri 1944 (**22**); Colchester 1971 (**20**). 'Hutchinson is thinking of buying the "Boxers". As I did it, in spite of its size, in a comparatively short time, I am only asking £35 for it.' (Gertler, Dec. 1918). *See* p. 345 and Plate **27**

'Ballet Dancers' (H. M. Goldberg) 23½ × 19½″; n.d. *exh.* London Group Apr. 1919 (**41**). (*Sunday Times*: 'One of the most important pictures in the exhibition.') Painted in the autumn of 1918. Roger Fry bought for £8 a charcoal study for this picture. *See* p. 345

'Circus' (unknown) *Exh.* London Group Nov. 1919 (**121**). *Times*: 'The violence of this picture seems to be misapplied energy!' *Observer*: 'His most important contribution, "The Circus" is neither representation nor interpretation nor decoration.') 'Yesterday I started a fairly large thing of a circus – a sort of outcome of my ballet.' (Gertler, Nov. 1918) 'I shall now call it finished – it has a sort of completion: it is not without interest, but I am far from satisfied . . . In my "Circus" I have already exhausted that manner which came to birth in the "Ballet" and pen drawings.' (Gertler, Dec. 1918) 'I have brought my "Circus" up to what I think is an interesting state and so I've left it now. No doubt you will think my last things unfinished – well they are – but I have decided that it is better to leave them so, rather than go on with no particular notion of how to better them.' (Gertler, 23 Dec. 1918)

'Harlequin, Clown & Columbine' (Private coll. London) 39″ × 41″; d. 1918; coll. M. Shearman; *exh.* Ben Uri 1957 (**9**); Colchester 1971 (**21**)

'Harlequinade' (Anthony Fry) Charcoal; 18″ × 18″; d. Oct. 1918; repro. *Woodcuts by various Artists* Omega Workshops 1918. Roger Fry made a woodcut of this picture.

'Reclining Nude' (unknown) Charcoal; d. 1918

'The Tea Set' (Private coll. London) 18″ × 20″; d. 1918. This may be the 'Still Life' exhibited at the London Group Apr. 1919 (**24**). Comments then included: *Sunday Times*: 'One of the most important pictures in the exhibition ... what has this clever young painter got into his head? ... Should he perhaps abandon painting for a while and yield his passion for solidity and plastic quality to sculpture?' *Observer*: 'It is not easy to keep patience with the distortions of the *saucers* in the Still Life. Is it really necessary to bash and twist crockery out of shape to prove one's allegiance to the advanced movement?' *See* p. 345

'Valentine Dobrée' (unknown). 'In town I finished off the large portrait of Mrs Dobree and a still life; both were important to me as by their completion they proved the reality of certain ideas that I have recently discovered. I think I certainly have in some points made a definite step forward.' (Gertler, June 1919)

'Geranium' (Private coll. London) 16″ × 20″; d. July 1919; coll. Miss Ethel Sands; *exh.* Whitechapel 1949 (**22**); Ben Uri 1957 (**10**); Colchester 1971 (**23**). *See* p. 346

'The Pigeon House, Garsington' (private coll.) *Exh.* Ben Uri 1944 (**62**). Started in the summer of 1919

'Horse in an Orchard' (Ralph Charrington) coll. Luke Gertler. Painted at Garsington in summer 1919. *See* note on 'Petroushka' 1919

'Petroushka' (unknown). 'The little "Horse" you saw at Garsington was the first step to a new ladder, which seems to me an important one and likely to last, perhaps even the beginning of my final path. And these two (1) "Bathers", (2) "Petroushka", seem to me important evidence of the fact and important also in enabling you to understand the work to come. The important thing really is that I have at last evolved a sort of charcoal drawing which is so explanatory to me that I can paint almost the whole picture afterwards from it. You will remember having seen the charcoal drawing of the "Bathers" at Garsington.' (Gertler, Dec. 1919). Petroushka was one of the most popular of the Russian ballets which Diaghilev was presenting in London at the time

'Nudes' (Sheffield) Drawing; d. 1919

'Figure Study' (Northampton) d. 1919; pres. by Sir Kenneth Clarke. Close to Picasso's 1906 'La Toilette' in pose and composition; the brushwork and tones recall Cézanne's work

'Circus Scene' (unknown) *Exh.* London Group May 1920 (**9**) (*Sunday Times:* 'Considerable distinction of design.' *Observer*: 'One need not be an Academician to experience discomfort and annoyance at such artistic abortions as Mr Mark Gertler's circus scenes . . . he has proved years ago that he is a painter of enormous ability. His sole object now seems to be to hide this ability under an assumed cloak of incompetence. What is he driving at? His pictures bear the evidence of great labour and of the striving after a quality of paint akin to Cézanne's. The result is merely defiled paint that bears the livid, greenish hues of putrefaction. And as it is with this colour so it is with his form. The blown out limbs of his monstrous nude female circus nudes and tightrope walkers invite deflation by means of a pen.')

'Footballers' (unknown) *Exh.* Grosvenor Galleries May 1921. (*Daily Telegraph*: 'Footballers – a pas de quatre obviously by Mr Max Gertler.'); London Group Oct. 1931 (**282**) (£10). 'My "Footballers" only just needed finishing off, but, alas, yesterday it all went wrong, and now it's done for – five weeks' solid work gone. I may take it up again, but at present I am very depressed and unhinged.' (Gertler, 2 Jan. 1920) 'I remember Gertler showing Ottoline at lunch one day a photo in the *Daily Mirror* of a man kicking a football, rather an extraordinary pose, and I have an idea he used it in a picture.' (Mrs Julian Vinogradoff). *See* p. 345

'The Red Jug' (Baron von den Heuvel, in 1949) 18″ × 20″; d. Apr. 1920; *exh.* Whitechapel 1949 **(26)**

'Self-Portrait' (Arts Council) 16¾″ × 11¾″; d. May 1920; *exh.* Goupil Febr. 1921 **(12)** (repro) (£40); Colchester 1971 **(25)**; repro. *Selected Letters*, fac. p. 177; 'M. Gertler', Fleuron pl 1. Lit. *Architect*, March 1921, *Morning Post*. 'To pass away time, when there is no one to sit for me I'm painting a small portrait of myself.' (Gertler, May 1920) *See* Plate **25**

'The Mantelpiece' (unknown) *Exh.* Goupil Feb. 1921 **(13)** (£60); London Group Retrospective 1928 **(63)**. Painted between May and July 1920 in Penn Studio

'Reclining Nude' (unknown) 15″ × 29″; d. July 1920; *exh.* Goupil Feb. 1921 **(17)** (£45); Leic. G. 1941 **(26)**; Whitechapel 1949 **(27)**

'The Bokhara Coat – Mrs Valentine Dobree' (unknown) 28″ × 28″; d. 1920; *exh.* Goupil Febr. 1921 **(5)** (£55); Leic. G 1941 **(27)**; Ben Uri 1944 **(28)**; Whitechapel 1949 **(25)**; Repro. *Colour*, Feb. 1921, p. 2. Lit. *Architect*, March 1921. Completed in July 1920. *See* p. 346

'Flowers in a Vase' (unknown) 21″ × 15″; d. July 1920; *exh.* Whitechapel 1949 **(28)**

'The Statue' (unknown) *Exh.* Goupil Febr. 1921 **(6)** (£50). Scene from a window at Garsington. Painted in July 1920

'Mr St John Hutchinson' (private coll.) d. Aug. 1920; repro. Birrell & Garnett *Modern Painters* (1921). Painted on a ten-day visit to the Hutchinsons at Wittering, Sussex. 'I think the portrait of Jack was a success.' (Gertler, Sept. 1920). *See* Plate **63**

'China Ornament' (private coll.) d. Aug. 1920; *exh.* Goupil Febr. 1921 **(1)** (£38). Painted during a ten-day visit to the Hutchinsons at Wittering, Sussex. 'They have such a good collection. I love them. I'm going to try and collect them myself.' (Gertler, Aug. 1920)

'Head of a Girl' (Mrs Julian Vinogradoff) 20″ × 15½″; d. Sept. 1920; *exh.* Whitechapel 1949 **(24)**. A portrait of Mrs Julian Vinogradoff, nee Morrell, painted at Garsington between 28 Aug. and 12 Sept. 'It was a struggle and she was so bored sitting. I didn't succeed in getting a likeness, but as a picture it's not bad. She's almost too good-looking to paint.' (Gertler, 12 Sept. 1920)

'The Pigeon House, Garsington' (Fitzwilliam Museum, Cambridge)

24″ × 18″; d. Sept. 1920; ex-Balston coll.; *exh.* Goupil Febr. 1921 (**4**) (£48); Whitechapel 1949 (**29**); Colchester 1971 (**24**); repro. *M. Gertler*, Fleuron, 1925, pl 2. 'From my bedroom window, [looking] over at the cottage 'gris clair' one of the pigeon house, with miles of distant country behind it. I shan't leave until I finish it.' (Gertler, 12 Sept. 1920). The style recalls the work of John Nash

'The Artist in his Studio' (Lord Killanin) 23″ × 28″; d. 1920

'Bust of a Young Girl' (unknown) d. 1920; repro. *M. Gertler*, Fleuron 1925, Plate 9

'Tulips' (Bradford) 25″ × 18″; d. 1920; *exh.* Goupil Febr. 1921 (**3**) (£50); Colchester 1971 (**26**) Lit. *Observer*, Febr. 1921

'Trees at Sanatorium, Scotland' (unknown). 'I could not manage to get quite the right spacing. It began to grow over the top edge of the canvas, and I should have liked a band of sky.' (Gertler, Dec. 1920) One of three landscapes (see below) painted from a window

'Paysage Ecossais' (Rutland Gallery) d. Febr. 1921; *exh.* Paris 1927 (British exh.) 'I have got another landscape going of the same subject [as 'Trees at Sanatorium' 1920] with a different and rather better spacing.' (Gertler, 1 Jan. 1921)

'Daffodils' (Mr Langdon) 16″ × 20″; d. 6 March 1921; coll. Gwendoline, Lady Melchett; *exh.* Whitechapel 1949 (**32**). Painted at Banchory Sanatorium

'Self-Portrait' (unknown) d. March 1921; *exh.* Goupil Febr. 1922 (**21**) (£35); Carnegie Inst., Pittsburg 1926; repro. *The Arts*, Nov. 1926, p. 264. Painted at Banchory Sanatorium

'The Scotch Girl' (unknown) d. 1920 Exh. Goupil Febr. 1922 (**14**) (£35) (*Daily Telegraph*: 'A quiet intensity of life, a bloom as of some healthy flower in a cottage garden, marks "The Scottish Maid".') Repro. *M. Gertler*, Fleuron, Plate 5. Sold to Walter Taylor for £35 in May 1921. 'There is a servant girl whom I long to paint. She's about seventeen, extremely plump, with a face like a doll. Only her eyes, black instead of blue, and the red parts of her cheeks are absolutely scarlet. She has all the beauty of an apple with the additional charm of being human – a living apple. What could be more desirable!' (Gertler, Nov. 1920 at Banchory Sanatorium). 'I have, after much manoeuvering, got one of the

serving maids, that I've had my eye on ever since I came, to sit
for me. She is really wonderful to paint – a typical rustic type –
sturdy as an ox, and cheeks like vermilion straight from the tube!
I have never seen such a thing – I am doing only a little head of
her, though my real desires are to take her away with me and
paint her for a year without stopping – and how I should like to
do her nude!' (Gertler, March 1921)

'Trees at Sanatorium – Scotland' (Luke Gertler) 43″ × 19″; d. 1921;
exh. Colchester 1971 (**27**); repro. *Selected Letters*, fac. p. 192. 'I
have a theme for even a third landscape from my window which
intrigues me, if only for its shape alone – it is to be 44″ × 20″, a
panel shape and upright.' (Gertler, 18 Febr. 1921) 'The doctor
said I could leave any time – that is before May, if I wanted to.
But the reason I am staying on till the beginning of next month is
that I want to finish a certain rather large landscape . . . In fact I
could not bear to leave it unfinished.' (Gertler, 11 Apr. 1921)

'The Jockey' (Mrs F. C. Speyer) d. June 1921; *exh*. Goupil Febr. 1922
(**7**) (£50); repro. *M. Gertler*, Fleuron 1925, Plate 4

'Staffordshire Group' (Ashmolean Museum, Oxford) 21½″ × 16½″;
d. Aug. 1921; ex-Balston coll.; *exh*. Whitechapel 1949 (**33**) or (**42**)

'The Hunter' (Luke Gertler) 27″ × 27″; d. Nov. 1921; coll. M.
Shearman, Lord Blanesburgh, Royal Caledonian Schools; *exh*.
Goupil Febr. 1922 (**11**) (£40); Colchester 1971 (**29**) Lit. Herbert
Furst: *The Art of Still Life Painting* (1927), p. 256. Repro. *M.
Gertler*, Fleuron 1925, Plate 7

'Ottoline Morrell' (private coll.) 8″ × 6″; pencil inscription: 'To
Ottoline Xmas 1921'

'Landscape with Cypress – Garsington' (unknown) 31″ × 25″; d.
1921; coll. Mr & Mrs Samuels; *exh*. Leic. G. 1941 (**3**); Ben Uri
1944 (**54**); Whitechapel 1949 (**31**)

'The Manor House, Garsington' (Mrs Julian Vinogradoff)
22″ × 30″; n.d.; *exh*. Ben Uri 1944 (**57**); Goupil, Whitechapel
1949 (**30**); Colchester 1971 (**28**); repro. *Selected Letters*, fac. p. 193;
M. Gertler, Fleuron, Plate 6. *See* Plate **46**

'Adolescence' (Hon. Sir Jasper Ridley, in 1949) 32″ × 22½″; d.
1922; *exh*. Whitechapel 1949 (**23**); repro. *M. Gertler*, Fleuron,
Plate 8

'The Queen of Sheba' (Tate Gallery) 37″ × 42″; d. 1922; *exh*.

London Group Oct. 1922 (**40**) (£60); repro. *Selected Letters*, fac. p. 193. The painting indicates Gertler's interest in the work of Renoir and Derain. A study for it was exhibited at the Goupil Gallery in Febr. 1923 (**13**). *See* Plate **41**

'China and Roses' 16½" × 20½"; coll. John Mavrogordato; *exh.* Whitechapel 1949 (**34**); repro. *Studio*, 1928, Plate 40. *See* p. 348

'Fruit' (Manchester) 6½" × 13½"; d. 1922

'Girl in an Armchair' (Mrs Blundell) 42" × 31"; d. 1922. A portrait of Mrs Christine Mavrogordato

'Head of a Boy' (Nottingham Castle) d. 1922

'The Jockey' (Mrs Speyer) d. 1922. A piece of Staffordshire pottery in a window at Garsington Manor

'The Straw Hat' (Sir Augustus M. Daniel, in 1941) 1922? *Exh.* Leic. G. 1930 (**1**) and 1941 (**28**)

'Adolescence' (unknown) d. 1922? Repro. *M. Gertler*, Fleuron 1925, Plate 8

'Cottages on Hillside' (S. Oppenheimer, in 1957) 16½" × 12½"; d. 1922; *exh.* Ben Uri 1957 (**11**)

'A Basque Shepherdess' (unknown) d. 1922; *exh.* Goupil 1923 (**23**)

'Self-Portrait with Spectacles' (unknown) d. 1922; *exh.* Goupil 1923

'Young Girlhood' (Mrs D. Cuthbert) 41" × 26"; d. 1923; coll. Edward le Bas; *exh.* Whitechapel 1949 (**38**); lit. C. Marriott: *Modern Masterpieces*, p. 19; repro. *M. Gertler*, Fleuron, Plate 10; M. Chamot: *Modern Painting in England*, (1937), fac. p. 98 (in colour). When this picture was painted Mrs Valentine Dobrée acted as a chaperone. The model, Alice Edwards, who lived in East London often sat at the Slade in the 1920s. *See* Plate **44**

'The Servant Girl' (Tate Gallery) 24" × 18½"; d. 1923; *exh.* Goupil summer 1923 (**77**); Leic. G. 1941 (**10**); Whitechapel 1949 (**35**); Colchester 1971 (**30**). Lit. *Daily Telegraph*, 30 May 1923; repro. *Selected Letters*, fac. p. 200. The model was a young Jewish girl who worked in a tobacconist's shop in the East End. The picture recalls some of Renoir's work of the 1880s. *See* Plate **40**

'The Servant Girl' (Tate Gallery) Pencil; 16" × 12¼"; d. 1923; *exh.* Goupil Febr. 1923 (**2**) as study for 'The Maid' and bought by E. Marsh; Ben Uri 1944 (**40**); Whitechapel 1949 (**D 13**); repro. *Selected Letters*. A study for the above. *See* notes on 'The Coster Family on Hampstead Heath' (1924)

'The Coster Woman' (Luke Gertler) 23″ × 16″; d. 1923; coll. W. J. Turner, Peter Pears; *exh.* Whitechapel 1949 (**36**); Colchester 1971 (**31**); Lit. *Daily Telegraph*, 31 Oct. 1923; repro. *M. Gertler*, Fleuron, Plate 11; *Selected Letters*, fac. p. 224. *See* Plate **47**

'Italian Peasants' (unknown) Pencil; d. 1923; *exh.* Leic. G. 1941 (**3**); Ben Uri 1944 (**35**)

'Peasants Standing' (unknown) Red chalk; d. 1923; *exh.* Ben Uri 1944 (**32**)

'Q.6. Tamar' (Nude) (unknown) d. 1923; *exh.* Goupil Febr. 1923 (**18**) (85 guineas); B. E. Exh. 1925 Lit. *The Times*, 1 Febr. 1923

'The Pond, Garsington' (Mr J. L. Behrend, in 1949) 26″ × 22″; d. 1923; *exh.* Whitechapel 1949 (**37**); repro. *M. Gertler*, Fleuron 1925, Plate 12

'Basket of Fruit' (D. Pearce) d. 1923

'A Basque Boy' (unknown) coll. Contemporary Art Society; *exh.* Goupil Febr. 1923 (**36**)

'Female Nude' (R. A. Bevan) 13½″ × 9″; d. 1923; *exh.* Colchester 1971 (**55**)

'Seated Nude Figure' (Leeds) Brown chalk; 12½″ × 14″; d. 1923

'Nude Tying up Shoe' (Luke Gertler) Pencil; 14″ × 11″; d. 1923

'The Coster Family on Hampstead Heath' (Tel-Aviv) d. 1924; *exh.* Goupil May 1924 (**1**) (500 guineas); Carnegie Inst. Pittsburgh 1925 (**185**); lit. *Daily Telegraph*, 14 July 1924; repro. *Studio*, June 1924; R. H. Wilenski, *The Modern Movement in Art* (1927), Plate 40, fac. p. 186; *Artwork* 6–8 1927, p. 100; *Apollo*, Nov. 1930, Vol. 12, no. 71. This picture was first planned in 1913. Apart from 'The Sisters' it is Gertler's only multifigure subject after 1916. The girl on the left was the model for 'The Servant Girl' (Tate Gallery), the woman was the subject of 'The Coster Woman' (Luke Gertler), and the girl on the right posed for 'After Bathing', 'Young Girlhood I' and others. *See* p. 347 and Plate **48**

'After Bathing' (Manchester) 39½″ × 24½″; d. 1924; *exh.* Goupil summer 1924 (**205**) (£210); Whitechapel 1949 (**40**); Colchester 1971 (**33**). The artist stated to the gallery in May 1924 that he wished to express the charm of young girlhood, and to combine that with the beauty of the landscape. 'I wanted my picture to be absolutely finished and realized in every respect so that the result should be monumental like the Old Masters and the combination of figure and landscape appear inevitable.' The model sat also for 'Young Girlhood' (1923). A drawing for the picture was exhibited by the Goupil in May 1924 (**11**) (50 guineas). *See* Plate **49**

'Gipsy at her Toilet' (Southampton) 40″ × 28″; d. 1924; coll. Lady Herbert; *exh.* Whitechapel 1949 (**39**); Colchester 1971 (**35**); repro. *M. Gertler*, Fleuron, Plate 13. The model was Miss May Spencer. The style relates closely to Matisse and Dreain. *See* p. 347 and Plate **42**

'The Artist's Mother' (Holding Scarf) (R. A. Bevan) 30″ × 28″; d. 1924; *exh.* Goupil spring 1925 (**57**); Leic. G. Apr. 1928 (**91**); Colchester 1971 (**32**); lit. *Daily Telegraph*, 23 Mar. 1925; *Observer*, 1 Mar. 1928; *Daily Mail*, 12 Mar. 1928; *New Statesman*, 17 Mar. 1928; *Manchester Guardian*, 19 Mar. 1928; *Spectator*, 24 Mar. 1928; *The Times*, 12 Apr. 1928; repro. *M. Gertler*, Fleuron 1925, Plate 14; *Apollo*, May 1928, Vol. 7, Nov. 1941, p. 242; *Artwork*, summer 1928. 'I was so anxious to keep the picture for myself that I stipulated with Marchant (of the Goupil gallery) that I would only let it go for £200, and he sold it for that price, the largest sum I ever received for a picture.' (Gertler, 24 Feb. 1925). *See* Plate **39**

'Dessert' (private coll.) d. 1924; *exh.* Ben Uri 1944 (**25**)

'Standing Nude' (Tate Gallery) Charcoal; 23″ × 10½″; d. 1924; coll. Contemporary Art Society E. Marsh; *exh.* Whitechapel 1949 (**D 5**); repro. *Selected Letters*, fac. p. 209

'Head of a Girl' (Bradford) Drawing; d. 1924

'The Artist's Mother (with Arm on Chair)' (University of Hull) Pencil; 21″ × 17½″; d. 1924 coll. M. Shearman, W. A. Evill; *exh.* Redfern G. May 1940, Shearman coll.; Ben Uri 1944 (45); Whitechapel 1949 (**D 14**) Plate **17**

'Garden Flowers' (unknown) 17½″ × 14½″; d. 1925; *exh.* Whitechapel 1949 (?)

'South of France' (private coll.) Painted in St Tropez Febr. 1925; *exh.* Ben Uri 1944 (**23**)

'St Tropez' (John Mavrogordato) 16″ × 24″; d. 1925; *exh.* Whitechapel 1949; Ben Uri 1957 (**13**); repro. *M. Gertler*, Fleuron 1925, Plate 15

'Portrait of Zena' (the artist's niece) (Irving Joseph) 36″ × 27″; d.

1925; repro. *M. Gertler*, Fleuron 1925, Plate 16. Quite close to
Derain in style

'Young Girlhood II' (Ashmolean Museum, Oxford) 53″ × 25″; d.
1925; pres. by Thomas Balston; *exh*. Goupil 1926 (**43**) (£200);
Whitechapel 1949 (**41**); Colchester 1971 (**34**); repro. *Selected
Letters*, Plate 18, fac. p. 209; *Apollo*, Nov. 1953, Page 134; *Mark
Gertler*, Fleuron, Plate 10. Quite close to Derain in style. The
same model as 'Young Girlhood I' (1923). *See* p. 347 and Plate **45**

'Basket of Fruit' (Large still life with china parrot) (Tate Gallery)
32″ × 40″; d. 1925; coll. acquired by Walter Taylor from the
artist, sold by him to Thomas Balston. *exh*. Whitechapel 1949
(**43**); Colchester 1971 (**36**) (repro.); repro. *Selected Letters*, fac.
p. 226; *M. Gertler*, Fleuron 1925, Plate 17. 'Taylor wasn't altogether anxious to part with it, but I told him how much you
liked it . . . It is one of my biggest and highest priced pictures
. . . you have the best Still Life I've done.' (Gertler to T. Balston,
Oct. 1928). *See* p. 348 and Plate **52**

'China Bird' (private coll.) 8½″ × 7″; inscription on back: 'Mark
Gertler 1925'; *exh*. Ben Uri 1944 (**39**); Whitechapel 1949 (**46**)

'Apples in a Bag' (Ashmolean Museum, Oxford) Oil on cardboard;
10½″ × 11¾″; d. 1925; coll. T. Balston; *exh*. Whitechapel 1949
(**42**); Colchester 1971 (**37**)

'Bouquet of Flowers' (Department of the Environment) d. 1925. 'I
have been absorbed in painting flowerpieces – one each day –
which means painting all day long with hardly a stop. I have just
finished my second so now I have two almost dead certs as far as
sales are concerned – also fairly nice looking pictures.' (Gertler, 22
Aug. 1925)

'A Bouquet of Flowers' (private coll.) *c.* 1925

'Flower Piece' (Miss Daphne Sanger) 21″ × 16″; d. 1925. Similar to
above

'Head of a Girl' (Richard Carline) Oil on panel; 20″ × 16″;
unfinished, n.d. *c.* 1925

'Still Life' (unknown) 18″ × 23″; d. 1926; *exh*. Ben Uri 1957 (**14**)
(Lender J. Mathias)

'Russian Peasant Girl' (Bradford) 26½″ × 21⅝″; d. 1926. A painting
of Mrs Catherine Carrington (née Alexander)

'Still Life With Aspidistra' (M. G. Farquharson) 38½″ × 44½″; d.

1926; *exh.* Whitechapel 1949 (**47**); Colchester 1971 (**38**) Lit and repro. *Apollo*, Nov. 1935; repro. *Selected Letters*, fac. p. 226. *See* Plate **53**

'The Dutch Doll' (Brighton) 30″ × 30″; *exh.* Colchester 1971 (**39**); repro. *Selected Letters*, fac. p. 128. Gertler made several paintings of this doll, the first being in the spring of 1915. This version was painted in 1926

'Dahlias' (Miss Dorothy Hart), d. 1927

'Everlasting Flowers and Pottery Horse' (Mrs Dorothy Hart) d. 1927

'Lydia Sherwood' (Mrs Margaret Aronson) coll. Sidney Schiff; *exh.* Leic. G. Mar. 1928 (**60**); repro. *Artwork*, summer 1928. Lydia Sherwood says: 'When we met in 1927 Gertler asked if he could paint my portrait. It was a head and shoulders. He put me into an embroidered peasant smock and I wore a red spotted scarf round my head. I told Sidney Schiff about the picture and he bought it.'

'Second Portrait of Lydia Sherwood' (unknown) *Exh*: Leic. G. Mar. 1928; lit. *Daily Mail*, 12 Mar. 1928. Lydia Sherwood says, 'This was the second portrait of me, painted soon after the first, again a head and shoulders facing front; but this time I was wearing an orange Russian shirt and my black velvet dress laced up.'

'Head of Girl' (Ralph Charrington) Drawing; 11″ × 9½″; d. 1927; coll. Luke Gertler; *exh.* Colchester 1971 (**56**)

'Red Curtains and Lady Rider' (Mrs Dorothy Hart) 1928

'Still Life with Book of Poems' (Mrs Dorothy Hart) d. 1928

'Sir Julian Huxley' (Sir Julian Huxley) 25″ × 21″; *exh.* Leic. G. 1928 (**68**), 1941 (**29**); Colchester 1971 (**40**); lit. *Modernist*, 13 Mar. 1928; repro. *Lady's Pictorial*, 28 Mar. 1928. Painted in 1927

'Still Life with Chrysanthemums' (Luke Gertler) 23″ × 17″; d. 1927; *exh.* Leic. G. 1928 (**63**); Colchester 1971 (**41**)

'Mrs John Mavrogordato' (unknown) d. 1927; *exh.* Leic. G. 1928; Ben Uri 1944 (**19**); lit. *Observer*, 1 Mar. 1928; *The Times*, 12 Mar. 1928; *Modernist*, 13 Mar. 1928; *Nation*, 24 Mar. 1928; *Apollo*, Mar. 1928; *The Times*, 12 Apr. 1928 ('His portrait of Mrs John Mavrogordato, reclining on a blue and gold striped sofa, is, indeed, almost comic in its disregard of pictorial depth, the recession of the bookcase being valued only as an aid to the pattern.'); *Jewish Chronicle*, 20 Apr. 1928; repro. *Artwork*, 1929, IV, 14, p. 71

'The Shakespeare Memorial at Stratford' (unknown) *Exh.* Leic. G. Mar. 1928 (**77**). 'I have nearly finished a picture of [this] which in itself is hideous.' (Gertler, 4 May 1927). Painted on a visit to Stratford to see Lydia Sherwood

'Nude' (unknown). 'I am very glad and encouraged by what you say of my work. The main thing one wants is to be steadily improving and, if one succeeds in this, one is sure to reach something worth while in the end. I agree with you. I too think that I am making headway, though one does not seem to do so continuously as much as by sudden spurts – every now and then one beats one's own record, as it were, and this is what I believe I've done with the nude. It is better than the best before it.' (Gertler, 5 July 1927 to T. Balston)

'Miss Julia Godby' (unknown) *Exh.* London Group June 1927 (**71**) (£65)

'Dahlias' (unknown) coll. G. Geoffrey Hart; *exh.* Leic. G. 1928 (**76**); *c.* 1927

'Standing Nude' (Mrs Blundell) Red crayon; 27″ × 18½″; d. 1927

'Torso of Female Nude' (Mrs R. Diamond) Pencil; 15″ × 10″; d. 1927

'Seated Girl' (Manchester) Black crayon; 13″ × 13″; d. 1927, coll. J. Mavrogordato

'Resting Nude' (Mr Daniel Macmillan) 26½″ × 21½″; n.d. *c.* 1927; coll. Mrs Hill; *exh.* Leic. G. 1928 (**71**); Whitechapel 1949 (**48**); lit. *Daily Mail*, 12 Mar. 1928; *The Times*, 12 Mar. and 4 Apr. 1928; *Graphic*, 17 Mar. 1928; repro. *Graphic*, Jan. 1928

'Girl with the Violin' (unknown) *c.* 1927. 'I've sold the "Girl with the Violin'', £85, all mine!' (Gertler, 29 Febr. 1928)

'Flowers and Chintz' (E. Betjemann in 1928) *c.* 1927; *exh.* Leic. G. Mar. 1928 (**72**)

'Pomegranates and Handkerchief' (E. L. Franklin, in 1928) *c.* 1927; *exh.* Leic. G. Mar. 1928 (**70**)

'The Stage' (Lord Birkenhead, in 1928) *c.* 1927; *exh.* Leic. G. Mar. 1928 (**65**)

'Tulips and Tapestry' (Mrs H. Lawrence) Wooden panel *c.* 1927; coll. J. E. Pollak; *exh.* Leic. G. Mar. 1928 (**66**)

'Chrysanthemums and Fruit' (R. Cockburn in 1928) *c.* 1927; *exh.* Leic. G. Mar. 1928 (**63**)

'The King of Prussia' (unknown) coll. G. G. Hart, in 1928 *c.* 1927; *exh.* Leic. G. Mar. 1928 (**67**), 1930 (**28**); lit. *Daily Telegraph*, 12 Mar. 1928; *Daily Mail*, 12 Mar. 1928; *Nation*, 12 Mar. 1928; *Jewish Chronicle*, 20 Apr. 1928; *Artwork*, summer 1928; *Manchester Guardian*, 1 Nov. 1930

'The Harvester' (G. G. Hart in 1928) *c.* 1927; *exh.* Leic. G. Mar. 1928 (**73**); lit. *Nation*, 24 Mar. 1928; repro. *Artwork*, summer 1928

'Flowerpiece' (unknown) 'I have been struggling with my flower piece. I believe I've discovered how to do flowers without having to be in such a desperate hurry, which is simply by replacing the faded ones – I have for instance replaced the mimosa – and other tricks I've discovered too, such as, when a flower has grown to about twice as tall as it was, cut its stem. Then it is in its old place again, etc! I really believe I am acquiring something that my work needed. My experiments in working higher in key, brighter in colour and more fluid in the contour are I think repaying me.' (Gertler, 4 Febr. 1928 to Marjorie Hodgkinson) 'I have finished my flowers and I really do believe they are *very* nice. In fact there are moments when I'm enthusiastic. They are so nice and bright, and just the effect I've been trying to get for ages. I believe all my future work will be beneficially affected by them. I really believe that I have at last added something to my work which was wanting, but we shall see.' (Gertler, 10 Febr. 1928 to Marjorie Hodgkinson)

'Lydia Sherwood' (Peter Rhodes) Sanguine; d. 1927; coll. E. Marsh; *exh.* Leic. G. Mar. 1928

'Supper' (Portrait of Miss Natalie Denny) (R. A. Bevan) 42″ × 28″; *exh.* Leic. G. Nov. 1930 (**13**); Colchester 1971 (**43**); lit. *Jewish Chronicle*, 21 Nov. 1930 ('a magnificent picture'); *Evening Standard* ('The most striking painting in the Leicester Galleries Exhibition is "Supper", a portrait of a beautiful young woman seated in a characteristically modern attitude'); *Truth*, 5 Nov. 1930; *New Statesman*, 8 Nov. 1930 ("Supper", at once impressive and magnificent'); *Sunday Times*, 2 Nov. 1930 ('The term "full-blooded" best describes the quality of his painting, which over and above all others makes itself felt. "Woman seated at a table" epitomizes this warm luxuriant aspect of life which is peculiar to Gertler.'). 'I have finished a portrait of Miss Denny. I believe I like it very much.' (Gertler, 29 Febr. 1928). Gertler met her at a party of Augustus John's, and asked her to sit for him. *See* p. 348, and Plate **50**

'Miss Natalie Denny in an Armchair' (Mr G. K. Beaulah) (Sold by Abbott & Holder *c.* 1965) A second portrait of Miss Denny

'Reclining Nude' (Belfast) 30″ × 40″; d. 1928; coll. T. Balston; *exh.* Leic. G. Nov. 1930 (**15**); Whitechapel 1949 (**50**); Colchester 1971 (**42**); lit. *Apollo*, Nov. 1953 (repro.) ('One of his best figure compositions'); *The Times*, 5 July 1949; *Nation*, 15 Nov. 1930; *New Statesman*, 8 Nov. 1930; repro. *Selected Letters*, fac. p. 225. The subject was Alice Edwards, a professional model. *See* Plate **51**

'Flowers in a Silver Vase' (unknown) d. 1928; coll. S. Samuels; lit. *Nation*, 15 Nov. 1930: repro. (in colour) *Apollo*, 1930, XII 71 Nov., p. 358

'Flower Piece' (Hon. Sir John Ridley) 35½″ × 27″; d. 1928; *exh.* Whitechapel 1949 (**51**)

'Bust of a Girl' (unknown) *c.* 1928; *exh.* Carnegie Institute, Pittsburgh 1928 (repro.). The same model as 'Resting Nude' (Mrs Hill)

'Still Life Before Lacquer Tray' (unknown) *c.* 1928; *exh.* Leic. G. 1928; repro. *Artwork*, 1928, IV 14, p. 71

'Still Life' (Plate, grapes, pears, etc.) (Manchester) d. 1928; repro. Gallery Art Report 1928

'Seated Nude' (unknown) Pencil; 16½″ × 12½″; d. 1928; *exh.* Ben Uri 1957 (**28**)

'Seated Nude' (unknown) Pencil; 15″ × 12″; s. & d. 1928; sold at The Little Gallery 'The Early Years' (**12**) in 1970. Note: most likely the same as above

'Cabbage and Rhubarb' (Dr Markovicz) d. 1929; coll. Luke Gertler; *exh.* Leic. G. Nov. 1930; lit. *Jewish Chronicle*, 21 Nov. 1930 ('In his most important and finished pictures a very definite range of colours is chosen, and the manner in which these colours are used is largely influenced by Renoir, the colours of the projection of one thing being that of the recession of another, and the colours in the whole range of his palette being used all over his picture. This is especially noticeable in . . . Savoy Green.') Repro. (colour) *Studio*, 1930 XCIX 453, December. Bought by Dr Markovicz

'The Pineapple' (J. Mavrogordato) 24″ × 32″ d. 1928; *exh*. Leic G. Nov. 1930 (**14**) Whitechapel 1949 (**49**); repro. *Apollo*, Nov. 1930; 'Fine Art' (*Studio*) 1931 p. 95

'The Back' (Mrs V. S. Pritchett) 31″ × 23″; d. 1929

'Ferns and Hyacinths' (Fine Art Society) 21″ × 25½″; d. 1929; coll. Gwendoline, Lady Melchett; *exh*. Leic. G. 1930 (**18**), 1941 (**23**)

'Head of a Girl' (Glasgow) 17″ × 14″; d. 1929; *exh*. Whitechapel 1949 (**52**). The dancer Greville Foster, a friend of Marjorie Hodgkinson's

'Artificial Flowers in a Sèvres Vase' (S. Samuels 1941) *c*. 1929; *exh*. Leic. G. May 1941 (**30**); repro. (in colour) *Apollo*, Nov. 1930

'The Sisters' (unknown) d. 1929; *exh*. Leic. G. Nov. 1930 (**17**); Carnegie Inst. Pittsburgh 1931 (**266**); *lit*. *Manchester Guardian*, 1 Nov. 1930; *Scotsman*, 1 Nov. 1930; *Daily Express*, 4 Nov. 1930 (repro.); *The Times*, 5 Nov. 1930; *Nation*, 15 Nov. 1930; *Jewish Chronicle*, 21 Nov. 1930; *Evening Standard*, Nov. 1930; *New Statesman*, 8 Dec. 1930; repro. *Apollo*, Nov. 1930. Two of the artist's nieces, Sally (left) and Renee, daughters of Harry Gertler. *See* pp. 347, 348 and plate **68**

'Mimosa and Tulips' (Lord Henry Bentinck, in 1930) d. 1929; *exh*. Leic. G. Nov. 1930 (**3**); *lit*. *Nation*, 15 Nov. 1930

'Clytie and Melon' (Mrs Jean Crick) 28″ × 36″; d. 1929: *exh*. Leic. G. Nov. 1930 (**21**); Carnegie Inst. Pittsburgh 1931 (**267**); Colchester 1971 (**44**); repro. *Studio*, Vol. 100, p. 357, Nov. 1930. *See* Plate **76**

'The Green Beret' (J. Mavrogordato) 16″ × 12″; d. 1929; *exh*. Leic. G. Nov. 1930 (**10**), Whitechapel 1949 (**52**), Ben Uri 1957 (**15**)

'Violin Case and Flowers' (Tate Gallery) 28″ × 36″; d. 1930: *exh*. Whitechapel 1949 (**53**); Ben Uri 1957 (**16**); repro. *Studio*, CIV 32, p. 13; *Selected Letters*, fac. p. 627

'Violin Case and Flowers' (Eric Holder) Pencil; 11″ × 14½″; inscribed: 'To my dear Friend Walter Taylor from Mark Gertler.' This is a study for the picture in the Tate Gallery.

'Bouquet of Flowers' (S. L. Major, in 1930) *c*. 1930; *exh*. Leic. G. Nov. 1930 (**5**); *lit*. *Manchester Guardian*, 1 Nov. 1930; *Morning Post*, 4 Nov. 1930; *The Times*, 5 Nov. 1930; *Truth*, 5 Nov. 1930; *Jewish Chronicle*, 21 Nov. 1930

'Study of a Head' (E. Hodgkinson, in 1930) *Exh*. Leic. G. Nov. 1930 (**9**)

'L'Amour de L'Art' (P. Morrell, in 1930) *c.* 1930; *exh.* Leic. G. Nov. 1930 (**19**); lit. *Morning Post*, 4 Nov. 1930

'S. S. Koteliansky' (Dr Markovicz) 28″ × 36″ d. 1930; *exh.* Leic. G. Nov. 1930 (**26**)

'Landscape, Bandol' (unknown) d. 1930; coll. Leic. G. 1930

'Bandol' (unknown) coll. Leic. G. 1930; repro. *Studio*, Nov. 1930. Painted on the artist's honeymoon in the spring of 1930. *See* Plate **70**

'Bouquet and Sun Shade' (Nottingham) 18″ × 22″; d. 1931; coll. T. Balston; *exh.* Leic. G. Oct. 1932 (**21**); Whitechapel 1949 (**56**); lit. *Sunday Times*, 9 Oct. 1932; *Jewish Chronicle*, 21 Oct. 1932

'Peaches and a Green Bottle' (unknown), *exh.* Agnews Nov. 1931; Lit. *Time and Tide* 'An important still life . . . he has always something which arrests attention, something beneath the suavity of his paint, something as hard and square as a stone, and as unmeltable. It is not agreeable, it is ugly and unpleasant; but it *matters*' (G. Raverot). *See* p. 351

'Still Life with Mandoline' (Belfast) d. 1931

'Thomas Balston' (Ashmolean Museum, Oxford) 20″ × 16″; d. 1931; coll. T. Balston; *exh.* Leic. G. Oct. 1932 (**2**); Lefevre G. 1937 (**6**); Whitechapel 1949 (**57**)

'Anemones and Autumn Leaves' (Dr Markovicz) 18″ × 14″; d. 1931; coll. Luke Gertler, Balston; *exh.* Leic. G. Oct. 1932 (**16**); Whitechapel 1949 (**54**); lit. *Sunday Times*, 9 Oct. 1932

'Fontainebleau' (Gwendoline, Lady Melchett) painted in 1931; *exh.* Leic. G. Oct. 1932 (**8**)

'The Statue Fontainebleau' (Contemporary Art Society) painted in 1931; *exh.* Leic. G. Oct. 1932 (**7**)

'Spring' (Victoria & Albert Museum) 38″ × 58″; repro. *Studio*, Sept. 1932. One of three fruit compositions painted as poster designs for the Empire Marketing Board in 1931

'Summer' (Victoria & Albert Museum) 38″ × 58″; repro. *V & A Review* (1934), p. 21. *See* above

'Autumn' (Victoria & Albert Museum) 38″ × 58″. *See* above

'Seated Nude' (Mrs Blundell) Drawing; d. 1931

'The Virgin and St Anne' (after El Greco) (D. Thoms) 20″ × 30″; n.d. 1931; coll. T. Balston; *exh.* Leic. G. Oct. 1932 (**18**); Whitechapel 1949 (**55**); Colchester 1971 (**45**); lit *Morning Post*, 10 Oct. 1932; *Observer*, 15 Oct. 1932

'Portrait of a Young Woman' (unknown); painted in July 1932; the model was Miss Jean Kemp

'The Song' (New Grafton Coll.) d. 1932; *exh.* Leic. G. Oct. 1932 (**5**); Carnegie Inst. Pittsburgh 1933 (**171**); Ben Uri 1944 (**30**); lit. *Jewish Chronicle*, 21 Oct. 1932 (repro.); repro. *Studio*, Sept. 1932. The model was Cecilia Dennis. *See* Plate **69**

'Arthur Bliss' (Sir Michael Sadler in 1932) d. 1932; *exh.* Leic. G. Oct. 1932 (**24**), Ben Uri 1944 (**26**); lit. *Time & Tide*, 15 Oct. 1932; *Observer*, 15 Oct. 1932; *Jewish Chronicle*, 21 Oct. 1932; *Apollo*, Oct.–Nov. 1932; Arthur Bliss, *As I Remember*, Faber, 1970, p.108 repro. *Studio*, Sept. 1932. 'I started Bliss's portrait. It's rather an interesting composition and they were excited from the start.' (Gertler, 15 May 1931)

'Hampstead Heath' (Gwendoline,, Lady Melchett) d. 1932; *exh.* Leic. G. Oct. 1932 (**22**)

'Clytie and Autumn Leaves' (Glasgow) 31″ × 43″ d. 1932; coll. J. Conway; *exh.* Leic. G. Oct. 1932 (**12**) (sold for £100); lit. *Sunday Times*, 9 Oct. 1932

'Girl with Ear-Rings' (Gilbert Spencer, in 1932) *c.* 1932; *exh.* Leic. G. Oct. 1932 (**23**); lit. *Time & Tide*, 15 Oct. 1932

'Peaches and Laurel Leaves' (Mrs J. B. Priestley, in 1932) *c.* 1932; *exh.* Leic. G. Oct. 1932 (**15**); lit. *Apollo*, Oct.–Nov. 1932; *The Times*, 11 Oct. 1932; *Weekend Review*, 15 Oct. 1932

'Flowers in Green Vase' (Mrs J. B. Priestley, in 1932) *c.* 1932; *exh.* Leic. G. Oct. 1932 (**20**); lit. *Apollo*, Oct.–Nov. 1932

'The Brown Jug' (Lord Bernstein, in 1932) *c.* 1932; *exh.* Leic. G. Oct. 1932 (**9**)

'Head of a Girl' (W. A. Evill, in 1932) *c.* 1932; *exh.* Leic. G. Oct. 1932 (**1**)

'Seated Nude' (Sir Michael Sadler, in 1932) *c.* 1932; *exh.* Leic. G. Oct. 1932 (**4**); lit. *Apollo*, Oct.–Nov. 1932; *Observer*, 19 Oct. 1932; *Jewish Chronicle*, 21 Oct. 1932

'Japanese Mask' (Ashmolean Museum, Oxford) *c.* 1932; coll. Lord Clark; *exh.* Leic. G. Oct. 1932 (**13**)

'The Benin Head' (Sir Michael Sadler, in 1932) *c.* 1932; *exh.* Leic. G. Oct. 1932 (**10**)

'Mrs Beddington Behrens' (unknown) *c.* 1932; *exh.* Leic. G. Oct. 1932 (**19**)

'Seated Nude' (unknown) Pastel; *c.* 1932; repro. *Studio,* Sept. 1932. The model was Cecilia Dennis

'Nude – Seen From Behind' (Dr Markovicz) 24″ × 18″; d. 1932

'Woman With Mandolin' (unknown) Pencil; d. 1932; repro. *Black and White,* by Arnold Haskell (frontispiece). This is the same subject as 'The Song'

'A Wooded Landscape – Hampstead' (D. Leslie) 14¾″ × 23¾″; d. 1932

'A Classical Head' (unknown) 20″ × 16″; d. 1933; coll. T. Balston, Luke Gertler. Abbott & Holder

'Musical Thought' (unknown) 1933

'Flowers in a Brown Vase' (Department of the Environment) d. 1933; *exh.* Leic. G. Oct. 1934 (**89**); lit. *The Times,* 9 Oct. 1934

'Golden Pheasant' (unknown); *exh.* Heffers gallery Feb. 1933, Leic. G. Oct. 1934 (**94**)

'The Artist's Wife' (Kendall, Westmorland) Pastel; 24¾″ × 32½″; d. 1933; *exh.* Whitechapel 1949 (**60**) Ben Uri, 1957 (**18**)

'Lord Derwent' (York) 31½″ × 25½″; d. 1933; *exh.* Leic. G. Oct. 1934 (**99**); lit. *Sunday Times,* 7 Oct. 1934; repro. *Apollo,* Oct. 1934. Painted at Lord Derwent's House in Scarborough. 'A young lord inspired by your [Balston's] portrait and Bliss's wants me to do him. But not before early next year.' (Gertler to T. Balston, 11 Oct. 1932) 'I have just finished a long day's work on the Portrait. Do you know – I really think I shall never again accept a commissioned portrait. It's a dreadful and degrading work. It drags one back. There were times when it was alright but now – for to-day – it is antipathetic to my outlook. I am longing to get back to real work.' (Gertler, 21 Aug. 1933 to T. Balston)

'Lord Derwent' (unknown) Pastel; d. 1933; *exh.* Leic. G. Oct. 1934 (**106**)

'Mandolin and Fruit' (A. Margulies) 25″ × 30″; d. 1933; *exh.* Leic. G. May 1941 (**21**); Ben Uri 1957 (**17**)

'The Passing of Time' (sold Christie's 19 Mar. 1971 (**131**)) 37″ × 45″; d. 1933; *exh.* London Group Nov. 1933 (**105**); Leic. G. Oct. 1934 (**96**); Brussels Universal International Exhibition 1935; lit. *Yorkshire Observer,* 6 Oct. 1934

'The Birth of Classical Music' (Sir Michael Sadler in 1934) Pastel; d. 1933; *exh.* Leic. G. Oct. 1934 (**104**)

'Meditation' (unknown) (Girl with head resting on hand) d. 1933; *exh.* Leic. G. Oct. 1934 (**103**)

'Standing Nude with Mandolin' (Mrs R. Diamond) Charcoal; 19″ × 12″; d. 1933

'Music' (Mrs M. Kostenz) Charcoal; 29½″ × 21″; d, 1933; coll. Mrs Dorothy Morland; *exh.* Ben Uri 1944 (**9**); Whitechapel 1949 (**D 15**)

'The Mandolinist' (Tate Gallery) 30″ × 22″; d. 1934; coll. T. Balston; *exh.* Leic. G. Oct. 1934 (**92**); Whitechapel 1949 (**62**). The painting was done direct from the model (Miss Jean Kemp, later Mrs Hogh, a schoolfriend of Gertler's landlady's daughter) in sittings of about one hour each. This was one of several pictures of her executed in 57 sittings during 1933. Lit. Quentin Bell, Introduction to *Selected Letters* ('In his last years Gertler does recover. This is both massive and psychologically right. The design is as impressive as anything in his work and yet easy flowing and unforced. He was beginning to do in paint what he had so magnificently done in sculpture.'); *The Times*, 9 Oct. 1934; *New Statesman & Nation*, 20 Oct. 1934 ('There is no denying that Mr Gertler can on occasion produce an admirably arranged painting which does impress the spectator and to some extent transport him from the realms of the flesh – as in the "Mandolinist".'); *Spectator*, 19 Oct. 1934 ('The painting "Mandolinist" clearly owes much to Picasso. The particular massiveness of the limbs and the simplification of the forms of the head are in a convention created by that artist, but yet there is something about the paintings which is entirely different from anything which is to be found in Picasso. The close fittingness of the figure in the frame, the peculiar effect of the leg cutting across the lower part of the composition with one of its sides reduced to almost a straight line, the exact observation of the light falling on the bust – all these make the painting an individual achievement. It is derivative, but the borrowings have been developed into something original.') Repro. *Selected Letters*, fac. p. 238. 'I am very glad you chose the "Mandolinist". It is the last thing I did before the [summer] holiday and one of my favourites. You must have noticed that I've kept it considerably

higher in key than the other – with – I think – a satisfactory result.'
(Gertler, 5 Oct. 1934 to T. Balston) Recalls the work of Henry
Moore with whom Gertler was very friendly at the time. *See*
p. 324, 348 and Plate **72**

'Homage to Roger Fry' (Peyton Skipworth) Pastel; 28″ × 38″; d.
1934; coll. Dr Andrew Morland; *exh.* London Group Nov. 1934
(**70**) (£100); Ben Uri 1944 (**59**); Ben Uri 1957 (**19**). *See* pp. 296,
348, Plate **73**

'Thomas Balston' (Newcastle) 8½″ × 6″; commissioned for £25 by
T. Balston and painted in Spain in 1934

'Nude with Mandolin' (Mrs Blundell) 36″ × 24″; d. 1934. The
model was Miss Jean Kemp

'Chromatic Fantasy' (Lord Beaverbrook) *c.* 1934; *exh.* Leic. G.
Oct. 1934 (**98**); Pittsburgh 1935 (repro. in catalogue); lit. *The
Times*, 9 Oct. 1934; *Apollo*, Oct. 1934; *Studio*, Oct. 1934

'The Sonata' (Mrs R. Diamond) n.d.; coll. D. Macmillan in 1934;
exh. Leic. G. Oct. 1934 (**102**); lit. *The Times*, 9 Oct. 1934. An oil
version of 'Birth of Classical Music'

'The Fugue' (J. Mavrogordato) *c.* 1934; *exh.* Leic. G. 1934 (**100**); lit.
Morning Post, 6 Oct. 1934

'Musical Bather' (Sir Michael Sadler in 1934) *c.* 1934; *exh.* Leic. G.
Oct. 1934 (**101**); lit. *Sunday Times*, 7 Oct. 1934; *Spectator*, 19 Oct.
1934

'Violin and Bust' (Fitzwilliam Museum, Cambridge) 14″ × 18″;
n.d. *c.* 1934; coll. T. Balston; *exh.* Leic. G. Oct. 1934 (**85**);
Whitechapel 1949 (**61**). The picture recalls the late work of Juan
Gris

'Stormy Sea' (Mrs A. P. Herbert in 1934) *c.* 1934; *exh.* Leic. G. 1934 (**87**)

'The Tent' (J. Mavrogordato) *c.* 1934; *exh.* Leic. G. Oct. 1934 (**93**)

'A Village in Spain' (S. Samuels in 1934) *c.* 1934; *exh.* Leic. G. May
1941 (**34**)

'Nude with Mandolin' (Fitzwilliam Museum, Cambridge) Drawing; 29½″ × 21″; *c.* 1934; *exh.* Colchester 1971 (**57**). Shows the
influence of Picasso

'Nude Seated on Ground' 'The Model' (unknown) *c.* 1934; *exh.*
Leic. G. Oct. 1934 (**88**); lit. *The Times*, 9 Oct. 1934

'The Sail' (Mrs Blundell) Pastel; 30″ × 22″; n.d. *c.* 1934; *exh.* Leic.
G. Oct. 1934 (**109**) Ben Uri 1944 (**27**)

'Nude Lying on Couch' (unknown) d. 1934

'Still Life with Head' (Richard Morphet) on panel $22\frac{1}{2}'' \times 28\frac{1}{2}''$; d. 1935; *exh.* Colchester 1971 (**46**). Painted with palette knife. Plate **71**

'Still Life, Guitar and Fruit' (Department of the Environment) d. 1935

'The Conversation' (Mrs Blundell) $25'' \times 30''$; d. 1935; *exh.* London Group Nov. 1935 (**54**), before 1937 (**23**), Ben Uri 1944 (16)

'Still Life with Bust' (Southampton) $42'' \times 51\frac{1}{2}''$; d. 1936

'Sanatorium Garden in Norfolk' (Mrs D. Morland in 1949) $23\frac{1}{2}'' \times 30''$ d. 1936; *exh.* Lefevre 1937 (**8**); Ben Uri 1944 (**61**); Whitechapel 1949 (**63**)

'Fish' (Leeds) $28'' \times 42''$; d. 1936; coll. T. Balston; *exh.* Lefevre 1937 (**18**); Whitechapel 1949 (**65**)

'The Harpists' (Harvane Gallery) $30'' \times 24\frac{1}{2}$; d. 1936; coll. Luke Gertler; *exh.* Lefevre 1937 (**25**)

'Hautbois, Norfolk' (Mrs Speyer) $18\frac{1}{2}'' \times 31''$; n.d. *c.* 1936; *exh.* Lefevre 1937 (**29**) 'Whitechapel 1949 (**64**)

'After Giotto' (Glasgow) $26\frac{1}{2}'' \times 31\frac{1}{4}''$; n.d. *c.* 1936; coll. J. Mathias; *exh.* Lefevre May 1939 (**17**); Whitechapel 1949 (**72**); repro. Glasgow Art Gallery Bull., Vol. IV, no. 1

'The Monastery – Castelltersol' (Mrs R. Diamond) $31'' \times 24''$ *c.* 1937; *exh.* Lefevre May 1937 (**20**)

'The Balcony' (unknown) *c.* 1936; *exh.* Lefevre May 1937 (**7**)

'Portrait of Dorothy Morland' (Mrs D. Morland) Panel; $27'' \times 22''$; d. 1937; coll. Dr A. Morland; *exh.* Ben Uri 1944 (**5**); Whitechapel 1949 (**66**); Ben Uri 1957 (**22**); Colchester 1971 (**48**)

'The Mantilla (Head of a Woman)' (Luke Gertler) $17\frac{1}{2}'' \times 12\frac{1}{2}''$; d. 1937. The same model as 'The Bride' below. The painting itself is included in 'The Bride'

'The Bride' (Mrs Blundell) $36'' \times 30''$; d. 1937; *exh.* London Group Nov. 1937 (**145**) (£80); Lefevre May 1939 (**28**); Colchester 1971 (**50**); lit. *The Times*, 13 May 1939. The model was one of the artist's students at the Westminster Technical Institute, a Jewish girl from the East End. *See* Plate **75**

'Still Life with Benin Head' (Mrs Blundell) $30'' \times 37''$; d. 1937

'Still Life with Benin Head' (Mrs Blundell) $24'' \times 20''$; d. 1937

'Flower Piece' (Mr Farquharson) $31'' \times 36\frac{1}{2}''$; d. 1937; *exh.* Lefevre 1939; Ben Uri 1944 (**2**); Whitechapel 1949 (**67**)

'Through the Window' (Mrs R. Diamond) $21\frac{1}{2}'' \times 31''$ d. 1937; *exh.* London Group Oct. 1937 (**10**) (£60); Lefevre 1937; Ben Uri 1944 (**29**)

'Fishes' (Mrs Blundell) $34'' \times 44''$; d. 1937

'Garden' (Miss Maria Donska) $20'' \times 29''$; *exh.* Ben Uri 1957 (**21**) M. G.

Study for 'Fish in Glass Case' (Mrs Gurney in 1941) Pastel; *c.* 1937; *exh.* Leic. G. May 1941 (**40**)

'The Balcony' (Mr Hofman) on panel; $15\frac{1}{2}'' \times 12''$; *c.* 1937

'Benin Head, Fan and Fruit' (Miss C. Duckworth-King in 1941) Pastel; *c.* 1937; *exh.* Leic. G. May 1941 (**39**)

'Miss Sylvia Lynd' (unknown) *c.* 1937; *exh.* Lefevre May 1937 (**4**)

'Standing Nude' (Mrs Blundell) Drawing; d. 1939

'Seated Nude' (Peter Stone) $20'' \times 16''$; d. 1939; *exh.* Ben Uri 1957 (**25**)

'Still Life with Benin Head' (Mrs Blundell) $28'' \times 34''$; d. 1939. Quite close in style to the late work of Juan Gris. *See* p. 348

'The Spanish Fan' (Mrs Blundell) $42'' \times 48''$; d. 1938; *exh.* Lefevre May 1939 (**7**); Whitechapel 1949 (**71**); Repro: Leic. G. 1941 (**33**), Ben Uri 1944 (**13**), Ben Uri 1957 (**24**) Colchester 1971 (**49**); lit. *World of Art*) repro.) 17 May 1939 ('The background is divided into three areas. It is the placing of the dividing lines, the relative proportions, that go to making the picture. The picture is all planned out like that. It is architectural.' – Mark Gertler); *The Times*, 13 May 1939. Repro. *Selected Letters*, fac. p. 239. *See* Plate **74**

'The Red Shawl' (Mrs Renée Diamond) $36'' \times 24''$; d. 1938; *exh.* Lefevre May 1939 (**3**); Whitechapel 1949 (**69**); Colchester 1971 (**47**); lit. *The Times*, 13 May 1939; repro. *World of Art*, 17 May 1939, p. 11. *See* p. 348

'The Sari' (Mrs R. Diamond) $36'' \times 23''$ d. 1938

'Head of a Girl' (Mrs R. Diamond) $18'' \times 14\frac{1}{2}''$ d. 1938. One of a pair. The sitter's mother, Mrs Davis, owns the other

'Head of a Girl' (Mrs Davis) d. 1938. A painting of the owner's daughter

Study for 'The Spanish Fan' (Mrs Blundell) d. 1938

DATES UNKNOWN

'Nude with Mandolin' (Mrs Blundell) Drawing

'Still Life' (Dizingoff Gallery, Tel Aviv, presented in 1950 by
    Samuels)
'Nude' (Franklyn, bought from the Redfern Gallery in 1934)
    18″ × 14″
'Flowers in a Vase' (Miss Maria Donska) Pastel; *exh.* Leic. G. May
    1941 (**38**)
'Head of a Negro Girl' (Phillip Hugh Jones)
'Portrait of a Young Girl' (Miss Georgina Dobrée) 13″ × 16″.
    The model was Miss Alice Edwards
'Tulips' (Department of the Environment)
'Cypresses' (Department of the Environment) *Exh.* Lefevre 1937 (**5**)
'Tea Things with Daily Mirror' (Mrs Jean Criel) 25″ × 21″
'Violin and Flowers' (Mrs Blundell) 44″ × 29″
'Still Life' (Pietermaritzburg) 13½″ × 14½″
'Apples' (Pietermaritzburg) 13″ × 18″
'Landscape' (Mrs Blundell)
'Nude Girl' (R. A. Bevan) Drawing; 13½″ × 9″; *exh.* Colchester
    1971 (**55**)
'Iris Tree' (coll. D. Carrington) Drawing

THE WHEREABOUTS OF THE FOLLOWING PAINTINGS ARE
UNKNOWN:

Exhibition Leicester Galleries 1930: 'The Straw Hat' (**1**); 'Street
    Scene' (**2**); 'Flowers in Papers' (**6**); 'The Pink House' (**8**); Girl
    Reading' (**11**); 'Tangerine and Pomegranates' (**20**); 'The Waiting
    Bouquet' (**22**); 'A Basket of Pomegranates' (**23**); 'Nude' (**24**);
    'The Rider' (**25**)
Exhibition Lefevre Galleries 1937: 'Napoleon II' (**1**); 'Landscape –
    Catalonia' (**3**); 'Cypresses' (**5**); 'Composition' (**10**); 'Portrait of
    Miss Jocelyn Herbert' (**11**); 'The Guitar' (**12**); 'The Profile' (**14**);
    'Design' (**16**); 'The Yellow Shawl' (**17**); 'Castelltersol' (**22**); 'The
    Hunter' (**21**); 'Still Life on a Balcony' (**24**); 'Nude Study' (**26**);
    'Etruscan Head' (**27**); 'Still Life and Flowers' (**28**)
Exhibition Lefevre Galleries 1939: 'The Garden' (**10**); 'The Ukelele'
    (**2**); 'Tree', 'Ashford Hill' (**6**); 'Through the Window' (**8**); 'Fish'
    (**5**); 'Seated Nude' (**12**); 'The Barn' (**13**); 'Flowers on Bandana'
    (**14**)

Select Bibliography

Books and articles about Mark Gertler
1916   Gilbert Cannan, *Mendel*, Fisher Unwin
1918   Clive Bell, 'Pot Boilers', Chatto & Windus
1921   Roger Fry, *New Statesman*, 12 February
1925   Hubert Wellington, 'Mark Gertler', Fleuron Press
1928–9   Roger Fry, *New Statesman* and *Nation* articles
1930   H. Furst, *Apollo*, Nov.
1932   Anon., *Studio*, Sept. (Interview)
1937   Aldous Huxley, Intro. to Lefevre Gallery Exhibition
1939   *World of Art Illus.*, 17 May
1940   St John Hutchinson, Intro. to Redfern Gallery Exhibition (Montague Shearman Collection)
1941   Valentine Dobrée, *Listener*, 15 May
1941   Sylvia Lind, Intro. to Leicester Galleries Exhibition
1949   Thomas Balston, Intro. to Whitechapel Gallery Exhibition
1953   Mary Sorrell, *Apollo*, Nov.
1956   Sir John Rothenstein, 'Modern English Painters', Eyre and Spottiswoode (includes chapter, 'Mark Gertler')
1965   Mark Gertler, 'Selected Letters', Edited by N. Carrington, Intro. by Quentine Bell, Rupert Hart-Davies
1971   John Woodeson, Intro. to exh. at Colchester, Ashmolean Museum Oxford, etc.

Books with useful references to Mark Gertler
Quentin Bell, *Bloomsbury*, Weidenfeld & Nicolson, 1968
David Garnett, *Carrington, Letters and Extracts from her Diaries*, with biogr. note by Noel Carrington, Jonathan Cape, 1971
Beatrice, Lady Glenavy, *Today we will only Gossip*, Constable, 1964
Christopher Hassall, *Edward Marsh*, Longmans, 1959
Michael Rolroyd, *Lytton Strachey*, Heinemann 1968. Penguin, 1971
Edward Marsh, *A Number of People*, Heinemann, 1939
C. W. R. Nevinson, *Paint and Prejudice*, Methuen, 1937
Ottoline, The Early Memoirs of Lady Ottoline Morrell, edited by Robert Gaythorne-Hardy, Faber and Faber, 1963
William Rothenstein, *Men and Memories*, Faber and Faber, 1932

Notes and References

CHAPTER 1

1 Biographical information in this book has been supplied by Mark Gertler's relatives, drawing on family papers and recollections (see Author's Note). Where possible it has been verified by consulting official records and many unpublished letters of which the following are the principal collections: Gertler to Carrington and Carrington to Gertler, Gertler to Thomas Balston, Gertler to Dorothy Brett (all at Texas University), Gertler to Koteliansky (British Museum), Gertler to Marsh (New York Public Library) and Gertler to William Rotherstein (Harvard University).

2 Quotations ascribed to Mark Gertler throughout the book are drawn from three sources, (1) Fragments of autobiography and journals (unpublished); (2) Letters (some published in *Selected Letters* – see Bibliography); (3) Published books and articles by various authors.

   Full details are given in each case for quotations from (3), but recipients and dates of letters are only listed where the information appears especially interesting. Gertler was a prolific letter writer, and often duplicated descriptions of events in letters to different people.

3 George R. Sims, *Living London* (Cassell, London, 1902).

4 Charles Booth, *Life and Labour of the People of London*, Macmillan & Co, 1896 p. 33.

CHAPTER 2

5 Lloyd P. Gartner, *The Jewish Immigrant in England 1870–1914*; (George Allen and Unwin, London, 1960), p. 46.

6 C. D. 1742 Min. 1724, statement by James Lawson Silver to the Royal Commission on Sweating, quoted in Gartner, op. cit., p. 160.

7 Charles Booth, op. cit. *The Jewish Community*, p. 177.

8 Usually they consisted of one room, often very shabby, in the teacher's home, where a dozen or so boys would sit in their praying shawls. A survey by the *Jewish Chronicle* in 1891 (10 April) had found considerably more than 200 *chaidarim* in the East End. At least 2,000 boys between five and fourteen years old attended for a fee of 6d. to 1s. 6d. a week. They were not popular with British Jewry. At the time Mark was attending, an attack was mounted on them at the 1898 conference on religious education, mainly on the grounds that since the teaching was in Yiddish the isolation of the child from English life would be intensified.

9 Charles Booth, op. cit., Intro., p. 29.

10 C. Russell and H. S. Lewis, *The Jew in London* (T. Fisher Unwin, London, 1900), p. 94.

11 Charles Booth, op. cit., *The Jewish Community*, op. 17
12 Charles Booth, op. cit., *The Community*, p. 168
13 *The Lancet*, 5 March 1884.
14 C. Russell and H. S. Lewis, op. cit., p. 194.
15 Lloyd P. Gartner, op. cit., p. 72.

CHAPTER 3

16 The records at Settles Street were left discreetly empty for his attainments
    under the headings of writing, spelling and arithmetic.
17 When it was opened, the *East London Observer* had commented on its
    superiority over some of the older schools and praised its 'modern improve-
    ments'. The paper reported, on 15 February 1896, that 'With a view of doing
    away with the noise arising from the large amount of traffic ... double
    windows had to be constructed.'
18 C. Russell and H. S. Lewis, op. cit., p. 139.
19 Anon., Mark Gertler, *Studio*, September 1932.
20 Charles Booth, op. cit., East London, p. 30.
21 David F. Schloss, 'Healthy Homes for the Working Classes', *The Fortnightly
    Review*, N.S. XLIII, 1 April 1888, pp. 533–5.
22 Charles Booth, op. cit.
23 Information from Mrs Silver *née* Plaskowsky.
24 Information from Mrs Hellerman.
25 Anon., 'Mark Gertler', *Studio*, September 1932.
26 Ibid.
27 Lloyd P. Gartner, op. cit., p. 160.

CHAPTER 4

28 *The Times*, 20 January 1903.
29 *The Times*, 19 July 1888.
30 F. A. McKenzie, *Windsor Magazine*, 1898, p. 544.
31 Ibid.
32 Born in Yorkshire in the small town of Keighley, Gaskell had done his basic
    student training at Ilkley art school, and won a place at the South Kensington
    School of Art, for two and a half years. A year in Paris (under Professor
    Bougrierlan and Ferrise) had given him closer contact with the most impor-
    tant work of eighteenth- and nineteenth-century Europe and after his return
    he got into the Paris Salon. He had been running the Polytechnic art school
    since 1896 and was no doubt a very good candidate for the job. No
    revolutionary, Gaskell saw art as an industry, which, like most, needed hard
    work and steady application. He had established himself securely in the
    world of official societies, being already on the council of the Royal Society
    of British Artists, a regular exhibitor at the Royal Academy, the Institute of
    Painters (in oil colours), and the Royal Institute of painters (in water colours).

From Mark's point of view it was lucky that Gaskell, unlike many practising painters, had a real interest in the art of the past. 'His interest in and enthusiasm for Art History have resulted in his becoming one of the foremost authorities in the country on all matters connected with Painting, Engraving, etc.,' commented an anonymous writer in his personal file at the Polytechnic. 'He has lectured for the Universities of Oxford and London on these subjects for many years and was once or twice tempted to take a Professorship (I believe definitely offered one in America and one in Ireland) ... In pursuit of his Art studies he has travelled a good deal and is familiar with most of the great European Galleries – with the most extra-ordinary memory of their contents. He has been Examiner to the Board of Education and several other bodies, President of the National Society of Art Masters, and has been frequently called into consultation on art and educa-tional matters by various influential societies.'

33 Anon., 'Mark Gertler', *Studio*, September 1932.
34 One was later acquired by the Fitzwilliam Museum in Cambridge.
35 A. B. Levy, *East End Story* (Constellation Books, London, 1951) p. 17.
36 Gaskell's school was a good one: it had gained 266 Board of Education Certificates. Students entering for the National Art Competitions had won one Gold medal (for book illustration) and three Bronze medals in design.
37 This put him in the top two per cent. Regent Street Polytechnic students won nine Bronze but most of them were for design (tapestry, book illus-trations, panels); only one other beside Mark's was for oil painting.
38 Sir John Rothenstein, *Summer's Lease* (Hamish Hamilton, London, 1965), p. 16.
39 For example, he had persuaded the Jewish Educational Aid Society to finance Epstein.

CHAPTER 5

40 Gilbert Spencer, *Stanley Spencer* (Victor Gollancz, London, 1961), p. 103.
41 George Charlton, 'The Slade' *Studio*, October, 1946.
42 Paul Nash, Outline (Faber and Faber, London, 1949), p. 89.
43 Adrian Allinson, *Memoirs* (unpublished).
44 Darsie Japp, letter to the author.
45 Paul Nash, op. cit., p. 89.
46 George Charlton, op. cit.
47 William Rothenstein, *Men and Memories*, vol. 2 (Faber and Faber, London, 1932), p. 166.
48 Randolph Schwabe, 'Three Teachers', *Burlington Magazine*, June 1943, p. 145.
49 Letter to J. B. Manson (unpublished).
50 Gilbert Spencer, op. cit., p. 104.
51 Adrian Allinson, op. cit.
52 Gilbert Spencer, op. cit., p. 116.

24*—MG *

53 C. R. W. Nevinson, *Paint and Prejudice* (Methuen, London, 1937), p. 19.
54 Darsie Japp, letter to the author.

CHAPTER 6

55 C. R. W. Nevinson, op. cit.
56 Adrian Allinson, op. cit.
57 Adrian Allinson, op. cit.
58 C. R. W. Nevinson, op. cit., p. 26.
59 Adrian Allinson, op. cit.
60 C. R. W. Nevinson, op. cit., p. 26.
61 Darsie Japp, letter to the author.
62 C. R. W. Nevinson, op. cit., p. 23.
63 Paul Nash, op. cit., p. 90.
64 Lightfoot had gone to the Chester School of Art and served an apprentice-ship as a chromo-lithographer. He got his chance to get to the Slade from Gerald Chowne who had been his teacher when he took part time art lessons at the Old Bluecoat School. In 1909 he won the coveted Melville Nettleship prize for figure composition.
65 Lightfoot continued, 'After a time, especially on a big canvas, one gets in knots and then a word or even a hint from a good friend who knows something about it may make all the difference to the result of your picture. Last year Gore came just as I had got in a frightful mess. The result was I turned the canvas upside down and started again on absolutely different lines. I learnt more from him than anybody. For I learnt nothing about painting at the Slade, and never met anybody yet who did. If you go away alone, you will have to be very wide awake. I cannot recommend a better way of carrying a big picture through than the way Gore told me. Work from nature on a small canvas, say 20 × 24 inches, in the morning say, then square it off [for the drawing], and carry the big one out from this and frightfully useful drawing of the details and figures, which you may bring in. In the hands etc., meet anything else in the picture, and do not draw figures as at the Slade with no background. The background, you will find, will place your figures – if they are well drawn-in in their proper position. Please do not take this as a lecture or sermon. I am merely endeavouring to help you as Gore and others have helped me . . .'
66 C. R. W. Nevinson, op. cit., p. 41.

CHAPTER 7

67 In the possession of David Burleigh, previously Berlinski.
68 In 1898, tiring of what they felt to be the laxity of the English Jews, the immigrants had broken away and established it as headquarters for the *Machzike Hadass v' Shomrie* (Strengtheners of the Law and Guardians of the Sabbath). The struggle was a bitter one. They had defied official Jewry by

setting up their own ritual slaughterers, a school for the study of the Jewish Law, and had even tried to appoint their own Chief Rabbi. 'It was at bottom a protest against the government of the foreign Jews, who are the most numerous section of the community, by English Jews, who are in imperfect sympathy with them . . . The foreign Jew complains that his native co-religionist preaches to him constantly about the duties of English citizenship, but is deplorably lacking in "yiddishkeit"–Jewish observance and Jewish feeling. He speaks contemptuously, in moments of bitterness, of the "West End" *goy* "and desires to be independent of him in religious matters". (C. Russell and H. S. Lewis, *The Jew in London*, p. 211.)

69 Information from David Burleigh. These drawings and paintings included such titles as: 'Old Jew', 'Head of an Old Man'; 'Jews Arguing', 'Jews Praying', 'Return of Jeptha', 'Jacob offering up his sacrifice', and 'Rabbi and Grandchild'.

CHAPTER 8

70 Darsie Japp, letter to the author.
71 The *Sunday Times*, *Pall Mall Gazette*, and *Morning Post* all mentioned them.
72 *Jewish Chronicle*, 9 February 1912. See p. 335.
73 Among several inches of praise *The Star* wrote of 'work full of hope for the future . . . patient concentration of effort. No romanticism or exaggeration or falsification of any kind . . . a triumph of artistic skill, won by thoroughness of workmanship governed by a sense of style, disciplined and developed by an intimate knowledge of the best work of the past. Mr Gertler's acceptance of reality is absolute and unconditioned. He takes what he finds and transmutes it into fine art by his perfect comprehension and insight and by the magic of a fastidious and lofty style.' Konody in the *Observer* spotted its 'affinity with the early German school' and praised its 'sureness of purpose, clear pure colour, a strong sense of pattern without loss of plastic roundness notwithstanding the even light and absence of strong shadows'.
74 Michael Sadleir, *M. E. Sadler* (Constable, London, 1949), p. 252.
75 C. R. W. Nevinson, op. cit., p. 26.
76 J. E. Blanche, *Portraits of a Lifetime* (J. M. Dent, London, 1939).
77 Beatrice Campbell, *Today we will only Gossip* (Constable, London, 1964), p. 75.
78 Augustus John, Foreword to C. Gray, *Peter Warlock*.
79 Adrian Allinson, op. cit.
80 C. R. W. Nevinson, op. cit., p. 33.

CHAPTER 9

81 Paul Nash, op. cit., p. 105.
82 St John Hutchinson, Introduction to 'The Collection of M. Shearman', Redfern Gallery, 1940.

24—MG * *

83 David Garnett, *Carrington, Letters and extracts from her diaries* with biographical note by Noel Carrington (Jonathan Cape, London, 1970), p. 12.

CHAPTER 10

84 Anon., 'Mark Gertler', *Studio*, September 1932.

85 Currie attracted the attention of the *Morning Post* ('nothing but praise for this exhibitor') and the *Standard*, who found his picture of a girl with a schoolbag 'one of the best things in the exhibition'. Originally trained at the Newcastle-under-Lyme and Hanley Schools of Art, he had won a national scholarship in 1903 and a British Institution scholarship in engraving from the Royal College of Art in 1905. His first interest had been ceramic art, and for the national competition in 1903 he had entered a pair of tile enamels. They had been picked out for praise in the *Studio* (September 1903, p. 258) as 'singularly dainty and pearly in character like the best kind of china painting'. For a time he painted figure subjects on porcelain in the Boullemeir style. Turning to fine art, he found a job as Master of Life Painting at Bristol, and married in 1907. In London he had found a place to live in Chiswick, and signed on at the Slade on 1 June 1910 for three days' instruction a week. At the end of the term a few weeks later he had departed. Making up his mind to paint full time, he gave up his two pounds a week job with the London County Council.

86 Michael Sadleir, op. cit., p. 254.

87 One of Currie's first successes was 'The Lament of Nicole', a painting which showed in its style Currie's strong interest in Gauguin. It was shown at the New English exhibition of November 1912.

88 William Marchant of the Goupil Gallery had started a yearly show of contemporary art in 1906; his autumn salons were assembled without the help of advisers: he simply backed his own judgement, and sent out invitations to any artists who in his opinion showed promise. The Baillie Gallery in Bruton Street exhibited modern work and the Stafford Gallery in Duke Street, St James's, had begun to show the British Fauves (J. D. Ferguson, Peploe, Ann Estelle Rice) and Sickert. The latter was also friendly with the proprietors of the little Carfax Gallery in Bury Street, St James's, which held exhibitions for him and his Camden Town group of friends, besides showing the New English painters. The latter were also welcome at the Chenil Gallery.

89 John Knewstub had two beautiful sisters of faintly pre-Raphaelite appearance: one had married Rothenstein, the other Orpen, and these, with friends such as John and McEvoy, were the star turns among the exhibitors. Others on show had been Innes, Eric Gill, Gore and Ann Estelle Rice. Knewstub himself was a strange personality. To one contemporary, Alan Gwynne Jones, he appeared 'pinkish and cherubic, with curly hair, very nice and kind with a very good eye for pictures'. To another, Mary Hutchinson, he was a 'small, fair haired, comic figure'. John thought he was 'a megalomaniac . . . -

[of] persuasive oratory, who when words failed him, as they often did, was in the habit of replacing them by an even more meaningful silence, accompanied by an expression of mystic rapture acquired in the neighbouring tavern'.

90 *Daily Chronicle*, 19 December 1911.
91 Alan Gwynne Jones, letter to the author.
92 Randolph A. Schwabe, *Burlington Magazine*, January 1943.

CHAPTER 11

93 Paul Nash, op. cit., p. 137.
94 He wrote to Marsh, saying 'Bomberg tells me he is extremely hard up; he said he would take £10 for 'The Nurse Cruiglea' and £15 for the Plaque and £20 for the other . . . They are undoubtedly extremely good drawings and certainly show great power. If you would care about buying one would you please let me know. You see it appears that he put an enormous amount of work into them and did innumerable studies for them! Please excuse me approaching you like this.' Marsh bought one for £10. This was the second time Mark had helped Bomberg; a year or two before he had loaned his studio when Bomberg needed space to paint a summer Slade Competition work.
95 Another was Jacob Kramer. A year or two later, Mark wrote to Marsh: 'This picture is the work of a young Jewish artist. He is almost penniless, and wants to go back into the country to see his people for next week, which is Passover week. He seems to be an artist of promise. His name is Kramer. He is a friend of Mr Sadler. I like this drawing, especially the figure of Christ which is so well drawn. He wants £5 for it. If you like it at all, and would care to help him, please write to me soon, as Passover is early next week. I feel very sorry for the poor fellow. Forgive me for bothering you so much. But he wrote to me and asked me to show you this. He has heard of you.'
96 Paul Nash, op. cit., p. 138.

CHAPTER 12

97 Sir John Rothenstein, *Modern English Painters*, (Eyre and Spottiswoode, London, 1956, Grey Arrow, 1962).
98 On 22 September 1931.
99 They included the Stafford Gallery's show of Gauguin and Cézanne in November 1911, the Sackville Gallery's Italian Futurists in March 1912 at 28 Sackville Street, and Fry's Second Post-Impressionist show at the Grafton Gallery in October 1912. Not to be outdone, Frank Rutter had put on a show at the Doré Gallery in October 1913, which covered every modern tendency he could think of. Meanwhile exotic contributions to the Allied Artists exhibitions poured in from overseas.

100 Lewis Hind, *Evening News*, 4 December 1912.
101 Gilbert Cannan, *Mendel* (T. Fisher Unwin, London, 1916).
102 Ibid.

CHAPTER 13

103 Ibid., pp. 308, 320.
104 Ibid.
105 Ibid., p. 390.
106 Ibid., p. 225.
107 Some of these paintings found their way to public collection and give an idea of the importance of his achievement at this time, but others became dispersed in private collection in England and overseas and the whereabouts of many of them is now unknown. 'Knewstub was very disappointed to have to go without that picture that you bought', ('A Jewish Family'), Mark told Marsh in September 1913, 'but as he sells everything to America I am glad that you had it first.' What became, for example, of the pictures shown at the Friday Club in February 1913? There was 'The Violinist' of which the *Observer* said, 'Thick lipped, with dense woolly black hair, it recalls Graeco-Roman encaustic paintings'. The same paper referred to a picture 'Woman Resting' ('a corpulent market woman'); this was described by Rothenstein, writing in the *Sunday Times*, as 'a fat elderly figure . . . [which] has been observed at first hand and with very considerable insight. Something of the sitter's mental outlook, something of her spiritual make-up, is conveyed.'

What became of 'The Furrier', which stirred up the critics? The *Pall Mall Gazette* said it recalled Van Gogh. The *Westminster Gazette* wrote, 'it has power though it can hardly be said to be pleasing'. The *Observer* praised it: 'The red sleeves, the green and purple striped waistcoat, the blue neckerchief with red spots and the dark green cap form a thoroughly pleasing pattern of pure unbroken colour in a perfectly balanced design'; but it was too much for the staid *Connoisseur*: 'If one applied the advanced critics' phrase "music of the paint", then Mr Gertler's paint has the volume and strength of a full powered German band.'

'The Market Woman and Children' (New English show, summer 1913); and 'Mother and Baby' (Whitechapel Art Gallery, May 1914) both vanished from sight.
108 The picture called 'Rabbi and his Grandchild' drew the comment from the *New Age*: 'It is a wonderful piece of painstaking and sympathetic observation with an undercurrent of deep understanding which alone could have selected and emphasized the tremendous gulf separating this old, knowing, self conscious, feeble and worn out Jew from this sublimely unconscious, slightly bored, robust and life-loving little girl . . . Mark Gertler has a way of compelling one's interest to descend below the surface. He is essentially a painter of ideas, a subject-picture painter.'

The girl, Dora Plaskowsky, later described her meeting with Mark. 'When I was a child I used to stand in my father's butcher's shop after school. One day Mark Gertler and his mother came into the shop. He went over to my father, enquiring if I were his daughter, remarked on my unusual colouring and asked if my father would allow me to sit for him. My father gave his permission and although my mother was rather reluctant, I used to go to the studio in Elder Street two or three times a week after school to sit until the light went. The floor was quite bare – just plain boards – but in one part of the room was a raised platform with a chair placed on top, where I would sit. He never spoke to me while he was working. Mark Gertler was quite thin; his hair was cut in a bob with a straight fringe over his forehead, and he had very deep set, rather intense and frightening eyes. He wore ordinary clothes, nothing eccentric, just a white shirt and trousers. Each time I received two shillings and sixpence.' She continued, 'He did several pencil drawings of me. I never actually saw him use paints. I think I went to the studio to sit for him for a period of about a year. However, I do remember seeing a very large painting of myself sitting on the knee of a rabbi. It was a full length picture. I remember particularly my socks! I also recall running home and asking my mother how Mark Gertler could possibly have painted this picture – I had never met or seen the old man.' (letters to the author).

109 Professor Quentin Bell. Introduction to '*Mark Gertler – Selected Letters*' edited by Noel Carrington (Rupert Hart-Davis, London, 1965.)

110 In the original system each adverse vote cancelled one favourable vote and the net number had to be greater than a half of all the members. Among those rejected were Bomberg, William Rothenstein and Therese Lessore. Epstein, who had originally proposed that election be by a bare majority, and Nevinson took the lead in getting the necessary proportion reduced from a half to a third. On 3 January Bomberg, Eric Gill, John Nash, Therese Lessore, Stanislava de Karlowska, Jessie Etchells and the minor painters, Walter Taylor, Fox-Pitt and Sylvia Gosse were elected. Paul Nash only just failed, beaten by the rules even though he had eleven votes for him and only four against. Another failure was William Rothenstein.

CHAPTER 14

111 Christopher Hassall, *Edward Marsh*, (Longmans, London, 1959), p. 241.

112 Including 'The Brawl' (acquired by Marsh in August 1913), 'Irish Market', 'Seaweed Gatherers', 'The Potator Digger', the 'Seamstresses' and 'Washing and Mending'.

113 Michael Sadleir, op. cit., p. 253. Currie painted the two girls in a picture called 'The Seamstresses'.

114 G. Cannan, op. cit., p. 359.

115 Michael Sadleir, op. cit., p. 253.

116 Evidence at the inquest on Dolly Henry in October 1914.

117 Ibid.

118 Ibid.
119 Michael Sadleir, op. cit.
120 Information from the late Hubert Wellington.
121 Michael Sadleir, op. cit., p. 255.
122 They were all to be featured and discussions were being held with others: 'Bobby [Roberts] is mixed up with the Omega workshops and has very little but things he's been doing specially to please Fry so that he could get work', Currie had told Marsh a few months before. But it was hoped to include him and others of the more advanced artists.

CHAPTER 15

123 *Ottoline, The Early Memoirs of Lady Ottoline Morrell*, edited by Robert Gathorne Hardy, (Faber and Faber, London, 1963).
124 Bertrand Russell, *Autobiography* (Allen and Unwin, London), p. 205.
125 Lord David Cecil, Ottoline Morrell; *Dictionary of National Biography*.
126 Ottoline Morrell, op. cit., p. 253.
127 Ibid.
128 Ibid., p. 253.
129 Ottoline Morrell, op. cit., p. 253.

CHAPTER 16

130 Professor Quentin Bell, Introduction to *Mark Gertler – Selected Letters*, op. cit.
131 Gilbert Cannan, op. cit.,p. 380.

CHAPTER 17

132 In his new outgoing mood Currie made friends with one of them – Frank Dobson – and sent a Dobson drawing for Marsh to consider for *Georgian Painters*.
133 Michael Sadleir, op. cit.
134 Ibid., p. 256.

CHAPTER 18

135 Frank Swinnerton, *The Georgian Literary Scene* (J. M. Dent, London, 1948), pp. 227, 324.
136 Beatrice Campbell, op. cit., p. 91.
137 David Garnett, *The Flowers of the Forest* (Chatto and Windus, London, 1955), p. 9.

CHAPTER 19

138 Beatrice Campbell, op. cit., pp. 75–9.
139 Ottoline Morrell, op. cit., p. 277.
140 Lord Bentinck bought two drawings for £15.

CHAPTER 21

141 They had bought this some time before from a relative of Gilbert Cannan's.
142 Anon., 'Mark Gertler', *Studio*, September 1932.
143 *Globe*, 10 October 1914.

CHAPTER 22

144 William and Lesley Jowitt accompanied them.
145 Rutter added, "The Fruit Stall" pushes the study of character to the point of caricature, while the methodical pyramids of fruit betray that the artist is subject to the prevailing concern with geometrical form; his imaginative and technical gifts are further demonstrated by his "Creation of Eve", a renaissance of the spirit of Blake among twentieth-century conventions.'
146 Clive Bell added, 'If I were to try and tell you why it moved me so much I should have to try to rewrite my book. Don't be uneasy. I'll only say that it holds one and so strongly that it put one's mind at rest, quite preventing the non-aesthetic part from asserting itself and asking silly questions. That, it seems to me, is what really satisfactory works of art do always.'

CHAPTER 25

147 Sir John Rothenstein, *Modern English Painters*, op. cit.
148 Adrian Allinson, op. cit.

CHAPTER 26

149 On 22 January he sent a full account of his progress to Richard Carline: 'I am working on a carving in wood of those acrobats that I showed you the design for in charcoal. You can't imagine what difficultise I've been through. First of all, for some time it was almost impossible to get the wood, which nearly drove me mad, I was so anxious to start. At last I got it and then commenced the "Craft" difficulties – which I found enormous! Now at last I have got it well on its way and so far have had only one mishap; in the sawing I broke off a piece, which was to be the hands on the left. That however can be glued on again afterwards. I really think now I shall be able to carry it through. If I do, it will be the best thing I've done. But whether I carry it through or not, it is terribly exciting to do – I have never been more excited about anything!'
150 The preliminary study for 'Bathers'.

CHAPTER 29

151 David Garnett, Introduction to *Carrington, Letters and Extracts from their Diaries* (Jonathan Cape, London, 1971).
152 Ibid.
153 Beatrice Campbell, op. cit., p. 102.

CHAPTER 30

154 Leonard Woolf, *New Statesman*, 5 February 1955.
155 J. Middleton Murry, *Between Two Worlds*, (Jonathan Cape, London, 1935), p. 253.

CHAPTER 31

156 Clive Bell, 'Pot Boilers' (Chatto & Windus, London, 1918).
157 Beatrice Campbell, op. cit., p. 79.

CHAPTER 33

158 David Garnett, *Letters of Carrington*. A full account of the relationship between Carrington and Lytton Strachey is given in Michael Holroyd's *Lytton Strachey* (William Heinemann Ltd., 1968, and Penguin Books, 1971). He says, 'Lytton's liaison with Carrington was more or less platonic, and the few attempts which were made later on to extend their relationship on to a physical plane were not successful' (Penguin, p. 646). Lytton Strachey and Carrington would both have preferred her to be a boy; they particularly enjoyed one trip when Carrington dressed as one and they passed as uncle and nephew. Throughout their lives, they had both had emotional and sexual relationships with others.
    Carrington gave up a great deal by living with Lytton Strachey and keeping house for him. He became very famous and much sought after by hostesses as a literary lion, but as David Garnett said, 'they would no more have thought of including Carrington than of asking him to bring his house-keeper or cook'. Dorothy Brett found it 'a mystery why she submerged her talent and whole life in him' (Holroyd, p. 669). Seeing very little of her early painter friends, and largely occupied with housework, Carrington's painting became a matter of an odd picture here and there. They indicate a fine talent which was never systematically developed. Carrington seems to have felt that she had discovered in Lytton a father substitute (her own father, an invalid, had been dominated by her mother and sister, both of whom she came to detest). 'In time her uppermost desire became to marry Lytton . . . She almost lost her own identity, caring for him as other people care for themselves. When he was with her she was alive; when he was away for a weekend, a day, she ceased to exist' (Holroyd, p. 647). Lytton did not marry her, but he gave her peace, understanding and humour, and 'a very deep and enduring affection'.

CHAPTER 34

159 Sylvia Lynd, Introduction to Leicester Galleries catalogue of Gertler Memorial Exhibition, 1941.
160 Beatrice Campbell, op. cit., pp. 163–4.

CHAPTER 35

161 Roger Fry, *New Statesman*, 12 February 1921.
162 Valentine Dobrée, *Listener*, 15 May 1941.
163 Beatrice Campbell, op. cit., p. 148.
164 Beatrice Campbell, op. cit.

CHAPTER 37

165 J. B. Priestley, in a letter to the author, said in 1971; 'The series of pictures, in a new manner, he had painted in Spain had been largely a failure – at least that is my impression, and I know I bought one not because I liked it but just to help him.'

CHAPTER 38

166 Beatrice Campbell, op. cit., 163–4.
167 Quentin Bell, Introduction to '*Mark Gertler – Selected Letters*', op. cit., p. 12.
168 Clive Bell, *New Statesman*, 24 May 1941.

PICTURES REFERRED TO IN THE TEXT
Numbers in bold type refer to the illustrations

169 'The Artist's Mother' (Tate Gallery). *See* p. 395 and **4**.
170 'Still Life with Melons' (Mrs Blundell). *See* p. 358.
171 'The Artist's Mother in her Kitchen' (Pietermaritzburg). *See* p. 359 and **6**.
172 'A Playful Scene' (Birmingham). *See* p. 359 and **3**.
173 'The Apple Woman and her Husband' (Melbourne). *See* p. 360 and **5**.
174 'Sir George Howard Darwin' (National Portrait Gallery). *See* p. 360.
175 'Portrait of a Girl' (Tate Gallery). *See* p. 360.
176 'Carrington' (Dr Krock). *See* p. 361 and **7**.
177 'A Jewish Family' (Tate Gallery). *See* p. 362 and **14**.
178 'The Artist's Mother' (Swansea). *See* p. 362 and **13**.
179 'The Rabbi and his Grandchild' (Southampton). *See* p. 361 and **12**.
180 'Family Group' (Southampton). *See* pp. 361, 362 and **8**.
181 'Rabbi and Rabbitzin' (Private collection). *See* p. 365 and **15**.
182 'The Doll' (Private collection). *See* p. 363 and **43**.
183 'The Fruit Sorters' (Leicester). *See* p. 363 and **16**.
184 'Black and White Cottage' (Mrs F. C. O. Speyer). *See* pp. 363, 364 and **24**.
185 'Gilbert Cannan at his Mill' (Ashmolean Museum, Oxford). *See* p. 363 and **38**.
186 'The Creation of Eve' (Private Collection). *See* p. 364 and **23**.

187 'Agapanthus' (Melbourne). *See* p. 364 and **37**.
188 'Portrait of Dorothy Brett' (Owner unknown). *See* p. 365.
189 'Swing Boats' (Owner unknown). *See* p. 366 and **28**.
190 'The Fruit Stall' (Owner unknown). *See* pp. 365, 366.
191 'Sir Michael Sadler' (Leeds). *See* p. 365.
192 'Apples' (Owner unknown). *See* p. 364.
193 'Merry-go-Round' (Ben Uri Gallery). *See* pp. 366, 367 and **26**.
194 'The Pond, Garsington' (Leeds). *See* p. 368.
195 'The Acrobats' (Tate Gallery). *See* p. 367 and **30**.
196 'The Bathers' (Gwendoline, Lady Melchett). *See* p. 368 and **32**.
197 'Portrait of Koteliansky' (Michael Campbell). *See* p. 367 and **62**.
198 'The Mandolinist' (Tate Gallery). *See* p. 387 and **72**.
199 'The Artist's Mother', 23″ × 18″ (Mrs Blundell). *See* p. 358.
200 'May Burleigh (*née* Berlinsky)' (David Burleigh). *See* p. 359.
201 'The Artist's Mother', pencil (Tate Gallery). *See* p. 360.
202 'Jews Arguing' (Owner unknown). *See* p. 358.
203 'The Violinist' (Fine Arts Society). *See* p. 361 and **9**.
204 'Mrs T. E. Harvey' (R. S. Rowntree). *See* p. 360 and **10**.
205 'Mr T. E. Harvey' (R. S. Rowntree). *See* p. 360.
206 'Coster Woman and Child' (Owner unknown). *See* p. 360.
207 'Vanity' (Private collection). *See* p. 360 and **11**.
208 'Daffodils in a Blue Bottle' (Richard Carline). *See* p. 366
209 'Still Life' (Hatton Gallery, King's College, Newcastle). *See* p. 362.
210 'Head of a Young Girl', black chalk (Manchester). *See* p. 362.
211 'Head of a Girl', black lead (Leeds). *See* p. 361.
212 'Woman Resting' (Owner unknown). *See* p. 361.
213 'Boxers' (Private collection). *See* p. 369 and **27**.
214 'Footballers' (Owner unknown). *See* p. 371.
215 'Ballet Dancers' (H. M. Goldberg). *See* p. 369 and **29**
216 'Still Life' (Manchester). *See* p. 368.
217 'The Tea Set' (Private collection). *See* p. 370.
218 'Geranium' (Private collection). *See* p. 370.
219 'The Teapot' (Tate Gallery). *See* p. 369.
220 'The Bokhara Coat' (Owner unknown). *See* p. 372
221 'The Coster Family on Hampstead Heath' (Tel Aviv). *See* p. 376 and **48**.
222 'The Sisters' (Owner unknown). *See* p. 383 and **68**.
223 'Young Girlhood – II' (Ashmolean Museum, Oxford). *See* p. 377 and **45**.
224 'Gipsy at her Toilet' (Southampton). *See* p. 376 and **42**.
225 'China and Roses' (Coll. Mavrogordato). *See* p. 374.
226 'Basket of Fruit' (Tate Gallery). *See* pp. 377, 378 and **52**.
227 'Supper' (Portrait of Miss Natalie Denny) (R. A. Bevan). *See* p. 381 and **50**.
228 'Homage to Roger Fry', pastel (Peyton Skipworth). *See* p. 387 and **73**.
229 'The Red Shawl' (Mr René Diamond). *See* p. 390.
230 'Still Life with Benin Head', 28″ × 34″ (Mrs Blundell). *See* p. 389.
231 'Peaches and a Green Bottle' (Owner unknown). *See* p. 384.

Index